Cooking Light. '86

Cooking Light '86

Oxmoor House®

Copyright 1986 by Oxmoor House, Inc.
Book Division of Southern Progress Corporation
P. O. Box 2463, Birmingham, Alabama 35201

ISBN: 0-8487-0677-3
ISSN: 0884-2922

Manufactured in the United States of America

Cooking Light '86

Executive Editor: Ann H. Harvey
Southern Living® Foods Editor: Jean W. Liles
Senior Editor: Joan E. Denman
Senior Foods Editor: Katherine M. Eakin
Assistant Editor: Ellen W. de Lathouder
Assistant Foods Editor: Susan L. Curtin, R.D.
Copy Editor: Melinda E. West
Editorial Assistants: Karen W. Hardegree, Donna A. Rumbarger
Director, Test Kitchen: Laura N. Massey
Test Kitchen Home Economists: Kay E. Clarke, Rebecca J. Riddle,
    Elizabeth J. Taliaferro, Elise Wright Walker
Production Manager: Jerry Higdon
Art Director: Bob Nance
Designer: Faith Nance
Production: Rick Litton, Jane Bonds, Diane Ridley

Cover: *Festive Dinner for Eight (menu begins on page 81).*

Back cover: *Poached Pears in Orange Sauce (page 83).*

Page ii: *Simmer tomato juice with seasonings for a delicious
72-calorie Tomato Bouillon (page 108), which may be served
either hot or cold.*

Contents

Living Well Is The Best Reward

Welcome to the good life.

Welcome to *Cooking Light '86* — a guide to the business of looking good and feeling better. This book is not just another diet book; it is a cookbook for those of you who want to take charge of your life with a more informed perspective on food choices and exercise options. It's an approach to better living that may start today, but one that you can continue to explore for the rest of your life.

Cooking Light '86 contains 500 light, nutritious recipes, including thirty delicious and attractive menus, ranging from quick breakfast ideas to company dinners and cocktail parties. As you sample these dishes and the other recipes in the sections that follow, you'll be inspired to see fresh, wholesome food in a new light. Fat, sugar, and sodium have been minimized, and vitamins, minerals, and fiber maximized — without sacrificing taste or texture. You'll also learn how to adapt your favorite recipes to make them more nutritious, yet still delicious and attractive.

In addition, *Cooking Light '86* provides the latest breakthroughs in nutrition and tips for applying those findings to the way you live. You will find valuable, updated information on nutrition and exercise and practical suggestions about what your workout should include for maximum efficiency. New foods and exercise equipment are highlighted in the "Marketplace."

With *Cooking Light '86*, you can meet the challenge of providing yourself and your family a healthier way of living. Read on — and enjoy your exploration of the food and fitness connection.

The natural flavor of fruit is enhanced with cream sherry to create a simple but delicious dessert. Spiked Fruit Bowl. The recipe (page 209) makes ten 80-calorie servings.

Update '86

Keeping up with health news — and separating sense from nonsense — can be a full-time job. The sheer volume of information can seem overwhelming, and conflicting reports about nutrition, fitness, and disease can create confusion about what's good for your body.

The following summaries put the latest and most significant scientific findings in perspective. These findings have influenced the content of *Cooking Light '86*, and as you use this book, you'll discover practical ways to put them into practice in your own life.

Toward a Healthy Heart

Medical research has proved conclusively that coronary disease, while still the leading cause of death in America, has been steadily on the decline. The decreasing number of deaths from heart disease over the past 20 years can be credited not only to improved medical and surgical treatments, but also to improved life-style habits: less smoking, more exercise, and reduced consumption of fat, salt, and cholesterol.

Blood Cholesterol Levels and Risk of Coronary Heart Disease		
AGE years	MODERATE RISK cholesterol greater than	HIGH RISK greater than
2 to 19	170 mg/dl	185 mg/dl
20 to 29	200 mg/dl	220 mg/dl
30 to 39	220 mg/dl	240 mg/dl
40 and over	240 mg/dl	260 mg/dl

THE CHOLESTEROL CONSENSUS

Recent studies indicate that the rate of heart disease drops 2 percent for every 1 percent drop in blood cholesterol, a major cause of the disease. Although your body needs cholesterol to make cell membranes and hormones, excess cholesterol is deposited along blood vessel walls, where it forms plaque that narrows and/or damages the blood vessels. The flow of oxygen is restricted, heart tissue dies, and a heart attack occurs.

A blood cholesterol level that rises above 200 to 260 milligrams per deciliter of blood is considered too high for an adult. More than 50 percent of Americans fall into this category.

Cholesterol levels can be significantly lowered by reducing the amount of saturated fat in your diet and by limiting your consumption of egg yolks and whole-milk dairy products. Regular exercise can significantly improve your blood cholesterol level and at the same time help control your weight.

A NEW WAY TO MEASURE STRESS

A new diagnostic techinque developed by Dr. Robert S. Eliot, author of *Is It Worth Dying For?*, offers additional insight into the relationship between stress and heart disease. His stress clinic has developed the concept of the "hot reactor" — someone who experiences extreme cardiovascular responses to standardized stress tests. Dr. Eliot's basic technique is to measure an individual's cardiovascular performance while he is doing quick mental arithmetic or trying for a high score on a video game. The results can indicate how well a person handles stress physiologically in everyday life.

Approximately one out of every five healthy persons, sometimes unknowingly, is a "hot reactor" who experiences such intense alarm and vigilance under stress that his body produces large amounts of "stress chemicals." These stress chemicals trigger a noticeable rise in blood pressure and other changes in the cardiovascular system.

LIVING LONGER WITH EXERCISE

A recent study by Dr. Ralph Paffenbarger has underscored the connection between exercise and longevity. After analyzing 17,000 Harvard graduates, ages 35 to 84, he found that those who exercised regularly were less likely to have heart disease and cancer than those who did not.

Harvard alumni who expended more than 2,000 calories each week — which is equal to running about 20 miles — had substantially lower risk of coronary disease. They also reported an improved quality of life, because exercise helped them maintain their weight, resist the urge to smoke, control blood pressure, and manage stress.

Calcium—Mineral of the Year

Osteoporosis, the loss of tissue that leaves bones porous and brittle, was the focus of much media attention during the past year. This degenerative bone condition affects 15 to 20 million Americans, and while it is more prevalent among older white women, men are also at risk.

About 45 percent of an adult's bone mass is formed between the ages of 11 and 17. At age 35, both men and women may begin to experience a slight, gradual loss of bone mass. After menopause, when estrogen levels decline, women lose bone mass more rapidly than men. Signs of osteoporosis include a decrease in height, the beginning of a "dowager's hump," and an increasing brittleness of the bones that can lead to serious hip and spine fractures.

Currently there is no reversal for osteoporosis, but it can be prevented or slowed by following a modest program of weight-bearing exercise, such as walking, and consuming enough calcium.

The average American woman consumes only 450 to 550 milligrams of calcium each day, according to the National Institutes of Health, but experts recommend increasing that intake to 1,000 to 1,500 milligrams. Milk, yogurt, cheese, and other dairy products are good sources, but calcium supplements may be needed to ensure the intake of the recommended levels. If you have had kidney stones, ask your doctor before taking a calcium supplement.

The Caffeine Controversy

Conflicting reports about the effects of caffeine on cholesterol levels, blood pressure, ulcers, breast disease, and various forms of cancer have created quite a bit of confusion.

Caffeine is found in coffee, tea, chocolate, many soft drinks, diet pills, cold, allergy and headache remedies, and in some baked goods, frozen desserts, and puddings. It stimulates the nervous system, warding off drowsiness and increasing alertness. The effects of caffeine depend on the source, quantity, frequency of consumption, and body weight. One soft drink can have the same effect for a child that four cups of coffee have for an adult. Caffeine seems to have a more pronounced effect on infrequent consumers than on regular coffee drinkers.

Some studies indicate that caffeine can temporarily elevate blood pressure, but the increase is not enough to cause hypertension. No conclusive evidence has been found to link caffeine and cancer, and recent research has contradicted earlier reports that coffee drinkers have higher blood cholesterol levels.

Research results are inconsistent, but some adverse effects have been proved:

— Although no link has been established to

breast cancer, caffeine is clearly associated with benign breast disease, according to a University of California-Berkeley study.

— Most doctors advise pregnant and nursing women to avoid caffeine or restrict their intake because the fetus is unable to metabolize it and because these women tend to metabolize it more slowly.

— Caffeine can produce irregular heartbeats, according to an Ohio State University study. If you are prone to such heartbeats or if you have had a heart attack, ask your doctor whether you should restrict your intake.

— People with ulcers or chronic heartburn may find that caffeine (and some decaffeinated products) can stimulate the secretion of stomach acid.

Because caffeine is a drug, you may experience drowsiness, lethargy, headaches, or irritability when you give it up. Prevent these withdrawal symptoms by reducing your intake gradually.

Fiber Facts and Fiction

Once considered nonessential, dietary fiber has gained new respect in the scientific community for its ability to prevent several diseases and conditions.

In the early 1970s, a study by British epidemiologist Dr. Denis Burkitt linked a high fiber diet to a low incidence of several diseases among rural Africans. Subsequent research has supported Dr. Burkitt's findings, and most doctors now recognize dietary fiber as a safe, effective way to reduce your risk of constipation, intestinal disorders, and colon cancer.

Colon cancer, the second most common form of cancer in the U.S., is rare among people who eat a high-fiber, low-fat diet. Fiber may reduce the bacteria that works with fat and bile acids to create cancer-causing substances in the intestinal tract. It also removes wastes sooner, thus lessening the exposure of those substances to the intestines.

Accumulating studies by Dr. James Anderson, a leader in diabetes-fiber research, have also linked fiber to better blood glucose control and reduced blood cholesterol levels. His diet includes fiber that comes largely from oat bran and legumes.

Fiber can be found in a wide variety of foods, including fresh fruits and vegetables, whole-grain versions of bread, cereal, and pasta (including wheat, oat, and rye products), brown rice, dried beans (legumes), nuts, and seeds.

Salt and Sodium

Starting in mid-1985, the U.S. Food and Drug Administration required nutrient labels on food packages to list sodium content. The meanings of terms such as "low-sodium" and "sodium-free" were standardized to help consumers keep track of their sodium consumption. Here are the new definitions:

Sodium-free: Less than 5 milligrams per serving.

Very low sodium: 35 milligrams or less per serving.

Low sodium: 140 milligrams or less per serving.

Reduced sodium: Sodium content has been reduced by 75 percent compared to the product it is replacing.

Unsalted, no salt added, without added salt: Salt has not been added as it usually would be during processing.

Although the words salt and sodium are often used interchangeably, they are not the same. Table salt is composed of 40 percent sodium and 60 percent chloride, and while it accounts for most of the sodium in American diets, many foods and drugs contain other forms.

Seeking the Perfect Sweetener

Opinions are divided over the merits of sugar substitutes. The Food and Drug Administration has been considering a ban on saccharin since 1977 because it may cause bladder cancer in laboratory animals. Products containing saccharin — a no-calorie petroleum product about 300 times sweeter than sugar — must now carry warning labels.

Aspartame, a combination of natural amino acids, has the same number of calories per gram as sugar, but because it's about 200 times sweeter, it can be used in smaller amounts. Consumer complaints, ranging from headaches to seizures, prompted an FDA investigation that declared aspartame safe, acknowledging that a small number of people may be sensitive to it.

Cyclamate dominated the artificial sweetener market until a 1969 study linked it to cancer in laboratory animals. Cheaper than saccharin and aspartame and a more effective sweetener when combined with either, cyclamate has no calories and is about 30 times sweeter than sugar. It is available around the world except in the United States and Great Britain. Manufacturers have petitioned the FDA to lift its ban on cyclamate, citing a 15-year study showing that cyclamate has no effects on primates.

Irradiation: Wave of the Future?

Preserving food has always been a controversial issue. Nitrates and nitrites have long been suspect. Salt is out of favor. Freezing has limited use. A new method may be on the horizon.

For almost 40 years, researchers have been working on a form of preservation called irradiation that exposes food to cobalt 60 or cesium 137. Irradiation helps keep insects out of grains and produce, prevents onions and potatoes from sprouting, and retards the ripening of fruits and vegetables to increase storage life. It can be used to sterilize certain foods, spices, and animal feeds, thus eliminating bacteria that cause salmonella, botulism, and trichinosis; it does not make food radioactive.

Because irradiation alters the chemical composition of food, not all foods can be preserved by this method. Cucumbers and other produce may turn mushy, and dairy products may develop off flavors.

The FDA has approved low-dosage use of cobalt 60, but higher doses are still being studied

New Dietary Allowances

The Food and Nutrition Board of the National Academy of Sciences updates its Recommended Dietary Allowances every 4 to 5 years. The tenth set of RDAs, originally scheduled for publication in mid-1985, has been delayed by a disagreement on the concept of prevention.

One side argues that the recommendations should be based on the amount of a certain nutrient needed to prevent a deficiency, while the other maintains that, with the exception of a few nutrients such as calcium and iron, deficiencies are not a problem in the United States; therefore, RDAs should be designed to offer protection against chronic diseases such as diabetes, cancer, heart disease, and hypertension.

The verdict is not expected until 1990.

The Food And
Fitness Connection

In the '80s, we're in a position to make significant decisions concerning our own health. Nutrition breakthroughs have identified many of the nutrients that make the body run more smoothly. At the same time medical research has connected the overconsumption of fat, cholesterol, sugar, and sodium with life-shortening diseases.

And the role of exercise in health maintenance can no longer be dismissed as optional. Whether you're already healthy and want to stay that way or still need to achieve your ideal weight, you'll reap the benefits of good health more successfully if you establish lifelong habits that include nutritious foods and adequate exercise.

This chapter, then, will show you how to make positive choices about the diet and exercise options available to you and your family. You will discover the nutrition basics behind the development of the menus and recipes in *Cooking Light '86*. You can also learn how to turn your kitchen into a *Cooking Light* kitchen by employing the same guidelines used to test and prepare the recipes in this volume. The result is delicious food that is lower in fat, sugar, sodium, and cholesterol. And you will discover some convenient exercises to increase your strength, flexibility, and cardiovascular endurance.

Finally, you will gain perspective on the only lasting solution to weight control and a healthier life-style: a careful balance of energy intake (food) and energy output (activity). *Cooking Light '86* emphasizes throughout the natural partnership that exists between a sound nutritional plan and exercise.

Feast without fasting with this nutritious lunch: Dilled Chicken Pasta Salad (page 177), Whole Wheat Popovers (page 110), and Vegetable Juice Appetizer (page 108).

Nutrition Basics for *Cooking Light*

Whether you want to lose weight or maintain your current size, you need a balanced mix of nutrients. A week-long regimen of bananas and hard-boiled eggs can't pack the same nutritional punch as a sensible selection of servings from the Basic Four Food Groups. How many times has hunger pushed you off the diet wagon? That's the downfall of most fad diets — skipping meals and skimping on nutrition are a sure prescription for failure.

At any given time, more than half of all Americans are trying to lose weight, yet some 34 million individuals still are at least 20 percent overweight. The key to counting calories is making those calories count. The *Cooking Light* menus are built around foods from the Basic Four that are high in nutrients and low in fat and sugar; therefore, you can eat to satisfaction without exceeding your desired calorie intake.

The Basic Four — Milk/Milk Products, Fruits/Vegetables, Meats/Eggs/Nuts/Legumes, and Breads/Cereals — provide more than 40 different nutrients that maintain healthy bones, teeth, and tissue; supply energy; and aid digestion.

energy value of food measured in terms of calories. The number of calories you need each day depends on your age, weight, sex, and level of physical activity. Most men need between 2,300 and 3,100 calories, and most women require 1,600 to 2,400 to maintain their weight and energy level. Keep in mind that if you eat less than 2000 calories, getting the percentage of nutrients you need becomes increasingly difficult.

Where then should these calories come from? Nutrient-dense foods that yield the most nutrients for the fewest calories are the essence of *Cooking Light*. Consider this: 1 gram of protein or 1 gram of carbohydrate has approximately 4 calories, while 1 gram of fat averages 9 calories. Because carbohydrates are the body's most efficient source of fuel, it is best to choose carbohydrates as the dietary mainstay. Meat or protein should be a secondary source of calories; eliminate empty calories by decreasing sugar, fat, and alcohol whenever possible.

Regardless of whether you want to maintain your ideal weight or reach it, the daily percentage of calories you derive from the three sources is important. Strive to make carbohydrates (particularly complex carbohydrates) at least 50 percent of your diet. Fat should be limited to 30 percent or less of the calories you consume and protein to no more than 20 percent.

Recommended Number Of Servings From The Four Basic Food Groups For Different Ages And Situations					
Group	Child	Teenager	Adult	Pregnant Woman	Lactating
Milk/Milk Products	3	4	2 to 4*	4	4
Meats/Eggs/Nuts/ Legumes	2	2	2	3	2
Fruits/Vegetables	4	4	4	4	4
Breads/Cereals	4	4	4	4	4

*Calcium needs for adult women are greater.

MAKING CALORIES COUNT

Specific needs can be met only by eating a balanced diet. This is the surest way of getting your calories from the proper mix of nutrients.

Throughout *Cooking Light '86,* you will find the

This proportion allows you the freedom to select from a wide variety of nutrient-dense foods for the bulk of your calories. But because the intention is not to live on bread alone, the formula allows for servings of lean meat, fish, and poultry to supply your protein needs. Nor is the intention to discount fat — an important nutrient when it is monitored as to type and proportion.

READING THE GRID

Each *Cooking Light '86* recipe contains calorie and nutrient information derived from a computer analysis based primarily on information from the U.S. Department of Agriculture. The values are as accurate as possible and reflect the standards below:

* All meats are trimmed of fat and skin before cooking.
* When a range is given for an ingredient (3 to 3½ cups flour), the lesser amount is calculated.
* When an ingredient alternate is suggested ("egg substitute or egg white"), the first ingredient is always calculated.
* Alcohol calories evaporate when heated, and this reduction is reflected in the calculations.
* When a marinade is used, the total amount of the marinade is calculated.
* Garnishes and other optional ingredients are not calculated.
* All fruits and vegetables listed in the ingredients are not peeled unless otherwise specified.

A closer look at the Oat Bran Muffin recipe below will help demonstrate the value each grid can have for determining your calorie source and nutrient consumption. Based on the information provided, you can see that 1 Oat Bran Muffin provides 124 calories (7 percent of a woman's daily calorie needs and 5 percent of a man's).

In addition to providing serving-size calorie counts for the recipes, *Cooking Light '86* has included a grid that gives values for 7 essential nutrients. Many other nutrients are necessary for maintaining good health; those represented on the grid are considered to be of most general interest.

Protein, fat, carbohydrate, and fiber values are expressed in grams. Cholesterol, sodium, and potassium are expressed in milligrams.

OAT BRAN MUFFINS

2½ cups unprocessed oat bran
½ cup raisins
1 tablespoon firmly packed brown sugar
1 tablespoon baking powder
⅛ teaspoon salt
½ cup chunky unsweetened applesauce
1 cup skim milk
½ cup egg substitute or 2 eggs, lightly
   beaten
1 tablespoon corn oil
Vegetable cooking spray

Combine oat bran, raisins, brown sugar, baking powder, and salt in a large bowl; make a well in center of mixture. Combine applesauce, milk, egg substitute, and oil, stirring well. Add applesauce mixture to dry ingredients, stirring just until moistened.

Coat muffin pans with cooking spray or line with paper baking cups. Spoon batter into pans, filling three-fourths full. Bake at 425° for 20 to 25 minutes or until golden brown. Yield: 1 dozen (124 calories each).

PRO 5.6 / FAT 3.1 / CARB 18.7 / FIB 5.3 / CHOL 0 / SOD 128 / POT 207

SEVEN ESSENTIAL NUTRIENTS

Protein (PRO) provides the amino acids your body depends on for tissue growth and repair. It helps supply the antibodies that combat disease and is a resource for enzymes and hormones that regulate body processes. You can determine the amount of protein you need by multiplying your ideal weight (see chart on page 18) by 0.4 grams of protein. For example, a 125-pound woman needs only 50 grams of protein each day. Another method is to allow for 40 grams of protein for every 1000 calories consumed. Sources of animal protein include meat, fish, eggs, milk, and cheese, while vegetable protein is found in peas, beans, and other legumes. Vegetable protein usually has less fat and more fiber than animal protein.

Fat helps your body absorb vitamins A, D, E, and K, insulates body tissue, and is used in the sheathing that covers nerves. Fatty acids such as linoleic acid are essential to growth and healthy skin. While 5 grams per day is enough, a more realistic range in the American diet is 40 to 80 grams per day. Although the saturated fats that come from eating meat and dairy products tend to elevate blood cholesterol, polyunsaturated fats such as vegetable oils can actually help lower cholesterol levels. Look for polyunsaturated margarine and safflower, soybean, and corn oils; limit your consumption of saturated fats such as lard and butter.

Carbohydrates (CARB) provide fuel for the brain, muscles, and central nervous system. Your body ideally needs approximately 150 to 300 grams each day, and up to 60 percent of your daily calorie intake can come from carbohydrates as long as protein and fatty acids provide the remaining 40 percent since they supply essential vitamins and minerals. Complex carbohydrates such as fresh produce, whole grain cereals, breads, and pasta contain more nutrients than simple carbohydrates such as sugar.

Fiber (FIB) or roughage aids the digestive process. The water-insoluble fiber found in wheat bran and whole grains is not broken down during digestion and provides the bulk that pushes food through the digestive tract. Water-soluble fiber (found in oat products, unpeeled fruit, vegetables, and legumes) can lower blood cholesterol levels and may improve blood glucose control. Because fiber affects your body's use of fat, it may help reduce fatty deposits that can lead to atherosclerosis. You need 20 to 25 grams of fiber for every 1,000 calories you eat.

Cholesterol (CHOL), used to make cell membranes and hormones, is packaged in envelopes of protein called lipoproteins. Low-density lipoproteins (LDLs) deliver fat and cholesterol to the cells, but too many LDLs can lead to atherosclerosis, a buildup of fatty deposits in the arteries that can cause heart attack and stroke. High-density lipoproteins (HDLs) appear to help reduce this risk by removing the cholesterol from the bloodstream. Therefore, you want to raise your HDL level and lower your LDL level by eating more fiber and less saturated fat. Your diet should include no more than 300 milligrams of cholesterol each day. One egg yolk contains 274 milligrams.

Sodium (SOD) helps maintain your body's fluid balance. Your daily requirement is 1,100 to 3,300 milligrams (about 1½ teaspoons of salt), but because sodium appears naturally in most foods, most Americans consume up to five times that amount. Too much sodium can lead to fluid retention and high blood pressure. The salt shaker isn't the only source of excess sodium: condiments such as catsup, chili sauce, prepared horseradish, pickles, and commercial salad dressings contain salt, too.

Potassium (POT) is critical to maintaining the heartbeat, contributes to growth and muscle strength, and works in close association with sodium to regulate body fluid and acid-base balance. The daily adult requirement is 1,875 to 5,625 milligrams, and primary sources are citrus fruits, bananas, raisins, carrots, unskinned potatoes, and dark green leafy vegetables. The higher your sodium intake, the more potassium you excrete, so potassium-rich foods can help compensate for too much sodium.

The chart on page 11 can give only ranges for these nutrients because recommended daily amounts depend on height, age, weight, sex, and general health conditions. However, it does provide the guidelines necessary for structuring your own daily needs.

Whether you're counting calories or just trying to make your calories count, you will find the recipe grids a valuable source for monitoring your diet.

Other current information appears throughout *Cooking Light '86*. All information is based on the newest findings of the medical and scientific communities and has been compiled to keep you apprised of the latest from the world of food and fitness. Nutrition and fitness facts are flagged by the following symbols:

NUTRITION   FITNESS

A Daily Guide To The Grid Nutrients					
Nutrients	Daily Nutrient Amounts*	×	Calories Per Gram	=	Calorie Range
PRO (Protein)	48 to 96 grams		4		192 to 384
FAT (Fat)	40 to 80 grams		9		360 to 720
CARB (Carbohydrate)	162 to 324 grams		4		648 to 1296
FIB (Fiber)	24 to 48 grams		0		0
CHOL (Cholesterol)	300 milligrams or less		0		0
SOD (Sodium)	1,100 to 3,300 milligrams		0		0
POT (Potassium)	1,875 to 5,625 milligrams		0		0

*Based on a range of 1200-2400 calories per day

The *Cooking Light* Kitchen

Put your pantry on a diet — permanently. "De-junking" your kitchen and restocking it with light, nutritious ingredients is the first step toward adapting your recipes and cooking style.

When shopping, don't just look for products tagged "diet" or "all natural"; instead, read and compare labels to determine which has the most nutritional value. Some imitation products may contain saturated palm or coconut oils, and others may not be significantly lower in fat or calories. A good rule of thumb: if a reduced fat item has at least 25 percent fewer calories than its regular counterpart, it's worth trying.

STAPLES AND SUBSTITUTIONS

For the *Cooking Light* kitchen, you'll find most of the following staples and substitutions on your supermarket shelves.

Bouillon granules — Chicken or beef granules can be added to water as a substitute for broth and are lower in fat and sodium than most canned broths or cubes.

Canned goods — Look for fruits packed in their own juice, unsweetened fruit juices, and low-sodium tomato and vegetable juice. No-salt-added canned vegetables are available when fresh produce isn't, and most tomato products are available in low- or no-sodium form. Use water-packed sea food, and rinse before using to reduce the sodium.

Cheese — A rich source of protein and calcium, cheese can be high in sodium and fat. But you'll find an array of low-fat processed cheeses on supermarket shelves, including several kinds made with skim milk. Buy Neufchâtel instead of cream cheese to save 30 calories per ounce. Low-fat cottage cheese can be substituted for ricotta in most recipes and can become an excellent substitution for sour cream when whirled in the blender with a little skim milk or plain yogurt.

Cocoa powder — Use plain or Dutch process cocoa powder instead of chocolate to reduce calories and saturated fat. Substitute ¼ cup of cocoa and 2 teaspoons of vegetable oil for one square baking chocolate.

Corn products — Stone ground white or yellow cornmeal has more nutrients than finer grinds.

Cornstarch — It can be used instead of cream, butter, or flour to thicken a sauce. Use half as much cornstarch as you would flour.

Egg substitute — All of the cholesterol is in the egg yolk, so when possible substitute two egg whites for each whole egg in a recipe. Cholesterol-free egg substitutes are also available; use ¼ cup egg substitute for a whole egg.

Herbs and spices — Fresh herbs and spices provide a good way to enhance a recipe's flavor. Use four parts fresh to one part dry herbs.

Legumes — Beans and peas are an inexpensive source of vegetable protein and fiber, and they don't contain fat or cholesterol.

Margarine — It's just as caloric as butter, but is a better nutritional buy because it's made with unsaturated fat. Try cutting back on the amount of margarine in stir-fry and casserole recipes by a third or a half.

Milk — Skim and nonfat dry milk are virtually fat-free and are fortified with fat-soluble vitamins A, D, E, and K, making them a good nutritional buy. Use nonfat dry milk in coffee and tea to save fat and cholesterol. Equal amounts of skim or low-fat milk can be substituted for whole milk to cut fat calories in recipes, and evaporated skim milk (184 calories per cup) will often work in place of whipping cream (838 calories per cup).

Oil — Always use vegetable oil, preferably sunflower, safflower, or corn oil.

Pasta and noodles — These versatile carbohydrates come in a wide variety of shapes and sizes. Stick to plain flour types where possible — egg noodles contain egg yolks.

Rice — Most white rice has been polished for a longer shelf life and then enriched with vitamins and minerals. Because these nutrients are applied to the outside of the grain, they can easily be lost by rinsing or by using too much water in the cooking process.

Sugar — It's lower in calories than you think: one teaspoon of firmly packed brown sugar has 17 calories; the same amount of granulated sugar has 16; and powdered sugar has 10. In *Cooking Light '86*, we've chosen to cut back on the amount of sugar rather than use artificial sweeteners. Try using one-third less sugar and adding more cinnamon,

nutmeg, almond or vanilla extract.

Tofu — An excellent source of vegetable protein, calcium, and iron that may help lower cholesterol, tofu (soybean curd) can be added to stir-fry dishes, tossed in salads, and mixed into spreads and dips. Tofu is similar in nutritional value to cottage cheese, but has less sodium and more iron than the dairy product.

Vegetable cooking spray — A must for the *Cooking Light* kitchen! Sauté in this low-fat spray instead of butter or oil, and use it to coat baking sheets, casseroles, or muffin tins.

Yogurt — Plain low-fat yogurt has been used throughout *Cooking Light '86* as a calcium-rich base for dips and dressings and even in desserts. Some people with lactose intolerance can eat yogurt instead of milk or milk-based products.

COOKING IT LIGHT

Keeping nutrients in and calories out takes a light touch: try stir-frying instead of deep-frying, steaming instead of boiling, rack-roasting instead of cooking in fatty drippings. These are the methods used in *Cooking Light '86*, and as you master them, your meals will take on new character. Vegetables will retain their color and crunch. Meats, fish, and chicken will taste tender and juicy without heavy sauces and gravies. Desserts will stay special but will be devoid of excessive calories.

One rule to remember: the shorter the cooking time for fruits and vegetables, the fewer nutrients you will lose. Stir-frying and steaming are quick methods that seal in vitamins and minerals rather than letting them escape into cooking liquid. Nonstick cookware is ideal for stir-frying, and if you don't have a steamer, use an aluminum colander set in a saucepan over an inch or two of water.

Grill or broil meats on a rack so that fat drains away, and be sure to trim all visible fat before cooking. Freeze steaks for an hour before slicing thinly across the grain for stir-frying. As you skin chicken parts, also remove the whitish fat pads beneath the skin.

Add more fish to your diet; it's a rich source of nutrients, and at about 10 minutes per inch of thickness, its quick cooking time is a bonus.

Defat soups, stews, and gravies by making them

ahead of time and chilling them until the fat congeals. You'll save 100 calories for each tablespoon of fat you lift off.

Remove excess sodium and oil from canned vegetables and tuna by rinsing before cooking. Flavor your dishes with herbs and spices instead of salt. Chives, parsley, and tarragon are good with most vegetables, while onion, garlic, thyme, sage, rosemary, and oregano can perk up meats, fish, and poultry. When a recipe calls for wine, remember that the flavor remains intact during cooking while alcohol evaporates and calories are reduced.

Can you really change the way you cook without sacrificing your favorite foods? Absolutely. The Strawberry Cheesecake pictured below is the *Cooking Light* version (see the complete recipe on page 211). Compare the ingredients with those of its traditional counterpart:

Margarine and ground almonds replaced the butter, graham cracker crumbs, and sugar for a lighter crust. To yield low-fat benefits, Neufchâtel was substituted for cream cheese and skim milk for whipping cream. The sugar was reduced by ½ cup and entirely eliminated in the glaze since fresh whole strawberries served as the topping.

The result? Cheesecake with 240 calories per serving, compared with 484 calories in the classic recipe. That's *Cooking Light!*

Strawberry Cheesecake

Traditional	Cooking Light
½ cup butter	1 teaspoon unsalted margarine
2 cups graham cracker crumbs	¼ cup finely ground almonds
3 tablespoons sugar	
4 (8-ounce) packages cream cheese	4 (8-ounce) packages Neufchâtel cheese
½ cup whipping cream	½ cup skim milk
1½ cups sugar	1 cup sugar
4 eggs	4 eggs
1 teaspoon vanilla extract	1 teaspoon vanilla extract
2 tablespoons grated orange rind	2 tablespoons grated orange rind
1 tablespoon grated lemon rind	1 tablespoon grated lemon rind
2 cups strawberries	2 cups strawberries
1 cup sugar	
Yield: one 8-inch cheesecake with 16 servings	Yield: one 8-inch cheesecake with 16 servings
Calories: 484 per serving	Calories: 240 per serving

Traditional

PRO 6.9 / FAT 31.0 / CARB 46.6 / FIB 0.4 / CHOL 157 / SOD 326 / POT 155

Cooking Light

PRO 8.0 / FAT 16.1 / CARB 17.0 / FIB 0.5 / CHOL 112 / SOD 248 / POT 142

Exercise — The Perfect Partner

Many people equate exercise with weight control, and rightly so: it's half of the battle against extra pounds. But the benefits of fitness reach far beyond the numbers on your bathroom scale.

Consider these facts:

Exercise increases your body's ability to burn fat and utilize oxygen more efficiently, which leads to more energy and better weight control.

Exercise keeps joints supple, strengthens muscles, and improves cardiovascular fitness by conditioning the heart.

Exercise helps you let go of the day's tensions — relaxing your mind and your muscles.

Still not convinced? Over a five-year period, you can gain an extra 50 pounds by eating just 100 excess calories each day (a plain doughnut, for example). But a brisk 25-minute walk each day would offset those calories, allowing your weight to stay the same.

In short, exercise is the perfect partner to eating right. A regular workout that includes all three components of fitness — aerobics, flexibility, and strength — will yield short- and long-term benefits. You'll look and feel better, and you'll enhance your chances for living a longer, healthier life.

YOUR PERSONAL FITNESS TEST

Just as your body requires nutrients from a variety of foods (energy intake), it needs a varied menu of exercises (energy output) to perform at peak efficiency. And if "spot reducing" is your aim, the only way to trim your thighs, waist, arms, or anything else is by reducing the overall proportion of fat to lean tissue in a regular program that combines all three types of exercise: aerobic, flexibility, and strength.

Test your personal fitness level in the three areas before embarking on the modified exercise program illustrated on the following pages.

Aerobic exercise is any sustained, vigorous activity that elevates the heart rate to a target heart rate or training level (see target heart rate formula on page 19). Your heart is a muscle, and as any muscle, it becomes stronger with routine exercise. Activities such as swimming, dancing, running, cross-country skiing, and even brisk walking are options for improving your aerobic fitness.

You can test your aerobic fitness with the walk/jog test. Warm up with gentle stretches for 5 to 10 minutes; then cover the distance of 1.5 miles for men or 1.25 miles for women as quickly as you can by walking, running, or jogging. Compare your time to the chart below.

Flexibility exercises stretch connective tissues and muscles and help relieve tension. Tired shoulder muscles unwind as you work through gentle, slow stretches. A wise workout includes flexibility stretches as part of the warm-up and cool-down phases. Bouncing during a stretch can strain your muscles; it's better to hold each stretch for 10 to 30 seconds.

Check the flexibility of your lower back and hamstrings — two areas vulnerable to strain — by placing a yardstick on the floor and putting a long

Walk-Jog Chart					
Aerobic Fitness Category	Under 30	30-39	40-49	50-59	60+
Very poor	15:00	15:30	16:00	17:00	18:30
Poor	15:00	15:30	16:00	17:00	18:30
Fair	13:30	14:00	14:45	15:45	17:00
Good	12:00	12:30	13:15	14:15	15:30
Excellent	10:45	11:15	12:00	13:00	14:00
Superior	9:30	10:00	10:30	11:15	12:30

Cundiff, David E. and Paul Brynteson. *Health Fitness Guide to a Lifestyle*, © 1979. Reprinted with permission of Kendall/Hunt Publishing Co.

strip of masking tape across it at a right angle to the 15-inch mark. (See photograph at right.)

After warming up with gentle stretches, remove your shoes, and sit on the floor with the yardstick between your legs. Place your heels near the edge of the tape line about 10 to 12 inches apart. With both hands parallel, bend forward and touch the yardstick with your fingertips, keeping your knees straight. Hold the position briefly; then relax and repeat twice. Check your score against the scores on the following chart.

Flexibility Chart

SIT AND REACH TEST SCORES (scores in inches)

Age	Males					Females				
	Excellent	Good	Average	Fair	Poor	Excellent	Good	Average	Fair	Poor
35 and under	21	19	15	9	7	23	21	18	14	11
36 to 45	21	19	14	10	5	23	21	17	12	10
45 and above	20	17	13	8	5	22	19	15	11	9

Reprinted from *The Y's Way to Physical Fitness*, © 1982, with permission of the YMCA of the USA, 101 N. Wacker Dr., Chicago, IL 60606.

Strength exercises can result in stronger abdominal muscles, helping to prevent back pain. As you increase your overall strength, you can decrease your chances of injury from both sudden and sustained exertion. Both weight training and calisthenics are strength-builders; whichever form you choose, proper posture and breathing techniques are as important as the amount of weight you lift or the number of repetitions. Breathe *in* when you are ready to start and muscles are relaxed, breathe *out* when you push or lift, and never hold your breath. This increases blood pressure and places an unnatural strain on your heart.

To measure muscle strength, try the one-minute sit-up test. Lie on your back with your knees bent and your feet flat. Have a partner hold your ankles firmly as you count the number of sit-ups you can do in 60 seconds. Make sure that your elbows touch the floor in the ''down'' position. Match your total to the scores below:

Strength Chart

ONE-MINUTE SIT-UP TEST SCORES

Age	Males					Females				
	Excellent	Good	Average	Fair	Poor	Excellent	Good	Average	Fair	Poor
35 and under	45	41-44	31-40	23-30	0-22	39	34-38	24-33	15-23	0-14
36 to 45	42	38-41	28-37	18-27	0-17	35	28-34	18-27	10-17	0-9
46 and above	38	33-37	23-32	15-22	0-14	24	20-23	12-19	7-11	0-6

Reprinted from *The Y's Way to Physical Fitness*, © 1982, with permission of the YMCA of the USA, 101 N. Wacker Dr., Chicago, IL 60606.

A Modified Fitness Program

This program of exercise illustrates how you can include activities for flexibility, strength, and aerobic fitness to create your own program. The first five exercises serve as a warm-up and include conditioning for flexibility and strength. Jumping rope conditions for aerobic fitness, and the last three exercises, which include more flexibility and strength conditioning, serve as a cool-down. Keep in mind that you will want to add another set of 8 to 12 repetitions to your strength exercises until you can complete 3 sets using good form. You will also want to include additional activities for flexibility and strength conditioning.

Flexibility and Strength—*Slowly rotate arms forward making larger and larger circles until they complete a full range of motion. Pause and rotate arms in opposite direction. Complete 8 to 12 repetitions in each direction.*

Strength—*Lie face down with hands clasped behind waist. Tuck chin, and contract buttocks muscles as you raise your head and chest off of floor. Complete 8 to 12 repetitions.*

Flexibility—*Sit on floor, and clasp hands together under knees. Bring knees up to chest near tucked chin. Slowly rock back and forth 8 to 10 times.*

Strength—*Position yourself across a bench or table, with hips off of bench. Slowly raise legs parallel to floor. Pause and slowly lower legs to within one inch of floor. Complete 8 to 12 repetitions.*

Flexibility—*Lie on back and bend one knee, placing foot flat on floor. Grab opposite leg below calf, and pull straightened leg to head until you feel a slight discomfort. Hold for 10 to 30 seconds; relax and repeat 2 to 6 times. Switch legs, and repeat the stretch.*

Aerobic—*For any aerobic exercise (skipping rope, walking, jogging, etc.), the goal is to work up to keeping your heart beat at 60 to 90 percent of its maximum predicted rate for 20 to 30 minutes at a time, 3 to 5 times a week. (See page 19.)*

Flexibility—*Assume sitting position shown, with one foot tucked in and the other extended out in front. Lean forward from the waist, keeping back straight and foot upright. Aim your chin between the knee and ankle (do not bend head toward knee). Slowly stretch until you feel a slight discomfort, and hold for 10 to 30 seconds. Relax and repeat 2 to 6 times. Switch leg positions, and repeat the stretch.*

Flexibility—*Lie on back with legs straight; pull one knee to chest, keeping head and shoulders relaxed on floor. Rotate ankle in both directions for 10 to 30 seconds. Relax and repeat 2 to 6 times. Switch legs, and repeat the stretch.*

Strength—*Lie on floor with arms crossed in front of chest and knees bent. Tuck chin, and roll up to a sitting position. Slowly lower trunk to floor, taking 4 counts. Hook feet only if necessary. Complete 8 to 12 repetitions. (Don't be concerned if you have trouble rolling up; just concentrate on lowering the trunk slowly.)*

OTHER FITNESS FACTORS

Of course, no one program is suitable for every individual. A number of factors come into play, notably your age, size, sex, physical activity level, and basal metabolic rate (BMR).

How much should you weigh? Traditional weight charts are based on height and frame size, but a more accurate measurement of your ideal weight takes into account the ratio of lean body tissue (muscle and bone) to fat. Experts recommend a body fat percentage of no more than 20 percent for women and 15 percent for men (hormonal balances make the difference). Your ratio can be estimated in two ways: a skinfold caliper test that measures areas such as your arm, chest, back, hip, and thigh, and an underwater test that is considered a more precise calculation. The underwater test is available at university and wellness centers.

However, you can calculate your approximate ideal body weight by using the formula below.

Ideal Body Weight Formula

Women: Allow 100 lbs. for the first 60 inches plus 5 pounds for each inch over 60 inches.
Men: Allow 106 lbs. for the first 60 inches plus 6 pounds for each inch over 60 inches.

An advantage to regular exercise, particularly aerobic, is that it may increase your basal metabolic rate (BMR), the rate at which your body burns calories when at rest. When aerobic exercise elevates your BMR, it can remain elevated for several hours — even burning calories while you sleep. Exercising for 30 minutes a day three times a week for a year can latently burn enough calories to shave 10 pounds of fat beyond the calories expended during the workout.

Many experts believe that the body has a "set point" for regulating metabolism, not unlike a home thermostat that controls temperature by turning the heating and cooling system on and off. When you try to lose weight only by reducing calories, your body reacts by lowering your BMR — that's "dieter's plateau," and the only way to get off of that plateau is by increasing your BMR through routine exercise.

Contrary to myth, both moderate and vigorous exercise reduce rather than increase the appetite by triggering appetite-suppressing hormones.

The chart that follows demonstrates how different aerobic activities use up calories.

Aerobic Activity Chart

CALORIES EXPENDED IN 30 MINUTES OF EXERCISE

Activity	Weight in Pounds		
	130 lbs.	150 lbs.	180 lbs.
Badminton	171	198	240
Calisthenics	128	149	178
Cycling (9 mph)	177	204	249
Fencing	128	149	178
Gardening			
Digging	213	258	312
Mowing	198	228	276
Raking	96	111	132
Judo/Karate	293	338	405
Rowing (Machine)	351	405	486
Skating			
Moderate	148	171	205
Vigorous	265	306	367
Skipping Rope	370	428	513
(70 skips/min.)			
Soccer	230	266	319
Stationary Running	358	414	497
(70 counts/min.)			
Swimming	276	318	387
Tennis	192	222	267
Volleyball	90	102	127
Walking			
(2mph-30 min./mile)	90	104	124
(4 mph-15 min./mile)	156	180	216
Waterskiing	199	230	275

To make a workout safe, it is recommended that you exercise within a range of 60 to 90 percent of your maximum heart rate (MHR = 220 minus your age). Which percentage is appropriate for you is determined by how long you have been active and your present level of fitness. A sedentary person's target heart rate (THR) would be at the lower end of the range (60 to 70 percent of the maximum heart rate), while fit individuals would train at the 85 to 90 percent range.

Once you determine your THR, you can check your pulse during your workout to see if you have reached it or exceeded it. Speed up your pace if your pulse is below your THR, and slow down if your pulse is above your THR. No additional benefit is achieved from training above your THR, and it could place unnecessary strain on your heart. Always end your workout by exercising slowly until your pulse falls below 100.

To Find Your Target Heart Rate

Maximum Heart Rate = 220 minus Age
Target Heart Rate = Maximum Heart Rate x 60 to 90%

A training range of 60 to 90% of your maximum heart rate allows you to improve and maintain aerobic fitness.

- Maximum Heart Rate x 60 to 70% = Sedentary or out-of-shape person

- Maximum Heart Rate x 70 to 80% = Someone who has been exercising for 4 to 6 weeks

- Maximum Heart Rate x 85 to 90% = Fit individuals who wish to maximize aerobic fitness

To Find Your Rate

Resting Pulse: Take your wrist (radial) pulse for 30 seconds, and multiply by 2.

Workout Pulse: Take your wrist (radial) pulse or neck (carotid) pulse for 6 seconds right after exercising, and multiply by 10.

NO MORE "BUTS"

Don't have time to exercise? Work a workout into your life, and you'll add time to your week. Make it something you can't live without, and you'll find new energy and enthusiasm for other activities.

Find the hidden workouts in your day: take the stairs instead of the elevator, don't ride if you can walk, or hand-deliver the memo you might have sent through the office mail.

Three half-hour sessions of vigorous activity each week are recommended as a starting point for overall fitness. Choose activities you enjoy — aerobic dancing, racquetball, swimming — and if one becomes a chore, choose another. Set a regular time for your workout and resolve to stick with it. If you need group support, check out the classes at your local workout facility, YMCA, school or community center. If you prefer to go it alone, check out some workout records or videos from the public library, and find one that suits your style.

But do check with your doctor before starting an exercise program if you are over the age of 35,

have a history of heart trouble, are more than 20 percent overweight, or have any chronic medical problems.

Don't disappoint yourself by setting unrealistic goals for weight loss or activity levels. Can't run a mile? Alternate jogging with walking, and don't sabotage your chance for success by smoking, which drastically increases your risk for cancer and heart disease. If you drink alcoholic beverages, do so in moderation.

Make fitness fun through periodic rewards: not a chocolate sundae, but a new sweatshirt or a book you've been wanting to read. Don't expect overnight success, but if you set up a realistic dietary plan that includes a healthy mix of nutrients and a convenient exercise routine that makes calories consumed compatible with calories expended, you will see results.

The menu and recipe sections that follow will help you in choosing calorie-conscious foods that are both nutritious and delicious. As your body becomes firmer and your step becomes lighter, be proud of your new look — and your new outlook.

Healthy American Meals

American cuisine in the '80s is dedicated to freshness and light-ness, celebrating our national wealth of fruits, vegetables, and herbs. The health food of the '60s and '70s has merged with classic *haute cuisine* to produce a light, elegant style that underscores our growing interest in nutrition and health; our desire to be slim, trim, and firm; and the increasing maturity of the American palate.

Although American cuisine is becoming somewhat of a culinary melting pot, it still retains much of its regional flavor. The thirty menus in this chapter are drawn from a variety of regional and eth-nic foods found throughout the country and, therefore, offer a wide selection of foods. Eclectic is the key word.

From New England are included seafood specialties, such as Seafood-Rice Salad and Shellfish en Papillote. From the mid-Atlantic area come German Apple Pancakes and Crab Crêpes with Spinach Mornay Sauce. Unpretentious farm foods, such as Cube Steak with Peppers and Onions and Braised Pork Loin with Apples and Cider, are Midwestern in flavor. Southern Cajun-Creole tastes get credit for the Chicken Scallop Grillades with Grits and the Praline Thins. Tex-Mex dishes that abound in the Southwest inspired the ''Mexican Special'' menu: Scallops Seviche, Fajitas, Guacamole Salad, and Frozen Piña Colada. And in the West, much of the cuisine relies on the readily available produce and domestic wines to create a truly unique and versatile style that can be found in ''Dinner from the Wok'' and ''Easy Vegetarian Supper.''

Light cooking combines the best of all culinary worlds without

A Light Cocktail Party can be a healthy affair. Clockwise from front: Lemon-Cheese Dip with Vegetables, Sesame-Pepper Vinaigrette, Skewered Marinated Pork, Fruit Kabobs, and Seafood Cocktail Sauce to serve with Deviled Shrimp (menu begins on page 90).

sacrificing flavor for health. In fact, many cooks have found that a light touch actually makes old favorites taste better, because it allows the real flavor of fresh food to come through. Gone is the dependency on heavy cream and butter. Emphasis is now on the bounty of fresh produce available to you in the neighborhood market and on some new, lighter techniques of preparation. As one California chef put it: "The better the cook you are, the easier it is to hold the butter and the cream." The result is that food in the '80s is higher in nutrients, fiber, and complex carbohydrates and lower in fat, cholesterol, sugar, and salt.

Each menu in this section punctuates the philosophy of this evolving American cuisine: that properly prepared food is healthy; that many interesting things can be done with fresh fruits, vegetables, and whole grains; that salt tends to mask the true flavor of food; and that fat is not so hard to reduce if lean protein sources are chosen.

In addition, standards were set for the overall mix of nutrients in each menu: calories derived from fat were limited to no more than 30 percent of the total meal, protein to no more than 20 percent, and carbohydrates to at least 50 percent.

Although many of the menus were created for entertaining, they can also be used to give family meals a boost and get everyone involved in the *Cooking Light* approach to healthy American cuisine. "Quick and Easy" menus, for example, can help you serve a delicious meal to unexpected guests or allow you to enjoy a simple but elegant Sunday supper with the family. Look for tips on make-aheads and planning ahead in all the menu sections.

Whether the meal is for family or guests, the visual impact of food is as important as its taste. Attention to such details as garnishes, color combinations, and the shapes of food, as well as the arrangement of the food on the plate, is very important when creating a beautiful meal. The color photographs which accompany each menu may suggest to you new ways to make the food look inviting when you present the meals at your table.

In order to shop more efficiently, remember to plan your menu in advance; make a shopping list so you won't overbuy or underbuy; avoid leftovers by purchasing required amounts; look for seasonal produce to add variety and freshness; use the Calorie/Nutrient Chart to find a substitute for food that is out of season (be sure that the food is similar and contains about the same number of calories).

The goal of *Cooking Light* is to present healthy meals for your family and guests alike. The menus that follow are not designed for a one-time or occasional diet. Calories are cut, but not so drastically that the menus cannot be used for pleasurable dining. Guidelines for the total calories in each menu remain within such a range as to allow for meals that are nutritious, delicious, festive, appealing, and satisfying — the kinds of meals that will continue to give pleasure on any day on any occasion throughout the years.

For a change of pace on your Weekend Retreat, enjoy Potato and Bacon Omelet, Stir-Fry Broccoli, and Poppy Seed-Cheddar Bread with your morning coffee. Each serving of the omelet has only 190 calories, yet is special enough for a fancy brunch (menu begins on page 28).

From the first sip of Hot Cocoa to the last bite of German Apple Pancake, this breakfast is tops.

Saturday Country Breakfast

The best way to pry open the eyes is with steaming mugs of hot cocoa (1 cup per serving), whipped up in minutes, thanks to a make-ahead mix.

As the next step in this menu, broil the tomatoes with their tasty topping, and grill the ham. (We used a ridged grill pan to create the attractive crosshatch pattern on the ham, but a regular skillet works equally well.)

German Apple Pancake
Grilled Ham
Broiled Tomatoes
Hot Cocoa

Serves 6
Total calories per serving: 347

Keep the tomatoes and ham warm while you make the German apple pancake.

It's okay to go ahead and make the pancake filling, but wait until everyone has appeared to put the pancake itself in the oven; it takes only 12 to 15 minutes to bake. Its airy puffiness makes such a spectacular centerpiece that everyone should be on hand to ooh and aah. And this pancake supplies a healthy dose of vitamins and fiber as well as a nutritious helping of complex carbohydrates.

GERMAN APPLE PANCAKE

3 medium Golden Delicious apples,
   peeled and cored
2 teaspoons lemon juice
Vegetable cooking spray
2 teaspoons unsalted margarine
2 eggs, lightly beaten
½ cup skim milk
½ cup unbleached or all-purpose
   flour
1 teaspoon vanilla extract
½ teaspoon grated lemon rind
⅛ teaspoon ground cinnamon
1 tablespoon sifted powdered sugar

Cut each apple into 16 pieces. Combine apples and lemon juice in a small bowl, tossing well. Coat a large skillet with cooking spray; add apples. Cover and cook over low heat 5 minutes or until apples are tender. Uncover and cook 2 minutes or until lightly browned; set aside, and keep warm.

Place margarine in a 10-inch cast-iron skillet coated with cooking spray. Bake at 425° for 4 minutes or until margarine melts and skillet is hot. Combine eggs, milk, flour, vanilla, lemon rind, and cinnamon in a medium bowl. Beat at medium speed of an electric mixer until smooth. Pour immediately into hot skillet. Bake at 425° for 12 to 15 minutes.

Remove from oven; top with apple slices, and sprinkle with powdered sugar. Cut into 6 equal wedges. Serve immediately. Yield: 6 servings (122 calories per serving).

PRO 3.9 / FAT 3.4 / CARB 19.6 / FIB 1.5 / CHOL 92 / SOD 34 / POT 142

GRILLED HAM

Vegetable cooking spray
1 (¾-pound) ham steak, ½-inch thick

Coat a large skillet or ridged grill pan with cooking spray. Place skillet over medium heat until hot; add ham to skillet, and cook 3 to 4 minutes on each side. Cut ham into 6 equal portions to serve. Yield: 6 servings (94 calories per serving).

PRO 12.5 / FAT 4.3 / CARB 0.3 / FIB 0.0 / CHOL 32 / SOD 785 / POT 205

BROILED TOMATOES

3 tablespoons fine, dry breadcrumbs
2 teaspoons dried whole basil or 3 tablespoons
   minced fresh basil
1 tablespoon plus 1 teaspoon chopped fresh parsley
¼ teaspoon pepper
⅛ teaspoon dried whole thyme
2 tablespoons unsalted margarine, melted
6 medium tomatoes
Vegetable cooking spray
Additional fresh basil leaves (optional)

Combine first 6 ingredients in a small bowl; mix well, and set aside. Cut off top of each tomato; sprinkle 1 tablespoon breadcrumb mixture onto cut sides of tomatoes. Place tomatoes on a broiler pan coated with cooking spray. Broil 6 inches from heat 3 to 5 minutes. Garnish with additional basil leaves, if desired. Yield: 6 servings (73 calories per serving).

PRO 1.7 / FAT 4.2 / CARB 8.7 / FIB 1.2 / CHOL 0 / SOD 35 / POT 311

HOT COCOA

¾ cup instant non-fat dry milk powder
¼ cup sugar
¼ cup Dutch process or unsweetened cocoa
¼ teaspoon ground cinnamon
Boiling water

Combine first 4 ingredients in a small bowl; stir well. Store mix in an airtight container.

For each serving, place 2 tablespoons cocoa mix in a mug. Add 1 cup boiling water, stirring well. Yield: 10 servings (58 calories per serving).

PRO 3.6 / FAT 0.6 / CARB 10.7 / FIB 0.1 / CHOL 2 / SOD 64 / POT 176

> Breakfast is an important meal; it gives you a mental and physical boost, making you more alert in the morning.
>
> In addition, scientists are rethinking their belief that it's what you eat that is important; it's also when you eat, suggesting that the time of day may be as significant as the food you eat. Calories consumed early in the day are more likely to be burned up, and those consumed in the evening are more likely to be stored as fat.

Complement the rich creaminess of Eggs Florentine with the tart freshness of Mixed Fruit with Lime for a special breakfast.

Special Breakfast For Four

Eggs Florentine
Mixed Fruit with Lime
Whole Wheat Biscuits
Blueberry-Orange Spread
Cinnamon Coffee

Serves 4
Total calories per serving: 428

Mix up the biscuit dough for this breakfast while blissfully inhaling the aroma of brewing cinnamon coffee. If you have timed it well, the biscuits should be coming out of the oven just as the hungry throngs appear at the breakfast table.

The sauce for the eggs Florentine takes only ten minutes. Cook the spinach; poach the eggs, and assemble the goodies in individual gratin dishes. Another three minutes under the broiler and it's straight to the table.

Two elements of this menu require no morning preparation. The iron-rich blueberry-orange spread can be made days ahead and kept in the refrigerator.

Time needn't be wasted on the mixed fruit with lime either. Cut up the fruit ahead; toss the mixture, and let it chill overnight.

EGGS FLORENTINE

1 tablespoon unsalted margarine
1 tablespoon all-purpose flour
1¼ cups skim milk
2 tablespoons (½ ounce) shredded Swiss cheese
¼ cup grated Parmesan cheese, divided
1 teaspoon Dijon mustard
¼ teaspoon pepper
⅛ teaspoon ground nutmeg (optional)
1 (10-ounce) package frozen chopped spinach
4 eggs, poached

Melt margarine in a heavy saucepan over low heat; add flour, stirring until smooth. Cook 1 minute, stirring constantly. Gradually add milk; cook over medium heat, stirring constantly, until mixture is thickened and bubbly. Add Swiss cheese, 2 tablespoons Parmesan, mustard, pepper, and nutmeg, if desired; cook over medium heat until cheese melts, stirring constantly. Remove from heat, and set sauce aside.

Cook frozen spinach according to package

directions, omitting salt; gently squeeze to remove as much moisture as possible. Divide spinach evenly among four 6-ounce custard cups; spoon 2 tablespoons sauce over spinach in each cup. Place 1 poached egg in each cup; top each with 3 tablespoons sauce and 1½ teaspoons Parmesan cheese.

Place custard cups on a broiler pan. Broil 6 inches from heat 2 minutes or until lightly browned. Serve immediately. Yield: 4 servings (193 calories per serving).

PRO 14.2 / FAT 11.3 / CARB 9.3 / FIB 1.6 / CHOL 283 / SOD 301 / POT 435

MIXED FRUIT WITH LIME

1½ cups diced cantaloupe
1½ cups diced honeydew
1 cup sliced fresh strawberries
2 kiwi, peeled and sliced
2 tablespoons lime juice
2 teaspoons sugar
1 teaspoon grated lime rind

Combine all ingredients in a large bowl; toss lightly. Cover and chill thoroughly. Yield: 4 servings (89 calories per 1¼-cup serving).

PRO 1.6 / FAT 0.6 / CARB 18.6 / FIB 1.7 / CHOL 0 / SOD 14 / POT 540

WHOLE WHEAT BISCUITS

½ cup unbleached or all-purpose
   flour
½ cup whole wheat flour
2 teaspoons baking powder
¼ teaspoon salt
2 tablespoons unsalted margarine
¼ cup skim milk
Vegetable cooking spray

Combine first 4 ingredients in a bowl; cut in margarine with a pastry blender until mixture resembles coarse meal. Add milk, stirring until dry ingredients are moistened. Turn dough out onto a lightly floured surface, and knead 4 to 5 times.

Roll dough to ½-inch thickness, and cut into rounds with a 2-inch biscuit cutter. Place biscuits on a baking sheet coated with cooking spray, and bake at 425° for 12 minutes or until golden.

Serve each biscuit with 1 tablespoon Blueberry-Orange Spread, if desired. Yield: 10 biscuits (125 calories per 2-biscuit serving).

PRO 3.2 / FAT 4.9 / CARB 18.0 / FIB 0.9 / CHOL 0 / SOD 245 / POT 81

BLUEBERRY-ORANGE SPREAD

1 teaspoon unflavored gelatin
¼ cup unsweetened orange juice
2 cups fresh blueberries
½ cup water
2 tablespoons sugar
2 teaspoons lemon juice
1½ teaspoons grated orange rind
¼ teaspoon ground ginger

Combine gelatin and orange juice, stirring well; set aside.

Combine blueberries, water, sugar, lemon juice, orange rind, and ginger in a medium saucepan; bring to a boil. Reduce heat; simmer, uncovered, 6 minutes, stirring occasionally.

Add gelatin mixture to blueberry mixture, stirring well. Cook over medium heat 2 minutes or until gelatin is completely dissolved, stirring constantly. Remove from heat, and cool to room temperature.

Pour into glass jars, and cover tightly. Refrigerate 4 to 6 hours or until mixture is thoroughly chilled. Store in refrigerator up to 2 weeks. Yield: 2 half pints (9 calories per tablespoon).

PRO 0.2 / FAT 0.0 / CARB 2.3 / FIB 0.3 / CHOL 0 / SOD 1 / POT 12

CINNAMON COFFEE

1 cup ground coffee (not instant)
1 teaspoon ground cinnamon
½ teaspoon vanilla extract

Combine coffee, cinnamon, and vanilla, mixing well. For each cup of coffee desired, use 1 tablespoon plus 1 teaspoon coffee mixture per cup of water. Brew until coffee reaches desired strength. Yield: 12 servings (3 calories per 1-cup serving).

PRO 0.0 / FAT 0.0 / CARB 0.2 / FIB 0.0 / CHOL 0 / SOD 0 / POT 142

Weekend Retreat Breakfast

The piping hot potato and bacon omelet makes a delectable impromptu breakfast after an early morning walk. By combining the egg whites with the whole eggs, cholesterol is reduced, yet the entrée still retains its creamy richness.

We recommend accompanying this hearty omelet with toasted slices of poppy seed Cheddar bread (1 slice per serving), baked the day before and

**Potato and Bacon Omelet
Stir-Fry Broccoli
Poppy Seed-Cheddar
Bread
Frozen Pineapple Yogurt
with Raspberries**

Serves 4
Total calories per serving: 424

waiting in the refrigerator. Steamed broccoli is another

easily pulled together dish. Stir-frying quickly prior to steaming keeps it crisp and full of vitamins. An added plus to broccoli is its high calcium content.

Like the bread, frozen pineapple yogurt is another make-ahead item. And like the broccoli, it's another rich source of calcium. Let the yogurt soften slightly before serving, if desired, and top it with raspberries or other seasonal fruit.

POTATO AND BACON OMELET

½ pound baking potatoes, peeled and diced
1 teaspoon vegetable oil
1 medium onion, thinly sliced
2 slices lean bacon, cut into 1-inch pieces
4 eggs
2 egg whites
¼ cup skim milk
2 tablespoons chopped fresh parsley
1 tablespoon chopped fresh chives
¼ teaspoon salt
⅛ teaspoon pepper
1 teaspoon unsalted margarine

Place potato and water to cover in a small saucepan; bring to a boil. Boil 3 minutes, and drain well.

Heat oil in a 10-inch nonstick skillet over medium heat; sauté potato and onion just until tender and browned. Transfer mixture to a small bowl, and set aside.

Cook bacon over medium heat until browned and crisp. Drain well on paper towels. Add to potato mixture, and set aside.

Combine eggs, egg whites, milk, parsley, chives, salt, and pepper in a medium mixing bowl; beat well.

Heat a 6-inch nonstick skillet or omelet pan over medium heat until hot enough to sizzle a drop of water; pour in half of egg mixture. As mixture starts to cook, gently lift the edges of

omelet with a spatula, and tilt pan to allow uncooked portions to flow underneath. When egg mixture is set, spoon half of potato mixture over half of omelet; loosen omelet with a spatula, and carefully fold in half. Slide onto a warm serving platter; keep warm. Repeat procedure with remaining egg and potato mixtures.

Cut each omelet in half; serve immediately. Yield: 4 servings (190 calories per serving).

PRO 11.2 / FAT 9.7 / CARB 14.6 / FIB 0.6 / CHOL 277 / SOD 313 / POT 507

Low-fat yogurt is a boon for calorie counters.

STIR-FRY BROCCOLI

1 pound fresh broccoli
1 teaspoon vegetable oil
½ cup boiling water
½ teaspoon chicken-flavored bouillon
  granules
4 slices lemon

Trim off large leaves of broccoli. Remove tough ends of lower stalks. Separate into spears.

Heat oil in a large nonstick skillet over medium-high heat until hot. Add broccoli; stir-fry 1 minute. Combine water and bouillon granules, stirring well; add to broccoli. Cover and cook 3 minutes or until crisp-tender. Garnish with lemon slices to serve. Yield: 4 servings (44 calories per serving).

PRO 3.5 / FAT 1.6 / CARB 6.1 / FIB 2.4 / CHOL 0 / SOD 67 / POT 285

POPPY SEED-CHEDDAR BREAD

1 package dry yeast
2 teaspoons sugar
1 cup warm water (105° to 115°)
½ teaspoon salt
¼ teaspoon ground red pepper
2½ cups unbleached or all-purpose flour, divided
1 cup (4 ounces) finely shredded sharp
  Cheddar cheese
Vegetable cooking spray
1 egg white, lightly beaten
1 teaspoon water
1 teaspoon poppy seeds

Dissolve yeast and sugar in 1 cup warm water; let stand 5 minutes or until bubbly. Combine yeast mixture, salt, red pepper, and half the flour in a large mixing bowl. Beat mixture at low speed of an electric mixer until smooth. Stir in enough remaining flour to make a soft dough.

Turn dough out onto a lightly floured surface,

and knead in cheese. Knead dough 8 minutes or until smooth and elastic. Place dough in a bowl, coated with cooking spray, turning to grease top. Cover and let rise in a warm place (85°), free from drafts, 1 hour or until dough is doubled in bulk.

Punch dough down. Turn dough out, and shape into a loaf; place in an 8½- x 4½- x 3-inch loafpan, coated with cooking spray. Combine egg white and 1 teaspoon water; beat well, and gently brush mixture over top of loaf. Sprinkle with poppy seeds. Cover and let rise in a warm place (85°), free from drafts, 1 hour or until doubled in bulk. Bake at 375° for 30 minutes or until loaf sounds hollow when tapped. Remove bread from pan immediately; cool on a wire rack. Yield: 1 loaf or 16 (½-inch) slices (97 calories per slice).

PRO 4.1 / FAT 2.6 / CARB 14.3 / FIB 0.0 / CHOL 7 / SOD 121 / POT 42

FROZEN PINEAPPLE YOGURT WITH RASPBERRIES

1 (20-ounce) can unsweetened pineapple
  chunks, drained
½ cup plain low-fat yogurt
2 tablespoons sifted powdered
  sugar
1 tablespoon lemon juice
1 cup fresh raspberries
Fresh mint leaves

Arrange pineapple on a baking sheet, and

freeze 2 hours or until frozen.

Combine yogurt, sugar, and lemon juice in container of a food processor or electric blender, and process until well combined. Add pineapple, and process until smooth. Divide yogurt among sherbet glasses, and garnish with raspberries and mint leaves. Yield: 4 servings (93 calories per serving).

PRO 2.1 / FAT 1.0 / CARB 20.8 / FIB 2.8 / CHOL 2 / SOD 21 / POT 220

After Workout Breakfast

According to exercise experts, morning workouts are great because our bodies burn calories most efficiently at that time of day. In addition, the exertion speeds up our metabolic rate for the rest of the day.

This high-energy menu, loaded with complex carbohydrates, is an ideal complement to morning

Whole Wheat Waffles with Welsh Rarebit Sauce
Chunky Applesauce
Tomato Cocktail Refresher

Serves 6
Total calories per serving: 453

exercise. The tomato cocktail refresher supplies a bounty of vita-

min A and helps replenish some of the water you might have lost during your workout.

The whole wheat waffles, in combination with their cheesy Welsh rarebit sauce, are high in both calcium and fiber. Fiber also turns up in the chunky applesauce, a sweet but nutritious ending note.

A morning workout followed by this nutrient-rich breakfast will set you up for a positively exhilarating day.

WHOLE WHEAT WAFFLES

2 eggs
2 cups skim milk
3 tablespoons vegetable oil
1 cup unbleached or all-purpose flour
1 cup whole wheat flour
1 teaspoon sugar
¼ teaspoon salt
Vegetable cooking spray
Welsh Rarebit Sauce

Beat eggs in a medium bowl at medium speed of electric mixer until light and fluffy; add milk and oil, mixing well. Combine flour, sugar, and salt; gradually add to milk mixture, beating until smooth.

Spoon 1⅓ cups batter into a preheated waffle iron coated with cooking spray. Cook 6 to 8 minutes or until steaming stops and waffle is crisp. Remove waffle; keep warm. Repeat procedure with remaining batter. Serve with 3 tablespoons Welch Rarebit Sauce. Yield: 6 servings (251 calories per 2-waffle serving plus 96 calories per 3 tablespoons sauce).

Welsh Rarebit Sauce:

¾ cup evaporated skim milk
1 cup (4 ounces) shredded Monterey Jack cheese
1 teaspoon Dijon mustard
½ teaspoon Worcestershire sauce
⅛ teaspoon lemon juice
Dash of salt
Dash of red pepper

Place milk in a small saucepan; cook over medium-low heat until hot (do not allow to boil). Gradually stir in cheese; stir until cheese melts and mixture is smooth. Add remaining ingredients. Reduce heat to low, and cook 2 minutes or until slightly thickened, stirring frequently. Yield: 1⅛ cups (32 calories per tablespoon).

PRO 16.6 / FAT 15.2 / CARB 37.3 / FIB 1.5 / CHOL 109 / SOD 356 / POT 381

CHUNKY APPLESAUCE

4 medium-size cooking apples, peeled and quartered
¾ cup unsweetened apple juice
½ teaspoon ground cinnamon
⅛ teaspoon ground nutmeg

Combine apples and apple juice in a medium saucepan. Cover and cook over medium heat 15 minutes or until tender, stirring occasionally. Remove from heat, and stir in spices. Serve warm or cold. Yield: 6 servings (67 calories per ½-cup serving).

PRO 0.2 / FAT 0.4 / CARB 17.2 / FIB 1.9 / CHOL 0 / SOD 1 / POT 139

TOMATO COCKTAIL REFRESHER

1 (46 ounce) can tomato juice
2 to 3 teaspoons drained prepared horseradish
¼ to ½ teaspoon hot sauce
Ice cubes
1 lemon, sliced and seeded

Combine first 3 ingredients in a serving pitcher; stir well. Pour over ice cubes in serving glasses; garnish with lemon slices. Yield: 6 cups (39 calories per 1-cup serving).

PRO 1.7 / FAT 0.1 / CARB 9.8 / FIB 0.9 / CHOL 0 / SOD 822 / POT 824

 With a growing interest in physical fitness, exercise testing has become an important part of periodic health evaluations. A heart stressed by exercise provides the precise information needed for a professional to assess your fitness and develop a safe exercise program.

An exercise test should be given to people older than 35, to anyone with heart problems, high blood pressure, high cholesterol, a family history of heart disease, and to those who smoke cigarettes. People who are on medication that affects the heart rate should also have this test before starting an exercise routine.

Today's exercise tests usually involve walking or running on a motor-driven treadmill at various speeds and inclines.

After the test, the individual sits quietly or lies down for 5 minutes. Often during this recovery period, changes show up that were not apparent even during maximal exercise.

Springtime Brunch

Welcome spring with a brunch centered around an Italian dish named for it: pasta with primavera sauce.

Our primavera ("spring" in Italian) sauce offers up a bounty of tempting produce, from crunchy snow peas and asparagus to succulent yellow squash. We used the tubular pasta known as *penne* because of its interesting shape, but any macaroni-type

Primavera Pasta
Tuscan Bread
Almond-Peach Tart

Serves 8
Total calories per serving: 406

pasta works well.

A crusty loaf of Tuscan bread (1 slice per serving for correct calorie count) makes the meal even more tasty and satisfying.

But don't forget to save room for dessert. With finely ground almonds as a base for the tart, it's worth saving room for. Fresh peaches are the highlight, adding yet another seasonal touch. We've kept the sugar to a minimum to let the radiant peach flavor shine through, so be sure to use the ripest fruit you can find. Both the bread and the tart can be made ahead.

PRIMAVERA PASTA

½ pound fresh asparagus spears
¼ pound fresh snow peas
2 medium-size yellow squash, halved lengthwise and sliced
Vegetable cooking spray
1 shallot, minced
2 cloves garlic, minced
½ pound fresh mushrooms, sliced
¼ cup minced fresh parsley
1 tablespoon dried whole basil or ¼ cup minced fresh basil
⅓ cup evaporated skim milk
1 tablespoon unsalted margarine
¼ cup grated Parmesan cheese
½ pound tubular pasta, cooked al dente without salt or fat
3 medium tomatoes, diced and drained
1 tablespoon plus 1½ teaspoons Parmesan cheese

Snap off tough ends of asparagus. Remove scales with a knife or vegetable peeler. Cut spears into 1½-inch pieces; set aside. Trim ends of snow peas, and remove strings; set aside.

Bring 3 to 4 inches of water to a boil in a large Dutch oven. Add asparagus to water; return to a boil. Add squash to mixture; return to a boil. Add snow peas to mixture; return to a boil. Remove from heat, and drain; rinse under cold running water. Drain well, and set aside.

Coat a large skillet with cooking spray; place over medium-high heat until hot. Add shallot

and garlic, and sauté 1 minute; add mushrooms, and sauté 3 minutes. Add drained vegetable mixture, parsley, and basil; cook, stirring frequently, 3 minutes. Remove from heat, and set aside.

Combine evaporated milk and margarine in a small saucepan; cook over medium heat until thoroughly heated. Gradually add ¼ cup Parmesan cheese; stir until well blended. Set aside.

Combine pasta, tomatoes, reserved vegetable mixture, and reserved sauce in a large bowl; toss gently to combine well.

Transfer mixture to a large serving platter; sprinkle with remaining Parmesan cheese. Yield: 8 servings (106 calories per serving).

PRO 6.0 / FAT 2.9 / CARB 15.6 / FIB 1.6 / CHOL 3 / SOD 83 / POT 466

Regular exercise is often the treatment of choice for individuals attempting to manage their stress. For thousands of years, human beings were required to be physical just for survival. This daily active life-style provided an outlet for the tensions and frustrations of daily living.

In the past 50 years, our society has become more technical, and as a result people have become more sedentary. Inactivity is now the norm; many people have eliminated exercise, an important stress outlet, from their lives.

The colorful array of vegetables in Primavera Pasta enhances the springlike look of this brunch.

TUSCAN BREAD

1 package dry yeast
1 teaspoon sugar
1¼ cups warm water (105° to 115°),
   divided
4 to 4½ cups unbleached or all-purpose
   flour, divided
½ teaspoon salt
Vegetable cooking spray

Dissolve yeast and sugar in ¾ cup warm water in a large bowl; let stand 5 minutes. Add ¾ cup flour, and stir well; cover and let rise in a warm place (85°), free from drafts, 30 minutes or until doubled in bulk.

Stir yeast sponge down; add ½ cup warm water and salt, stirring well. Add enough remaining flour to make a stiff dough. Turn dough out onto a lightly floured surface; knead 8 to 10 minutes or until smooth and elastic. Place dough in a bowl coated with cooking spray, turning to grease top. Cover and let rise in a warm place (85°), free from drafts, 1 hour and 15 minutes or until doubled in bulk.

Punch dough down; let rest 5 minutes. Shape dough into a 14-inch-long loaf. Dust loaf lightly with flour, and place on a baking sheet. Cover and let rise in a warm place (85°), free from drafts, 30 minutes or until doubled in bulk.

Bake at 400° for 30 minutes or until loaf sounds hollow when tapped. Remove bread from baking sheet; cool on a wire rack. Yield: 1 loaf or 16 (1-inch) slices (103 calories per slice).

PRO 3.2 / FAT 0.3 / CARB 22.0 / FIB 0.0 / CHOL 0 / SOD 75 / POT 44

ALMOND-PEACH TART

1 cup unbleached or all-purpose flour
¼ cup finely ground almonds
1 tablespoon sugar
Dash of salt
¼ cup plus 1 tablespoon unsalted margarine,
   chilled
½ teaspoon vanilla extract
¼ teaspoon almond extract
3 tablespoons cold water
3½ cups sliced, peeled fresh peaches
2 tablespoons reduced-calorie peach spread
1 tablespoon Amaretto or Cognac
1 tablespoon sugar

Combine flour, almonds, 1 tablespoon sugar, and salt in a small bowl; cut in margarine with a pastry blender until mixture resembles coarse meal. Sprinkle flavorings and water evenly over surface; stir with a fork until dry ingredients are moistened. Shape dough into a ball; chill.

Roll dough to ⅛-inch thickness on a lightly floured surface; fit into a 9½-inch tart pan. Prick bottom and sides of tart shell with a fork. Bake at 350° for 30 minutes or until golden brown. Cool completely on a wire rack, and remove from tart pan. Arrange peach slices in tart shell, and set aside.

Heat peach spread in a small saucepan over low heat until melted; remove from heat, and stir in Amaretto, mixing well. Brush evenly over peaches in tart shell; sprinkle 1 tablespoon sugar over peaches. Cover edges of tart shell with aluminum foil to prevent overbrowning. Broil 5 to 6 inches from heat 5 minutes or until edges of peaches are lightly browned. Cool. Cut into wedges to serve. Yield: 8 servings (197 calories per serving).

PRO 2.8 / FAT 9.4 / CARB 25.6 / FIB 2.0 / CHOL 0 / SOD 21 / POT 203

A fitting finale to a New Orleans Brunch, Lemon Sorbet and Praline Thins.

New Orleans Brunch

Creole cooks are experts on using herbs and spices for maximum flavor, a technique that makes it possible to cut more calorie-rich ingredients out and at the same time keep the taste-testers happy.

For instance, over half a dozen herbs and spices (including Cajun favorites, paprika and red pepper) give a savory lift to our recipe for chicken grillades.

We substituted chicken for the traditional beef in the grillades to make a lighter dish, but we never dreamed of fiddling with the grits. They're a welcome

Chicken Grillades
Spinach Salad with
Cucumber Vinaigrette
Praline Thins
Lemon Sorbet

Serves 6
Total calories per serving: 427

switch from the popular standby of mashed potatoes made with milk and butter. Nutritionally speaking, grits are a richer source of fiber, too.

The salad is simply a nutritious mélange of crisp greens and other vegetables tossed with a delicate vinaigrette dressing — a combination that doesn't fight with the spicy grillade sauce.

The tart lemon sorbet can be made ahead and is so easy to put together that it will probably become a mainstay in your repertoire of desserts.

Another make-ahead is the lacy praline thins (1 cookie per serving), which are reminiscent of New Orleans cuisine. They may be served as a flat or rolled cookie. In any case, a serving of this dessert twosome will leave your guests content.

CHICKEN GRILLADES

6 (¼-pound) boneless chicken breast halves, skinned
2 tablespoons all-purpose flour
⅛ teaspoon salt
⅛ teaspoon pepper
1 tablespoon vegetable oil
1½ teaspoons unsalted margarine
¼ cup minced onion
¼ cup minced celery
¼ cup minced green pepper
1 clove garlic, minced
¼ teaspoon paprika
¼ teaspoon dried whole thyme
⅛ teaspoon dried whole oregano
⅛ teaspoon dried whole basil
⅛ teaspoon red pepper
1 small bay leaf
1 tablespoon all-purpose flour
½ cup plus 2 tablespoons beef broth
¼ cup plus 2 tablespoons tomato paste
2 cups hot cooked regular grits (cooked without salt or fat)

Place chicken between 2 sheets of waxed paper; pound to ¼-inch thickness, using a meat mallet or rolling pin.

Combine 2 tablespoons flour, salt, and pepper; dredge chicken in flour mixture. Heat oil and margarine over medium-high heat in a large nonstick skillet until hot. Add chicken, and cook 30 seconds on each side; transfer to a plate, and keep warm.

Add next 10 ingredients to skillet, and cook over medium heat until onion is tender, stirring occasionally. Add 1 tablespoon flour, and cook 3 minutes, stirring constantly. Add broth and tomato paste; cover and simmer 10 minutes. Add chicken; simmer 5 minutes or until chicken is tender and thoroughly heated, stirring occasionally. Remove and discard bay leaf. Serve immediately with hot grits. Yield: 6 servings (208 calories per serving plus 49 calories per ⅓ cup cooked grits).

PRO 29.2 / FAT 6.6 / CARB 19.0 / FIB 0.8 / CHOL 75 / SOD 292 / POT 459

SPINACH SALAD WITH CUCUMBER VINAIGRETTE

1 medium cucumber, peeled and seeded
1 shallot, chopped
2 tablespoons water
2 tablespoons cider vinegar
2 teaspoons vegetable oil
½ teaspoon sugar
⅛ teaspoon salt
⅛ teaspoon pepper
¾ pound spinach, washed, trimmed, and torn
  into pieces
6 ounces Belgian endive, sliced diagonally
2 cups sliced fresh mushrooms
8 radishes, trimmed and sliced
1 green onion, chopped

Combine first 8 ingredients in container of an electric blender or food processor, and process until smooth. Chill at least 30 minutes. Combine spinach, endive, mushrooms, radishes, and onion in a salad bowl. Pour dressing over vegetables. Toss gently. Yield: 6 servings (48 calories per serving).

PRO 2.9 / FAT 2.0 / CARB 6.5 / FIB 3.0 / CHOL 0 / SOD 102 / POT 561

Many people feel overwhelmed with the idea of giving up salt. But by adjusting the flavorings and developing the art of seasoning foods with lemon juice, garlic, spices, and fresh herbs, you can fool the palate and introduce yourself to a whole new world of interesting flavors.

As a bonus, herbs and spices contain few calories and add greatly to the taste and enjoyment of cooking. Fresh herbs usually impart a better flavor than the dried variety and should be used when available. In substituting fresh for dry, 4 parts of fresh herbs are equal to 1 part dried. Therefore, allow 1 teaspoon fresh herbs for ¼ teaspoon of dried.

Store dried seasonings in a cool, dry area to maintain their flavor. Keep them tightly covered away from the stove, and use within one year. To release the oils and to increase their verve, crush or crumble herbs in your hands or with a mortar and pestle before using.

Above all, don't be afraid to experiment. Try new and different combinations of seasonings, remembering to taste as you go.

PRALINE THINS

½ cup finely chopped pecans
½ cup firmly packed brown sugar
2 tablespoons all-purpose flour
2 tablespoons unsalted margarine, melted
½ teaspoon vanilla extract
¼ teaspoon ground cinnamon
1 egg white, lightly beaten
Vegetable cooking spray

Combine first 6 ingredients in a bowl; stir in egg white until just blended. Line a baking sheet with aluminum foil, shiny side down, and coat foil with cooking spray. Drop batter by heaping teaspoonfuls 3 inches apart onto foil; bake at 350° for 7 to 9 minutes or just until firm. Lift cookies off foil with a metal spatula; curl around a rolling pin. Let cool 1 to 2 minutes or until hard. Remove to wire racks to cool completely. Store in an airtight container. Yield: 20 cookies (48 calories each).

PRO 0.5 / FAT 3.1 / CARB 4.8 / FIB 0.1 / CHOL 0 / SOD 4 / POT 27

LEMON SORBET

2½ cups water
½ cup sugar
1 cup fresh lemon juice
Candied violets (optional)

Combine water and sugar in a medium saucepan; bring to a boil. Cook 5 minutes, stirring occasionally. Remove from heat; let cool to room temperature, and chill.

Add lemon juice, stirring well. Pour mixture into an 8-inch square baking pan. Freeze.

Transfer mixture to container of an electric blender, and process until smooth. Spoon into serving dishes. Garnish with candied violets, if desired. Yield: 3 cups (74 calories per ½-cup serving).

PRO 0.2 / FAT 0.0 / CARB 20.1 / FIB 0.0 / CHOL 0 / SOD 1 / POT 51

Avocado and alfalfa sprouts make these Dagwood Sandwiches special. Packed in a hamper as a wholesome Bike Trip Take-Along, they will add pleasure to a leisurely two-wheeling day (menu begins on page 48).

Seashore Delight

Come summertime, the beach is really the only place to be. Our picnic suggestion is a seafood-rice salad with fresh shrimp and bay scallops that can be made the day before and chilled overnight. It will be a refreshing respite from the heat.

In combination with some crispy bagel thins (4 thins per serving for the correct calorie

Seafood-Rice Salad
Roasted Peppers
Bagel Thins
Pears Poached in Red Wine

Serves 6
Total calories per serving: 530

count), the salad will provide enough carbohydrates to stoke

you up for an afternoon of volleyball on the sand.

The roasted peppers (green, yellow, or red) can also be prepared ahead and served chilled or at room temperature. They add color and crunch to this menu, while the poached pears sate your sweet tooth without betraying your waistline in that slim-line swim suit.

SEAFOOD-RICE SALAD

2 quarts water
2 tablespoons lemon juice
1 bay leaf
¼ teaspoon salt
¾ pound fresh large shrimp, peeled and deveined
¾ pound fresh bay scallops, rinsed and drained
1⅓ cups water
1½ teaspoons chicken-flavored bouillon granules
⅔ cup regular rice, uncooked
⅔ cup uncooked wild rice
1⅓ cups water
¼ pound snow peas
¼ cup lemon juice
1 tablespoon tarragon vinegar
1 tablespoon olive oil
3 tablespoons minced fresh parsley
1 clove garlic, minced
½ teaspoon salt
¼ teaspoon crushed red pepper
Leaf lettuce

Combine 2 quarts water, 2 tablespoons lemon juice, bay leaf, and ¼ teaspoon salt in a Dutch oven; bring to a boil. Add shrimp; cook 30 seconds. Add scallops, and cook 2 minutes. Drain; discard bay leaf, and rinse. Cover and chill.

Combine 1⅓ cups water and bouillon granules in a medium saucepan; bring to a boil, and stir in regular rice. Reduce heat; cover and simmer 25 minutes or until liquid is absorbed. Remove from heat, and fluff with a fork; let cool completely.

Rinse wild rice thoroughly under cold running water. Bring 1⅓ cups water to boil in a medium saucepan; stir in wild rice. Reduce heat; cover and simmer 50 minutes or until rice is tender. Remove saucepan from heat, and let rice cool completely.

Trim ends of snow peas, and remove strings. Arrange snow peas in a steaming rack; place over boiling water. Cover and steam 1 minute or until crisp tender. Let cool.

Combine reserved seafood, rice, and snow peas in a large bowl, tossing until well combined; set aside.

Combine ¼ cup lemon juice, vinegar, oil, parsley, garlic, ½ teaspoon salt, and pepper in a small bowl; mix well. Pour over seafood mixture; toss thoroughly. Cover and chill thoroughly.

Transfer salad to a large lettuce-lined serving platter to serve. Yield: 6 servings (275 calories per serving).

PRO 25.5 / FAT 3.8 / CARB 35.7 / FIB 1.1 / CHOL 94 / SOD 602 / POT 497

Made with fresh seafood and chilled, Seafood-Rice Salad will lure the family from the beach at lunchtime.

ROASTED PEPPERS

3 medium-size green peppers
1 medium-size yellow pepper
1 tablespoon lemon juice
¼ teaspoon salt
¼ teaspoon pepper

Arrange peppers on a rack in a shallow roasting pan. Broil 6 inches from heat 12 minutes or until peppers are charred and blistered, turning frequently. Remove from oven. Place peppers in a paper bag; seal bag, and let stand until cool. Cut peppers in half; peel and discard seeds. Cut peppers into ¼-inch strips.

Combine peppers, lemon juice, salt, and pepper in a small bowl; toss well. Serve chilled or at room temperature. Yield: 6 servings (39 calories per serving).

PRO 1.3 / FAT 0.7 / CARB 8.3 / FIB 1.7 / CHOL 0 / SOD 102 / POT 299

BAGEL THINS

2 (1-day-old) plain bagels

Cut each bagel in half crosswise with a serrated knife to form 2 U-shaped pieces. Cut each piece into 6 thin slices. Arrange slices on an ungreased baking sheet. Bake at 325° for 25 minutes or until lightly browned. Yield: 24 thins (15 calories each).

PRO 0.6 / FAT .08 / CARB 2.9 / FIB 0.0 / CHOL 0 / SOD 30.8 / POT 3.4

PEARS POACHED IN RED WINE

6 medium pears
2 tablespoons plus 1½ teaspoons
  lemon juice
1 cup dry red wine
½ cup port wine
2 tablespoons sugar
½ teaspoon grated lemon rind
½ teaspoon vanilla extract
1 (3-inch) stick cinnamon
2 whole cloves

Peel pears, removing core from bottom end but leaving stems intact. Slice ¼-inch from bottom of each pear to make a flat base. Brush pears with lemon juice to prevent browning.

Combine remaining ingredients in a Dutch oven; bring to a boil. Place pears in Dutch oven in an upright position; spoon wine mixture over pears. Cover; reduce heat, and simmer 20 minutes or until tender. Remove from heat, and let pears cool in wine mixture. Cover and chill 1 hour, turning pears occasionally. Strain wine; discard spices. Place pears in individual dessert bowls; spoon equal amounts of wine mixture over each pear. Serve chilled. Yield: 6 servings (156 calories per serving).

PRO 0.8 / FAT 0.7 / CARB 34.2 / FIB 4.2 / CHOL 0 / SOD 3 / POT 274

Noontime Surprise

Fusilli with Ratatouille Sauce
Ricotta Green Salad
Herbed Flat Bread
Ambrosia

Serves 8
Total calories per serving: 470

When planning a picnic, choose dishes that taste even better when made ahead. The eggplant with pasta gains in flavor when chilled overnight.

Kept wrapped airtight in foil and plastic, the herbed flat bread tastes just as good a day later as it does fresh out of the oven.

Toss the salad greens before you leave, and put the dressing in a separate container. Combine them before serving.

The ambrosia recipe is equally accommodating. Combine everything but the coconut before leaving, and sprinkle it on later.

Noontime Surprise, packed and ready to go.

FUSILLI WITH RATATOUILLE SAUCE

1 (1-pound) eggplant, cut into 1-inch cubes
1 teaspoon salt
Vegetable cooking spray
1 medium onion, chopped
½ teaspoon dried whole basil
½ teaspoon dried whole thyme
¼ teaspoon dried fennel seeds, crushed
1 bay leaf
1 (28-ounce) can whole tomatoes, undrained and chopped
2 teaspoons minced garlic
½ cup chopped fresh parsley
1 (16-ounce) package fusilli

Place eggplant in a colander; sprinkle with salt, and toss lightly. Let stand 30 minutes; rinse and pat dry.

Coat a large skillet with cooking spray; place over medium-high heat until hot. Add onion, and sauté until tender. Add eggplant, basil, thyme, fennel seeds, and bay leaf; cook over medium heat 3 minutes, stirring occasionally. Add tomatoes and garlic; cover and simmer 20 minutes, stirring occasionally. Remove from heat, and discard bay leaf. Stir in parsley; set aside, and keep warm.

Cook fusilli according to package directions,

omitting salt and fat; drain well.

Combine eggplant mixture and pasta. Let stand at room temperature 10 minutes. Yield: 8 servings (260 calories per serving).

PRO 9.4 / FAT 1.0 / CARB 54.0 / FIB 2.9 / CHOL 0 / SOD 484 / POT 577

RICOTTA GREEN SALAD

1 (½-pound) head romaine, torn
1 (¼-pound) head escarole, torn
1 (¼-pound) chicory, torn
1 medium-size red onion, thinly sliced and
separated into rings
1 medium cucumber, thinly sliced
Ricotta Dressing

Combine first 5 ingredients in a large bowl; toss lightly. Divide salad among 8 salad plates; top each with 2 tablespoons Ricotta Dressing. Yield: 8 servings (58 calories per serving).

Ricotta Dressing:

¼ cup red wine vinegar
1 clove garlic, minced
1 teaspoon Dijon mustard
¼ teaspoon salt
¾ cup part-skim ricotta cheese
2 tablespoons grated Parmesan cheese
1 teaspoon dried whole basil or 2 tablespoons
minced fresh basil

Combine all ingredients in container of an electric blender; process until smooth. Cover and chill. Yield: 1 cup (20 calories per tablespoon).

PRO 4.3 / FAT 2.4 / CARB 4.9 / FIB 0.8 / CHOL 8 / SOD 150 / POT 240

HERBED FLAT BREAD

1 package dry yeast
⅛ teaspoon sugar
1 tablespoon vegetable oil
1 cup warm water (105° to 115°)
½ teaspoon salt
¼ teaspoon pepper
3 cups unbleached or all-purpose flour
Vegetable cooking spray
½ teaspoon dried whole rosemary, crushed
1 teaspoon vegetable oil
½ teaspoon dried whole rosemary, crushed

Combine yeast, sugar, 1 tablespoon oil, and warm water in a large bowl, mixing well. Let stand 10 minutes or until foamy. Stir in salt and pepper. Gradually add enough flour to make a stiff dough.

Turn dough out onto a lightly floured surface, and knead 8 to 10 minutes or until dough is smooth and elastic. Place dough in a large bowl coated with cooking spray, turning to grease top. Cover and let rise in a warm place (85°), free from drafts, 30 minutes or until dough is doubled in bulk.

Punch dough down. Turn dough out onto a lightly floured surface, and knead ½ teaspoon rosemary into dough. Divide dough in half, and shape each half into an 8-inch round, with edge of round slightly thicker than center. Make several indentations in top of each round with finger tip. Place rounds on a baking sheet coated with vegetable cooking spray and lightly dusted with flour.

Bake at 400° for 10 minutes. Remove from oven; brush top of each round lightly with 1 teaspoon oil, and sprinkle with ½ teaspoon rosemary. Reduce heat to 375°, and bake an additional 10 to 15 minutes or until rounds sound hollow when tapped. Yield: 2 rounds or 32 slices (87 calories per 2-slice serving).

PRO 2.4 / FAT 1.3 / CARB 16.4 / FIB 0.0 / CHOL 0 / SOD 74 / POT 36

AMBROSIA

4 medium oranges
1 (15¼-ounce) can unsweetened pineapple
chunks, drained
¼ cup grated fresh coconut

Peel oranges, removing white membrane from outer edge; section oranges over a medium bowl, reserving juice and membranes. Squeeze membranes to extract juice; discard membranes.

Combine reserved orange juice, orange sections, and pineapple chunks in bowl. Cover and chill 1 hour. Spoon ambrosia into individual serving dishes, and sprinkle each serving with ½ tablespoon coconut. Yield: 8 servings (65 calories per serving).

PRO 0.9 / FAT 1.4 / CARB 13.8 / FIB 1.9 / CHOL 0 / SOD 9 / POT 181

Lunch For The Neighbors

Asparagus Quiche
Herbed Cherry
Tomatoes
Escarole Salad
Cat's Tongue Cookies
Pineapple Boats

Serves 6
Total calories per serving: 426

Quiche is ideal company food. It requires a minimum of tending once it goes in the oven, and everyone loves it.

This quiche is extra high in calcium, thanks to an abundance of low-fat cheese and milk — and pleasing to look upon, too.

The cherry tomatoes with basil and the escarole, orange, and walnut salad require very little fussing. They make a tasty twosome that boasts a high-vitamin

Asparagus Quiche is the focal point of this neighborly fare.

content.

The cat's tongue (1 cookie per serving for the correct calorie count) can be made ahead and

stored in airtight containers. The pineapple can be cut up in the morning and kept in the refrigerator until lunchtime.

ASPARAGUS QUICHE

1¼ cups all-purpose or unbleached flour
¼ teaspoon salt
3 tablespoons unsalted margarine
1 tablespoon vegetable shortening
4 to 5 tablespoons ice water
¾ pound fresh asparagus
3 eggs
⅔ cup evaporated skim milk
⅓ cup low-fat cottage cheese
3 tablespoons grated Parmesan cheese
2 tablespoons grated onion
¼ teaspoon salt
⅛ teaspoon pepper

Combine flour and ¼ teaspoon salt in a small bowl; cut in margarine and shortening with a pastry blender until mixture resembles coarse

meal. Sprinkle water evenly over surface of flour mixture; stir with a fork until dry ingredients are moistened. Shape dough into a ball; cover and chill at least 30 minutes.

Roll dough to ⅛-inch thickness on a lightly floured surface. Line a 9-inch quiche dish with pastry; trim edges. Prick bottom and sides of pastry with a fork. Bake at 425° for 10 minutes; remove from oven, and gently prick with a fork. Bake 5 minutes. Cool on a wire rack.

Snap off tough ends of asparagus. Remove scales with a knife or vegetable peeler, if desired. Cover and cook asparagus in a small amount of boiling water 6 minutes or until crisp-tender. Drain; refresh under cold water, and pat dry. Cut off top 3 inches of each stalk, and set aside. Dice stems, and place in pastry shell.

Combine eggs, milk, cottage cheese, Parmesan, onion, ¼ teaspoon salt, and pepper in a medium bowl; beat well. Pour into prepared shell; arrange reserved asparagus tips on top of egg mixture in a spokes pattern.

Bake at 375° for 30 minutes or until set. Cover edges of quiche with foil; broil 4 to 5 inches from heat 2 minutes or until golden. Yield: 6 servings (268 calories per serving).

PRO 12.8 / FAT 11.6 / CARB 28.3 / FIB 1.5 / CHOL 141 / SOD 362 / POT 348

HERBED CHERRY TOMATOES

¾ pound cherry tomatoes
2 tablespoons water
½ teaspoon dried whole basil or 1 tablespoon minced fresh basil
1 clove garlic, crushed
⅛ teaspoon salt
⅛ teaspoon pepper
⅛ teaspoon dried whole thyme
Vegetable cooking spray
Fresh basil sprig (optional)

Combine first 7 ingredients in a small saucepan coated with cooking spray. Cover and cook over medium heat 4 minutes or until tender, stirring occasionally. Transfer to a serving dish; garnish with fresh basil, if desired. Serve immediately. Yield: 6 servings (12 calories per serving).

PRO 0.6 / FAT 0.1 / CARB 2.7 / FIB 0.5 / CHOL 0 / SOD 53 / POT 122

ESCAROLE SALAD

1 (¾-pound) head escarole, torn
2 medium oranges, peeled, seeded, and sectioned
1 small cucumber, thinly sliced
¼ cup unsweetened orange juice
3 tablespoons water
2 tablespoons cider vinegar
1 tablespoon lemon juice
1 tablespoon minced shallot
1 teaspoon poppy seeds
1 teaspoon honey
⅛ teaspoon salt
⅛ teaspoon pepper
¼ cup chopped walnuts

Combine escarole, orange sections, and cucumber slices in a large bowl; toss gently.

Combine orange juice, water, vinegar, lemon juice, shallot, poppy seeds, honey, salt, and pepper in container of an electric blender. Process until well blended. Pour dressing over salad; toss gently. Sprinkle with walnuts. Transfer to individual salad plates to serve. Yield: 6 servings (85 calories per serving).

PRO 2.9 / FAT 3.4 / CARB 13.0 / FIB 2.1 / CHOL 0 / SOD 63 / POT 384

CAT'S TONGUE COOKIES

2 tablespoons unsalted margarine, softened
2 tablespoons sugar
1 egg white
¾ teaspoon vanilla extract
¼ cup unbleached or all-purpose flour

Cream margarine in a small bowl; gradually add sugar, beating until light and fluffy. Add egg white, beating well. Add vanilla and flour, stirring well.

Spoon batter into a pastry bag fitted with a No.7 round tip. Pipe mixture in 3-inch fingers onto aluminum foil-lined baking sheets, making ends slightly thicker.

Bake at 425° for 4 to 5 minutes or until edges are lightly browned. Cool 1 minute on baking sheets; remove cookies from baking sheets, and cool completely on a wire rack. Yield: 18 cookies (23 calories each).

PRO 0.4 / FAT 1.3 / CARB 2.7 / FIB 0.0 / CHOL 0 / SOD 3 / POT 5

PINEAPPLE BOATS

1 (2-pound) fresh pineapple

Cut pineapple in half lengthwise. Scoop out pulp, leaving shells ¼- to ½-inch thick. Reserve one pineapple shell.

Cut pineapple pulp into bite-size cubes, discarding core. Spoon pineapple cubes into reserved shell. Chill. Spoon into individual serving dishes to serve. Yield: 6 servings (38 calories per serving).

PRO 0.3 / FAT 0.3 / CARB 9.7 / FIB 1.2 / CHOL 0 / SOD 1 / POT 89

Rainy Day Luncheon

A sophisticated oriental menu doesn't have to be time consuming. The beef salad can be assembled earlier in the morning and finished just before serving.

Just as convenient are the green onion pancakes (a traditional Chinese bread), which can be made the day before and

Oriental Beef Salad
Green Onion Pancakes
Sliced Mangos with Lime

Serves 4
Total calories per serving: 657

wrapped up airtight at coil stage. While cooking the noodles for

the salad, roll out the pancakes, and bake.

The sliced mangos with lime are the easiest of all. A secret about mangos: the colder they are, the better they taste. After slicing them, keep them in the freezer rather than the refrigerator until ready to serve.

ORIENTAL BEEF SALAD

¼ teaspoon chicken-flavored bouillon granules
¼ cup warm water
2 tablespoons white wine vinegar
2 tablespoons chopped green onion
1 clove garlic, minced
2 teaspoons minced, peeled gingerroot
2 teaspoons reduced-sodium soy sauce
½ teaspoon sugar
⅛ teaspoon pepper
¾ pound lean round steak
2 teaspoons peanut oil
Vegetable cooking spray
¼ pound snow peas
1 teaspoon dry mustard
1 tablespoon hot water
2 tablespoons chopped fresh parsley
2 tablespoons sour cream
1 tablespoon peanut butter
⅛ teaspoon crushed red pepper
4 ounces bean thread noodles or other oriental spaghetti-type pasta
2 cups boiling water
1 teaspoon sesame seeds, toasted
1 cup coarsely grated carrot
1 medium cucumber, sliced

Combine bouillon granules and warm water in a 10- x 6- x 2-inch baking dish. Add next 7 ingredients, stirring well; set aside. Trim excess fat from steak; add steak to marinade, turning to coat well. Cover and marinate in refrigerator

overnight, turning occasionally.

Remove steak from marinade, reserving marinade; pat dry. Heat oil in a skillet or grill pan coated with cooking spray over medium-high heat until hot. Add steak to skillet; cook 2 minutes on each side for rare meat or to desired degree of doneness. Remove meat, reserving pan drippings; slice diagonally across the grain into ¼-inch-thick slices. Set aside; keep warm.

Trim ends of snow peas, and remove strings. Place in a steaming basket. Plunge basket into boiling water, and remove immediately. Place peas in a bowl of ice water to cool quickly. Remove from water, and refrigerate.

Combine mustard and hot water in a small bowl. Combine mustard mixture, reserved marinade, reserved pan drippings, parsley, sour cream, peanut butter, and red pepper in container of an electric blender; process until smooth. Set sauce aside.

Place noodles in a large bowl; add boiling water, and let stand 10 minutes or until softened. Drain.

Place noodles on a serving platter; sprinkle with sesame seeds. Arrange steak, snow peas, and carrot attractively on noodles. Arrange cucumber around outside edge of platter. Serve meat and vegetables with reserved sauce. Yield: 4 servings (369 calories per serving).

PRO 34.1 / FAT 11.6 / CARB 31.0 / FIB 2.3 / CHOL 58 / SOD 210 / POT 683

GREEN ONION PANCAKES

1¼ cups unbleached or all-purpose flour
½ cup hot water
¼ teaspoon salt
2 teaspoons sesame oil
⅓ cup minced green onion
¼ teaspoon salt
2 teaspoons peanut oil

Combine first 3 ingredients in a bowl. Turn out onto a lightly floured surface; knead 5 minutes. Roll and stretch dough into an 8-inch log; divide into 4 equal pieces. Cover with an inverted bowl; let rest 30 minutes.

Shape each piece of dough into a ball; flatten balls into 7½-inch rounds. Brush one side with sesame oil; sprinkle evenly with green onion and ¼ teaspoon salt. Roll up rounds; pinch seams and ends to seal. Coil rolls into a tight spiral, tucking ends under. Roll coils into 7-inch rounds using a rolling pin, and place on a floured plate, separating pancakes with floured sheets of waxed paper.

Brush a small amount of peanut oil on a non-stick skillet, and place over medium-high heat until hot. Add 1 pancake, and cook 3 to 4 minutes on each side or until golden brown, brushing skillet with more oil before turning. Repeat procedure with remaining pancakes. Cut pancakes into wedges to serve. Yield: 4 servings (168 calories per serving).

PRO 3.9 / FAT 4.9 / CARB 27.6 / FIB 0.3 / CHOL 0 / SOD 295 / POT 63

SLICED MANGOS WITH LIME

2 medium mangos, peeled and sliced
¼ cup lime juice
1 lime, thinly sliced

Combine mangos and lime juice in a medium bowl; toss gently. Cover and refrigerate 2 hours.

Arrange mango slices on a serving platter; garnish with lime slices. Serve chilled. Yield: 4 servings (120 calories per serving).

PRO 1.1 / FAT 0.5 / CARB 32.1 / FIB 1.9 / CHOL 0 / SOD 4 / POT 299

Oriental Beef Salad, Green Onion Pancakes, and Sliced Mangos with Lime add up to an exotic luncheon.

Light Summer Repast

Soufflé-Topped Flounder
Farmer's Cheese Potatoes
Pickled Vegetables
Minted Melon Balls

Serves 2
Total calories per serving: 464

Flounder is at its most delicious in summer. Add a yogurt topping to two choice fillets; pop them under the broiler, and you have a light but satisfying main course that's ready in minutes.

Steam the potatoes early in the morning, and chill them until lunchtime. Then slice them, and top with a calcium-loaded farmer's cheese dressing.

Cook the pickled vegetables at the same time you do the potatoes. Their brightness will add a jolt of color to the repast.

For dessert, melon flavored with citrus juice and a touch of créme de menthe is just what the weatherman ordered.

Minted Melon Balls have a touch of créme de menthe.

SOUFFLÉ-TOPPED FLOUNDER

2 (4-ounce) flounder fillets
2 teaspoons unsalted margarine, melted
1 tablespoon reduced-calorie mayonnaise
1 tablespoon plain low-fat yogurt
½ teaspoon lemon juice
⅛ teaspoon curry powder
⅛ teaspoon paprika
Dash of red pepper
1 egg white

Place fish, skin side down, in a broiler pan coated with cooking spray; brush fish with margarine. Broil 4 to 5 inches from heat 4 minutes.

Combine next 6 ingredients in a small bowl, stirring well. Beat egg white (at room temperature) until stiff peaks form; fold into mayonnaise mixture. Spoon evenly over fish. Broil 4 to 5 inches from heat 2 minutes or until puffed and golden. Serve immediately. Yield: 2 servings (157 calories per serving).

PRO 21.1 / FAT 6.8 / CARB 1.5 / FIB 0.1 / CHOL 60 / SOD 174 / POT 435

FARMER'S CHEESE POTATOES

4 small new potatoes (about 10 ounces)
¼ cup (2 ounces) curd-style farmer's cheese
3 tablespoons skim milk
1 tablespoon plus 1½ teaspoons minced
   green onion
⅛ teaspoon salt
⅛ teaspoon pepper
1 tablespoon minced fresh chives or parsley

Arrange potatoes in a steaming rack, and place over boiling water. Cover and steam 15 to 20 minutes or until tender. Let cool to touch. Peel and cut into ¼-inch slices. Divide potatoes evenly between 2 salad plates.

Combine cheese, milk, onion, salt, and pepper in container of an electric blender; process until smooth. Spoon sauce evenly over potatoes. Garnish with chives. Serve at room temperature. Yield: 2 servings (162 calories per serving).

PRO 7.8 / FAT 3.2 / CARB 28.1 / FIB 0.8 / CHOL 2 / SOD 320 / POT 838

PICKLED VEGETABLES

8 coriander seeds
6 whole peppercorns
1 bay leaf
1 cup water
¼ cup dry white wine
1 teaspoon chicken-flavored bouillon granules
1 medium carrot, scraped and thinly sliced
¼ pound cauliflower flowerets
1 medium zucchini, cut into 1/4-inch slices
2 tablespoons distilled white vinegar
1 tablespoon lemon juice
¼ teaspoon sugar
¼ teaspoon celery seeds
⅛ teaspoon crushed red pepper

Combine first 3 ingredients in a square of cheesecloth; tie with a string to form a bag. Place cheesecloth bag, water, wine, and bouillon granules in a medium saucepan; bring to a boil. Add carrot; cover and boil 2 minutes. Add cauliflower; cover and boil 2 minutes. Add zucchini; cover and continue boiling 2 minutes. Drain vegetables, reserving cooking liquid and cheesecloth bag; set vegetables aside. Return cooking liquid and cheesecloth bag to saucepan; cook until liquid is reduced to ¼ cup. Discard cheesecloth bag. Cool liquid. Add remaining ingredients and reserved vegetables to cooled cooking liquid; toss lightly. Cover and chill overnight. Drain. Yield: 2 servings (52 calories per serving).

PRO 2.4 / FAT 0.6 / CARB 11.7 / FIB 1.4 / CHOL 0 / SOD 216 / POT 513

MINTED MELON BALLS

1 large orange
1 cup watermelon balls
1 cup honeydew balls
1 tablespoon white crème de menthe
1 tablespoon lemon juice
Fresh mint leaves

Cut orange in half crosswise. Gently squeeze orange halves, reserving ¼ cup juice. Carefully remove orange pulp (do not puncture shells); discard pulp, and set shells aside.

Combine ¼ cup orange juice, watermelon, honeydew, crème de menthe, and lemon juice in a small bowl; mix well. Cover and chill.

Scallop reserved orange shells, if desired. Fill shells with equal amounts of melon mixture. Garnish with mint leaves. Serve immediately. Yield: 2 servings (93 calories per serving).

PRO 1.4 / FAT 0.6 / CARB 18.4 / FIB 0.7 / CHOL 0 / SOD 12 / POT 373

Americans ate 143 pounds of fruit per person in 1984; more than half of it was fresh. Bountiful supplies, low prices, greater variety, and increased consumer concerns about health and nutrition have all played a part in the growth of fresh fruit in the nation's diet.

Another important trend is the increased consumption of fruit in the form of juice. However, it is best to eat the natural whole fruit with skin, if it's eatable, rather than juicing or drying it; you take in more fiber and achieve a greater feeling of satiety, thus consuming fewer calories. One orange will usually satisfy your hunger, but you might want more than one glass of orange juice which is made from three to four oranges.

Because of its natural sugar content, fruit can also satisfy a sweet tooth without the fat and calories that make up most sweets.

Bike Trip Take-Along

Making lunch portable enough to take on an extended bike trip is simple with a bit of planning. For instance, tea, or whatever beverage you select, stays chilled longer if the portable water bottle has been one-fourth filled with water and frozen.

Wrap your Dagwood sand-

Dagwood Sandwiches
Marinated Zucchini Spears
Iced Tea

Serves 4
Total calories per serving: 252

wiches individually in foil with some tangy marinated zucchini

spears (a low-sodium version of dill pickles) wrapped in separate foil pouches.

Pack everything carefully in a basket or, better still, a knapsack, and then bequeath it to the most willing cycler, or divide into individual portions, and let each cycler carry his own.

DAGWOOD SANDWICHES

½ medium avocado, peeled and sliced
1 tablespoon fresh lemon juice
8 slices thin-sliced whole wheat bread
1 tablespoon plus 1 teaspoon reduced-calorie mayonnaise
4 large escarole lettuce leaves
4 (⅔-ounce) slices low-fat process American cheese
2 medium tomatoes, sliced
2 ounces alfalfa sprouts, washed and drained

Combine avocado and lemon juice in a small bowl; toss well. Set aside.

Spread 4 slices of bread with 1 teaspoon mayonnaise each. Top with lettuce leaves, cheese, and avocado and tomato slices. Divide alfalfa sprouts among sandwiches; cover with remaining bread slices. Cut each sandwich in half. Yield: 4 servings (229 calories per serving).

PRO 11.8 / FAT 8.3 / CARB 31.1 / FIB 4.3 / CHOL 3 / SOD 582 / POT 496

MARINATED ZUCCHINI SPEARS

1½ cups water
½ cup dry white wine
¼ cup lemon juice
2 cloves garlic, sliced
⅛ teaspoon salt
8 sprigs fresh parsley
¼ teaspoon fennel seeds
12 whole peppercorns
8 coriander seeds
1 bay leaf
2 medium zucchini (about ¾ pound), quartered lengthwise

Combine water, wine, lemon juice, garlic, and salt in a small saucepan. Tie next 5 ingredients in a cheesecloth bag, and add to saucepan. Bring to a boil. Cover, reduce heat, and simmer 10 minutes. Uncover and cook until marinade is reduced to 1 cup.

Place zucchini in bottom of a shallow baking dish; pour hot marinade over zucchini. Cover and chill overnight. Drain; discard cheesecloth bag. Serve chilled. Yield: 4 servings (23 calories per serving).

PRO 1.2 / FAT 0.1 / CARB 5.5 / FIB 0.4 / CHOL 0 / SOD 78 / POT 263

Turn a Simple Sunday Supper into a special occasion with Artichoke Cheese Strata (page 68) and Spinach-Radish Salad (menu begins on page 67).

Family Night Supper

Chicken and Squash Soup
Beet and Lettuce Salad
Whole Wheat Loaf
Stuffed Baked Apples

Serves 6
Total calories per serving: 447

The chicken and squash soup can be made ahead and then reheated just before the family settles in at the supper table.

As a salad, nothing could be simpler than curly endive, white radishes, and beets tossed with horseradish yogurt.

Make the whole wheat loaf ahead, and try toasting it (1 slice per serving). Of special interest to the children will be the nutritious baked apples.

Make-aheads: Chicken and Squash Soup and Whole Wheat Loaf.

CHICKEN AND SQUASH SOUP

1 (2½-pound) broiler-fryer, skinned
2 quarts water
1 medium onion, sliced
½ teaspoon dried whole rosemary
½ teaspoon salt
½ teaspoon pepper
1 bay leaf
6 (2½-inch) strips orange rind
1 (1½-pound) spaghetti squash
1 (1-pound) butternut squash, peeled and sliced
2 tablespoons lemon juice
Fresh parsley sprigs (optional)

Combine first 8 ingredients in a large stockpot. Bring to a boil. Cover; reduce heat, and simmer 1 hour. Remove chicken from broth; let cool to touch. Remove meat from bones, discarding bones; coarsely chop meat, and refrigerate. Remove and discard bay leaf and orange rind from broth. Refrigerate broth overnight.

Pierce spaghetti squash several times with a large fork; place on a jellyroll pan. Bake at 350° for 1 hour or until tender. Allow squash to cool; cut squash in half, and remove seeds. Using a fork, remove spaghetti-like strands; measure 2 cups of strands, reserving remaining pulp for other uses. Coarsely chop strands, and set aside.

Skim off, and discard fat from broth. Combine broth and butternut squash in a large Dutch oven; bring to a boil. Reduce heat, and simmer 15 minutes or until squash is tender.

Place 2 cups of broth mixture in container of

an electric blender; process until smooth. Strain mixture into a small Dutch oven, discarding pulp. Repeat with remaining broth mixture.

Add reserved chicken, 2 cups chopped spaghetti squash, and lemon juice to pureed mixture. Cook over medium heat until thoroughly heated. Ladle soup into individual serving bowls, and garnish with fresh parsley sprigs, if desired. Yield: 7 cups (171 calories per 1-cup serving).

PRO 16.8 / FAT 4.2 / CARB 17.7 / FIB 2.5 / CHOL 46 / SOD 231 / POT 597

BEET AND LETTUCE SALAD

1½ cups sliced, cooked beets or 1 (16-ounce) can sliced beets, rinsed and drained
¼ pound curly endive, torn
¼ pound Boston lettuce, torn
¼ pound white icicle radishes, thinly sliced
1 medium-size red onion, thinly sliced
½ cup plain low-fat yogurt
2 tablespoons reduced-calorie mayonnaise
1 tablespoon cider vinegar
2 teaspoons prepared horseradish
½ teaspoon sugar
⅛ teaspoon salt
⅛ teaspoon white pepper

Cut beet slices into ¼-inch strips. Combine beets, endive, lettuce, radishes, and onion in a large salad bowl; toss gently. Combine remaining ingredients, and pour over vegetables; toss until well coated. Spoon onto individual plates. Yield: 6 servings (58 calories per serving).

PRO 2.4 / FAT 2.0 / CARB 8.8 / FIB 1.0 / CHOL 3 / SOD 131 / POT 372

WHOLE WHEAT LOAF

1 package dry yeast
½ teaspoon sugar
1 cup warm water (105° to 115°)
1¼ cups whole wheat flour
1½ cups unbleached or all-purpose flour
½ teaspoon salt
Vegetable cooking spray
1 tablespoon cornmeal
1 egg white
1 teaspoon water

Dissolve yeast and sugar in 1 cup warm water in a large bowl; let stand 5 minutes.

Combine flour and salt. Add enough flour mixture to yeast mixture to make a stiff dough.

Turn dough out onto a lightly floured surface; knead 8 minutes or until smooth and elastic. Place in a bowl coated with cooking spray, turning to grease top. Cover and let rise in a warm place (85°), free from drafts, 30 minutes or until doubled in bulk.

Punch dough down; shape dough into a 14-inch loaf. Place loaf in a baguette pan or on a baking sheet coated with cooking spray and sprinkled with cornmeal. Cover and let rise in a warm place (85°), free from drafts, 30 minutes or until doubled in bulk. Cut 3 slashes, ¼-inch deep, across top of loaf. Combine egg white and 1 teaspoon water, mixing well. Brush loaf with egg white mixture. Bake at 400° for 15 minutes; reduce heat to 350°, and bake 10 additional minutes or until loaf sounds hollow when tapped. Remove bread from baguette pan immediately; cool on a wire rack. Yield: 1 loaf or 16 (1-inch) slices (73 calories per slice).

PRO 2.8 / FAT 0.3 / CARB 15.4 / FIB 0.8 / CHOL 0 / SOD 77 / POT 61

STUFFED BAKED APPLES

6 medium Granny Smith apples
⅓ cup golden raisins
2 tablespoons chopped walnuts
½ teaspoon ground cinnamon
⅛ teaspoon mace
½ cup unsweetened apple juice
½ cup water
2 tablespoons lemon juice
1 tablespoon plus 1½ teaspoons honey

Core apples; peel top one-third of each, and place in a 12- x 8- x 2-inch baking dish.

Combine raisins, walnuts, cinnamon, and mace; stuff 1 tablespoon plus 1½ teaspoons raisin mixture into cavity of each apple. Combine apple juice, water, lemon juice, and honey; pour into baking dish. Cover and bake at 350° for 45 minutes or until apples are tender, basting occasionally with pan liquid. Serve warm. Yield: 6 servings (145 calories per serving).

PRO 1.1 / FAT 2.0 / CARB 34.1 / FIB 3.5 / CHOL 0 / SOD 3 / POT 262

Vegetarian Pizza Supper

In the health-conscious '80s, vegetarianism can be a valid alternative life-style. Vegetarians rarely have cholesterol problems, for instance.

While the dough for the pizzas rises, unwind with a mug of cider rather than a cocktail. You'll be getting more vitamins and fewer empty calories.

After sampling how yummy homemade pizza can be, you may never eat the takeouts

Individual Vegetable Pizzas
Grapefruit and Lettuce Salad
Cappuccino Parfaits

Serves 4
Total calories per serving: 469

again. The zucchini, eggplant, and green pepper topping adds a Mediterranean touch.

Grapefruit is breaking out of the breakfast-only mold these days. Choose pink or white, depending upon your personal taste, and toss with it some Bibb lettuce, watercress, and vinegar for a unique salad.

Prepare the cappuccino parfaits through the first freezing the night before. Then whip the mixture up in the food processor or blender; add the liqueur, and freeze one more time.

INDIVIDUAL VEGETABLE PIZZAS

1 package dry yeast
1/8 teaspoon sugar
1/2 cup warm water (105° to 115°)
1 cup unbleached or all-purpose flour
1/2 cup whole wheat flour
1/8 teaspoon salt
Vegetable cooking spray
1 tablespoon cornmeal
1/2 cup chopped onion
1/2 cup chopped green pepper
1/2 cup diced zucchini
1/2 cup diced eggplant
1 (16-ounce) can whole tomatoes, undrained
1 clove garlic, minced
1/4 teaspoon dried whole oregano
1/4 teaspoon dried whole basil
1/8 teaspoon salt
1 tablespoon plus 1 teaspoon grated Parmesan cheese, divided
1 cup (4 ounces) shredded part-skim mozzarella cheese, divided

Dissolve yeast and sugar in warm water; let stand 5 minutes or until bubbly.

Combine flour and 1/8 teaspoon salt in a medium bowl; add yeast mixture to flour mixture, stirring well.

Turn dough out onto a lightly floured surface;

knead 8 to 10 minutes or until smooth and elastic. Place dough in a large bowl coated with cooking spray, turning to grease top. Cover and let rise in a warm place (85°), free from drafts, 1 hour or until doubled in bulk.

Punch dough down. Divide dough into 4 equal portions. Roll each portion into a circle, 6 inches in diameter. Place circles on a baking sheet coated with cooking spray and sprinkled with cornmeal.

Coat a large skillet with cooking spray; place over medium heat until hot. Add onion and green pepper, and sauté until vegetables are tender. Add zucchini and eggplant; cook 2 minutes, stirring constantly.

Drain tomatoes, reserving 3 tablespoons liquid; chop tomatoes. Add tomatoes, reserved liquid, garlic, oregano, basil, and 1/8 teaspoon salt to vegetable mixture in skillet, stirring well. Cover and simmer 5 minutes; uncover and cook 5 minutes or until thickened.

Spoon sauce evenly over pizza crusts, leaving a 1/2-inch border around edges; sprinkle top of each pizza with 1 teaspoon grated Parmesan cheese and 1/4 cup mozzarella cheese. Bake at 425° for 20 minutes or until lightly browned. Yield: 4 individual pizzas (283 calories each).

PRO 15.3 / FAT 6.1 / CARB 43.9 / FIB 10.0 / CHOL 18 / SOD 499 / POT 550

One taste of this succulent Vegetable Pizza is convincing proof that homemade pizza is best.

GRAPEFRUIT AND LETTUCE SALAD

¼ cup plus 2 tablespoons unsweetened
    grapefruit juice
2 tablespoons vinegar
¼ teaspoon sugar
¼ teaspoon salt
¼ teaspoon pepper
¼ pound Bibb lettuce, separated into
    leaves
1 cup watercress leaves
2 cups grapefruit sections
¼ cup thinly sliced green onion

Combine grapefruit juice, vinegar, sugar, salt, and pepper in a small bowl; set aside.

Divide lettuce leaves and watercress leaves evenly among 4 individual salad plates. Arrange grapefruit sections on lettuce-lined plates, and sprinkle onion over top. Stir prepared dressing until well blended; spoon 2 tablespoons dressing over each salad. Yield: 4 servings (34 calories per serving).

PRO 1.2 / FAT 0.2 / CARB 8.2 / FIB 0.6 / CHOL 0 / SOD 154 / POT 241

CAPPUCCINO PARFAITS

1 package unflavored gelatin
2½ cups cold strong coffee, divided
¼ cup plus 2 tablespoons sugar
1 cup evaporated skim milk
2 tablespoons Kahlúa or other coffee-flavored
    liqueur

Combine gelatin and ½ cup coffee in a small bowl; let stand 1 minute.

Heat remaining 2 cups coffee to a simmer in a small saucepan. Add gelatin mixture and sugar to hot coffee; cook over low heat, stirring constantly, until gelatin and sugar dissolve. Remove from heat; stir in evaporated milk. Cool. Pour mixture into an 8-inch square baking pan; freeze until almost frozen.

Spoon mixture into container of an electric blender; add Kahlúa, and process until smooth. Return to pan; freeze until firm. Spoon into parfait glasses, and serve immediately. Yield: 4 servings (152 calories per serving).

PRO 6.4 / FAT 0.1 / CARB 27.9 / FIB 0.0 / CHOL 3 / SOD 77 / POT 267

Dinner On The Deck

Grilled Beef Kabobs
Roasted New Potatoes
Marinated Pepper Slaw
Commercial Whole Wheat
Pita Bread
Peach Ice
Chocolate Wafers

Serves 10
Total calories per serving: 517

No one is quite sure who invented the redwood deck, but he ought to be declared a national hero. Having dinner on a deck is like a two-hour vacation.

Share your deck with some cherished friends, and turn a regular summer meal into a real celebration with this menu.

Beef kabobs skewered with onions, mushrooms, and zucchini demand a grill. Keep them company with new potatoes nestled in foil and pita bread (½ pita per serving for correct calorie count). The technicolored pepper slaw is a great source of vegetable fiber.

Make the chocolate wafers (1 cookie per serving) and peach ice ahead. Select the ripest, juiciest peaches you can find for maximum flavor. Store the cookies in an airtight container.

GRILLED BEEF KABOBS

2½ pounds lean boneless sirloin tip steak
1 (8-ounce) bottle Italian reduced-calorie salad dressing
½ cup dry red wine
3 medium zucchini, cut into ½-inch pieces
1 medium onion, cut into 1-inch pieces
½ pound fresh mushrooms

Trim excess fat from steak, and cut into 1-inch cubes; place in a plastic zip-top bag. Add Italian dressing and wine; mix well. Marinate in refrigerator several hours or overnight.

Cook zucchini in a medium saucepan in boiling water to cover 3 minutes or until tender. Drain well.

Remove meat from marinade, reserving marinade. Alternate meat and vegetables on skewers. Grill 4 to 5 inches from medium coals 10 minutes or until desired degree of doneness. Turn and brush kabobs frequently with reserved marinade. Yield: 10 servings (191 calories per serving).

PRO 28.2 / FAT 4.7 / CARB 5.8 / FIB 0.5 / CHOL 55 / SOD 260 / POT 554

ROASTED NEW POTATOES

10 large new potatoes (about 2½ pounds potatoes)

Separate potatoes into 3 groups; wrap each group in aluminum foil. Place packages in hot coals, covering packages with coals. Roast 30 minutes or until tender. Serve hot. Yield: 10 servings (84 calories per serving).

PRO 2.5 / FAT 0.1 / CARB 18.8 / FIB 0.9 / CHOL 0 / SOD 8 / POT 578

MARINATED PEPPER SLAW

1 small head cabbage (about 1½ pounds), shredded
3 medium-size red peppers, seeded and thinly sliced
1 medium onion, grated
½ cup white wine vinegar
¼ cup reduced-calorie mayonnaise
1 tablespoon Dijon mustard
1 tablespoon sugar
1 clove garlic, minced
1 teaspoon celery seeds
½ teaspoon salt
½ teaspoon pepper
⅓ cup finely chopped fresh parsley

Combine cabbage, red pepper, and onion in a large bowl; mix well. Set aside.

Combine next 8 ingredients in container of an electric blender; process until smooth. Pour over cabbage, mix well. Cover; chill overnight, tossing occasionally. Add parsley; toss well. Yield: 10 servings (54 calories per serving).

PRO 1.4 / FAT 2.1 / CARB 8.3 / FIB 1.3 / CHOL 2 / SOD 222 / POT 267

PEACH ICE

½ cup sugar
3½ pounds ripe peaches
3 tablespoons lemon juice
1 teaspoon vanilla extract

Place sugar in container of an electric blender; process 1 minute or until sugar becomes light and powdery. Set aside.

Peel and slice peaches; immediately toss peaches with lemon juice in a medium bowl. Add peaches and vanilla to blender container; process until smooth.

Transfer mixture into freezer can of a 1-gallon hand-turned or electric freezer, and freeze according to manufacturer's instructions. Let ripen at least 1 hour before serving. Yield: 10 servings (101 calories per ½-cup serving).

PRO 1.0 / FAT 0.2 / CARB 25.9 / FIB 3.7 / CHOL 0 / SOD 2 / POT 327

CHOCOLATE WAFERS

¼ cup plus 2 tablespoons unsalted margarine, softened
⅓ cup sugar
1 egg
½ cup unbleached or all-purpose flour
2 tablespoons Dutch process or unsweetened cocoa
⅛ teaspoon salt
½ teaspoon vanilla extract
Vegetable cooking spray

Cream margarine in a medium mixing bowl; gradually add sugar, beating until light and fluffy. Add egg; beat well.

Sift together flour, cocoa, and salt; gradually add to creamed mixture, mixing well after each addition. Stir in vanilla.

Drop dough by teaspoonfuls 2 inches apart onto cookie sheets coated with cooking spray. Bake at 350° for 8 minutes. Cool 2 minutes on cookie sheets. Remove to wire racks to cool completely. Yield: 48 cookies (24 calories each).

PRO 0.3 / FAT 1.6 / CARB 2.4 / FIB 0.0 / CHOL 6 / SOD 9 / POT 4

Any type of rhythmic exercise such as walking, jogging, or cycling has been shown to be valuable in the release of tension. Dr. Herbert DeVries at the University of Southern California found that moderate exercise for 5 to 30 minutes can promote significant relaxation for tense individuals. Even a short 10-minute walk can reduce tensions.

There is also evidence that moderate exercise can actually condition your body to counteract stress; exercise simulates physical reactions to stress, helping your body adapt more quickly when stress arises.

Dressed Up Hamburger Dinner

Peppered Beef Patties
Vegetable Medley
Rye Rolls
Kiwi Custard Pie

Serves 6
Total calories per serving: 610

This menu keeps the ease and simplicity of serving hamburgers while catering to adult tastes. The crushed peppercorn and white wine sauce would also be worthy of filet mignon.

Rutabaga adds interest to the peas and carrots in the vegetable medley.

Rye rolls (1 roll per serving for correct calorie count) add fiber to the meal, and kiwis make the custard pie deliciously tart.

Peppered Beef Patties, Vegetable Medley, Rye Rolls, and Kiwi Custard Pie.

PEPPERED BEEF PATTIES

1½ pounds lean ground round
3 tablespoons grated onion
½ to ¾ teaspoon dried whole marjoram
⅛ teaspoon salt
1 tablespoon plus 1½ teaspoons cracked black pepper
Vegetable cooking spray
½ cup boiling water
½ teaspoon beef-flavored bouillon granules
2 teaspoons cornstarch
2 shallots, minced
1 teaspoon unsalted margarine, melted
½ cup dry white wine
¼ teaspoon Worcestershire sauce
Fresh parsley sprigs

Combine ground round, onion, marjoram, and salt in a medium bowl, mixing well. Shape mixture into 6 oval patties, 1½-inches thick. Sprinkle with pepper.

Place a medium skillet coated with cooking spray over medium heat until hot. Add patties, and cook 4 minutes on each side for rare meat or to desired degree of doneness. Drain; transfer to a warm platter, and keep warm.

Combine water and bouillon granules in a small bowl; add cornstarch, stirring well. Set mixture aside.

Sauté shallots in margarine in a medium skillet 1 minute or until tender. Add wine, and cook 1 minute, stirring frequently. Add reserved bouillon mixture and Worcestershire sauce; cook, stirring constantly, until mixture is thickened and bubbly. Spoon sauce over patties. Garnish with parsley sprigs, if desired. Yield: 6 servings (208 calories per serving).

PRO 23.7 / FAT 10.4 / CARB 3.9 / FIB 0.3 / CHOL 80 / SOD 133 / POT 454

VEGETABLE MEDLEY

1 cup diced carrot
1 cup diced, peeled rutabaga
½ cup sliced celery
2 tablespoons chopped onion
½ cup water
⅛ teaspoon salt
⅛ teaspoon pepper
1 cup frozen English peas, thawed

Combine first 7 ingredients in a medium saucepan; bring to a boil. Cover; reduce heat, and simmer 10 minutes. Add peas, and simmer 3 minutes or until peas are tender. Yield: 6 servings (42 calories per ½-cup serving.)

PRO 1.8 / FAT 0.1 / CARB 8.3 / FIB 1.9 / CHOL 0 / SOD 93 / POT 189

RYE ROLLS

2 packages dry yeast
1 teaspoon brown sugar
½ cup warm water (105° to 115°)
2½ cups unbleached or all-purpose flour
1½ cups rye flour
¼ teaspoon salt
1 cup warm water (105° to 115°)
⅓ cup instant non-fat dry milk powder
2 tablespoons honey
Vegetable cooking spray

Dissolve yeast and sugar in ½ cup warm water in a large bowl. Let stand 5 minutes.

Combine flour and salt in a medium bowl, stirring well. Add flour mixture, 1 cup warm water, milk powder, and honey to yeast mixture, stirring well.

Turn dough out onto a lightly floured surface; knead 10 minutes or until smooth and elastic. Place dough in a bowl coated with cooking spray, turning to grease top. Cover and let rise in a warm place (85°), free from drafts, 1 hour or until doubled in bulk.

Punch dough down. Divide dough into 12 portions; shape each portion into a ball. Place balls 2 inches apart in a 13- x 9- x 2-inch baking pan coated with cooking spray. Cover and let rise in a warm place (85°), free from drafts, 1 hour and 15 minutes or until doubled in bulk. Bake at 400° for 20 minutes or until rolls sound hollow when tapped. Yield: 12 rolls (150 calories each).

PRO 5.2 / FAT 0.4 / CARB 31.9 / FIB 0.4 / CHOL 1 / SOD 69 / POT 132

KIWI CUSTARD PIE

⅔ cup graham cracker crumbs
2 tablespoons unsalted margarine, melted
1 tablespoon sugar
1 envelope unflavored gelatin
¼ cup water
⅓ cup sugar
2 tablespoons water
½ cup evaporated skim milk, heated
2 teaspoons vanilla extract
1 (8-ounce) carton plain low-fat yogurt
4 kiwis, peeled and thinly sliced

Combine graham cracker crumbs, margarine, and 1 tablespoon sugar. Press mixture firmly onto bottom and sides of an 8-inch pieplate. Bake at 350° for 12 minutes. Let cool.

Dissolve gelatin in ¼ cup water in a small bowl; set aside.

Combine ⅓ cup sugar and 2 tablespoons water in a small heavy saucepan. Cook over medium heat, stirring occasionally, until golden brown. Add milk; cook over low heat, stirring constantly, until smooth. Add dissolved gelatin; cook, stirring constantly, until gelatin dissolves. Remove from heat; add vanilla, stirring well.

Pour mixture into a medium bowl; cover and refrigerate 30 minutes or until consistency of unbeaten egg white. Beat at medium speed of electric mixer 3 minutes or until light and fluffy; add yogurt, beating until smooth. Spoon mixture into prepared shell. Chill. Arrange kiwi slices on top of pie just before serving. Yield: 6 servings (210 calories per serving).

PRO 5.7 / FAT 5.5 / CARB 30.7 / FIB 0.6 / CHOL 3 / SOD 123 / POT 352

Grilled Salmon Fillets and
Roasted Corn-on-the-Cob
for lakeside dining.

Lakeside Dinner Party

Grilled Salmon Fillets
Vegetable Kabobs
Roasted Corn-on-the-Cob
Lettuce and Tomato Salad
Peach and Prune Compote

Serves 6
Total calories per serving: 476

An energetic afternoon of swimming and canoeing at the lake can work up quite an appetite. It's time for your grill to earn its keep.

Those lucky enough to have a bountiful garden will have no trouble filling their skewers for the vegetable kabobs and their salad bowls with Boston lettuce and tomatoes. The greenest thumbs will probably also be supplying their own corn.

Put the salmon packets and corn on first to grill — the foil will help keep them warm while the vegetable kabobs cook.

Buttermilk dressing has a summery tang to it. So does the juicy peach and prune compote (which can be make ahead). The compote and vegetable kabobs will give your iron consumption a boost.

Stand downwind from the grill, and inhale deeply. Summer even smells special.

GRILLED SALMON FILLETS

2 pink salmon fillets (about 1½ pounds)
1 tablespoon dry white vermouth
¼ teaspoon pepper
6 sprigs fresh dill

Cut two 12-inch square pieces of heavy-duty aluminum foil; place fillet, skin side down, in center of each piece of foil. Sprinkle fillets with equal amounts of vermouth and pepper; top with fresh dill sprigs.

Fold aluminum foil over fillets, and seal edges securely. Place foil packages on grill. Grill over medium coals 30 minutes or until fish flakes easily when tested with a fork.

Remove fish to a warm serving platter; cut into serving size pieces. Serve immediately. Yield: 6 servings (138 calories per serving).

Note: Foil packages may be placed on a baking sheet, and baked at 400° for 25 minutes or until fish flakes easily when tested with a fork.

PRO 22.7 / FAT 4.2 / CARB 0.2 / FIB 0.0 / CHOL 40 / SOD 73 / POT 349

VEGETABLE KABOBS

2 medium-size yellow squash (about ½ pound)
2 medium zucchini (about ½ pound)
6 small onions (about ½ pound)
1 medium-size sweet red pepper, seeded and
   cut into 18 pieces
6 large fresh mushrooms
¼ cup lemon juice
2 teaspoons Dijon mustard
1 clove garlic, minced
2 teaspoons dried whole basil
½ teaspoon dried whole thyme
½ teaspoon dried whole rosemary
1 bay leaf, crumbled
¼ teaspoon salt
¼ teaspoon pepper

Place first 3 ingredients in boiling water to
cover; cook 5 minutes or until crisp-tender. Drain
and cool. Cut vegetables into 1-inch pieces.
Combine cooked vegetables, red pepper, and
mushrooms in a shallow dish. Combine remaining ingredients. Pour over vegetables; toss.
Cover and marinate in refrigerator overnight.
Thread vegetables onto skewers, alternating
types; reserve marinade. Place kabobs 6 inches
from medium coals. Grill 30 minutes or until
tender, turning and basting with marinade.
Yield: 6 servings (51 calories per serving).

PRO 2.4 / FAT 0.6 / CARB 11.2 / FIB 1.6 / CHOL 0 / SOD 155 / POT 447

ROASTED CORN-ON-THE-COB

2 tablespoons unsalted margarine, melted
1 tablespoon minced fresh parsley
1 tablespoon minced fresh chives
2 teaspoons lemon juice
¼ teaspoon salt
¼ teaspoon pepper
6 ears fresh corn

Combine first 6 ingredients in a small bowl.
Peel back husks from corn; remove silks. Brush
corn with margarine mixture; replace husks.
Wrap each ear in aluminum foil. Place corn on
grill. Cover and cook over medium coals 45 minutes or until tender, turning frequently. Yield: 6
servings (99 calories per serving).

PRO 2.0 / FAT 4.5 / CARB 15.3 / FIB 0.4 / CHOL 0 / SOD 108 / POT 157

LETTUCE AND TOMATO SALAD

¾ pound Boston lettuce
2 medium tomatoes, cut into wedges
Buttermilk Salad Dressing

Arrange lettuce and tomatoes among 6 salad
plates. Spoon 2 tablespoons Buttermilk Dressing
over each salad. Yield: 6 servings (37 calories
per serving).

Buttermilk Salad Dressing:

½ cup buttermilk
3 tablespoons reduced-calorie salad dressing
1 tablespoon vinegar
½ teaspoon dried whole basil
¼ teaspoon dry mustard
¼ teaspoon minced garlic
⅛ teaspoon pepper

Combine all ingredients in container of an
electric blender; process until smooth. Yield: ¾
cup (10 calories per tablespoon).

PRO 2.0 / FAT 1.4 / CARB 5.0 / FIB 0.8 / CHOL 5 / SOD 37 / POT 279

PEACH AND PRUNE COMPOTE

6 ounces dried pitted prunes
¼ cup dry white wine
1 cup water
1 (3-inch) stick cinnamon
6 medium peaches, peeled and sliced
½ cup unsweetened orange juice
1 tablespoon lemon juice
2 tablespoons honey
¼ teaspoon ground allspice

Combine first 4 ingredients in a saucepan,
and bring to a boil. Reduce heat to medium,
and simmer 10 minutes or until prunes are
tender. Transfer prunes to a bowl, using a slotted spoon; reserve cooking liquid. Add peaches
to prunes; set aside.
Add orange juice, lemon juice, honey, and
allspice to cooking liquid, and cook over low
heat until mixture is reduced to 1 cup. Strain
through a fine sieve over fruit mixture, and cool.
Cover loosely, and chill. Yield: 6 servings (151
calories per ½-cup serving).

PRO 1.6 / FAT 0.9 / CARB 38.0 / FIB 3.3 / CHOL 0 / SOD 15 / POT 603

Last Minute Guests

Steak with Peppers and Onions
Shredded Potato Cake
Steamed Green Beans
Macaroon Baked Peaches

Serves 6
Total calories per serving: 427

When unexpected dinner guests appear at the door, the aptly named "minute" steak can be a lifesaver.

The message to be learned here is to have something ready in the pantry or freezer for an emergency. And, of course, minute or breakfast steaks qualify as a freezer candidate.

Braise the steaks with a color-

Steak with Peppers and Onions, Shredded Potato Cake, and Green Beans.

ful mix of red pepper, onion, and mushrooms. Then add crisp green beans, quickly steamed.

Let your food processor do all

the work for the shredded potato cake, and bake the peaches with macaroon topping while the guests enjoy the meal.

STEAK WITH PEPPERS AND ONIONS

6 (3-ounce) breakfast steaks, each ¼-inch thick
¼ teaspoon salt
¼ teaspoon pepper
Vegetable cooking spray
1 tablespoons vegetable oil
1 medium-size red or green pepper, seeded and cut into thin strips
1 medium onion, chopped
2 cups sliced fresh mushrooms
½ teaspoon dried whole thyme
½ teaspoon dried whole chervil
1 bay leaf
½ cup dry white wine
2 cups water
1 teaspoon beef-flavored bouillon granules
1 tablespoon cornstarch
2 tablespoons water
2 teaspoons Dijon mustard

Season steaks with salt and pepper; set aside.

Coat a large skillet with cooking spray; add oil, and place over high heat until hot. Add steaks, and cook 1 minute on each side. Drain on paper towels, and set aside.

Reduce heat to low, and add red pepper and onion to skillet. Cover and cook 4 minutes or until onion is tender. Add mushrooms, thyme, chervil, and bay leaf; cook 1 minute, stirring frequently. Add wine; cook 5 minutes, stirring frequently.

Add 2 cups water and bouillon granules to vegetable mixture; cook, uncovered, 15 minutes, stirring frequently.

Dissolve cornstarch in 2 tablespoons water, stirring well; add dissolved cornstarch and mustard to vegetable mixture, stirring well. Cook, stirring constantly, 1 minute or until thickened.

Add steaks, and cook until thoroughly heated. Remove bay leaf.

Transfer steaks to a warm serving platter; spoon vegetables and sauce over steaks. Yield: 6 servings (170 calories per serving).

PRO 21.5 / FAT 6.2 / CARB 6.7 / FIB 0.7 / CHOL 41 / SOD 266 / POT 470

SHREDDED POTATO CAKE

1½ pounds new potatoes
¼ teaspoon salt
¼ teaspoon pepper
Vegetable cooking spray
2 teaspoons vegetable oil, divided

Cook potatoes in boiling water to cover 20 minutes or until tender. Let cool to touch; peel and coarsely grate. Combine potatoes, salt, and pepper in a large bowl; toss lightly.

Coat a 10-inch heavy skillet with cooking spray; add 1 teaspoon oil, and place over medium heat until hot. Add potato mixture; press potato mixture down and spread evenly over bottom of skillet. Cook 2 minutes; reduce heat to low, and cook 10 minutes or until bottom is browned and crusty.

Remove skillet from heat. Place a large plate over skillet; invert potato cake onto plate.

Heat remaining 1 teaspoon oil in skillet over low heat; slide potato cake back into skillet. Cook 8 to 10 minutes or until bottom is browned and crusty. Invert onto a serving plate. Cut into wedges to serve. Yield: 6 servings (103 calories per serving).

PRO 2.4 / FAT 1.6 / CARB 20.4 / FIB 0.5 / CHOL 0 / SOD 104 / POT 617

STEAMED GREEN BEANS

1½ pounds fresh green beans
¼ teaspoon salt

Wash beans; trim ends, and remove strings. Arrange in a steaming rack.

Add salt to 1 inch water in pan. Bring water to a boil; place steaming rack in pan. Cover; steam 8 minutes or to desired degree of doneness. Yield: 6 servings (35 calories per serving).

PRO 2.1 / FAT 0.1 / CARB 8.1 / FIB 2.4 / CHOL 0 / SOD 104 / POT 237

MACAROON BAKED PEACHES

3 cups sliced, peeled fresh peaches
2 teaspoons lemon juice
½ teaspoon vanilla extract
2 teaspoons sugar
½ teaspoon ground cinnamon
6 coconut macaroons, crumbled (about ¾ cup)
1 tablespoon unsalted margarine

Toss peaches with lemon juice and vanilla; arrange in a 1-quart baking dish. Combine sugar and cinnamon, mixing well; sprinkle over peaches. Sprinkle crumbled macaroons evenly over mixture; dot with margarine.

Bake at 350° for 30 minutes or until lightly browned. Spoon into individual serving bowls, and serve warm. Yield: 6 servings (119 calories per serving).

PRO 1.0 / FAT 4.4 / CARB 20.3 / FIB 2.3 / CHOL 0 / SOD 9 / POT 201

 Establishing a regular walking program is an excellent way for sedentary people to start getting more aerobic exercise. Here are some tips that may help.

*Try to walk at the same time every day to help establish a routine (perhaps before breakfast or dinner).

*Drive your walking route once in the car to see how far you will be walking. Strive for a minimum of 2 miles.

*Walk at a pace that makes you perspire a little — without huffing and puffing.

*Swing your arms while you walk to burn up even more calories.

*Wear comfortable, well-cushioned shoes with plenty of support. If you wear lace-up shoes, lace them up normally, but at the top of each side make an extra loop, and thread the opposite lace through it. The heel of your shoe will fit better, making you less likely to get blisters.

*Apply the overload principle to your fitness program until you obtain desired results. Simply stated, continue to place more demands on your body than usual. For example, once your body has adapted to 1 mile, try walking 2, and so on.

*Train, don't strain is the best approach to improving fitness. Remember the purpose of your fitness program is to nurture and enhance your body. Work hard, but be gentle.

Chicken-In-A-Pot Dinner

Beet Salad
Chicken Breast Fricassee
Buttermilk Corn Muffins
Frozen Grapes
Oatmeal Raisin Cookies
Serves 4
Total calories per serving: 532

Chicken can be a lifesaver when time is at a premium, especially when it cooks in the same pot with the vegetables. Use the buttermilk corn muffins (1 muffin per serving) for catching some of the cooking juices.

The oatmeal-raisin cookies (1 cookie per serving) can be made ahead and stored. Frozen grapes (40 calories per ½-cup serving) get that frosty look when exposed to warm air. They are best if frozen overnight.

Chicken Breast Fricassee, Buttermilk Corn Muffins, and frozen grapes.

BEET SALAD

¾ pound beets
3 whole cloves
3 tablespoons cider vinegar
1½ teaspoons sugar
¼ teaspoon salt
⅛ teaspoon pepper
½ pound iceberg lettuce
½ pound Belgian endive, broken into spears
1 medium cucumber, peeled, halved lengthwise, seeded and sliced

Leave root and 1 inch stem on beets; scrub with a vegetable brush. Place beets with water to cover in a medium saucepan; add cloves. Bring to a boil. Cover; reduce heat, and simmer 30 minutes or until tender. Drain, reserving 3 tablespoons of cooking liquid; discard cloves. Peel and dice beets; chill.

Combine 3 tablespoons reserved cooking liquid, vinegar, sugar, salt, and pepper in a small bowl, stirring well; chill.

Divide lettuce evenly among 4 salad plates. Arrange endive, reserved beets, and cucumber on lettuce-lined plates. Spoon dressing evenly over salads. Yield: 4 servings (71 calories per serving).

PRO 2.9 / FAT 0.4 / CARB 15.9 / FIB 2.8 / CHOL 0 / SOD 229 / POT 652

CHICKEN BREAST FRICASSEE

4 (4-ounce) boneless chicken breast halves,
   skinned
1/8 teaspoon pepper
Vegetable cooking spray
1/2 pound small white onions
1/2 pound mushrooms, quartered
1/2 pound carrots, scraped and diagonally sliced
1 cup frozen whole kernel corn
1 cup water
1/4 cup dry white wine
1 teaspoon chicken-flavored bouillon granules
1 teaspoon dried whole tarragon
1/2 teaspoon dried whole thyme
1 bay leaf
1 tablespoon cornstarch
1/2 cup evaporated skim milk
1 teaspoon lemon juice
1 sprig fresh tarragon (optional)

Sprinkle chicken with pepper, and set aside. Coat a Dutch oven with cooking spray, and place over medium heat until hot. Add chicken, and cook 2 minutes on each side. Add next 10 ingredients; bring to a boil. Cover; reduce heat, and simmer 15 minutes or until vegetables are tender and chicken is done. Remove chicken to a serving platter, and keep warm.

Dissolve cornstarch in milk; add to Dutch oven, stirring well. Bring to a boil; reduce heat, and simmer until thickened. Remove from heat; stir in lemon juice. Discard bay leaf.

Arrange vegetables around chicken on platter; pour sauce over top, and garnish with fresh tarragon, if desired. Yield: 4 servings (262 calories per serving).

PRO 31.7 / FAT 3.9 / CARB 26.8 / FIB 2.3 / CHOL 72 / SOD 216 / POT 856

BUTTERMILK CORN MUFFINS

1 cup yellow cornmeal
1 cup all-purpose flour
2 teaspoons baking powder
1/4 teaspoon baking soda
1/4 teaspoon salt
1 1/2 cups buttermilk
1 egg, beaten
1 tablespoon unsalted margarine,
   melted
Vegetable cooking spray

Combine first 5 ingredients in a large mixing bowl. Combine buttermilk, egg, and margarine; add to dry ingredients, mixing well.

Coat muffin pans with cooking spray; spoon batter into muffin pans, filling each two-thirds full. Bake at 425° for 20 minutes or until muffins are golden brown. Yield: 12 muffins (107 calories each).

PRO 3.6 / FAT 1.9 / CARB 18.3 / FIB 1.4 / CHOL 24 / SOD 144 / POT 77

OATMEAL RAISIN COOKIES

1/2 cup regular oats, uncooked
1/2 cup unbleached or all-purpose flour
1/4 cup firmly packed brown sugar
1/4 teaspoon ground cinnamon
1/8 teaspoon baking soda
1/8 teaspoon salt
3 tablespoons unsalted margarine, melted
2 tablespoons skim milk
1/3 cup raisins
Vegetable cooking spray

Place oats on a baking sheet. Bake at 350° for 10 minutes. Remove from oven; set aside.

Combine flour, sugar, cinnamon, soda, and salt in a medium bowl. Combine margarine and milk in a small bowl; add to flour mixture, mixing until well blended. Fold in reserved oats and raisins.

Drop batter by rounded teaspoonfuls 2 inches apart onto cookie sheets coated with cooking spray. Bake at 350° for 10 to 12 minutes. Cool 1 minute on cookie sheets. Remove to wire racks to cool completely. Yield: 18 cookies (52 calories each).

PRO 0.8 / FAT 2.1 / CARB 8.0 / FIB 0.5 / CHOL 0 / SOD 21 / POT 42

Make a birthday memorable: Shellfish en Papillote and Parsleyed Potatoes.

Special Birthday Celebration

Eating smart, the way you will with this menu, will help keep you feeling young regardless of which birthday calls forth the celebration.

Make the aspics the night before, and reserve them in the refrigerator. Only the dill mayonnaise needs to be made at the last minute.

The shellfish and vegetables en papillote features cooking in parchment which makes for an elegant dish without a lot of

**Company Tomato Aspic
Shellfish en Papillote
Parsleyed Potatoes
Cherry-Filled Meringues**

Serves 2
Total calories per serving: 650

trouble. Precooking the vegetables keeps them from giving off too much liquid when they're baked in the parchment and cuts cooking time.

Slicing the potatoes into ovals isn't necessary, of course, but it does make for a more special presentation.

The meringue shells can also be made ahead and stored in an airtight container. The cherry filling cooks up in minutes. Let it stand in the refrigerator during dinner, and assemble the tarts just before serving (otherwise the shells get soggy). If tradition is important to you, place a candle in each meringue.

COMPANY TOMATO ASPIC

1½ teaspoons unflavored gelatin
2 tablespoons water
1⅓ cups tomato juice
¼ cup chopped celery
1 clove garlic, minced
1 bay leaf
¼ teaspoon dried whole basil
4 whole peppercorns
½ teaspoon lemon juice
¼ teaspoon Worcestershire sauce
2 to 3 drops hot sauce
Vegetable cooking spray
2 tablespoons reduced-calorie mayonnaise
1 tablespoon minced fresh dill or ¾ teaspoon dried whole dillweed
¼ teaspoon lemon juice
Fresh dill sprigs

Soften gelatin in water; set aside.

Combine tomato juice, celery, garlic, bay leaf, basil, peppercorns, ½ teaspoon lemon juice, Worcestershire sauce, and hot sauce in a small saucepan. Bring to a boil. Cover; reduce heat, and simmer 15 minutes. Strain tomato juice mixture, discarding vegetables and herbs; add softened gelatin, stirring until gelatin dissolves.

Coat two (8 ounce) individual molds with cooking spray. Pour tomato juice mixture into molds; chill 2 hours or until set.

Turn molds out onto individual serving plates. Combine mayonnaise, dillweed, and ¼ teaspoon lemon juice; mix well. Spoon 1 tablespoon on top of each aspic. Garnish with dill sprigs. Yield: 2 servings (77 calories per serving).

PRO 3.4 / FAT 4.1 / CARB 8.4 / FIB 0.7 / CHOL 5 / SOD 710 / POT 608

SHELLFISH EN PAPILLOTE

Parchment paper
¼ pound fresh green beans
¼ pound carrots, scraped and cut into 3- x ¼-inch strips
¼ pound sea scallops
¼ pound uncooked large fresh shrimp, peeled and deveined
2 teaspoons unsalted margarine
⅛ teaspoon pepper
¾ cup chopped fresh basil leaves
2 tablespoons white vermouth
1 tablespoon plus 1½ teaspoons lemon juice
1 tablespoon plus 1½ teaspoons grated Parmesan cheese
2 teaspoons vegetable oil
2 teaspoons pine nuts
1 clove garlic, minced
1 teaspoon pine nuts, toasted

Cut two 14- x 12-inch pieces of parchment paper; fold each piece of paper in half lengthwise. Cut each paper to form a large heart shape. Open out flat, and set aside.

Remove strings from beans; wash beans thoroughly. Cut into 2-inch pieces. Combine green beans, carrots, and water to cover in a medium saucepan. Bring to a boil. Cover; reduce heat, and simmer 3 minutes. Drain.

Divide vegetables in half, and arrange along one side of fold of each reserved parchment paper heart. Top vegetables on each heart with half of shrimp and scallops; dot with margarine, and sprinkle with pepper.

Fold paper edges over to seal securely. Carefully place parchment pouches on a baking sheet. Bake at 375° for 15 minutes or until pouches are puffed and lightly browned. Transfer pouches to serving plates.

Combine basil, vermouth, lemon juice, Parmesan, oil, 2 teaspoons pine nuts, and garlic in container of an electric blender. Process until smooth.

Cut an opening in each parchment pouch. Spoon sauce evenly over vegetable-seafood mixture, and sprinkle with toasted pine nuts. Serve immediately. Yield: 2 servings (291 calories per serving).

PRO 21.0 / FAT 14.4 / CARB 17.9 / FIB 2.6 / CHOL 87 / SOD 301 / POT 794

PARSLEYED POTATOES

½ pound small new potatoes, peeled
⅛ teaspoon salt
⅛ teaspoon pepper
1 tablespoon minced fresh parsley

Arrange potatoes in a steaming rack. Place over boiling water in a saucepan; sprinkle with salt and pepper. Cover and steam 15 minutes or until potatoes are tender. Transfer potatoes to a serving plate; sprinkle with parsley. Serve warm. Yield: 2 servings (91 calories per serving).

PRO 2.4 / FAT 0.1 / CARB 20.6 / FIB 0.5 / CHOL 0 / SOD 154 / POT 628

CHERRY-FILLED MERINGUES

1 egg white
¼ teaspoon vanilla extract
2 tablespoons sugar
1 teaspoon sifted powdered sugar
Cherry Filling

Beat egg white (at room temperature) and vanilla in a small bowl until soft peaks form. Gradually add 2 tablespoons sugar, beating until stiff peaks form and sugar dissolves. (Do not underbeat mixture.) Spoon meringue mixture into a pastry bag fitted with a star tip.

Draw 2 circles (3 inches in diameter) on a baking sheet covered with unglazed brown paper. (Do not use recycled paper.) Starting at center of each outlined circle, pipe meringue in a flat spiral fashion, using a circular motion that ends just inside each circle's outline. (This forms base of meringue cups.) Continue to pipe meringue atop outer ring of base, using a circular motion, to form 2 continuously attached and stacked meringue rings. (These form sides of meringue cup.) Repeat procedure with remaining meringue mixture. Sprinkle each shell with powdered sugar.

Bake at 200° for 2 hours. Turn oven off; cool meringue shells in oven at least 1 hour. (Do not open oven door.) Remove baked meringue shells from brown paper, and cool completely. Use immediately or store in airtight containers at room temperature up to 2 days.

Place baked meringue shells on individual dessert dishes. Spoon ½ cup Cherry Filling into each cup. Serve immediately. Yield: 2 servings (191 calories per serving).

Cherry Filling:

1 teaspoon cornstarch
1 tablespoon dark rum
1 cup fresh cherries, pitted and halved
3 tablespoons unsweetened orange juice
1 tablespoon honey
½ teaspoon grated lemon rind
½ teaspoon lemon juice

Combine cornstarch and rum in a small bowl; mix well, and set aside.

Combine next 4 ingredients in a small saucepan. Cook over low heat, stirring occasionally, 5 minutes. Bring to a boil; stir in cornstarch mixture. Reduce heat; cook, stirring constantly, until clear and thickened. Stir in lemon juice. Remove from heat; chill 1 hour. Yield: 1 cup.

PRO 2.9 / FAT 0.0 / CARB 40.4 / FIB 0.0 / CHOL 0 / SOD 37 / POT 74

The term aerobics is often misunderstood to mean dancing. Literally, aerobics means "with oxygen" — exercises that demand oxygen without producing an unbearable oxygen debt, so that they can be sustained nonstop for at least 15 minutes. Aerobic exercises are the basic activities on which any exercise program should be built. They range in intensity from brisk walking to vigorous cross-country skiing. Other aerobic activities include cycling, swimming, skating, jogging, rowing, rope jumping, stair climbing, racquetball, and dancing. Participating in one or more of these activities 3 to 5 days per week can significantly improve aerobic or cardiovascular fitness.

Aerobic fitness is influenced by a variety of factors, such as age, sex, genetic background, and training. Age has been shown to slightly decrease aerobic fitness every decade after the mid-twenties. However, the active person will always maintain a higher level of fitness than will the sedentary individual. An increase in aerobic fitness can occur at any age by starting an aerobic exercise program.

This Chocolate-Almond Fluff can be assembled ahead to help keep Sunday supper simple.

Simple Sunday Supper

Sunday dinner, right after church, is usually the big meal of the day. But sometimes Sunday night suppers are much more convenient, especially if you have invited guests.

Forget the roast beef and Yorkshire pudding. Instead, spend the entire afternoon biking or hiking, and return home to this easily pulled together meal.

Cold Cantaloupe Soup
Artichoke-Cheese Strata
Spinach-Radish Salad
Chocolate-Almond Fluff

Serves 6
Total calories per serving: 428

The cantaloupe soup, the strata, and the chocolate-almond fluff can all be assembled ahead

of time. On Sunday evening when you get home, it's just a matter of popping the strata in the oven.

For a special twist, the iron-rich spinach in the salad is combined with the fresh taste of watercress and radishes, creating an interesting accompaniment to the mildly sweet soup and the cheesy strata.

COLD CANTALOUPE SOUP

1 (3½-pound) ripe cantaloupe, peeled, seeded, and cut into pieces
⅔ cup unsweetened orange juice, divided
1 tablespoon lemon juice
1 teaspoon minced fresh mint
Fresh mint sprigs

Combine half of cantaloupe, ⅓ cup orange juice, and lemon juice in container of an electric blender; process until smooth. Transfer to a bowl; repeat procedure with remaining cantaloupe and orange juice. Stir in minced mint. Cover and chill at least 2 hours. Ladle into serving bowls, and garnish with mint sprig. Yield: 4½ cups (89 calories per ¾-cup serving).

PRO 2.1 / FAT 0.6 / CARB 21.4 / FIB 0.6 / CHOL 0 / SOD 18 / POT 696

SPINACH-RADISH SALAD

¾ pound fresh spinach, trimmed and torn
¼ pound fresh watercress, trimmed
1 (6-ounce) package radishes, trimmed and thinly sliced
½ medium onion, sliced and separated into rings
3 tablespoons fresh lemon juice
1 tablespoon vegetable oil
½ teaspoon salt
½ teaspoon pepper

Combine spinach, watercress, radishes, and onion in a large salad bowl. Combine remaining ingredients, stirring well. Pour dressing over salad; toss lightly. Serve immediately. Yield: 6 servings (46 calories per serving).

PRO 2.4 / FAT 2.7 / CARB 4.9 / FIB 2.2 / CHOL 0 / SOD 255 / POT 475

ARTICHOKE-CHEESE STRATA

½ cup chopped green onion
1 teaspoon unsalted margarine, melted
3 slices whole wheat bread, cubed
Vegetable cooking spray
¾ cup (3 ounces) shredded extra sharp Cheddar cheese
1 (14-ounce) can artichoke hearts, drained and quartered
1 (4-ounce) jar sliced pimientos, drained
2 eggs, lightly beaten
2 egg whites, lightly beaten
1 (12-ounce) can evaporated skim milk
½ teaspoon dry mustard
¼ teaspoon salt
⅛ teaspoon ground red pepper

Sauté green onion in margarine in a small skillet until tender. Remove from heat.

Arrange half of bread cubes in a 9-inch quiche dish coated with cooking spray. Top with half of cheese, half of artichokes, half of green onion, and half of pimiento. Repeat layers.

Combine remaining ingredients in a large bowl; stir well. Pour over ingredients in quiche dish. Cover and chill at least 3 hours.

Allow to stand at room temperature 30 minutes. Bake at 350° for 1 hour or until set. Yield: 6 servings (194 calories per serving).

PRO 13.5 / FAT 7.9 / CARB 18.6 / FIB 1.4 / CHOL 109 / SOD 386 / POT 427

CHOCOLATE-ALMOND FLUFF

1 envelope unflavored gelatin
2 cups skim milk
¼ cup plus 2 tablespoons sugar
¼ cup Dutch process or unsweetened cocoa
½ teaspoon almond extract
1 tablespoon sliced almonds, toasted

Soften gelatin in milk in a small saucepan; let stand 1 minute. Add sugar and cocoa; cook over low heat, stirring constantly, 5 minutes or until gelatin dissolves. Transfer to a large bowl; stir in almond flavoring. Cover and chill until consistency of unbeaten egg white.

Place bowl in a larger bowl of ice water; beat at high speed of an electric mixer until chocolate mixture is light and fluffy (about 5 minutes). Spoon evenly into dessert dishes; chill thoroughly. Garnish with almonds. Yield: 6 servings (99 calories per serving).

PRO 4.6 / FAT 1.6 / CARB 18.2 / FIB 0.2 / CHOL 2 / SOD 70 / POT 168

Veal Paupiettes make a classic entrée and, at the same time, let you try something delightfully different. Add the elegant simplicity of Poached Asparagus, Tomatoes Provençal, and Bowknot Rolls to create a Festive Dinner for Eight (menu begins on page 81).

Romantic Dinner For Two

Minted Lamb Chops
Lemon Pilaf
Baked Eggplant with Fresh
Tomato Sauce
Chocolate-Dipped
Strawberries
Café Brûlot

Serves 2
Total calories per serving: 580

Keep in mind that spending time in the kitchen is not the point of a romantic dinner. We suggest making the chocolate-dipped strawberries ahead of time and keeping them chilled until the moment is right.

Cook the pilaf mixture, and keep it warm while the eggplant is in the oven. You can mold the pilafs while the lamb chops are under the broiler.

The café brûlot can steep while you linger over your meal. Bring it to a simmer when the candles begin to taper.

Chocolate-Dipped Strawberries with Café Brûlot.

MINTED LAMB CHOPS

2 (5-ounce) lamb loin chops, ¾-inch thick
1 tablespoon finely chopped fresh mint leaves
¼ teaspoon dried whole rosemary, crushed
⅛ teaspoon salt
⅛ teaspoon pepper
Fresh mint leaves

Trim excess fat from chops. Sprinkle chops with chopped mint, rosemary, salt, and pepper.

Place chops on a rack in a shallow roasting pan. Broil 5 inches from heat 4 minutes on each side or until desired degree of doneness. Remove lamb chops to a warm serving platter; garnish with mint leaves. Yield: 2 servings (169 calories per serving).

PRO 25.8 / FAT 6.5 / CARB 0.2 / FIB 0.0 / CHOL 91 / SOD 211 / POT 268

LEMON PILAF

1 teaspoon unsalted margarine
Vegetable cooking spray
1 tablespoon minced green onion
1/3 cup regular rice, uncooked
3/4 cup plus 2 tablespoons water
1/2 teaspoon grated lemon rind
2 teaspoons lemon juice
1/2 teaspoon chicken-flavored bouillon granules
1 small bay leaf
1/8 teaspoon pepper
1 tablespoon minced fresh parsley

Melt margarine in a saucepan coated with cooking spray over medium heat. Add onion; cook, stirring constantly, until tender. Add rice; cook 1 minute, stirring constantly. Stir in next 6 ingredients. Bring to a boil. Cover; reduce heat, and simmer 15 minutes or until liquid is absorbed. Discard bay leaf.

Cool rice mixture 5 minutes. Add parsley; stir with a fork until fluffy. Press mixture evenly into two 1/2-cup molds coated with cooking spray. Invert onto serving plates. Serve warm. Yield: 2 servings (135 calories per serving).

PRO 2.3 / FAT 2.2 / CARB 26.2 / FIB 1.0 / CHOL 0 / SOD 98 / POT 59

BAKED EGGPLANT WITH FRESH TOMATO SAUCE

1 small eggplant, quartered lengthwise
1 large tomato, chopped
1/2 cup chopped onion
1 clove garlic, minced
1/2 teaspoon sugar
1/4 teaspoon ground cumin
1/8 teaspoon salt

Reassemble eggplant; wrap in aluminum foil. Place on a baking sheet, and bake at 400° for 40 minutes or until tender.

Combine remaining ingredients in a small saucepan. Cook over medium heat, stirring frequently, 5 minutes or until thickened.

Place 2 eggplant quarters on each plate; spoon sauce over eggplant. Serve immediately Yield: 2 servings (91 calories per serving).

PRO 3.7 / FAT 0.7 / CARB 21.0 / FIB 3.9 / CHOL 0 / SOD 167 / POT 740

CHOCOLATE-DIPPED STRAWBERRIES

12 medium-size fresh strawberries
1 (1-ounce) square semi-sweet chocolate, melted
1 tablespoon evaporated skim milk
1 teaspoon Triple Sec or other orange-flavored liqueur

Wash strawberries, leaving stems intact, and drain well.

Combine chocolate, milk, and Triple Sec in a small bowl; set bowl in a pan of boiling water. Beat with a small wire whisk until mixture is smooth.

Insert a wooden pick into stem end of each strawberry. Dip each strawberry halfway into chocolate mixture. Place picks in holes of an inverted sieve; refrigerate until chocolate is firm. Remove picks, and arrange chilled strawberries in a serving bowl; serve immediately. Yield: 2 servings (113 calories per serving).

PRO 2.0 / FAT 5.0 / CARB 17.1 / FIB 1.8 / CHOL 0 / SOD 10 / POT 227

CAFÉ BRÛLOT

2 cups hot brewed coffee
2 teaspoons brown sugar
1 (2-inch) stick cinnamon
2 whole cloves
1 tablespoon julienne orange rind
1 (2-inch) strip lemon rind
2 tablespoons Cognac
1 tablespoon Curaçao or other orange-flavored liqueur
2 (2-inch) strips lemon rind

Combine first 6 ingredients in a saucepan; cover and let stand 15 minutes. Bring to a simmer over medium heat, stirring occasionally. Add Cognac and Curaçao. Strain into coffee cups, and garnish with lemon rind strips. Yield: 2 servings (72 calories per serving).

PRO 0.0 / FAT 0.0 / CARB 5.1 / FIB 0.0 / CHOL 0 / SOD 3 / POT 97

Polished rice is enriched with vitamins and minerals which are applied to the outside of the grain. Therefore, avoid rinsing and cook in as little water as possible.

Curried Chicken with Cantaloupe and breadsticks make getting to the theater easy.

Before The Theater Dinner

An occasional night at the theater or movies is a psychological necessity. Events on the stage provide momentary escapes and let you return with a fresh perspective.

But you don't have to lace on your running shoes to be on time. We've planned an elegant but easy menu designed to be made ahead of time.

Make the sherried consommé the night before, and reheat it

Sherried Consommé
Curried Chicken with
Cantaloupe
Commercial Whole Wheat
Sesame Breadsticks
Plum Ice
Serves 4
Total calories per serving: 493

when dinner is served.

The curried chicken with cantaloupe needs no reheating at all.

Make the chicken the night before, and all that is left is to prepare the fruit and vegetable accompaniments.

You will find no quicker bread than whole wheat sesame breadsticks (3 breadsticks per serving for the correct calorie count); they go straight from the package to the table.

Dessert is equally obliging. Make it whenever you have time, and store it in the freezer.

SHERRIED CONSOMMÉ

Bones from 2 pounds chicken breast halves (reserved from Curried Chicken with Cantaloupe)
3½ cups water
1 (14½-ounce) can whole tomatoes, drained
1 medium onion, thinly sliced
1 carrot, scraped and sliced
1 stalk celery, sliced
¼ cup dry white wine
1 cup sliced fresh mushrooms
4 whole peppercorns
2 whole cloves
1 bay leaf
1 teaspoon beef-flavored bouillon granules
½ teaspoon dried whole thyme
2 tablespoons Sercial or medium-dry sherry

Combine all ingredients, except sherry, in a large saucepan. Bring to a boil. Cover; reduce heat, and simmer 1½ hours. Strain mixture through a fine sieve into a bowl; discard bones, vegetables, and spices. Cover; chill overnight.

Remove and discard hardened fat from top of consommé. Bring consommé to a simmer in a saucepan over medium heat. Remove from heat; stir in Sercial. Ladle into serving bowls. Yield: 2 cups (53 calories per ½-cup serving).

PRO 1.9 / FAT 0.4 / CARB 9.8 / FIB 0.9 / CHOL 0 / SOD 367 / POT 268

CURRIED CHICKEN WITH CANTALOUPE

2 pounds chicken breast halves, skinned
1½ cups water
1 teaspoon chicken-flavored bouillon granules
6 whole peppercorns
2 whole cloves
1 bay leaf
¼ pound fresh snow peas
⅓ cup reduced-calorie mayonnaise
⅓ cup plain low-fat yogurt
1 teaspoon curry powder
¼ teaspoon ground ginger
1 clove garlic, crushed
2 tablespoons chopped green onion
1 (1-pound) cantaloupe, peeled, and cut into very thin wedges
1 tablespoon diced red pepper
1 tablespoon sliced almonds, toasted
1 sprig fresh coriander or parsley

Bone chicken, reserving bones for use in Sherried Consommé; set chicken aside.

Combine water, bouillon granules, peppercorns, cloves, and bay leaf in a medium saucepan; bring to a boil. Add chicken; reduce heat, and simmer 8 minutes or until chicken is tender. Remove chicken, and let cool. Cut into ¼-inch-thick strips. Cover and chill.

Trim ends from snow peas, and remove strings. Place snow peas in a steaming basket. Plunge basket into a pan of boiling water, and remove immediately. Drain snow peas, and chill thoroughly.

Combine mayonnaise, yogurt, curry, ginger, and garlic; stir until well combined. Add reserved chicken breast halves and green onion, tossing lightly. Arrange cantaloupe and chilled snow peas on a large serving platter; top with chicken mixture. Garnish with red pepper, toasted almonds, and coriander. Yield: 4 servings (280 calories per serving).

PRO 34.5 / FAT 10.3 / CARB 12.0 / FIB 1.0 / CHOL 91 / SOD 333 / POT 570

PLUM ICE

1 pound ripe plums, pitted and quartered
1 cup dry red wine
1 cup water
¼ cup sugar
1 (1½-inch) stick cinnamon
⅛ teaspoon ground cloves
2 teaspoons grated orange rind
¼ cup unsweetened orange juice

Combine plums, wine, water, sugar, cinnamon, and cloves in a medium saucepan. Bring to a boil. Reduce heat, and simmer 10 minutes. Cool plum mixture, and process through a food mill. Place pureed plum mixture in a 9-inch square pan. Stir in orange rind and orange juice. Freeze 2 hours or until frozen.

Transfer frozen plum mixture to container of an electric blender, and process until smooth. Return plum mixture to pan, and freeze just until firm. Scoop out into stemmed glasses. Serve immediately. Yield: 4 servings (127 calories per serving).

PRO 1.1 / FAT 0.7 / CARB 31.6 / FIB 0.7 / CHOL 0 / SOD 3 / POT 281

Dinner From The Wok

The key to organizing a Chinese menu is to make the most of your preparation time.

Chinese cooking involves lots of chopping and mincing. Doing the cleaver and knife work for all the recipes before starting makes the cooking a breeze.

Once you peel and devein the shrimp and prepare the onion and tomato, the sour shrimp soup is simply a matter of combining the ingredients in one pot and simmmering until done.

Sour Shrimp Soup
Oriental Pork Stir-Fry
Sticky Rice
Almond Cookies
Orange Wedges

Serves 6
Total calories per serving: 464

For the stir-fried pork, soak the dried mushrooms while you cut up the pork, green onion, gingerroot, garlic, carrot, and tomato.

As with most stir-fried dishes, the wok time is minimal.

The rice needs no tending, and the almond cookies (2 cookies per serving) are just as tasty if they are made ahead. The orange wedges are decorative with the ends curled under.

Nutritionally, Chinese cuisine is hard to beat because of its emphasis on fresh vegetables. The one flaw in Chinese cooking, its high sodium content, has been controlled in these recipes.

SOUR SHRIMP SOUP

3½ cups water
1 (8-ounce) bottle clam juice
3 tablespoons lemon juice
¼ teaspoon salt
⅛ teaspoon pepper
1 bay leaf
1 cup diced, peeled tomato
½ cup chopped onion
¼ pound fresh spinach, cut into strips
10 whole radishes
½ pound large fresh shrimp, peeled and deveined

Combine water, clam juice, lemon juice, salt, pepper, and bay leaf in a small Dutch oven; bring to a boil. Add tomato and onion. Cover; reduce heat, and simmer 10 minutes, stirring occasionally. Add spinach and radishes; cook, uncovered, 4 minutes, stirring occasionally. Add shrimp, and cook 3 minutes or until shrimp are done. Remove bay leaf, and discard; ladle soup into serving bowls. Yield: 6 cups (52 calories per 1-cup serving).

PRO 7.1 / FAT 0.5 / CARB 5.3 / FIB 1.0 / CHOL 46 / SOD 317 / POT 280

Oriental fare that is easy to prepare: Sour Shrimp Soup, Oriental Pork Stir-Fry, Almond Cookies, and Orange Wedges with a new "twist."

ORIENTAL PORK STIR-FRY

1 pound lean boneless pork
1 cup dried shiitake mushrooms (about
  1 ounce)
3 cups hot water
2 teaspoons cornstarch
Vegetable cooking spray
1 tablespoon vegetable oil
¼ cup chopped green onion
1 tablespoon minced gingerroot
2 cloves garlic, minced
2 (7½-ounce) jars pickled baby corn, drained
  and rinsed
1 medium carrot, scraped and thinly sliced
½ cup water
½ teaspoon chicken-flavored bouillon
  granules
2 tablespoons dry sherry
1 tablespoon reduced-sodium soy sauce
1 medium tomato, cut into 12 wedges
2 tablespoons thinly sliced green onion
  tops
2 green onion fans

Trim excess fat from pork, cut pork into ¼-inch-thick strips, and set aside.

Combine mushrooms and 3 cups hot water; set aside 30 minutes. Drain mushrooms, reserving 1 tablespoon liquid; quarter mushrooms, and set aside. Dissolve cornstarch in reserved liquid, and set aside.

Coat a wok or large skillet with cooking spray; allow to heat at medium-high (325°) for 1 minute. Pour oil around top of wok. Add pork; stir-fry 4 minutes or until browned. Remove pork from wok, and set aside.

Add ¼ cup green onion, gingerroot, and garlic to wok; stir-fry 30 seconds. Add reserved mushrooms, corn, carrot, ½ cup water, bouillon granules, sherry, and soy sauce. Cover and simmer 5 minutes.

Add reserved cornstarch mixture to wok, stirring well. Add tomato wedges and reserved pork; cook, stirring gently, until thoroughly heated. Transfer mixture to a serving platter; garnish with green onion tops and green onion fans. Serve immediately. Yield: 6 servings (223 calories per serving).

PRO 18.6 / FAT 8.1 / CARB 19.4 / FIB 1.4 / CHOL 48 / SOD 182 / POT 581

STICKY RICE

1 cup regular rice, uncooked
2 cups water

Combine rice and water in a medium saucepan; bring to a boil. Cover; reduce heat to low, and cook 15 minutes or until water is absorbed. Remove rice from heat, and let stand, covered, 20 minutes. Yield: 6 servings (112 calories per serving).

PRO 2.1 / FAT 0.1 / CARB 24.8 / FIB 0.7 / CHOL 0 / SOD 2 / POT 28

ALMOND COOKIES

¼ cup plus 2 tablespoons unsalted
  margarine
¼ cup sugar
1 egg white
½ teaspoon almond extract
1 cup unbleached or all-purpose
  flour
½ teaspoon baking powder
1 tablespoon sliced almonds

Cream margarine; gradually add sugar, beating until light and fluffy. Add egg white, beating well; stir in almond extract.

Combine flour and baking powder; add flour mixture to creamed mixture, beating well. Shape into 1-inch balls. Place balls 2 inches apart on ungreased cookie sheets. Press an almond slice in center of each cookie. Bake at 350° for 10 to 12 minutes or until lightly browned. Remove cookies to wire racks to cool. Yield: 2 dozen (52 calories each).

PRO 0.7 / FAT 3.0 / CARB 5.8 / FIB 0.0 / CHOL 0 / SOD 9 / POT 10

ORANGE WEDGES

2 medium oranges

Cut each orange into 6 sections. Partially peel back ends of each section, but do not detach rind. Curl free ends under sections, and arrange sections on a platter. Yield: 6 servings (25 calories per 2-wedge serving).

PRO 0.5 / FAT 0.1 / CARB 6.1 / FIB 1.0 / CHOL 0 / SOD 1 / POT 101

Mexican Special

Seviche
Fajitas
Fresh Tomato Salsa
Guacamole Salad
Frozen Piña Colada

Serves 8
Total calories per serving: 586

This fiesta menu accommodates the cook so that more time can be spent with guests.

The seviche and fajitas can be started the day before and left in the refrigerator to "cook" overnight in the marinade.

The guacamole dressing whips up quickly in the blender. And the fresh tomato salsa is also easy. (Just don't make either one too far in advance. The avocado can turn dark, and the salsa may get watery.)

The piña coladas are saved for dessert — sort of like fruit sherbet with a kick.

This fiesta includes Fajitas (front), Seviche, and Guacamole Salad.

SEVICHE

1 quart water
6 whole peppercorns
3 slices lemon
1 bay leaf
½ pound fresh large shrimp, peeled and deveined
½ pound bay scallops
½ cup fresh lemon juice
¼ cup fresh lime juice
2 medium oranges, peeled, sectioned, and seeded
1 medium-size red onion, thinly sliced
1 (2½-inch) green chile, seeded and minced
1 teaspoon grated orange rind
3 tablespoons fresh orange juice

Combine first 4 ingredients in a medium saucepan; bring to a boil. Add shrimp and scallops; cook 1 minute or until opaque. Drain, discarding peppercorns, lemon slices, and bay leaf; rinse under cold water. Drain well.

Combine seafood, lemon juice, and lime juice in a shallow dish. Cover and marinate in refrigerator at least 4 hours or overnight. Drain.

Combine seafood and remaining ingredients in a bowl. Spoon onto individual dishes. Yield: 8 appetizer servings (86 calories per serving).

PRO 9.3 / FAT 0.4 / CARB 12.4 / FIB 1.4 / CHOL 42 / SOD 110 / POT 461

FAJITAS

2 pounds flank steak
¼ cup lemon juice
¼ cup lime juice
1 (2½-inch) green chile, seeded and minced
1 tablespoon vegetable oil
¼ teaspoon salt
¼ teaspoon pepper
¼ teaspoon ground cumin
8 (6-inch) flour tortillas

Trim excess fat from steak; place in a shallow baking dish, and set aside.

Combine lemon juice, lime juice, chile pepper, oil, salt, pepper, and cumin, stirring well; pour over steak. Cover and marinate in refrigerator 4 hours or overnight.

Drain steak, reserving marinade. Place on rack in a broiler pan. Broil 5 to 6 inches from heat 5 to 6 minutes on each side or until desired degree of doneness, basting often with reserved marinade. Transfer to a cutting board; slice steak diagonally across the grain into thin slices.

Place a skillet or griddle over medium heat until hot. Place tortillas in skillet 30 to 40 seconds on each side or until thoroughly heated. Divide steak slices evenly among tortillas. Wrap tortilla around steak; serve with Fresh Tomato Salsa, if desired. Yield: 8 servings (296 calories per serving).

PRO 29.9 / FAT 8.0 / CARB 26.2 / FIB 0.5 / CHOL 55 / SOD 132 / POT 494

FRESH TOMATO SALSA

2 cups peeled, seeded, and coarsely chopped tomato
½ cup minced green onion
½ cup tomato sauce
2 tablespoons chopped fresh parsley
2 to 3 teaspoons minced green chile
2 teaspoons lemon juice
¼ teaspoon salt
⅛ teaspoon pepper

Combine all ingredients in a small bowl, stirring gently. Cover and chill at least 4 hours. Serve with Fajitas, if desired. Yield: 2¼ cups (16 calories per ¼-cup serving).

PRO 0.7 / FAT 0.1 / CARB 3.4 / FIB 0.5 / CHOL 0 / SOD 125 / POT 164

GUACAMOLE SALAD

1 (10-ounce) avocado, peeled and chopped
½ cup evaporated skim milk
3 tablespoons lemon juice
2 tablespoons sour cream
1 clove garlic, crushed
¼ teaspoon salt
¼ teaspoon chili powder
¼ teaspoon Worcestershire sauce
⅛ teaspoon ground cumin
2 drops hot sauce
1 (1-pound) head iceberg lettuce, shredded
¼ pound fresh spinach, shredded
1 (15-ounce) can garbanzo beans, drained
1 (14-ounce) can hearts of palm, drained and sliced
1 small red or green pepper, seeded and chopped

Combine first 10 ingredients in container of an electric blender; process until smooth.

Combine lettuce, spinach, garbanzo beans, and hearts of palm in a large salad bowl; toss lightly. Spoon onto individual salad plates. Top evenly with avocado mixture, and garnish with red pepper. Yield: 8 servings (150 calories per serving).

PRO 5.5 / FAT 7.4 / CARB 19.6 / FIB 5.2 / CHOL 2 / SOD 307 / POT 675

FROZEN PIÑA COLADA

4 cups chopped fresh pineapple
1 teaspoon grated orange rind
½ cup unsweetened orange juice
3 tablespoons skim milk
3 tablespoons light rum
1 tablespoon plus 1½ teaspoons lemon juice
½ teaspoon coconut extract

Combine all ingredients in container of an electric blender, and process until smooth. Transfer mixture to a 9-inch metal pan. Freeze 3 hours or until almost frozen.

Place mixture in container of an electric blender; process until smooth. Return mixture to metal pan. Freeze until firm. Spoon into serving dishes, and serve immediately. Yield: 8 servings (54 calories per ½-cup serving).

PRO 0.6 / FAT 0.4 / CARB 11.9 / FIB 1.2 / CHOL 0 / SOD 4 / POT 130

Dinner With A French Accent

Crab Crêpes with
Spinach Mornay Sauce
Baby Carrots
Leek-Mushroom Salad
Strawberry-Orange
Spongecake

Serves 8
Total calories per serving: 648

French food does not have to be time consuming and laden with calories. The proof is in this menu that features the classic French entrée, crêpes.

The trick to the salad is not in the time spent, but in its careful arrangement on individual serv-ing plates. It's really no more complicated than a regular tossed salad.

Make the light crêpes the day before; stack them between sheets of waxed paper, and keep them in the refrigerator overnight. Mixing up the crab fill-ing and whirling up the spinach mornay sauce in the blender will take only minutes.

The baby carrots make a deli-cate complement to the entrée and are as easy as the grand fi-nale — an airy spongecake topped with fresh strawberries.

CRAB CRÊPES WITH SPINACH MORNAY SAUCE

⅔ cup chopped green onion
1 cup sliced fresh mushrooms
½ teaspoon dried whole thyme
2 teaspoons unsalted margarine, melted
1 tablespoon all-purpose flour
¾ cup skim milk
¼ cup dry white wine
1 pound fresh lump crabmeat, drained and flaked
2 tablespoons chopped fresh parsley
1 tablespoon lemon juice
¼ teaspoon dry mustard
¼ teaspoon salt
⅛ teaspoon ground red pepper
16 Light Crêpes
Vegetable cooking spray
Spinach Mornay Sauce
2 tablespoons grated Parmesan cheese

Sauté green onion, mushrooms, and thyme in margarine in a large skillet until vegetables are tender. Reduce heat to low, and add flour; cook 1 minute, stirring constantly. Gradually add milk and wine; cook over medium heat, stirring constantly, until thickened and bubbly. Remove from heat; stir in crabmeat, parsley, lemon juice, mustard, salt, and red pepper.

Spoon 1½ tablespoons crabmeat mixture down center of each Light Crêpe; roll up crêpes, and arrange in a 13- x 9- x 2-inch baking dish coated with cooking spray. Spoon Spinach Mornay Sauce over crêpes; sprinkle with Parmesan. Cover and bake at 350° for 25 minutes or until thoroughly heated. Broil crêpes 4 to 6 inches from heat 1 minute or until golden brown. Yield: 8 servings (293 calories per serving).

Light Crêpes:

1½ cups all-purpose flour
¼ teaspoon salt
3 eggs, beaten
2 cups skim milk
2 tablespoons unsalted margarine, melted
¼ teaspoon vegetable oil

Combine flour and salt. Gradually add eggs, milk, and margarine, beating until smooth. Refrigerate batter at least 2 hours. (This allows flour particles to swell and soften so that crêpes are light in texture.)

Brush the bottom of an 8-inch nonstick crêpe pan or skillet with oil; place pan over medium heat just until oil is hot, not smoking. Pour 3 tablespoons batter into hot pan; quickly tilt pan in all directions so that batter covers pan in a thin film. Cook crêpe 1 minute. Lift edge of crêpe to test for doneness. Crêpe is ready for flipping when it can be shaken loose from the pan. Flip crêpe, and cook 30 seconds on other side. (This side is rarely more than spotty brown and is the side on which the filling is placed.) Repeat procedure with remaining batter.

Place crêpes on a towel to cool. Stack crêpes between layers of waxed paper. Yield: 16 crêpes (85 calories each).

Spinach Mornay Sauce:

1½ cups skim milk
1 cup chopped fresh spinach leaves
¼ cup grated Parmesan cheese
1 tablespoon cornstarch
2 teaspoons lemon juice
¼ teaspoon dry mustard
⅛ teaspoon ground red pepper
⅛ teaspoon ground nutmeg

Combine all ingredients in container of an electric blender; process until smooth.

Transfer spinach mixture to a small saucepan. Cook, stirring constantly, over medium heat until mixture is thickened and bubbly. Yield: 1½ cups (11 calories per tablespoon).

PRO 21.6 / FAT 8.9 / CARB 30.6 / FIB 1.4 / CHOL 165 / SOD 437 / POT 502

BABY CARROTS

2 pounds baby carrots, scraped
½ teaspoon sugar
Fresh cilantro leaves

Combine carrots and sugar in a small Dutch oven; add water to cover. Bring to a boil; cover and simmer 10 minutes or until carrots are crisp-tender. Transfer carrots to a warm serving platter; garnish with cilantro. Yield: 8 servings (50 calories per serving).

PRO 1.2 / FAT 0.2 / CARB 11.8 / FIB 1.7 / CHOL 0 / SOD 40 / POT 366

LEEK-MUSHROOM SALAD

8 medium leeks, trimmed
2 heads Bibb lettuce, washed and separated
4 medium tomatoes, sliced
8 mushrooms, thinly sliced
Salad Dressing (recipe follows)
2 tablespoons chopped fresh parsley

Place leeks in a large saucepan; add water to cover. Bring to a boil. Cover, reduce heat, and simmer 5 minutes or until tender. Drain; cover and chill. Cut leeks in half lengthwise. Line chilled salad plates with lettuce; top with leeks, tomatoes, and mushrooms. Spoon 1½ table-spoons salad dressing over each salad; garnish with parsley. Yield: 8 servings (155 calories per serving).

Salad Dressing:

¼ cup white wine vinegar
¼ cup olive oil
1 tablespoon Dijon mustard
1 tablespoon water
½ teaspoon sugar
⅛ teaspoon pepper
1 shallot, chopped

Combine all ingredients in container of an electric blender; process until smooth. Cover and chill thoroughly. Yield: ¾ cup.

PRO 3.0 / FAT 7.5 / CARB 21.1 / FIB 2.3 / CHOL 0 / SOD 88 / POT 464

STRAWBERRY-ORANGE SPONGECAKE

2 tablespoons unsalted margarine
2 egg yolks
¼ cup sugar
1½ teaspoons grated orange rind
1 teaspoon vanilla extract
4 egg whites
½ teaspoon cream of tartar
¼ cup sugar
⅔ cup unbleached or all-purpose
   flour
⅛ teaspoon salt
Vegetable cooking spray
1 pint fresh strawberries
2 tablespoons powdered sugar, divided

Melt margarine in a small saucepan over low heat; set aside to cool.

Combine egg yolks and ¼ cup sugar in a large bowl; beat at medium speed of an electric mixer until mixture is thickened. Add orange rind and vanilla; beat until well blended.

Beat 4 egg whites (at room temperature) and cream of tartar in a medium bowl until foamy. Gradually add ¼ cup sugar, 1 tablespoon at a time, and beat until stiff peaks form. Gently fold beaten egg whites into yolk mixture.

Sift flour and salt together twice. Gently fold flour mixture and cooled margarine into egg mixture. Spoon batter into a 9-inch round cake-pan coated with cooking spray. Bake at 350° for 20 minutes or until a wooden pick inserted near center comes out clean. Cool in pan 10 minutes. Remove to a wire rack, and cool completely. Split cake in half horizontally. Slice strawberries, reserving 1 strawberry to use as a garnish. Arrange sliced strawberries over top of cut side of cake; sift 1 tablespoon powdered sugar over top. Cover with remaining half of cake. Sift remaining powdered sugar over top, and garnish with reserved strawberry. Yield: 8 servings (150 calories per serving).

PRO 3.6 / FAT 4.4 / CARB 24.4 / FIB 0.5 / CHOL 68 / SOD 80 / POT 94

Michel Guérard, famed chef of the luxurious restaurant Eugénie-les-Bains in France, coined the phrase "cuisine minceur" and established himself, ten years ago, as the father of healthy, low-fat, high-pleasure cooking. Chef Guérard discovered that his profession had made his body rotund and his apron strings too short for the traditional double wrap.

Thus, he set about the task of formulating new recipes and new techniques, creating the "cuisine of slimness." From then on, eating light but delicious has been fashionable in France and America.

Chef Guérard did not design a regimen of rabbit food, but rather recipes that are similar to those in this menu — Dinner with a French Accent. Remarkably, this meal contains only 648 calories. This type of "lean" cooking tries to deceive the taste buds by choosing nutrient-smart foods and seasoning them with wine, herbs, and other fresh ingredients.

Festive Dinner for Eight

Veal is a classic dinner party entrée and a wonderful meat to experiment with.

Seeking something different for a formal dinner party, we've come up with paupiettes, rolled veal scallops with a stuffing of mushrooms, breadcrumbs, parsley, Parmesan, and lemon rind — all enhanced with a lemon-parsley sauce.

Because the entrée has so

Veal Paupiettes
Poached Asparagus
Tomatoes Provençal
Bowknot Rolls
Poached Pears in
Orange Sauce

Serves 8
Total calories per serving: 651

many flavors, we kept the rest of the menu quite simple: poached asparagus, baked tomatoes with an herbed breadcrumb topping, and bowknot rolls (1 roll per serving) that can be made ahead and reheated.

Even the dessert gives you a chance to show off. Poached pears in orange sauce can be a festive dessert when the pears are cored leaving the stem end intact. Lemon rind and mint leaves add the finishing touch.

VEAL PAUPIETTES

Vegetable cooking spray
½ cup minced shallots
½ cup minced fresh mushrooms
½ cup minced fresh parsley, divided
½ cup fine, dry breadcrumbs
¼ cup grated Parmesan cheese
1 teaspoon grated lemon rind
⅛ teaspoon freshly ground black pepper
8 (4-ounce) veal cutlets
1 tablespoon unsalted margarine, divided
½ cup minced onion
½ cup minced celery
½ cup minced carrot
1¼ cups water
½ cup dry white wine
1 teaspoon chicken-flavored bouillon granules
¼ teaspoon dried whole thyme
¼ teaspoon dried whole rosemary
¼ teaspoon dried whole tarragon
1 bay leaf
1 egg yolk, lightly beaten
¼ cup evaporated skim milk
1 teaspoon cornstarch
⅛ teaspoon freshly ground black pepper
2 teaspoons lemon juice
Green onion strips

Coat a medium skillet with cooking spray; place over medium heat until hot. Add shallots, and sauté 1 minute. Add mushrooms, and cook 3 minutes, stirring frequently. Remove from heat, and stir in ¼ cup parsley, breadcrumbs, cheese, lemon rind, and ⅛ teaspoon pepper. Cool 10 minutes.

Place veal cutlets between 2 sheets of waxed paper, and flatten to ⅛-inch thickness, using a meat mallet or rolling pin; place 2 tablespoons stuffing mixture on each cutlet. Fold cutlet over stuffing mixture to form a roll, and tie securely with string. Brown veal rolls in 1½ teaspoons margarine in a large skillet over medium heat, adding remaining margarine as necessary. Transfer veal to a warm serving platter; cover.

Add onion, celery, and carrot to skillet; sauté 5 minutes or until tender. Add water, wine, bouillon granules, and herbs; cook over medium heat, stirring occasionally, 8 minutes or until volume is reduced by half. Add veal rolls; cover and simmer 10 to 15 minutes or until veal is tender. Transfer veal rolls to a warm serving platter, reserving cooking liquid. Cover.

Strain cooking liquid, discarding vegetables and bay leaf; place in a saucepan. Combine egg yolk and milk; gradually add to cooking liquid, stirring constantly. Cook over low heat, stirring constantly, until mixture is reduced to 1 cup. Add remaining ¼ cup parsley, cornstarch, ⅛ teaspoon pepper, and lemon juice. Cook, stirring constantly, until sauce thickens.

Remove string from veal rolls; garnish each roll with green onion strips. Serve with sauce. Yield: 8 servings (350 calories per serving).

PRO 33.5 / FAT 18.5 / CARB 10.8 / FIB 0.5 / CHOL 151 / SOD 254 / POT 757

Poached Pears in Orange Sauce look particularly dramatic in a formal setting.

POACHED ASPARAGUS

2 pounds fresh asparagus
¼ teaspoon salt
Pimiento strips (optional)

Snap off tough ends of asparagus. Remove scales with a knife or vegetable peeler, if desired. Cook asparagus with salt in a small amount of boiling water 6 to 8 minutes. Drain well, and place on a serving platter; garnish with pimiento, if desired. Yield: 8 servings (25 calories per serving).

PRO 3.5 / FAT 0.2 / CARB 4.2 / FIB 1.1 / CHOL 0 / SOD 76 / POT 342

TOMATOES PROVENÇAL

4 medium tomatoes
1 clove garlic, minced
¼ teaspoon salt
¼ teaspoon pepper
¼ teaspoon dried whole basil
¼ teaspoon dried whole thyme
1 tablespoon olive oil
¼ cup minced fresh parsley

Remove stem from tomatoes; cut in half crosswise. Place tomatoes, cut side up, in a 13- x 9- x 2-inch baking pan; sprinkle with garlic, salt, pepper, basil, and thyme. Drizzle oil evenly over each tomato half.

Bake at 350° for 30 minutes; sprinkle with parsley, and serve immediately. Yield: 8 servings (30 calories per serving).

PRO 0.7 / FAT 1.9 / CARB 3.4 / FIB 0.6 / CHOL 0 / SOD 80 / POT 161

BOWKNOT ROLLS

1 package dry yeast
1 tablespoon plus 1 teaspoon sugar, divided
½ cup warm water (105° to 115°)
2 cups warm skim milk (105° to 115°)
2 tablespoons unsalted margarine, melted
1 teaspoon salt
6½ to 7 cups unbleached or all-purpose flour, divided
Vegetable cooking spray
1 egg white
1 teaspoon water

Dissolve yeast and 2 teaspoons sugar in warm water in a large bowl. Let stand 5 minutes or until bubbly. Add remaining 2 teaspoons sugar, warm milk, margarine, salt, and 2 cups flour, mixing well. Cover and let rise in a warm place (85°), free from drafts, 1 hour to 1½ hours or until doubled in bulk.

Stir enough remaining flour into batter to make a stiff dough. Turn out onto a lightly floured surface; knead 8 to 10 minutes or until smooth and elastic. Divide dough into 24 equal portions; roll each portion into a 10-inch rope. Tie ropes loosely into knots, and place on baking sheets coated with cooking spray. Cover and let rise in a warm place (85°), free from drafts, 15 to 20 minutes or until doubled in bulk.

Combine egg white and 1 teaspoon water, stirring well. Brush rolls with egg white mixture, and bake at 425° for 12 minutes or until golden brown. Yield: 24 rolls (128 calories each).

Note: Extra rolls may be frozen for later use.

PRO 4.2 / FAT 1.2 / CARB 25.2 / FIB 0.0 / CHOL 0 / SOD 112 / POT 80

POACHED PEARS IN ORANGE SAUCE

8 pears
1¼ cups orange juice
½ teaspoon grated lemon rind
2 tablespoons lemon juice
½ teaspoon ground cinnamon
3 whole cloves
1½ teaspoons cornstarch
¼ cup cold water
Lemon rind strips
Mint leaves

Peel and core pears; leave stem end intact.

Combine next 5 ingredients in a Dutch oven; bring to a boil. Place pears, stem end up, in Dutch oven; spoon juices over pears. Reduce heat; cover and simmer 10 to 15 minutes or until pears are tender. Remove pears with a slotted spoon; set aside.

Combine cornstarch and water; stir well. Pour cornstarch mixture into pan juices; cook over low heat, stirring constantly, until thickened. Pour orange sauce over pears; garnish each with a strip of lemon rind and mint leaves. Yield: 8 servings (118 calories per serving).

PRO 0.9 / FAT 0.7 / CARB 30.1 / FIB 4.1 / CHOL 0 / SOD 1 / POT 285

Autumn Sonata

This menu is our tribute to vermillion and bronze trees, the smell of burning leaves, and rough and tumble touch football games in the backyard.

Start with a hot and savory tomato soup that needs little tending (getting the fire going successfully may require more of your attention).

Next, enjoy a juicy pork loin roast paired with two autumn favorites, apples and apple cider. On the side, steamed cabbage

Herbed Tomato Soup
Braised Pork Loin
Cider-Glazed Apples
Steamed Cabbage
Rice Spoonbread
Lime Mousse
Serves 6
Total calories per serving: 536

and a delicate rice and cornmeal spoonbread. Again, neither recipe will require much time in the kitchen.

The lime mousse for dessert is the least demanding of all. It can be made ahead and stored in its mold in the refrigerator. Unmold just before serving.

This menu is easy indeed — about as easy as falling in love with fall.

HERBED TOMATO SOUP

1 (28-ounce) can whole tomatoes, undrained
1¼ cups chopped onion
1¼ cups sliced celery
1 clove garlic, minced
3 cups water
2 teaspoons beef-flavored bouillon granules
1 teaspoon dried whole basil
½ teaspoon dried whole thyme
1 bay leaf
6 celery leaves

Combine tomatoes, onion, sliced celery, garlic, water, bouillon granules, basil, thyme, and bay leaf in a large Dutch oven, stirring well. Bring mixture to a boil. Cover; reduce heat, and simmer 1 hour, stirring occasionally. Remove and discard bay leaf.

Place 1 to 2 cups hot tomato mixture in container of an electric blender; process until smooth. Transfer pureed mixture to a large saucepan. Repeat procedure with remaining tomato mixture. Cook over medium heat until thoroughly heated.

Ladle soup into individual serving bowls. Garnish with celery leaves. Yield: 6 cups (45 calories per 1-cup serving).

PRO 1.8 / FAT 0.3 / CARB 9.9 / FIB 0.9 / CHOL 0 / SOD 661 / POT 431

BRAISED PORK LOIN

1 clove garlic, minced
⅛ teaspoon salt
⅛ teaspoon pepper
1 (1½-pound) boneless pork loin roast, rolled and tied
½ teaspoon dried sage
½ teaspoon dried whole rosemary
1 medium onion, quartered
1 stalk celery, sliced
1 medium Granny Smith apple, chopped
1 cup water
½ cup unsweetened apple cider
Fresh parsley sprigs

Combine first 3 ingredients. Untie roast; trim excess fat. Sprinkle inside with garlic mixture; retie roast with string at 2- to 3-inch intervals. Sprinkle with sage and rosemary. Place in a 12- x 8- x 2-inch baking dish; add onion and celery. Insert meat thermometer, if desired. Bake, uncovered, at 425° for 30 minutes.

Remove roast from oven; add apple, water, and cider. Reduce heat to 350°; cover and bake an additional 50 minutes or until meat thermometer registers 170°.

Transfer roast to a warm platter; discard fruit, vegetables, and broth. Garnish with parsley. Yield: 6 servings (134 calories per serving).

PRO 17.6 / FAT 6.4 / CARB 0.3 / FIB 0.0 / CHOL 51 / SOD 103 / POT 304

Braised Pork Loin and Cider-Glazed Apples make a fitting tribute to the fall season.

CIDER-GLAZED APPLES

Vegetable cooking spray
2 medium Granny Smith apples, cored and cut into
⅟4-inch slices
½ cup unsweetened apple cider
1 tablespoon brown sugar
1 teaspoon cornstarch

Coat a large skillet with cooking spray; place over medium heat until hot. Add apples, and sauté one minute. Combine remaining ingredients, stirring well. Add to apples. Cook over medium heat 3 minutes or until apples are tender, stirring occasionally. Serve warm. Yield: 6 servings (43 calories per serving).

PRO 0.1 / FAT 0.2 / CARB 11.0 / FIB 0.9 / CHOL 0 / SOD 1 / POT 80

STEAMED CABBAGE

1 (1¾-pound) head cabbage, coarsely chopped
(about 7 cups)
½ cup dry white wine
¼ teaspoon salt
¼ teaspoon pepper

Place cabbage in a Dutch oven; add wine, salt, and pepper. Cover and cook over medium heat 12 minutes or until tender, stirring occasionally. Transfer cabbage to a serving bowl; serve warm. Yield: 6 servings (45 calories per serving).

PRO 2.1 / FAT 0.3 / CARB 10.3 / FIB 1.9 / CHOL 0 / SOD 130 / POT 450

RICE SPOONBREAD

1 cup boiling water
⅓ cup yellow cornmeal
2 eggs, separated
1 cup skim milk
⅓ cup all-purpose flour
1 tablespoon sugar
2 teaspoons baking powder
¼ teaspoon salt
1 cup cooked regular rice (cooked without
salt or fat)
1 tablespoon unsalted margarine, melted
Vegetable cooking spray

Pour water over cornmeal in a large bowl, stirring well; set aside to cool.
Combine egg yolks and milk, beating well.
Combine flour, sugar, baking powder, and salt into a small bowl. Add to cornmeal mixture alternately with milk mixture, stirring well after each addition.
Beat egg whites (at room temperature) until stiff peaks form. Fold egg whites, rice, and margarine into cornmeal mixture. Spoon batter into a 1½-quart baking dish coated with cooking spray. Bake at 350° for 1 hour or until set. Yield: 6 servings (158 calories per serving).

PRO 5.6 / FAT 4.0 / CARB 24.3 / FIB 1.2 / CHOL 92 / SOD 243 / POT 117

LIME MOUSSE

1 envelope unflavored gelatin
3 tablespoons water
¼ cup plus 2 tablespoons sugar
¼ cup water
2 egg yolks
⅓ cup lime juice
1 teaspoon vanilla extract
1 (8-ounce) carton plain low-fat yogurt
3 egg whites
Vegetable cooking spray
Lime rind strips
Lime slices

Soften gelatin in 3 tablespoons water in a small bowl; set aside. Combine sugar and ¼ cup water in a small saucepan; bring to a boil, stirring constantly. Boil 2 to 3 minutes.
Beat egg yolks until thick and lemon colored. While beating, slowly add syrup mixture in a small, steady stream, beating until cool.
Place bowl of softened gelatin in a large bowl of hot water; stir until gelatin dissolves. Add dissolved gelatin to yolk mixture, beating well; stir in lime juice and vanilla. Chill until consistency of unbeaten egg white. Fold in yogurt.
Beat egg whites (at room temperature) until stiff peaks form. Fold into lime mixture; spoon into a 6-cup non-metallic mold coated with cooking spray. Chill until set. Unmold onto a serving plate. Garnish with lime. Yield: 6 servings (111 calories per serving).

PRO 5.7 / FAT 2.5 / CARB 16.8 / FIB 0.0 / CHOL 93 / SOD 56 / POT 131

Holiday Buffet

This year try a healthier holiday menu that doesn't skimp on taste or pleasure. Holidays are meant to be savored, and our spread will let you do just that.

The rye bread dressing for the turkey breast has a high-fiber bonus. Sweetened with a bit of apple juice, it is spiced up with caraway seeds and lemon rind.

Eating light is not a reason to exclude all the traditional foods in your holiday meal. Just roast the sweet potatoes rather than smothering them in marshmallows and pineapple. Sweet potatoes are filled with flavor that all

**Rye Bread Dressing
Baked Turkey Breast
Orange Sweet Potatoes
Herbed Brussels Sprouts
Cranberry-Orange Relish
Pumpkin Mousse
or
*Light Chocolate Roulage**

Serves 8
Total calories per serving: 689
or *778

too often gets covered up.

Cranberry-Orange Relish is a holiday must. Ours keeps the

sugar and salt to a minimum. All the brussels sprouts need is a creamy herb sauce to lend some elegance.

We haven't forgotten dessert — which means pumpkin, of course. Try our cold pumpkin mousse or just in case you want to offer a choice, we've included a second dessert: a light chocolate roulage (the asterisks indicate the alternate calorie count for the menu). The calorie count for the whole festive meal is remarkably low

Sensible holiday eating can also be pleasurable.

RYE BREAD DRESSING

¾ cup unsweetened apple cider
1 cup raisins
1½ cups minced onion
1½ cups chopped celery
2 tablespoons unsalted margarine
1 medium Red Delicious apple, cored and diced
½ teaspoon salt
½ teaspoon caraway seeds
½ teaspoon grated lemon rind
½ teaspoon ground cinnamon
¼ teaspoon ground allspice
¼ teaspoon freshly ground black pepper
7 slices rye bread, cubed and toasted

Combine cider and raisins in a small saucepan; bring to a boil. Remove from heat; cover and let stand 15 minutes.

Sauté onion and celery in margarine in a skillet until tender. Add apple; cover and cook 5 minutes.

Combine raisin mixture, sautéed mixture, salt, caraway seeds, lemon rind, cinnamon, allspice, pepper, and bread cubes in a large bowl, mixing well. Spoon mixture into a 13- x 9- x 2-inch baking dish. Cover and bake at 350° for 1 hour.

Uncover and bake an additional 20 minutes. Serve warm. Yield: 8 servings (168 calories per serving).

PRO 3.1 / FAT 3.3 / CARB 34.3 / FIB 2.8 / CHOL 0 / SOD 297 / POT 335

BAKED TURKEY BREAST

1 (6½-pound) turkey breast, skinned

Insert meat thermometer in turkey breast, if desired. Place in a browning bag prepared according to package directions. Place bag in bottom of a shallow roasting pan. Bake at 350° for 1 hour. Cut a slit in top of bag; bake 1 hour or until a meat thermometer registers 170°. Baste with pan drippings. Transfer to a platter. Let stand 15 minutes; carve into thin slices. Yield: 8 servings (138 calories per serving).

PRO 26.4 / FAT 2.8 / CARB 0.0 / FIB 0.0 / CHOL 61 / SOD 56 / POT 269

ORANGE SWEET POTATOES

3 medium-size sweet potatoes (about 2 pounds)
⅔ cup unsweetened orange juice
1 tablespoon unsalted margarine, melted
¼ teaspoon ground cardamom

Peel sweet potatoes, and cut crosswise into ½-inch-thick slices. Arrange potato slices in a single layer in a 13- x 9- x 2-inch baking dish. Combine orange juice, margarine, and cardamom in a small bowl, stirring well. Pour over sweet potato slices. Bake, uncovered, at 350° for 25 minutes or until tender, turning twice.

Broil 4 inches from heat 5 minutes or until top of potatoes are lightly browned. Yield: 8 servings (141 calories per serving).

PRO 2.0 / FAT 1.8 / CARB 29.8 / FIB 2.4 / CHOL 0 / SOD 15 / POT 271

HERBED BRUSSELS SPROUTS

2 pounds brussels sprouts
1 tablespoon plus 1½ teaspoons cornstarch
¼ cup skim milk
1 teaspoon unsalted margarine
Vegetable cooking spray
1 shallot, minced
1¾ cups skim milk
1 teaspoon chicken-flavored bouillon granules
½ teaspoon dried whole marjoram
⅛ teaspoon pepper
1 bay leaf
2 tablespoons minced fresh parsley

Cut a small cross in base of each brussels sprout; arrange in a steaming rack. Place rack in a saucepan over boiling water; cover and steam 10 minutes or until tender. Remove; set aside.

Dissolve cornstarch in ¼ cup milk; set aside.

Melt margarine in a medium saucepan coated with cooking spray over medium heat. Add shallot, and sauté until tender. Add 1¾ cups milk, bouillon granules, marjoram, pepper, and bay leaf; simmer 20 minutes, stirring constantly. Stir in cornstarch mixture; cook over low heat, stirring constantly, 2 minutes or until thickened. Remove bay leaf. Stir in brussels sprouts. Transfer to a serving bowl; garnish with parsley. Yield: 8 servings (65 calories per serving).

PRO 5.7 / FAT 0.8 / CARB 10.8 / FIB 2.6 / CHOL 1 / SOD 107 / POT 318

CRANBERRY-ORANGE RELISH

2 cups fresh cranberries, finely chopped
2 tablespoons grated orange rind
1 medium orange, peeled, sectioned, seeded, and chopped
1 medium-size green apple, cored and finely chopped
⅓ cup sugar
¼ teaspoon ground ginger
¼ teaspoon ground nutmeg

Combine all ingredients in a medium bowl; stir well. Cover and chill overnight. Yield: 8 servings (65 calories per ¼-cup serving).

PRO 0.4 / FAT 0.2 / CARB 17.1 / FIB 1.1 / CHOL 0 / SOD 1 / POT 81

PUMPKIN MOUSSE

1 (16-ounce) can pumpkin
1 (12-ounce) can evaporated skim milk
2 egg yolks, beaten
⅓ cup sugar
½ teaspoon ground cinnamon
¼ teaspoon ground ginger
⅛ teaspoon ground nutmeg
1 envelope unflavored gelatin
¼ cup cold water
3 egg whites
¼ teaspoon cream of tartar
1 teaspoon vanilla extract

Combine pumpkin, milk, egg yolks, and sugar in a large saucepan; beat well. Stir in cinnamon, ginger, and nutmeg. Cook over medium heat, stirring occasionally, until thoroughly heated. Remove from heat; set aside.

Combine gelatin and cold water in a small saucepan; let stand 1 minute. Cook over low heat 5 minutes or until gelatin completely dissolves. Stir into pumpkin mixture. Cool.

Combine egg whites (at room temperature) and cream of tartar in a medium bowl; beat until soft peaks form. Add vanilla; beat until stiff peaks form. Fold into pumpkin mixture. Spoon into a 1½-quart bowl, and chill thoroughly. Spoon into dessert dishes to serve. Yield: 8 servings (112 calories per serving).

PRO 6.6 / FAT 1.7 / CARB 18.2 / FIB 1.0 / CHOL 70 / SOD 80 / POT 284

LIGHT CHOCOLATE ROULAGE

Vegetable cooking spray
2 eggs
1 egg yolk
⅓ cup sugar
1 teaspoon vanilla extract
½ teaspoon almond extract
2 egg whites
½ cup Dutch process or unsweetened cocoa
2 tablespoons unbleached or all-purpose
  flour
1½ teaspoons Dutch process or unsweetened
  cocoa
Orange-Ricotta Filling
1 tablespoon sifted powdered sugar
Orange rind twists

Line a 15- x 10- x 1-inch jellyroll pan with waxed paper; coat waxed paper and sides of pan with cooking spray. Set pan aside.

Combine 2 eggs and 1 egg yolk in a medium bowl; beat at high speed of electric mixer until well blended. Gradually add ⅓ cup sugar, beat-

ing 4 minutes or until mixture is thick and lemon colored. Add flavorings; beat well.

Beat egg whites (at room temperature) in a small bowl until soft peaks form. Gradually add 2 tablespoons sugar, and beat until stiff peaks form. Fold into egg mixture.

Sift together ½ cup cocoa and flour; gently fold cocoa mixture into batter. Spread batter evenly in prepared pan. Bake at 375° for 10 minutes.

Sift 1½ teaspoons cocoa in a 15- x 10-inch rectangle on a linen towel. When cake is done, immediately loosen from sides of pan, and turn out onto cocoa. Peel off waxed paper. Starting at narrow end, roll up warm cake and towel together; let cake cool completely on a wire rack, seam side down.

Unroll cake; remove towel. Spread with Orange-Ricotta Filling; reroll cake. Chill until serving time.

Sift powdered sugar over cake in desired pattern. Garnish with orange twists. Cut into 1¼-inch slices to serve. Yield: 8 servings (201 calories per serving).

Orange-Ricotta Filling:

1½ cups part-skim ricotta cheese
⅓ cup sifted powdered sugar
1 tablespoon ground almonds, toasted
1 tablespoon Cointreau or other orange-flavored
  liqueur
½ teaspoon almond extract
¼ teaspoon vanilla extract

Combine all ingredients in a food processor bowl with metal blade; process until smooth. Yield: 1¾ cups.

PRO 9.3 / FAT 7.7 / CARB 24.9 / FIB 0.3 / CHOL 117 / SOD 130 / POT 135

A classic dessert for a traditional celebration: Light Chocolate Roulage relies on cocoa, a low-fat alternative to chocolate squares, for its rich flavor.

Light Cocktail Party

Americano*
or
French Wench
or
Vermouth Cassis
or
White Wine Spritzer
Skewered Marinated Pork
Deviled Shrimp
Seafood Cocktail Sauce
Sesame-Pepper Vinaigrette
Lemon-Cheese Dip with
Vegetables
Fruit Kabobs
Cornmeal-Cheddar Wafers
Cracker Bread

Serves 12
Total calories per serving: *614

Drinks make a cocktail party bubbly, especially if you serve club soda on ice, spiked with a shot of colorful liqueur — irresistable looking in a highball glass. (The asterisk represents the drink included in the calorie count.)

Enjoy a sampling of sesame-pepper vinaigrette or an asparagus spear that has been plunged into the lemon and cottage cheese dip. Or maybe your sweet tooth is active enough for naturally sweet pineapple, kiwi, and strawberries — chilled and threaded on a skewer.

Lots of beneficial calcium is hidden in the cornmeal-cheddar wafers as well as in the dip.

Most of this party fare can be made ahead. The skewered pork can be marinated overnight and popped under the broiler just before serving.

AMERICANO

2 tablespoons sweet red vermouth
2 teaspoons Campari
3 ice cubes
1 strip orange rind
⅔ cup club soda, chilled

Combine vermouth, Campari, and ice cubes in an 8-ounce glass. Twist orange rind over glass, and rub cut edge around inside of rim. Add orange rind and club soda to glass; stir. Yield: 1 serving (53 calories per serving).

PRO 0.0 / FAT 0.0 / CARB 5.4 / FIB 0.0 / CHOL 0 / SOD 9 / POT 20

FRENCH WENCH

1 tablespoon Dubonnet
½ cup ginger ale, chilled

Combine ingredients in a wine glass; stir gently. Yield: 1 serving (61 calories per serving)

PRO 0.0 / FAT 0.0 / CARB 12.2 / FIB 0.0 / CHOL 0 / SOD 8 / POT 11

VERMOUTH CASSIS

2 tablespoons dry white vermouth
¾ teaspoon crème de cassis
1 ice cube
½ cup club soda, chilled
1 strip lemon rind

Combine vermouth, crème de cassis, and ice in a wine glass; add club soda, stirring well. Garnish with lemon rind. Yield: 1 serving (40 calories per serving).

PRO 0.0 / FAT 0.0 / CARB 1.9 / FIB 0.0 / CHOL 0 / SOD 5 / POT 15

WHITE WINE SPRITZER

3 ice cubes
¼ cup dry white wine
¼ cup club soda, chilled
1 strip lime rind

Combine first 3 ingredients in a large wine glass; stir well. Garnish with lime rind Yield: 1 serving (39 calories per serving).

PRO 0.1 / FAT 0.0 / CARB 0.5 / FIB 0.0 / CHOL 0 / SOD 2 / POT 38

DEVILED SHRIMP

4½ cups water
½ cup chopped onion
¼ cup chopped celery
6 whole allspice
6 whole peppercorns
1 bay leaf
2 tablespoons lemon juice
1 tablespoon white wine vinegar
½ teaspoon dried whole thyme
½ teaspoon crushed red pepper
¼ teaspoon salt
1½ pounds unpeeled large fresh shrimp

Combine all ingredients, except shrimp, in a medium stockpot; bring to a boil. Add shrimp, and cook 3 minutes. (Do not boil.) Drain; rinse in cold water.
Peel and devein shrimp. Serve with Seafood Cocktail Sauce. Yield: 12 appetizer servings. Serving size: 3 shrimp (43 calories per serving).

PRO 7.8 / FAT 0.4 / CARB 1.6 / FIB 0.1 / CHOL 64 / SOD 111 / POT 117

SEAFOOD COCKTAIL SAUCE

1 cup reduced-calorie catsup
1 tablespoon lemon juice
2½ teaspoons prepared horseradish
1 teaspoon red wine vinegar
⅛ teaspoon pepper

Combine all ingredients in a bowl, mixing well; chill 30 minutes. Serve with fish or shellfish. Yield: 1 cup (6 calories per tablespoon).

PRO 0.2 / FAT 0 / CARB 1.1 / FIB 0.0 / CHOL 0 / SOD 3 / POT 14

Cocktails can be deceptively high in calories, and often they may push you over your daily caloric limit. The trend in America has been to drink lighter and less. One way to get half the calories and half the alcohol from a glass of wine is by diluting it with club soda. Most of the recipes in this Cocktail Party menu make use of club soda or the carbonated water of choice for a lighter beverage.

Another interesting tidbit to remember is that wine increases the iron absorption of a meal by 300 percent.

SKEWERED MARINATED PORK

1 pound lean boneless pork
½ cup minced onion
1 clove garlic, minced
2 teaspoons minced gingerroot
1 teaspoon sugar
½ teaspoon crushed red pepper
¼ teaspoon pepper
2 tablespoons lemon juice
1 tablespoon water
1 tablespoon reduced-sodium soy
  sauce
Vegetable cooking spray

Trim excess fat from pork; cut into 1-inch cubes, and set aside.

Combine next 9 ingredients in a small bowl, mixing well; add pork, tossing to mix well. Cover and marinate in refrigerator overnight, stirring occasionally.

Thread pork cubes on 12 small wooden skewers, using 2 pork cubes per skewer. Cook over medium heat in a large griddle or skillet coated with cooking spray 20 minutes or until pork is done, turning frequently. Yield: 12 appetizer servings. Serving size: 1 skewer (72 calories per serving).

PRO 9.3 / FAT 3.0 / CARB 1.4 / FIB 0.1 / CHOL 28 / SOD 71 / POT 137

SESAME-PEPPER VINAIGRETTE

2 medium-size green peppers, seeded and cut into thin strips
2 medium-size sweet red peppers, seeded and cut into thin strips
1 small yellow pepper, seeded and cut into thin strips
1 tablespoon sesame seeds, toasted
1 tablespoon plus 1 teaspoon reduced-sodium soy sauce
2 teaspoons white wine vinegar
2 teaspoons sesame oil

Combine all ingredients in a medium bowl, tossing to mix well. Cover and refrigerate 2 hours. Yield: 12 appetizer servings. Serving size: 5 strips (29 calories per serving).

PRO 0.8 / FAT 1.4 / CARB 3.9 / FIB 0.8 / CHOL 0 / SOD 67 / POT 133

Fruit Kabobs accent the natural beauty of fruit and provide a naturally sweet dessert.

LEMON-CHEESE DIP WITH VEGETABLES

1½ cups low-fat cottage cheese
2 teaspoons grated lemon rind
3 tablespoons lemon juice
1 tablespoon chopped green onion
1 teaspoon Dijon mustard
⅛ teaspoon red pepper
2 pounds fresh asparagus
½ pound fresh snow peas
2 medium heads Belgian endive

Combine first 6 ingredients in container of an electric blender or food processor; process until smooth. Cover and chill thoroughly.

Snap off tough ends of asparagus. Remove scales with a knife or vegetable peeler. Trim ends from snow peas. Add asparagus and snow peas to a large saucepan of boiling water, and cook 2 minutes or until crisp-tender. Drain and chill 30 minutes. Peel leaves from core of endive. Wash leaves, and pat dry with paper towels. Chill thoroughly.

Arrange asparagus, snow peas, and endive on a platter. Serve with reserved dip. Yield: 12 appetizer servings (65 calories per serving with 3 tablespoons dip per serving).

PRO 7.7 / FAT 0.9 / CARB 8.2 / FIB 1.8 / CHOL 2 / SOD 146 / POT 538

FRUIT KABOBS

8½ cups fresh strawberries
10 medium kiwis, peeled and cut into
    ¼-inch-thick slices
2 (15¼-ounce) cans unsweetened
    pineapple chunks, drained

Thread fruit alternately onto 48 (6-inch) wooden skewers. Cover, and chill thoroughly. Yield: 12 appetizer servings. Serving size: 4 skewers (101 calories per serving).

PRO 1.4 / FAT 0.8 / CARB 19.4 / FIB 3.4 / CHOL 0 / SOD 2 / POT 435

CORNMEAL-CHEDDAR WAFERS

¼ teaspoon dried whole oregano
⅛ teaspoon dried whole thyme
⅛ teaspoon dried parsley flakes
Dash of red pepper
⅓ cup stone-ground cornmeal
⅓ cup unbleached or all-purpose flour
⅛ teaspoon salt
2 tablespoons unsalted margarine, softened
1 cup (4 ounces) shredded sharp Cheddar cheese
2 tablespoons water

Crush oregano, thyme, parsley flakes, and red pepper with a mortar and pestle. Combine herbs, cornmeal, flour, and salt in a medium bowl. Cut in margarine with a pastry blender until mixture resembles coarse meal; cut in cheese until well blended. Sprinkle water evenly over flour mixture, stirring until dry ingredients are moistened. Shape dough into a roll, 1½ inches in diameter; wrap in waxed paper. Freeze at least 1 hour.

Remove waxed paper, and cut roll into ¼-inch-thick slices. Place slices 1 inch apart on ungreased baking sheets. Bake at 400° for 8 minutes or until lightly browned. Remove from baking sheets; cool on wire racks. Yield: 24 wafers. Serving size: 2 wafers (79 calories per serving).

PRO 3.0 / FAT 5.1 / CARB 5.2 / FIB 0.4 / CHOL 10 / SOD 83 / POT 19

CRACKER BREAD

5½ to 6 cups all-purpose flour, divided
1 package dry yeast
1 tablespoon sugar
1½ teaspoons salt
2 cups warm water (120° to 130°)
⅓ cup unsalted margarine, melted
Vegetable cooking spray
2 tablespoons poppy seeds

Combine 4 cups flour, yeast, sugar, and salt in a large bowl; stir well. Gradually add water to flour mixture, stirring well. Add margarine; beat at medium speed of an electric mixer until blended. Gradually stir in enough remaining flour to make a stiff dough.

Turn dough out on a floured surface, and knead 4 minutes or until dough is smooth and elastic. Place in a bowl coated with cooking spray, turning to grease top. Cover and let rise in a warm place (85°), free from drafts, 1½ hours or until doubled in bulk.

Punch dough down, and divide into 10 equal portions. Shape each portion into a ball on a lightly floured surface, and let dough rest 10 minutes.

Roll each ball into a 10-inch round. Place rounds on baking sheets coated with cooking spray. Brush lightly with cold water, and sprinkle with poppy seeds. Prick entire surface with a fork. (Do not allow to rise.) Bake at 350° for 25 minutes or until lightly browned and crisp. Remove from pans, and let cool on wire racks. Yield: ten 10-inch rounds. Serving size: ½ round (172 calories per serving).

PRO 4.3 / FAT 3.8 / CARB 29.7 / FIB 1.2 / CHOL 0 / SOD 177 / POT 50

Light Recipes

The key to the new healthy American cuisine is recipe modification. This may involve creating totally new dishes or adapting delicious old favorites by cutting empty calories and retaining the nutrients. In the ten recipe chapters that follow, you will find over 300 new light recipes created especially for *Cooking Light '86*. Included are many classic recipes that you will still be able to enjoy.

The various categories of foods in this section provide you with the kinds of recipes that will make you more successful in meeting the newly published *Dietary Guidelines* recommended for Americans by the United States Department of Agriculture. Your success with these recipes in preparing light meals will readily prepare you for success in adapting your own recipes to a more healthful cooking style.

Eat a variety of foods. Most foods have more than one nutrient, but no single food provides all the essential nutrients. That is achieved by eating a mix of foods supplied by the Basic Four.

The vegetarian meals in the "Meatless Main" chapter include variety in a single entrée and at the same time offer complete protein sources. You might find yourself serving meat less often when you find out how satisfying these dishes can be.

Maintain a desirable weight. The wide variety of beautiful fruits and vegetables now available at the market are tempting enough to help you comply with this guideline. The "Fruit and Vegetables" chapter compounds this temptation by offering creative ways to serve standbys like grapefruit and squash. You will be able to keep an eye on your weight and still satisfy your palate.

Energy-rich complex carbohydrates abound in these lusciously light recipes: Broccoli-Rice Quiche (page 134), Spice Cookies (page 221), and Double Raspberry Yogurt Parfait (page 206).

Avoid too much fat, saturated fat, and cholesterol. "Fish and Shellfish" is dedicated to a category of food that, in recent months, has taken on new significance in the world of health and nutrition. The polyunsaturated oils in fish are being linked to a decrease in the risk of heart disease, and shellfish are now associated with lower cholesterol values than those previously published.

Next to seafood, poultry is the best option for limiting saturated fat; just be sure to skin the bird and remove any excess fat before cooking. Check the "Poultry" chapter for some tempting combinations.

Eating more nutritiously does not necessarily mean that red meat has to become a memory. It does mean learning to choose smaller and leaner portions of meat that have been trimmed of excess fat. The recipes in the "Meats" chapter show how selecting lean cuts can reduce fat and cholesterol levels and at the same time let you enjoy a variety of beef, veal, pork, and lamb.

Eat foods with adequate starch and fiber. Nothing has had more of an impact on American eating habits in the '80s than the new emphasis on complex carbohydrates. They do more than just contribute fiber and nutrients to the diet — they are the body's preferred energy source.

Getting more complex carbohydrates (starchy foods) into your meals is really quite easy once you peruse the "Breads, Grains, and Pasta" chapter; it also contains delicious ways to get more fiber.

Avoid too much sugar. Desserts are the trickiest part of the meal when it comes to nutrition. Empty calories abound. Fruit dishes are a natural solution, and you will find them in "Desserts" prepared in a variety of ways: frozen, chilled, or grilled. Even the more indulgent desserts have a remarkably low calorie count.

Avoid too much sodium. Just the right salad dressing can turn an ordinary salad into something quite special, but these can be high in sodium, fat, and calories. The recipes in "Salads and Salad Dressings" have no salty additives like capers and olives. Reduced-calorie mayonnaise, yogurt, buttermilk, and low-fat cottage cheese are substituted for regular mayonnaise and sour cream to reduce fat and calories.

If you drink alcoholic beverages, do so in moderation — and don't drive. On the job and off, Americans are drinking less and enjoying it more. Adding bottled waters to alcoholic drinks is a popular alternative to "strong" drinks, and health spa mixtures, like Fruit Fling in "Appetizers and Beverages," are on the increase. You will also find in this section some great hors d'oeuvres, which are just as nutritious as the rest of the meal.

The *Dietary Guidelines* are intended to provide healthy Americans with sensible, uncomplicated guidance on the kinds of foods they should be eating. You can use the recipes in *Cooking Light '86* to help you establish a healthy pattern of eating that is compatible with these guidelines.

Make your first course festive and light: Chicken Drummette Appetizers (page 100) with a yogurt dip, Baked Potato Skins (page 105), Twisted Cheese Straws (page 105), and Spicy Tortilla Chips (page 105) with Tomato Salsa (page 102). Serve with fruity, fizzy Lime Sangría (page 107).

Appetizers & Beverages

AMBROSIA APPETIZER

4 medium oranges, peeled, sectioned, and
  seeded
1 medium grapefruit, peeled, sectioned, and
  seeded
1 medium-size Red Delicious apple, cubed
1 cup seedless red grapes
1 (8-ounce) can unsweetened pineapple
  tidbits, undrained
½ cup unsweetened orange juice
¼ cup dry sherry
2 teaspoons chopped fresh mint leaves
3 tablespoons plus 1 teaspoon grated
  fresh coconut

Combine oranges, grapefruit, apple, grapes,
and pineapple in a large bowl. Combine orange
juice, sherry, and mint; pour over fruit, and toss.
Chill. To serve, spoon into individual bowls, and
sprinkle with 1 teaspoon coconut. Yield: 10 appetizer servings. Serving size: ½ cup (84 calories
per serving).

PRO 1.1 / FAT 1.0 / CARB 18.1 / FIB 1.9 / CHOL 0 / SOD 2 / POT 253

PINK GRAPEFRUIT AND ORANGE
COMPOTE

3 medium navel oranges
2 medium-size pink grapefruit
1 tablespoon honey
Dash of ground cinnamon

Remove rind from ½ orange and ½ grapefruit
using a paring knife, being careful not to include membrane; cut rind into julienne strips.
Remove and discard remaining rind. Blanch julienne rind in a small saucepan of boiling water
3 to 4 minutes or until tender. Drain; set aside.
Peel and section fruit over a bowl, collecting
juice. Squeeze membranes to release as much
juice as possible.
Strain juice into a saucepan, reserving fruit in
bowl. Add reserved rind and honey; bring to a
boil. Reduce heat, and simmer 5 minutes. Stir in
cinnamon, and set aside to cool. Pour over fruit.
Spoon into individual bowls to serve. Yield: 6
servings (89 calories per serving).

PRO 1.9 / FAT 0.2 / CARB 22.5 / FIB 2.2 / CHOL 0 / SOD 1 / POT 313

PICKLED BABY CARROTS

1 cup white wine vinegar
1½ cups unsweetened apple cider
1 teaspoon mixed pickling spices
½ teaspoon dried whole dillweed
1 pound baby carrots, scraped (about 30 carrots)

Combine first 4 ingredients in a large saucepan; bring to a boil. Add carrots; cover and reduce heat. Simmer 10 to 12 minutes or until
crisp-tender. Remove from heat, and pour into a
plastic container; set container in a bowl of ice
water to cool quickly. Chill. Drain and arrange
on a serving platter. Yield: 6 to 7 servings. Serving size: 2 carrots (27 calories per serving).

PRO 0.3 / FAT 0.1 / CARB 6.1 / FIB 0.5 / CHOL 0 / SOD 13 / POT 134

An appetizer need not stimulate the
appetite so that you will want to eat
more. It can actually help you eat less.
Light appetizers and beverages start the digestive juices flowing and can help fill you up before the entrée is served. The key is to eat
slowly. The stomach starts signaling to the brain
that it is satisfied about 20 minutes after you
begin eating. So the more time you take to eat,
the less food you should need to make you feel
full. Enjoy those delicacies, but slow your pace.

CHEESE-STUFFED ENDIVE

2 small heads Belgian endive (about ¼ pound)
½ (8-ounce) package Neufchâtel cheese, softened
2 teaspoons prepared horseradish
Paprika

Peel leaves from core of endive. Wash leaves,
and pat dry with paper towels. Place in a plastic
food storage bag, and refrigerate.
Combine Neufchâtel cheese and horseradish;
stir until smooth. Chill at least 1 hour.
Spoon 1 teaspoon cheese mixture onto inside
of each endive leaf. Sprinkle with paprika. Cover
and refrigerate until ready to serve. Yield: 2
dozen appetizers. Serving size: 1 leaf (13 calories each).

PRO 0.5 / FAT 1.1 / CARB 0.3 / FIB 0.0 / CHOL 4 / SOD 20 / POT 21

CARROT-STUFFED ENDIVE

4 small heads Belgian endive (about ½ pound)
1 cup radishes, grated
2 cups grated carrot
⅓ cup thinly sliced green onion
¼ cup plain low-fat yogurt
1 teaspoon dried whole dillweed
1 tablespoon lemon juice
⅛ teaspoon pepper
⅛ teaspoon ground cinnamon

Peel leaves from core of endive. Wash leaves, and pat dry with paper towels. Place in a food storage bag, and refrigerate.

Squeeze grated radishes between paper towels to remove as much moisture as possible. Combine radishes and remaining ingredients in a bowl. Cover and chill at least 30 minutes. Spoon 1 tablespoon vegetable mixture onto inside of each endive leaf, and arrange on a serving platter. Yield: 4 dozen appetizers. Serving size: 1 leaf (4 calories each).

PRO 0.2 / FAT 0.1 / CARB 0.9 / FIB 0.2 / CHOL 0 / SOD 4 / POT 41

TARRAGON VEGETABLE APPETIZER

2 small carrots, scraped and diagonally sliced
1 (6-ounce) package frozen snow peas, thawed and drained
6 cherry tomatoes
1 medium cucumber, sliced
⅓ cup Italian reduced-calorie salad dressing
3 tablespoons tarragon vinegar
2 tablespoons water
¼ teaspoon dried whole tarragon
¼ teaspoon freshly ground black pepper
¼ teaspoon garlic powder

Cook carrots in a small amount of boiling water 3 to 4 minutes or until crisp-tender; drain.

Combine carrots, snow peas, tomatoes, and cucumber in a large shallow dish. Combine remaining ingredients in a jar; cover tightly, and shake vigorously. Pour over vegetables, tossing lightly to coat. Cover and chill overnight. Arrange on individual plates to serve. Yield: 6 servings (37 calories per serving).

PRO 1.5 / FAT 0.2 / CARB 8.0 / FIB 1.2 / CHOL 0 / SOD 132 / POT 237

The crisp texture of fresh vegetables is enhanced by the zest of tarragon in the Tarragon Vegetable Appetizer.

SPICY TEA EGGS

6 hard-cooked eggs
2 tablespoons Earl Grey tea leaves
¼ cup reduced-sodium soy sauce
4 (3-inch) sticks cinnamon
2 whole star anise
1 tablespoon chopped fresh chives

Gently crack entire surface of each egg shell, using the back of a spoon; do not remove shells from eggs.

Place eggs in a 2-quart casserole; add cold water to cover. Add tea, soy sauce, cinnamon, and star anise, stirring well; cover and refrigerate overnight. Drain. Leave eggs in shells to store. Wrap securely in plastic wrap, and refrigerate until ready to serve.

To serve, remove shells, and cut each egg in quarters; sprinkle with chopped chives. Yield: 6 servings (88 calories per serving).

PRO 6.9 / FAT 5.6 / CARB 1.7 / FIB 0.0 / CHOL 274 / SOD 457 / POT 67

NACHOS

24 unsalted tortilla chips (about 2 ounces)
Vegetable cooking spray
½ cup (2 ounces) shredded part-skim farmer's cheese
3 tablespoons plus 1½ teaspoons chopped green chiles

Spread a single layer of tortilla chips in a jellyroll pan coated with cooking spray. Sprinkle with cheese and chiles. Bake at 350° for 5 minutes or until cheese melts. Yield: 2 dozen appetizers. Serving size: 1 nacho (20 calories each).

PRO 0.8 / FAT 1.3 / CARB 1.5 / FIB 0.0 / CHOL 2 / SOD 53 / POT 7

ITALIAN STUFFED MUSHROOMS

30 medium-size fresh mushrooms
½ cup (2 ounces) shredded mozzarella cheese
¼ cup minced fresh parsley
¼ cup Italian reduced-calorie salad dressing

Clean mushrooms with damp paper towels. Remove mushroom stems, and finely chop; set caps aside.

Combine chopped mushroom stems, cheese, parsley, and salad dressing in a bowl, stirring well. Spoon mixture into reserved caps. Place in a shallow baking pan. Bake at 350° for 15 to 20 minutes or until cheese melts. Yield: 2½ dozen appetizers. Serving size: 1 mushroom (12 calories each).

PRO 0.7 / FAT 0.7 / CARB 1.0 / FIB 0.1 / CHOL 2 / SOD 24 / POT 67

TUNA HORS D'OEUVRES

1 (6½-ounce) can water-packed tuna
½ (8-ounce) package Neufchâtel cheese, softened
2 tablespoons minced celery
2 teaspoons lemon juice
1 teaspoon Worcestershire sauce
⅔ cup minced chives

Rinse tuna in a colander under cold running water 1 minute; drain well. Combine tuna and next 4 ingredients, mixing well; cover and chill. Shape mixture into balls, using 2 teaspoons mixture for each. Roll in chives.

Place hors d'oeurves on a serving platter. Cover and refrigerate until thoroughly chilled. Yield: 32 appetizers. Serving size: 1 hors d'oeurve (15 calories each).

PRO 1.3 / FAT 0.9 / CARB 0.3 / FIB 0.0 / CHOL 3 / SOD 16 / POT 10

CHICKEN DRUMMETTE APPETIZERS

1½ pounds chicken drummettes, skinned
Vegetable cooking spray
2 tablespoons unsalted margarine, melted
2 tablespoons hot sauce
1½ teaspoons cider vinegar
½ cup plain low-fat yogurt
¼ cup sour cream
¼ cup crumbled blue cheese

Arrange drummettes on a rack coated with cooking spray; place rack on a broiler pan, and bake at 475° for 30 minutes. Combine margarine, hot sauce, and vinegar in a small bowl. Brush drummettes with half of mixture, and broil 2 inches from heat 1 to 2 minutes or until tops are golden brown and crisp. Turn drummettes, and brush with remaining mixture; broil an additional 1 to 2 minutes or until drummettes are golden brown and crisp.

Combine yogurt, sour cream, and blue cheese in a serving bowl, mixing well. Serve drummettes hot with yogurt sauce. Yield: 20 appetizers. Serving size: 1 drummette plus 2 teaspoons sauce (65 calories each).

Note: The drummettes can be baked in advance and broiled just before serving.

PRO 4.4 / FAT 4.9 / CARB 0.6 / FIB 0.0 / CHOL 14 / SOD 47 / POT 49

SWEET-AND-SOUR MEATBALLS

1 pound lean ground beef
2 tablespoons fine, dry breadcrumbs
1 tablespoon skim milk
½ teaspoon pepper
¼ teaspoon salt
⅛ teaspoon dried whole thyme
⅛ teaspoon ground cinnamon
Dash of ground red pepper
1 clove garlic, minced
Vegetable cooking spray
½ cup chopped onion
1 (10¾-ounce) can tomato puree
½ cup unsweetened pineapple juice
2 tablespoons red wine vinegar
2 tablespoons lemon juice
1 teaspoon Worcestershire sauce

Combine first 9 ingredients; mix well. Shape into 48 meatballs, using 1½ teaspoons mixture for each meatball; arrange on rack of a broiler pan coated with cooking spray. Bake at 400° for 10 minutes or until browned; set aside.

Coat a Dutch oven with cooking spray; place over medium heat until thoroughly heated. Add onion, and sauté until tender. Add tomato puree, pineapple juice, vinegar, lemon juice, and Worcestershire sauce. Add meatballs; cover and simmer over low heat 20 minutes. Serve hot. Yield: 4 dozen appetizers. Serving size: 1 meatball (35 calories each).

PRO 1.8 / FAT 2.4 / CARB 1.4 / FIB 0.1 / CHOL 9 / SOD 47 / POT 70

CHUNKY GUACAMOLE

2 medium avocados (about 1½ pounds), cubed
½ cup diced tomato
¼ cup minced onion
1 tablespoon minced fresh parsley or coriander
1 teaspoon minced garlic
2 to 3 tablespoons lime juice
¼ teaspoon salt
⅛ teaspoon ground red pepper

Coarsely mash avocado; add remaining ingredients, mixing well. Spoon into a serving bowl, and serve immediately with unsalted tortilla chips. Yield: 2 cups. Serving size: 1 tablespoon (27 calories per serving).

PRO 0.4 / FAT 2.5 / CARB 1.5 / FIB 0.5 / CHOL 0 / SOD 20 / POT 106

BLACK-EYED PEA RELISH

1 (16-ounce) package frozen black-eyed peas
½ cup diced red pepper
½ cup sliced green onion
3 tablespoons cider vinegar
1 clove garlic, minced
¼ teaspoon salt
¼ teaspoon hot sauce
⅛ teaspoon pepper

Cook peas according to package directions, omitting salt and fat; drain. Combine peas and remaining ingredients in a large bowl; cover and chill overnight. Serve with unsalted tortilla chips. Yield: 4½ cups. Serving size: 1 tablespoon (9 calories per serving).

PRO 0.6 / FAT 0.1 / CARB 1.7 / FIB 0.1 / CHOL 0 / SOD 9 / POT 32

Serve Black-Eyed Pea Relish as a delicious appetizer or with dinner as an interesting side dish.

Tomato Salsa will appeal to those who like their relish with a zip of Latin American flavor.

TOMATO SALSA

3 medium tomatoes, diced
¼ cup chopped green chiles, rinsed and drained
¼ cup diced red onion
¼ cup diced green pepper
2 tablespoons chopped fresh parsley
1 tablespoon lime juice
¼ teaspoon cumin
¼ teaspoon hot sauce
⅛ teaspoon salt
⅛ teaspoon garlic powder

Combine all ingredients in a bowl, mixing well; let stand 15 minutes to blend flavors. Serve with unsalted tortilla chips or with grilled chicken or fish. Yield: 3 cups. Serving size: 1 tablespoon (3 calories per serving).

PRO 0.1 / FAT 0.0 / CARB 0.6 / FIB 0.1 / CHOL 0 / SOD 8 / POT 23

EGGPLANT RELISH

1 cup chopped onion
3 cloves garlic, minced
1 tablespoon vegetable oil
1 (1-pound) eggplant, diced (about 5 cups)
1 cup diced celery
1 cup diced red pepper
1 cup diced green pepper
1 cup diced, seeded tomato
⅛ teaspoon dried whole thyme
⅛ teaspoon pepper
Dash of crushed red pepper
1 tablespoon red wine vinegar

Combine onion, garlic, and oil in a large Dutch oven; cover and cook over low heat 10 minutes, stirring occasionally. Add eggplant; cook, covered, over low heat 10 minutes, stirring occasionally. Stir in celery and red and green pepper; cover and cook 5 minutes.

Add tomato, thyme, pepper, and crushed red pepper; cook 10 minutes. Remove from heat, and stir in vinegar. Cover; let stand 10 minutes to blend flavors. Serve warm or at room temperature with melba toast. Yield: 4½ cups. Serving size: 1 tablespoon (6 calories per serving).

PRO 0.2 / FAT 0.2 / CARB 1.0 / FIB 0.2 / CHOL 0 / SOD 2 / POT 36

CUCUMBER-YOGURT DIP

1 (16-ounce) carton plain low-fat yogurt
1 medium cucumber, peeled, seeded, and thinly sliced
⅛ teaspoon salt
¼ cup fresh parsley sprigs
1 clove garlic
½ teaspoon white wine vinegar
¼ teaspoon dried whole oregano
⅛ teaspoon pepper

Line a colander or sieve with a double layer of cheesecloth that has been rinsed out and squeezed dry; allow cheesecloth to overlap at the sides. Place colander in a large pan. Stir yogurt until smooth; pour into colander, and fold edges of cheesecloth over to cover yogurt. Refrigerate 12 to 24 hours. Remove yogurt from colander, and set aside; discard liquid.

Toss cucumber with salt in a small bowl; cover with plastic wrap. Chill 1 hour.

Rinse and drain cucumber; squeeze out excess moisture with paper towels. Combine cucumber and remaining ingredients in container of an electric blender; process 2 minutes or until finely pureed. Transfer cucumber mixture to a bowl; add drained yogurt. Stir with a whisk until smooth. Chill 30 minutes. Serve with melba toast. Yield: 2 cups. Serving size: 1 tablespoon (10 calories per serving).

PRO 0.8 / FAT 0.2 / CARB 1.3 / FIB 0.1 / CHOL 1 / SOD 20 / POT 47

PEPPER-HERB YOGURT DIP

1 (16-ounce) carton plain low-fat
  yogurt
2 tablespoons minced onion
Vegetable cooking spray
¼ teaspoon pepper
⅛ teaspoon dried whole thyme
Dash of dried whole rosemary
1 tablespoon chopped fresh parsley
1 tablespoon thinly sliced green onion tops
¼ teaspoon dried whole dillweed or
  1 teaspoon chopped fresh dill

Line a colander or sieve with a double layer of cheesecloth that has been rinsed out and squeezed dry; allow cheesecloth to overlap at the sides. Stir yogurt until smooth; pour into sieve, and fold edges of cheesecloth over to cover yogurt. Place colander in a large pan; refrigerate 12 to 24 hours. Remove yogurt from colander, and set aside; discard liquid.

Sauté onion in a small skillet coated with cooking spray over low heat 8 to 10 minutes or until tender. Stir in pepper, thyme, and rosemary, and set aside to cool. Combine drained yogurt, onion mixture, and remaining ingredients in a small bowl; cover and chill. Serve with melba toast or crackers. Yield: ¾ cup. Serving size: 1 tablespoon (25 calories per serving).

PRO 2.0 / FAT 0.6 / CARB 2.9 / FIB 0.0 / CHOL 2 / SOD 27 / POT 96

YOGURT FRUIT DIP

1 (8-ounce) package Neufchâtel cheese,
  softened
2 (8-ounce) cartons vanilla low-fat yogurt
1 teaspoon lemon juice
1 (8-ounce) can unsweetened crushed
  pineapple, drained
½ teaspoon coconut extract
½ teaspoon grated orange rind

Beat Neufchâtel cheese at medium speed of an electric mixer until fluffy; add yogurt and lemon juice, and beat until smooth. Stir in pineapple, coconut extract, and orange rind; cover and chill thoroughly. Serve with assorted fresh fruit. Yield: 3½ cups. Serving size: 1 tablespoon (20 calories per serving).

PRO 0.8 / FAT 1.1 / CARB 1.9 / FIB 0.0 / CHOL 3 / SOD 22 / POT 28

SPINACH DIP

1 (10-ounce) package frozen chopped
  spinach, thawed and drained
Vegetable cooking spray
½ cup chopped onion
2 cloves garlic, minced
¼ teaspoon dried whole thyme, crushed
1 (8-ounce) package Neufchâtel cheese,
  softened
¼ teaspoon salt
⅛ teaspoon pepper
1 hard-cooked egg, chopped

Place spinach on paper towels, and squeeze until barely moist; set aside.

Coat a medium skillet with cooking spray; place over low heat until hot. Add onion and garlic; sauté until tender. Add thyme, and cook 1 minute, stirring constantly. Add spinach to onion mixture, and cook 2 to 3 minutes, stirring constantly.

Transfer spinach mixture to a bowl; cool to room temperature. Add cheese, salt, and pepper, mixing well. Cover and chill thoroughly. Stir in chopped egg just before serving. Serve with melba toast or Baked Potato Skins (recipe on page 105). Yield: 3½ cups. Serving size: 1 tablespoon (14 calories per serving).

PRO 0.7 / FAT 1.1 / CARB 0.5 / FIB 0.1 / CHOL 8 / SOD 32 / POT 25

CHILE-CHEESE DIP

½ (4-ounce) can green chiles, undrained
1 cup canned pinto beans, undrained and mashed
1 cup (4 ounces) shredded Monterey Jack cheese
1 clove garlic, minced
½ cup minced onion

Drain and chop chiles, reserving 1 tablespoon juice. Combine chiles, 1 tablespoon chile juice, beans, cheese, and garlic in top of a double boiler; bring water to a boil. Reduce heat to low; cook, stirring frequently, until cheese melts. Place cheese mixture in container of an electric blender, and process until pureed. Transfer to a chafing dish, and stir in onion. Serve warm with unsalted tortilla chips. Yield: 1½ cups. Serving size: 1 tablespoon (29 calories per serving).

PRO 1.7 / FAT 1.5 / CARB 2.1 / FIB 0.0 / CHOL 4 / SOD 58 / POT 13

CRAB DIP

1 (6-ounce) package frozen crabmeat, thawed, drained, and flaked
1 (8-ounce) package Neufchâtel cheese, softened
¼ cup reduced-calorie mayonnaise
2 tablespoons dry white wine
½ teaspoon dried whole thyme
1 drop hot sauce
1 tablespoon chopped fresh parsley

Combine first 6 ingredients in container of an electric blender, and process at low speed until smooth. Transfer to a serving bowl; cover and chill 2 hours. Garnish with chopped parsley. Serve with melba toast. Yield: 1¾ cups. Serving size: 1 tablespoon (29 calories per serving).

PRO 1.6 / FAT 2.3 / CARB 0.4 / FIB 0.0 / CHOL 11 / SOD 54 / POT 20

CLAM DIP

1 (16-ounce) carton plain low-fat yogurt
Vegetable cooking spray
1 clove garlic, minced
1 (6½-ounce) can minced clams, rinsed and drained
1 tablespoon chopped fresh parsley
1 teaspoon grated Parmesan cheese
⅛ teaspoon dried whole oregano
⅛ teaspoon pepper

Line a colander or sieve with a double layer of cheesecloth that has been rinsed out and squeezed dry; allow cheesecloth to overlap at the sides. Place colander in a large pan. Stir yogurt until smooth; pour into colander, and fold edges of cheesecloth over to cover yogurt. Refrigerate 12 to 24 hours. Remove yogurt to a medium bowl, and set aside. Discard liquid.

Coat a small heavy saucepan with cooking spray; place over medium heat until hot. Add garlic, and sauté 1 minute or until golden brown, stirring constantly. Add sautéed garlic and remaining ingredients to reserved yogurt, stirring well; chill 30 minutes. Serve with crackers or melba toast. Yield: 1 cup. Serving size: 1 tablespoon (30 calories per serving).

PRO 3.3 / FAT 0.7 / CARB 2.3 / FIB 0.0 / CHOL 9 / SOD 35 / POT 85

CHICKEN LIVER PÂTÉ

1 medium onion, chopped
2 cloves garlic, minced
1 pound chicken livers
3 tablespoons unsalted margarine, melted
1 tablespoon all-purpose flour
¼ teaspoon salt
1 teaspoon white pepper
1 bay leaf
⅛ teaspoon dried whole oregano
2 tablespoons minced fresh parsley
2 hard-cooked eggs
1 medium apple, peeled, cored, and diced

Sauté onion, garlic, and chicken livers in margarine in a large skillet over medium-high heat 5 minutes or until livers are browned.

Add flour, salt, pepper, bay leaf, oregano, and parsley. Cover; reduce heat, and simmer 5 minutes or until livers are tender. Remove and discard bay leaf.

Combine liver mixture, eggs, and apple in a food processor; process until coarsely chopped. Pack in crocks or a pâté tureen; cover and chill thoroughly. Serve on crackers or party rye bread. Yield: about 3 cups. Serving size: 1 tablespoon (22 calories per serving).

PRO 1.7 / FAT 1.3 / CARB 0.9 / FIB 0.1 / CHOL 47 / SOD 18 / POT 20

VEGETABLE-CHEESE SPREAD

1 cup low-fat cottage cheese
2 tablespoons minced fresh chives
2 tablespoons minced radish
2 tablespoons minced, peeled cucumber
1 teaspoon Dijon mustard
1 teaspoon lemon juice
¼ teaspoon Worcestershire sauce
Dash of ground red pepper

Combine all ingredients in a bowl; stir gently until well blended. Chill; serve with melba toast or as a sandwich spread. Yield: 1¼ cups. Serving size: 1 tablespoon (11 calories per serving).

PRO 1.6 / FAT 0.2 / CARB 0.5 / FIB 0.0 / CHOL 1 / SOD 54 / POT 16

If you can't tolerate milk, yogurt may be a good substitute according to a study from the University of Minnesota.
Many people lack the enzyme lactase, which breaks down lactose, the main sugar in milk. If lactose is not digested, it remains in the intestines and causes gastrointestinal problems within an hour after consuming milk products.
Yogurt, a rich source of calcium, contains the enzyme lactase, thus making yogurt a good source of milk for the milk intolerant.

BAKED POTATO SKINS

7 medium-size baking potatoes
1 tablespoon plus 1½ teaspoons unsalted margarine, melted
½ teaspoon pepper

Bake potatoes at 400° for 45 minutes to 1 hour or until done. Remove from oven, and let stand 20 minutes or until cool to touch. Halve potatoes lengthwise; scoop out pulp, leaving a thin shell. (Reserve potato pulp for another use.) Cut each potato skin shell in half lengthwise into 2 wedges; cut wedges in half crosswise.
Place potato skin pieces, skin side down, on a jellyroll pan. Brush with margarine, and sprinkle with pepper. Bake at 450° for 20 minutes or until browned and crispy. Yield: 56 appetizers. Serving size: 1 wedge (5 calories each).

PRO 0.1 / FAT 0.3 / CARB 0.6 / FIB 0.1 / CHOL 0 / SOD 0 / POT 20

TWISTED CHEESE STRAWS

2 tablespoons unsalted margarine, softened
1 cup (4 ounces) shredded Gruyère cheese
1½ cups unbleached or all-purpose flour
¼ teaspoon salt
⅛ teaspoon pepper
⅛ teaspoon ground red pepper
½ cup skim milk
Vegetable cooking spray

Combine margarine and cheese in a large bowl; add flour, salt, pepper, and red pepper, mixing well. Gradually add milk, stirring with a fork to form a soft dough.
Turn dough out onto a lightly floured surface, and roll into a 16- x 7-inch rectangle (about ¼-inch-thick). Cut into 7- x ½-inch strips; twist strips several times, and arrange on baking sheets coated with cooking spray. Bake at 350° for 15 minutes; reduce heat to 300°, and continue baking 15 minutes or until golden brown. Remove to wire racks to cool. Yield: 32 appetizers. Serving size: 1 straw (41 calories each).

PRO 1.8 / FAT 1.9 / CARB 4.3 / FIB 0.0 / CHOL 4 / SOD 32 / POT 16

SPICY TORTILLA CHIPS

3 tablespoons vegetable oil
1 tablespoon water
3 cloves garlic
½ teaspoon dried whole oregano
½ teaspoon ground cumin
¼ teaspoon paprika
⅛ teaspoon salt
⅛ teaspoon pepper
⅛ teaspoon ground red pepper
1 (8-ounce) package 8-inch corn tortillas

Combine first 9 ingredients in container of an electric blender, and process 1 to 2 minutes or until pureed. Brush both sides of tortillas with mixture; stack tortillas, and cut into 8 wedges. Arrange wedges in a single layer in jellyroll pans, and bake at 400° for 10 minutes or until crisp and lightly browned. Serve warm or store in airtight containers. Yield: 8 dozen appetizers. Serving size: 1 chip (13 calories each).

PRO 0.2 / FAT 0.5 / CARB 1.8 / FIB 0.0 / CHOL 0 / SOD 6 / POT 1

SESAME PITA TRIANGLES

4 (6-inch) whole wheat pita pockets
2 teaspoons unsalted margarine, melted
2 teaspoons sesame seeds

Split each pita in half crosswise; quarter each half, making 8 wedges; place in a jellyroll pan, smooth side down. Brush with margarine, and sprinkle with sesame seeds. Bake at 350° for 10 to 15 minutes or until crisp and lightly browned. Yield: 32 appetizers. Serving size: 1 triangle (34 calories each).

PRO 0.7 / FAT 0.6 / CARB 6.0 / FIB 0.0 / CHOL 0 / SOD 72 / POT 22

PARMESAN MELBA TOASTS

1 (8-ounce) loaf day-old whole wheat French bread
1 tablespoon unsalted margarine, melted
1 tablespoon grated Parmesan cheese

Cut bread into ¼-inch thick slices. Arrange in a single layer in a jellyroll pan; bake at 250° for 30 to 40 minutes or until lightly browned. Combine margarine and cheese; brush on toast. Bake at 350° for 5 minutes or until crisp. Repeat baking procedure with remaining bread slices. Yield: 35 appetizers. Serving size: 1 toast (22 calories each).

PRO 0.6 / FAT 0.5 / CARB 3.6 / FIB 0.2 / CHOL 0 / SOD 40 / POT 6

 Drink plenty of water when you exercise. Water composes one-half to three-fourths of an individual's body weight, and 1 hour of strenuous exercise can reduce that weight by as much as 2 pounds.
It is also a good idea to drink more water than you think you need in order to help prevent muscle cramps and faintness. In a recent study, young men who were deprived of water for 24 hours drank enough to replenish the amount of water lost during that time; whereas, the older men, under the same conditions — even though they were thirsty — failed to drink enough water to compensate for the amount lost.
Whenever possible, try to drink water for liquid replacement. Sweetened drinks are much more slowly absorbed. Caffeine and alcohol will only increase water loss because they are diuretics.

MIXED VEGETABLE DRINK

2 cups tomato juice, chilled
3 to 4 ice cubes
½ cup sliced carrot
¼ cup sliced cucumber
¼ cup sliced celery
2 teaspoons lemon juice
4 drops hot sauce
3 sticks celery

Combine tomato juice and ice cubes in container of an electric blender; process until smooth. Add next 5 ingredients, and process until smooth. Pour into glasses, and garnish with celery sticks; serve immediately. Yield: 3 cups (41 calories per 1-cup serving).

PRO 1.6 / FAT 0.2 / CARB 10.0 / FIB 1.2 / CHOL 0 / SOD 612 / POT 718

MELON SLUSH

1 medium-size ripe cantaloupe, chilled
2 teaspoons vanilla extract
1 teaspoon sugar
3 slices lime

Peel and seed cantaloupe; cut into small pieces. Combine cantaloupe, vanilla, and sugar in container of an electric blender; process until smooth. Pour into chilled glasses, and garnish with lime slices. Serve immediately. Yield: 3 cups (95 calories per 1-cup serving).

PRO 2.0 / FAT 0.6 / CARB 21.3 / FIB 0.7 / CHOL 0 / SOD 20 / POT 701

FRUIT FLING

1 cup unsweetened orange juice, chilled
1 cup unsweetened pineapple juice, chilled
1 tablespoon grated fresh coconut
1 banana, sliced
1 tablespoon honey
1 cup crushed ice

Combine all ingredients in container of an electric blender, and process until smooth and slushy. Pour into glasses, and serve immediately. Yield: 3 cups (152 calories per 1-cup serving).

PRO 1.5 / FAT 1.4 / CARB 35.6 / FIB 0.7 / CHOL 0 / SOD 3 / POT 448

CANTALOUPE COOLER

1 medium-size ripe cantaloupe (about 3 pounds), chilled
1 (8-ounce) carton vanilla low-fat yogurt
¾ cup skim milk
Dash of ground allspice

Peel and seed cantaloupe; cut into small pieces. Combine cantaloupe and remaining ingredients in container of an electric blender. Process until smooth. Pour into glasses, and serve immediately. Yield: 5 cups (99 calories per 1-cup serving).

PRO 4.7 / FAT 1.0 / CARB 19.4 / FIB 0.4 / CHOL 3 / SOD 61 / POT 581

MIXED FRUIT SHAKE

2 cups unsweetened orange juice, chilled
1 banana, chilled and sliced
1 cup sliced, peeled fresh peaches, chilled
¼ cup instant non-fat dry milk powder
½ teaspoon vanilla extract

Combine all ingredients in container of an electric blender, and process until smooth and frothy. Pour into glasses, and serve immediately. Yield: 4 cups (129 calories per 1-cup serving).
Note. 1 cup frozen unsweetened peaches may be substituted for fresh peaches.

PRO 4.1 / FAT 0.4 / CARB 28.5 / FIB 1.4 / CHOL 2 / SOD 42 / POT 570

STRAWBERRY FROSTY

3 cups sliced fresh strawberries
1 cup unsweetened orange juice
1 tablespoon sugar
½ cup club soda
2 cups ice cubes
¼ teaspoon almond extract

Combine strawberries, orange juice, and sugar in container of an electric blender, and process until smooth. Add remaining ingredients, and process until smooth and slushy. Pour into glasses, and serve immediately. Yield: 5 cups (66 calories per 1-cup serving).

PRO 1.0 / FAT 0.5 / CARB 15.3 / FIB 1.7 / CHOL 0 / SOD 1 / POT 239

GRAPE JUICE SPRITZER

½ cup unsweetened white grape juice
½ cup club soda
1 tablespoon lemon juice
1 slice lemon
1 sprig fresh mint

Combine first 3 ingredients in a glass filled with crushed ice. Garnish with lemon and mint, and serve immediately. Yield: 1 cup (90 calories per 1-cup serving).

PRO 0.6 / FAT 0.0 / CARB 22.7 / FIB 0.0 / CHOL 0 / SOD 4 / POT 180

FRUIT JUICE SPRITZER

1 (6-ounce) can frozen orange juice concentrate, thawed and undiluted
1 (6-ounce) can frozen apple juice concentrate, thawed and undiluted
4½ cups club soda, chilled
6 thin slices lime
6 thin slices orange

Combine orange juice, apple juice, and club soda in a pitcher, mixing well. Pour over ice in serving glasses, and garnish with lime and orange slices before serving. Yield: 6 cups (110 calories per 1-cup serving).

PRO 1.3 / FAT 0.5 / CARB 26.0 / FIB 0.1 / CHOL 0 / SOD 9 / POT 394

LIME SANGRÍA

4 cups dry white wine, chilled
1½ cups club soda, chilled
¼ cup Cognac
¼ cup Triple Sec or other orange-flavored liqueur
¼ cup lime juice
3 tablespoons sugar
1 orange, thinly sliced
1 lime, thinly sliced

Combine first 6 ingredients, stirring until sugar dissolves. Pour over crushed ice in serving glasses, and garnish with lime and orange slices. Yield: 6 cups (187 calories per ¾-cup serving).

PRO 0.2 / FAT 0 / CARB 11.0 / FIB 0 / CHOL 0 / SOD 6 / POT 107

APPLE CIDER PUNCH

1 quart unsweetened apple cider
2 (3-inch) sticks cinnamon
8 whole cloves
1 cup unsweetened pineapple juice, chilled
2¾ cups unsweetened orange juice, chilled
¼ cup lemon juice, chilled
3 cups club soda, chilled

Combine first 3 ingredients in a saucepan; bring to a boil. Cover; reduce heat, and simmer 15 minutes. Strain cider, discarding spices. Chill.
Just before serving, combine spiced cider, juice, and club soda in a punch bowl. Serve over crushed ice, if desired. Yield: 10½ cups (44 calories per ½-cup serving).

PRO 0.3 / FAT 0.1 / CARB 10.9 / FIB 0.1 / CHOL 0 / SOD 2 / POT 138

SPICED FRUIT TEA

2 quarts water
2 (3-inch) sticks cinnamon
2 whole cloves
8 regular tea bags
¾ cup sugar
1¾ cups unsweetened orange juice
¼ cup lemon juice

Combine first 3 ingredients in a large Dutch oven; bring to a boil. Cover; reduce heat, and simmer 10 minutes. Remove from heat, and add tea bags; cover and let stand 10 minutes. Strain liquid, discarding tea bags and spices. Add sugar and juice; cook over low heat until thoroughly heated, stirring until sugar dissolves. Pour into cups to serve. Yield: 10 cups (80 calories per 1-cup serving).

PRO 0.4 / FAT 0.0 / CARB 20.2 / FIB 0.0 / CHOL 0 / SOD 1 / POT 103

HOT SPICED CIDER

2 cups unsweetened apple cider
1 (3-inch) stick cinnamon
2 whole cloves
2 lemon slices

Combine first 3 ingredients in a saucepan. Bring to a boil. Cover; reduce heat, and simmer

5 minutes. Strain into mugs, and garnish with lemon slices. Yield: 2 cups (117 calories per 1-cup serving).

PRO 0.1 / FAT 0.3 / CARB 29.0 / FIB 0.5 / CHOL 0 / SOD 7 / POT 295

VEGETABLE JUICE APPETIZER

1 (24-ounce) can cocktail vegetable juice
1 cup brewed tea
⅛ teaspoon ground cinnamon
1 tablespoon honey
Lemon slices

Combine vegetable juice, tea, and cinnamon in a saucepan. Cook over low heat until thoroughly heated, stirring occasionally. Stir in honey. Pour into mugs to serve; garnish with lemon slices. Yield: 4 cups (49 calories per 1-cup serving).

PRO 1.1 / FAT 0.2 / CARB 12.4 / FIB 0.4 / CHOL 0 / SOD 621 / POT 346

TOMATO BOUILLON

2 cups tomato juice
1 medium onion, sliced
1 stalk celery, chopped
2 bay leaves
4 whole peppercorns
2 lemon wedges

Combine first 5 ingredients in a medium saucepan; cover and let stand for 1 hour.
Bring mixture to a boil. Cover; reduce heat, and simmer 10 minutes. Strain mixture; discard vegetables. Serve hot or chilled; garnish with lemon wedges. Yield: 2 cups (72 calories per 1-cup serving).

PRO 2.9 / FAT 0.4 / CARB 17.0 / FIB 2.0 / CHOL 0 / SOD 900 / POT 1053

Cranberry-Orange Bread (page 112), Vermicelli with Tomato-Basil Sauce (page 124), Potato Crescents (page 115), Pear-Almond Muffins (page 112), Apple Danish (page 116), and Brown Rice Pilaf (page 120).

Breads, Grains & Pastas

BUTTERMILK CORN STICKS

1½ cups cornmeal
1½ teaspoons baking powder
¾ teaspoon baking soda
½ teaspoon sugar
½ teaspoon salt
1 egg, lightly beaten
1½ cups buttermilk
Vegetable cooking spray

Combine first 5 ingredients in a large bowl. Combine egg and buttermilk in a small bowl, beating well; add to flour mixture, and stir just until combined.

Place cast-iron cornstick pans coated with cooking spray in a 400° oven 3 minutes or until very hot. Remove from oven; spoon batter into pans, filling three-fourths full. Bake at 400° for 25 minutes or until golden brown. Yield: 17 corn sticks (48 calories each).

PRO 2.1 / FAT 0.9 / CARB 7.6 / FIB 1.6 / CHOL 17 / SOD 138 / POT 68

WHOLE WHEAT POPOVERS

2 eggs
1 cup skim milk
½ cup all-purpose flour
½ cup whole wheat flour
1 tablespoon unsalted margarine, melted
¼ teaspoon salt
Vegetable cooking spray

Place eggs and milk in container of an electric blender; process until bubbly. Add flour, margarine, and salt; process until smooth.

Place a muffin pan coated with cooking spray in a 450° oven 3 minutes or until very hot. Spoon batter into muffin pan, filling two-thirds full. Bake at 425° for 20 minutes; reduce heat to 350°, and bake 10 minutes. Prick each popover with a fork to let steam escape, and bake an additional 5 minutes. Yield: 9 popovers (88 calories each).

PRO 4.0 / FAT 2.7 / CARB 12.0 / FIB 0.7 / CHOL 61 / SOD 95 / POT 92

OATMEAL BISCUITS

¾ cup regular oats, uncooked
1½ cups unbleached or all-purpose flour
2 teaspoons baking powder
½ teaspoon baking soda
1 tablespoon brown sugar
¼ teaspoon salt
⅓ cup unsalted margarine
1 cup buttermilk
Vegetable cooking spray

Place oats in container of an electric blender, and process until oats are ground to a powder. Combine oat powder and next 5 ingredients in a bowl; cut in margarine until mixture resembles coarse meal. Add buttermilk, stirring until dry ingredients are moistened.

Turn dough out onto a lightly floured surface, and knead 10 to 12 times. Roll dough to ½-inch thickness, and cut into rounds with a 1½-inch biscuit cutter. Place biscuits on baking sheets coated with cooking spray; bake at 400° for 12 to 15 minutes or until lightly browned. Yield: 3 dozen (42 calories each).

PRO 1.0 / FAT 1.9 / CARB 5.4 / FIB 0.2 / CHOL 0 / SOD 45 / POT 23

OAT BRAN MUFFINS

2½ cups unprocessed oat bran
½ cup raisins
1 tablespoon firmly packed brown sugar
1 tablespoon baking powder
⅛ teaspoon salt
½ cup chunky unsweetened applesauce
1 cup skim milk
½ cup egg substitute or 2 eggs, lightly
   beaten
1 tablespoon corn oil
Vegetable cooking spray

Combine oat bran, raisins, brown sugar, baking powder, and salt in a large bowl; make a well in center of mixture. Combine applesauce, milk, egg substitute, and oil, stirring well. Add applesauce mixture to dry ingredients, stirring just until moistened.

Coat muffin pans with cooking spray or line with paper baking cups. Spoon batter into pans, filling three-fourths full. Bake at 425° for 20 to 25 minutes or until golden brown. Yield: 1 dozen (124 calories each).

PRO 5.6 / FAT 3.1 / CARB 18.7 / FIB 5.3 / CHOL 0 / SOD 128 / POT 207

CARROT MUFFINS

1 cup unbleached or all-purpose flour
¾ cup whole wheat flour
1 teaspoon baking powder
¼ teaspoon salt
½ teaspoon ground cinnamon
¼ teaspoon ground nutmeg
1 cup grated carrot
½ cup chopped walnuts
2 eggs, beaten
1 cup buttermilk
⅓ cup maple syrup
¼ cup unsalted margarine, melted
Vegetable cooking spray

Combine first 6 ingredients in a large bowl; stir in carrot and walnuts. Make a well in center of mixture. Combine eggs, buttermilk, maple syrup, and margarine in a bowl. Add to flour mixture, stirring just until moistened. Spoon batter into muffin pans coated with cooking spray, filling two-thirds full. Bake at 400° for 20 to 25 minutes or until golden brown. Yield: 15 muffins (137 calories each).

PRO 4.1 / FAT 6.5 / CARB 16.8 / FIB 0.8 / CHOL 37 / SOD 89 / POT 124

APPLE-BRAN MUFFINS

2 cups whole wheat flour
1 cup seven-grain cereal
½ cup raw bran
1½ teaspoons baking powder
¼ teaspoon salt
1 teaspoon ground cinnamon
½ teaspoon ground nutmeg
¼ teaspoon ground allspice
1 cup skim milk
½ cup unsweetened apple juice
¼ cup plus 1 tablespoon honey
¼ cup unsalted margarine, melted
2 eggs
1 teaspoon vanilla extract
1 cup finely chopped apple
Vegetable cooking spray

Combine first 8 ingredients in a large bowl; make a well in center of mixture. Combine milk, apple juice, honey, margarine, eggs, and vanilla in a mixing bowl; beat at medium speed of an electric mixer until well combined. Add to flour mixture, stirring just until moistened. Stir in apple. Spoon batter into muffin pans coated with cooking spray, filling two-thirds full. Bake at 400° for 20 to 25 minutes. Yield: 1½ dozen (141 calories each).

PRO 4.4 / FAT 3.9 / CARB 23.5 / FIB 1.3 / CHOL 31 / SOD 74 / POT 158

Wheat bran, the richest source of water-insoluble fiber, is already well known for aiding digestion, but water-soluble fiber, found in oat bran, beans, prunes, green peas, corn, and oatmeal, is the "new fiber."

Almost 10 years ago, Dr. James Anderson, at the University of Kentucky Medical Center, found that diets high in water-soluble fiber helped diabetics control blood glucose. Now he is finding that this new fiber helps lower blood cholesterol.

Anderson's recent studies discovered that a diet which included 100 grams of oat bran daily, in the form of muffins and cereal, reduced blood cholesterol by 13 percent in just 10 days and by 19 percent in 3 weeks.

PEANUT BUTTER-BANANA MUFFINS

1½ cups unbleached or all purpose flour
¼ cup firmly packed brown sugar
1 tablespoon baking powder
½ teaspoon salt
¾ cup skim milk
½ cup smooth peanut butter
⅓ cup unsalted margarine, melted
2 medium bananas, mashed
1 egg
Vegetable cooking spray

Combine first 4 ingredients in a large bowl; make a well in center of mixture. Combine milk, peanut butter, margarine, banana, and egg in a mixing bowl; beat at medium speed of an electric mixer until smooth. Add to flour mixture, stirring just until moistened. Spoon into muffin pans coated with cooking spray, filling two-thirds full. Bake at 400° for 20 to 25 minutes or until golden brown. Yield: 16 muffins (150 calories each).

PRO 4.4 / FAT 8.4 / CARB 15.8 / FIB 0.5 / CHOL 17 / SOD 181 / POT 159

PEAR-ALMOND MUFFINS

¼ cup plus 1 tablespoon slivered almonds
1½ cups unbleached or all-purpose flour
1 tablespoon baking powder
¼ teaspoon salt
½ teaspoon ground cinnamon
⅛ teaspoon ground mace
2 eggs
½ cup buttermilk
¼ cup honey
¼ cup unsweetened pear juice
¼ cup unsalted margarine, melted
½ teaspoon almond extract
1 cup grated pear
Vegetable cooking spray
¼ cup sliced almonds

Place slivered almonds in container of an electric blender, and process to a powder. Combine almond powder, flour, baking powder, salt, cinnamon, and mace in a large bowl; make a well in center of mixture. Combine eggs, buttermilk, honey, pear juice, margarine, and almond extract in a bowl; beat at medium speed of an electric mixer until smooth. Add to flour mixture, stirring just until moistened. Fold in pear. Spoon batter into muffin pans coated with cooking spray, filling two-thirds full. Sprinkle sliced almonds over batter. Bake at 400° for 20 to 25 minutes or until golden brown. Yield: 15 muffins (139 calories each).

PRO 3.3 / FAT 6.3 / CARB 18.6 / FIB 0.8 / CHOL 37 / SOD 118 / POT 98

LEMON-BLUEBERRY BREAD

1¾ cups unbleached or all-purpose
  flour
2 teaspoons baking powder
¼ teaspoon salt
¼ cup unsalted margarine, softened
¼ cup plus 2 tablespoons firmly packed
  brown sugar
2 eggs, lightly beaten
½ cup skim milk
1 cup fresh blueberries
1 tablespoon plus 1 teaspoon grated
  lemon rind
Vegetable cooking spray

Combine flour, baking powder, and salt in a medium bowl; set aside. Cream margarine in a large bowl; gradually add sugar, beating until light and fluffy. Add eggs, one at a time, beating well after each addition. Add flour mixture alternately with milk, beginning and ending with flour mixture. Mix just until blended after each addition. Stir in blueberries and lemon rind. Pour batter into a 8½- x 4½- x 3-inch loafpan coated with cooking spray. Bake at 350° for 40 to 45 minutes or until a wooden pick inserted in center comes out clean. Cool bread in pan 10 minutes; remove from pan, and cool completely. Yield: 1 loaf or 17 (½-inch) slices (94 calories per slice).

PRO 2.3 / FAT 3.4 / CARB 13.8 / FIB 0.3 / CHOL 32 / SOD 84 / POT 54

CRANBERRY-ORANGE BREAD

1¾ cups unbleached or all-purpose flour
1 teaspoon baking powder
1 teaspoon baking soda
¼ teaspoon salt
¼ cup plus 2 tablespoons unsalted margarine,
  softened
¼ cup plus 2 tablespoons sugar
2 eggs, lightly beaten
1 tablespoon grated orange rind
1 cup unsweetened orange juice
1 cup cranberries, chopped
¼ cup chopped walnuts
Vegetable cooking spray

Combine flour, baking powder, soda, and salt in a medium bowl; set aside. Cream margarine in a large bowl; gradually add sugar, beating until light and fluffy. Add eggs and orange rind, beating well. Add flour mixture alternately with orange juice, beginning and ending with flour mixture. Mix just until blended after each addition. Stir in chopped cranberries and walnuts. Pour batter into a 9- x 5- x 3-inch loafpan coated with cooking spray. Bake at 350° for 50 to 55 minutes or until a wooden pick inserted in center comes out clean. Cool in pan 10 minutes; remove from pan, and cool completely before slicing. Yield: 1 loaf or 18 (½-inch) slices (117 calories per slice).

PRO 2.4 / FAT 5.5 / CARB 15.1 / FIB 0.2 / CHOL 30 / SOD 77 / POT 61

SWEET POTATO BREAD

2 cups unbleached or all-purpose flour
2½ teaspoons baking powder
½ teaspoon salt
¼ teaspoon ground allspice
¼ teaspoon ground nutmeg
1 cup mashed, cooked sweet potatoes
½ cup firmly packed brown sugar
¼ cup unsalted margarine, melted
3 tablespoons skim milk
2 eggs
1 teaspoon grated orange rind
¼ cup chopped pecans
Vegetable cooking spray

Combine first 5 ingredients in a large bowl; set aside. Combine potatoes, sugar, margarine, milk, eggs, orange rind, and nuts, beating well. Add to dry ingredients, stirring just until moistened. Pour batter into a 9- x 5- x 3-inch loafpan coated with cooking spray. Bake at 350° for 45 minutes or until a wooden pick inserted in center comes out clean. Cool in pan 10 minutes; remove from pan, and cool completely. Yield: 1 loaf or 18 (½-inch) slices (122 calories per slice).

PRO 2.5 / FAT 4.4 / CARB 18.6 / FIB 0.2 / CHOL 30 / SOD 120 / POT 82

PUMPKIN-DATE BREAD

1 cup whole wheat flour
½ cup unbleached or all-purpose flour
1 teaspoon baking powder
1 teaspoon baking soda
¼ teaspoon salt
1 teaspoon ground cinnamon
½ teaspoon ground nutmeg
¼ teaspoon ground cloves
¼ teaspoon ground allspice
¼ cup plus 2 tablespoons unsalted
   margarine, softened
3 tablespoons brown sugar
2 eggs
1 cup canned pumpkin
½ cup buttermilk
1 cup regular oats, uncooked
½ cup chopped dates
Vegetable cooking spray

Combine first 9 ingredients, set aside. Cream margarine in a large bowl; gradually add sugar, beating until light and fluffy. Beat in eggs and pumpkin. Add flour mixture alternately with buttermilk, beginning and ending with flour mixture; stir in oats and dates. Pour batter into an 8½- x 4½- x 3-inch loafpan coated with cooking spray. Bake at 350° for 1 hour and 15 minutes or until a wooden pick inserted in center comes out clean. Cool in pan 10 minutes; remove from pan, and cool completely. Yield: 1 loaf or 17 (½-inch) slices (127 calories per slice).

PRO 3.2 / FAT 5.3 / CARB 18.0 / FIB 1.7 / CHOL 33 / SOD 90 / POT 137

Sweet Potato Bread is a delicious treat that's quick to make but also quick to disappear.

BUTTERMILK BUCKWHEAT PANCAKES

½ cup buckwheat flour
¼ cup unbleached or all-purpose flour
1 tablespoon sugar
2 teaspoons baking powder
1 egg, beaten
½ cup buttermilk
¼ cup water
1 tablespoon unsalted margarine, melted
Vegetable cooking spray

Combine flour, sugar, and baking powder in a large bowl; set aside. Combine next 4 ingredients, stirring with a wire whisk until smooth; add to flour mixture, stirring well. Heat a griddle or skillet coated with cooking spray over medium heat until hot. For each pancake, pour 2 tablespoons batter onto griddle. Turn pancakes when tops are bubbly and edges are slightly dry. Yield: 8 (4-inch) pancakes (69 calories each).

PRO 2.1 / FAT 2.3 / CARB 10.1 / FIB 0.0 / CHOL 35 / SOD 100 / POT 56

WHOLE WHEAT-APPLE PANCAKES

1 cup unbleached or all-purpose flour
1 cup whole wheat flour
2 tablespoons brown sugar
1 tablespoon baking powder
½ teaspoon baking soda
½ teaspoon salt
½ teaspoon ground cinnamon
1½ cups buttermilk
¾ cup unsweetened apple juice
3 tablespoons unsalted margarine, melted
2 eggs
1 cup grated cooking apple
Vegetable cooking spray

Combine first 7 ingredients in a large bowl. Combine buttermilk, apple juice, margarine, and eggs in a bowl, and mix well. Add to flour mixture, stirring until smooth. Stir in apple. Heat a griddle or skillet coated with cooking spray over medium heat until hot. For each pancake, pour 2 tablespoons batter onto griddle. Turn pancakes when tops are bubbly and edges are slightly dry. Yield: 23 (4-inch) pancakes (71 calories each).

PRO 2.3 / FAT 2.3 / CARB 10.7 / FIB 0.5 / CHOL 24 / SOD 121 / POT 73

OATMEAL-WHOLE WHEAT WAFFLES

1½ cups plus 2 tablespoons whole wheat flour
2¼ teaspoons baking powder
¼ teaspoon salt
2 cups skim milk
2 eggs, beaten
2 tablespoons unsalted margarine, melted
2 tablespoons honey
1 cup regular oats, uncooked
Vegetable cooking spray

Combine first 3 ingredients in a medium mixing bowl. Add milk, eggs, margarine, and honey; beat at medium speed of an electric mixer until smooth. Stir in oats.
Pour about 1 cup batter into preheated waffle iron coated with cooking spray. Bake 5 minutes or until done. Yield: 12 (4-inch square) waffles (136 calories each).

PRO 5.5 / FAT 3.7 / CARB 21.2 / FIB 2.2 / CHOL 46 / SOD 139 / POT 165

WHOLE WHEAT YEAST BISCUITS

1 package dry yeast
¼ cup plus 2 tablespoons warm water (105° to 115°)
2½ cups whole wheat flour
½ cup unbleached or all-purpose flour
1 tablespoon sugar
2 teaspoons baking powder
½ teaspoon baking soda
½ teaspoon salt
½ teaspoon dried whole oregano
½ teaspoon dried whole basil
3 tablespoons unsalted margarine, softened
1 cup buttermilk
Vegetable cooking spray

Dissolve yeast in warm water, and set aside. Combine next 8 ingredients; cut in margarine until mixture resembles coarse meal. Add yeast mixture and buttermilk, mixing well. Turn dough out onto a lightly floured surface. Roll dough to ½-inch thickness; cut into rounds with a 2-inch cutter. Place biscuits on baking sheets coated with cooking spray. Bake at 400° for 12 to 15 minutes. Yield: 22 biscuits (78 calories each).

PRO 2.6 / FAT 1.9 / CARB 13.4 / FIB 1.1 / CHOL 0 / SOD 101 / POT 78

POTATO CRESCENTS

1 cup skim milk
¼ cup unsalted margarine
1 cup mashed, cooked potatoes (cooked without salt or fat)
2 tablespoons brown sugar
1 package dry yeast
½ teaspoon salt
1 egg
3 cups unbleached or all-purpose flour, divided
1 tablespoon minced fresh chives
Vegetable cooking spray

Combine milk and margarine in a small saucepan; cook over low heat until margarine melts. Let cool to 105° to 115°.

Combine milk mixture, potatoes, sugar, yeast, salt, egg, and 1 cup flour in a large bowl; beat at low speed of an electric mixer until moistened. Beat at medium speed 3 minutes. Stir in chives and enough remaining flour to make a soft dough.

Turn dough out onto a lightly floured surface, and knead until smooth and elastic (about 8 to 10 minutes). Place in a bowl coated with cooking spray, turning to grease top. Cover and let rise in a warm place (85°), free from drafts, 1 hour or until doubled in bulk.

Punch dough down, and turn out onto a lightly floured surface; roll into a 16-inch circle, and cut into 20 wedges. Roll up each wedge tightly, beginning at wide end. Seal points; place rolls, point side down, on baking sheets coated with cooking spray. Cover and let rise in a warm place (85°), free from drafts, 45 minutes or until doubled in bulk. Bake at 400° for 15 to 18 minutes or until lightly browned. Yield: 20 rolls (103 calories each).

PRO 2.9 / FAT 3.1 / CARB 16.0 / FIB 0.2 / CHOL 14 / SOD 75 / POT 85

MUSHROOM-SWISS CHEESE ROLLS

1 cup skim milk
¼ cup unsalted margarine
¼ cup honey
½ teaspoon salt
1 teaspoon dried whole thyme
1 package dry yeast
1 egg
3½ cups unbleached or all-purpose flour, divided
2 cups sliced fresh mushrooms
1 cup (4 ounces) finely shredded Swiss cheese
Vegetable cooking spray

Combine milk, margarine, and honey in a small saucepan. Cook over low heat until margarine melts; let cool to 105° to 115°.

Combine milk mixture in a large bowl with salt, thyme, yeast, egg, and 1 cup flour; beat at low speed of an electric mixer until moistened. Beat at medium speed 3 minutes. Stir in mushrooms and enough remaining flour to make a soft dough.

Turn dough out onto a lightly floured surface, and knead in cheese. Knead until smooth and elastic (about 4 to 6 minutes). Place in a bowl coated with cooking spray, turning to grease top. Cover and let rise in a warm place (85°), free from drafts, 1 hour or until doubled in bulk.

Punch dough down, and divide into 4 portions. Shape each portion into 12 rolls, and place in two 13- x 9- x 2-inch baking pans coated with cooking spray. Cover and let rise in a warm place (85°), free from drafts, 45 minutes or until doubled in bulk. Bake at 350° for 25 to 30 minutes or until golden brown. Yield: 4 dozen (56 calories each).

PRO 2.0 / FAT 1.8 / CARB 8.3 / FIB 0.0 / CHOL 8 / SOD 35 / POT 38

Carbohydrates are the most efficient energy foods. Some athletes involved in endurance activities, such as marathon running or cross-country skiing, often rely on a diet-exercise technique called carbohydrate loading to maximize the amount of stored energy. The process begins 1 week before an event with the athlete eating a diet of 70 percent to 80 percent carbohydrates and training as usual. After three days, the athlete continues the high carbohydrate diet and either cuts back on training or terminates it until the event.

Carbo-loading is not recommended as a regular dietary pattern, but one could experiment before a prolonged or continuous activity by eating a concentrated diet of whole grains, pasta, and fresh fruit and vegetables. Remember, its effect will benefit your endurance, not your speed.

APPLE DANISH

½ cup sliced almonds
½ cup skim milk
½ cup unsweetened apple juice, divided
¼ cup plus 2 tablespoons honey, divided
¼ cup unsalted margarine
4½ cups unbleached or all-purpose
   flour
½ teaspoon salt
½ teaspoon ground cinnamon
2 eggs
1 package dry yeast
1 cup grated cooking apple
½ teaspoon almond extract
Vegetable cooking spray
Baked Apple Filling
1 egg white, beaten

Place almonds in an electric blender, and process until ground to a powder; set aside. Combine milk, ¼ cup apple juice, ¼ cup honey, and margarine in a saucepan, and cook until margarine melts; let cool to 105° to 115°. Combine almond powder, flour, salt, and cinnamon. Combine 2 cups almond-flour mixture with milk mixture, eggs, yeast, apple, and almond extract. Beat at medium speed of an electric mixer 3 minutes; stir in enough almond-flour mixture to make a smooth dough.

Turn dough out onto a lightly floured surface, and knead until smooth and elastic (about 8 to 10 minutes). Place in a bowl coated with cooking spray, turning to grease top. Cover and let rise in a warm place (85°), free from drafts, 1 hour or until doubled in bulk.

Punch dough down; turn out onto a lightly floured surface, and roll into a 24- x 16-inch rectangle. Cut into 4-inch squares. Spoon 2 tablespoons Baked Apple Filling onto center of each square, and fold corners toward center, overlapping slightly. Pinch corners and edges together to seal. Place pastries on 2 baking sheets coated with cooking spray; cover and let rise in a warm place (85°), free from drafts, 45 minutes or until doubled in bulk.

Brush pastries with egg white. Bake at 350° for 20 minutes. Combine remaining apple juice and honey in a small saucepan; cook until thoroughly heated. Brush hot pastries with glaze. Serve warm. Yield: 2 dozen (154 calories each).

Baked Apple Filling:

6½ cups sliced, peeled cooking apples
Vegetable cooking spray
1 tablespoon plus 1½ teaspoons brown sugar
1 teaspoon ground cinnamon
2½ teaspoons vanilla extract

Arrange apples in a deep baking dish coated with cooking spray. Combine remaining ingredients; sprinkle over apples, and toss. Cover and bake at 350° for 45 to 50 minutes or until softened. Yield: 3 cups (9 calories per tablespoon).

PRO 3.7 / FAT 3.8 / CARB 27.2 / FIB 0.9 / CHOL 23 / SOD 62 / POT 110

CINNAMON-ALMOND SWEET ROLLS

1 cup skim milk
¼ cup honey
3 tablespoons unsalted margarine, softened
¼ teaspoon salt
1 package dry yeast
1 egg
2½ to 3 cups unbleached or all-purpose flour,
   divided
Vegetable cooking spray
2 tablespoons unsalted margarine, melted
½ cup chopped almonds
2 tablespoons plus 1½ teaspoons brown sugar
½ teaspoon ground cinnamon
½ cup sifted powdered sugar
¼ teaspoon ground cinnamon
⅛ teaspoon ground nutmeg
1 tablespoon skim milk
¼ teaspoon almond extract

Combine first 3 ingredients in a saucepan; cook over low heat until margarine melts. Let cool to 105° to 115°. Combine milk mixture, salt, yeast, egg, and 1 cup flour; beat at low speed of an electric mixer until moistened. Beat at medium speed 3 minutes. Stir in enough flour to make a soft dough.

Turn dough out onto a lightly floured surface, and knead until smooth and elastic (about 8 to 10 minutes). Place in a bowl coated with cooking spray, turning to grease top. Cover and let rise in a warm place (85°), free from drafts, 1 hour or until doubled in bulk.

Punch dough down, and turn out onto a

lightly floured surface; roll into an 18- x 12-inch rectangle. Brush with 2 tablespoons melted margarine. Sprinkle with almonds, brown sugar, and ½ teaspoon cinnamon. Roll up dough, jellyroll fashion, beginning with long side. Pinch edges of seam together. Cut into ½-inch slices, and arrange in two 13- x 9- x 2-inch baking pans coated with cooking spray. Cover and let rise in a warm place (85°), free from drafts, 45 minutes or until doubled in bulk. Bake at 375° for 15 to 20 minutes or until lightly browned.

Combine powdered sugar, ¼ teaspoon cinnamon, and nutmeg in a bowl. Stir in 1 tablespoon milk and almond extract. Spread over hot rolls. Yield: 3 dozen (77 calories each).

PRO 1.0 / FAT 3.1 / CARB 11.0 / FIB 0.1 / CHOL 8 / SOD 40 / POT 46

OATMEAL FRENCH BREAD

3¼ cups regular oats, uncooked and divided
4½ to 4¾ cups unbleached or all-purpose flour, divided
2¼ cups warm water (105° to 115°)
2 packages dry yeast
¼ cup wheat germ
1 tablespoon brown sugar
½ teaspoon salt
1 tablespoon cornmeal
Vegetable cooking spray

Place 3 cups oats in container of an electric blender, and process until oats are ground to a powder. Combine oat powder and 2½ cups flour in a bowl; set aside. Combine 2 cups flour, water, yeast, wheat germ, sugar, and salt in a large bowl. Beat at medium speed of an electric mixer 3 minutes or until well combined. Stir in enough reserved oat-flour mixture to make a stiff dough.

Turn dough out onto a lightly floured surface, and knead until smooth and elastic (about 8 to 10 minutes). Place in a bowl coated with cooking spray, turning to grease top. Cover and let rise in a warm place (85°), free from drafts, 1 hour or until doubled in bulk.

Punch dough down; divide in half. Shape each half into a 14-inch loaf; place on a baking sheet coated with cooking spray and sprinkled with cornmeal. Make ¼-inch-deep diagonal slits

in loaves; cover and let rise in a warm place (85°), free from drafts, 45 minutes or until doubled in bulk. Brush loaves lightly with water; sprinkle with ¼ cup oats. Bake at 400° for 25 to 30 minutes or until loaves sound hollow when tapped. Yield: 2 (16-inch) loaves or 64 (½-inch) slices (47 calories per slice).

PRO 1.7 / FAT 0.4 / CARB 9.4 / FIB 0.6 / CHOL 0 / SOD 19 / POT 33

HONEY-GRAIN BREAD

2 packages dry yeast
½ cup warm water (105° to 115°)
½ cup plus 2 tablespoons honey, divided
1 cup skim milk
¼ cup unsalted margarine
1 egg, beaten
½ cup bulgur wheat, uncooked
½ cup wheat germ
1 teaspoon salt
½ teaspoon ground nutmeg
1½ cups whole wheat flour
4¼ cups unbleached or all-purpose flour, divided
Vegetable cooking spray

Dissolve yeast in warm water in a large bowl; add 2 tablespoons honey, and let stand 5 minutes or until foamy. Combine remaining ½ cup honey, milk, and margarine in a saucepan. Cook over low heat until margarine melts; let cool to 105° to 115°. Add milk mixture, egg, bulgur, wheat germ, salt, nutmeg, whole wheat flour, and 2 cups unbleached flour to yeast mixture. Stir in enough remaining unbleached flour to make a stiff dough.

Turn dough out onto a lightly floured surface, and knead until smooth and elastic (about 8 to 10 minutes). Place in a large bowl coated with cooking spray, turning to grease top. Cover and let rise in a warm place (85°), free from drafts, 1 hour or until doubled in bulk.

Punch dough down, and divide in half; shape each half into a loaf. Place loaves in two 8½- x 4½- x 3-inch loafpans coated with cooking spray. Repeat rising procedure 45 minutes or until doubled in bulk. Bake at 350° for 30 to 35 minutes or until browned. Yield: 2 loaves or 34 (½-inch) slices (118 calories per slice).

PRO 3.6 / FAT 2.0 / CARB 22.8 / FIB 0.6 / CHOL 8 / SOD 76 / POT 80

PULL-APART RYE LOAF

1 package dry yeast
¼ cup warm water (105° to 115°)
3 tablespoons light molasses, divided
1¾ cups skim milk
¼ cup unsalted margarine
1 teaspoon salt
1 teaspoon caraway seeds
3 cups unbleached or all-purpose flour, divided
2 cups rye flour
Vegetable cooking spray

Dissolve yeast in warm water in a large bowl; add 1 tablespoon molasses, and let stand 5 minutes or until foamy.

Combine milk, margarine, and 2 tablespoons molasses in a small saucepan. Cook over low heat until margarine melts; set aside and let cool to 105° to 115°. Add cooled milk mixture, salt, caraway seeds, and 2 cups unbleached flour to yeast mixture, stirring until well combined. Combine remaining unbleached flour and rye flour, and add enough to yeast mixture to make a stiff dough.

Turn out onto a floured surface, and knead until smooth and elastic (about 5 minutes). Place in a large bowl coated with cooking spray, turning to grease top. Cover and let rise in warm place (85°), free from drafts, 1 hour or until doubled in bulk.

Punch dough down, and divide in half. Divide each half into 17 equal balls. Place a row of 6 balls along each long side of a 9- x 5- x 3-inch loafpan coated with cooking spray. Place a row of 5 balls down center. Repeat with other half of dough in a second loafpan. Cover and let rise in warm place (85°), free from drafts, 45 minutes or until doubled in bulk. Bake at 375° for 30 to 35 minutes. Let cool in pans 10 minutes. Remove from pans, and cool completely on wire racks. Yield: 2 loaves or 34 (½-inch) slices (71 calories per slice).

PRO 2.0 / FAT 1.4 / CARB 12.8 / FIB 0.2 / CHOL 0 / SOD 72 / POT 60

GREEN ONION RYE BREAD

½ cup water
1 teaspoon chicken-flavored bouillon granules
2 cups minced green onion
1 cup skim milk
¼ cup unsalted margarine
¼ cup light molasses
2 cups unbleached or all-purpose flour
2 tablespoons brown sugar
2 packages dry yeast
1 teaspoon dried whole rosemary
½ teaspoon salt
4½ cups rye flour
Vegetable cooking spray

Combine water, bouillon granules, and green onion in a saucepan. Cover and cook 5 minutes or until onion is tender; set aside to cool.

Combine milk, margarine, and molasses in a small saucepan; cook over low heat, stirring occasionally, until margarine melts. Set aside, and let cool to 105° to 115°.

Combine milk mixture, reserved green onion mixture, unbleached flour, sugar, yeast, rosemary, and salt in a large bowl. Beat at low speed of an electric mixer until moistened. Beat at medium speed 3 minutes. Stir in enough rye flour to make a stiff dough.

Turn dough out onto a lightly floured surface, and knead until smooth and elastic (about 8 to 10 minutes). Place in a large bowl coated with cooking spray, turning to grease top. Cover and let rise in a warm place (85°), free from drafts, 45 minutes or until doubled in bulk.

Punch dough down. Turn dough out onto a lightly floured surface, and divide in half. Shape each half into a round loaf, and place on a baking sheet coated with cooking spray. Cover and let rise in a warm place (85°), free from drafts, 45 minutes or until doubled in bulk. Cut 3 slashes, ¼-inch deep, in top of loaf.

Bake at 350° for 40 to 45 minutes or until browned. Cut each loaf into 16 wedges. Yield: 2 loaves or 32 wedges (97 calories per wedge).

PRO 2.4 / FAT 1.6 / CARB 18.3 / FIB 0.6 / CHOL 0 / SOD 54 / POT 90

Made with a touch of red wine, honey, and mozzarella cheese, Eggplant Bread tastes just as good as it looks.

EGGPLANT BREAD

1½ cups finely chopped, peeled eggplant
½ cup finely chopped onion
¾ cup dry red wine
¾ teaspoon dried whole oregano
¾ teaspoon dried whole basil
1 cup plus 2 tablespoons skim milk
2 tablespoons unsalted margarine
1 tablespoon plus 1½ teaspoons honey
1 package dry yeast
¼ teaspoon salt
1 egg white
3½ cups unbleached or all-purpose flour, divided
Vegetable cooking spray
¾ cup (3 ounces) finely shredded part-skim
   mozzarella cheese

Combine first 5 ingredients in a saucepan, and bring to a boil. Cover; reduce heat, and simmer 5 minutes. Drain well; set aside.

Combine milk, margarine, and honey in a small saucepan. Cook over low heat until margarine melts, and let cool to 105° to 115°. Combine milk mixture, yeast, salt, egg white, and 1 cup flour in a large bowl. Beat at low speed of an electric mixer just until dry ingredients are moistened. Beat at medium speed 3 minutes.

Stir in enough remaining flour to make a soft dough.

Turn dough out onto a lightly floured surface, and knead until smooth and elastic (about 8 to 10 minutes). Place in a bowl coated with cooking spray, turning to grease top. Cover and let rise in a warm place (85°), free from drafts, 1 hour or until doubled in bulk.

Punch dough down, and divide in half. Roll each half into an 18- x 10-inch rectangle. Spread half of eggplant mixture on each rectangle, leaving a ½-inch border on all sides; sprinkle with cheese. Roll up dough jellyroll fashion, beginning with long side. Pinch edges of seam together, and seal ends.

Place 2 rolls side by side on a baking sheet coated with cooking spray; twist rolls together several times. Shape twisted roll into a ring, pinching ends together. Cover and let rise in a warm place (85°), free from drafts, 45 minutes to 1 hour or until doubled in bulk. Bake at 400° for 30 to 35 minutes or until golden brown. Slice with an electric knife. Yield: 1 ring or 50 (½-inch) slices (46 calories per slice).

PRO 1.7 / FAT 0.8 / CARB 7.5 / FIB 0.1 / CHOL 1 / SOD 25 / POT 46

SAUSAGE AND PEPPER BRAID

1 cup skim milk
2 tablespoons unsalted margarine
2 tablespoons honey
1 package dry yeast
1 tablespoon dried whole sage
¼ teaspoon salt
1 egg
3½ to 4 cups unbleached or all-purpose flour, divided
Vegetable cooking spray
1 pound sweet Italian sausage, cooked and well drained
1 cup finely chopped green pepper
1 cup finely chopped red pepper

Combine milk, margarine, and honey in a small saucepan. Cook over low heat until margarine melts; let cool to 105° to 115°. Combine milk mixture, yeast, sage, salt, egg, and 1 cup flour in a large bowl; beat at low speed of an electric mixer until moistened. Beat at medium speed 3 minutes. Stir in enough remaining flour to make a soft dough.

Turn dough out onto a lightly floured surface, and knead until smooth and elastic (about 8 to 10 minutes). Place in a large bowl coated with cooking spray, turning to grease top. Cover and let rise in a warm place (85°), free from drafts, 1 hour or until doubled in bulk.

Punch dough down, and divide into 3 equal portions. Roll 1 portion into an 18- x 10-inch rectangle. Sprinkle with sausage, and roll up jellyroll fashion, starting with long side. Pinch edges of seam together; set aside. Repeat procedure with second portion of dough, sprinkling dough with green pepper; set aside. Repeat procedure with remaining dough, sprinkling with red pepper.

Place dough rolls on a baking sheet coated with cooking spray. Braid dough rolls together, gently stretching to 22 inches in length. Fold ends under.

Cover and let rise in a warm place (85°), free from drafts, 45 minutes or until doubled in bulk. Bake at 400° for 20 minutes or until golden brown. Cool 10 minutes. Slice with an electric knife; serve warm. Yield: 1 (20-inch) loaf or 26 (¾-inch) slices (119 calories per slice).

PRO 5.0 / FAT 4.6 / CARB 14.4 / FIB 0.1 / CHOL 21 / SOD 150 / POT 106

BROWN RICE PILAF

¾ cup diced onion
1 (10¾-ounce) can chicken broth, undiluted and divided
1⅓ cups water
1 cup brown rice, uncooked
¾ cup finely chopped red pepper
¾ cup finely chopped green pepper
¼ teaspoon dried whole thyme

Combine onion and ¼ cup chicken broth in a 2-quart ceramic ovenproof dish; cover and cook over medium heat 3 minutes or until onion is translucent, stirring frequently. Stir in remaining ingredients, and bring to a boil. Remove from heat. Cover and bake at 350° for 50 minutes or until liquid is absorbed. Yield: 8 servings (102 calories per ½-cup serving).

PRO 2.9 / FAT 0.8 / CARB 20.7 / FIB 2.1 / CHOL 0 / SOD 124 / POT 162

MUSHROOM RISOTTO

2 cups sliced fresh mushrooms
2 tablespoons minced shallot
1 tablespoon lemon juice
Vegetable cooking spray
1 cup Italian Arborio rice
2 cups hot water
1 teaspoon chicken-flavored bouillon granules
2 tablespoons grated Parmesan cheese
¼ teaspoon pepper

Combine mushrooms, shallot, and lemon juice in a nonstick saucepan coated with cooking spray. Cover and cook over medium heat 5 minutes or until tender, stirring occasionally. Stir in rice, and cook 3 minutes, stirring occasionally.

Combine hot water and bouillon granules; add ½ cup bouillon mixture to saucepan. Cook 2 to 3 minutes or until liquid is absorbed, stirring occasionally. Repeat procedure with remaining bouillon mixture, adding ½ cup at a time and making sure each portion is absorbed before adding the next.

Remove from heat; stir in cheese and pepper. Spoon into a serving bowl to serve. Yield: 6 servings (138 calories per ½-cup serving).

PRO 3.6 / FAT 0.8 / CARB 28.8 / FIB 1.0 / CHOL 1 / SOD 98 / POT 136

FRUITED WILD RICE

1 cup wild rice, uncooked
4 cups water
½ teaspoon salt
¼ pound pearl onions, peeled
1 (10¾-ounce) can chicken broth, undiluted
¼ cup currants
¼ cup golden raisins

Wash rice in cold water several times, and drain well. Bring water and salt to a boil in a medium saucepan; add rice. Cover; reduce heat, and simmer 1 hour. Drain and set aside.

Combine onions and broth in a medium saucepan; bring to a boil. Cover; reduce heat, and simmer 25 minutes or until tender. Add currants, raisins, and reserved rice; cover and cook over low heat 2 to 3 minutes or until thoroughly heated, stirring occasionally. Spoon into a serving bowl to serve. Yield: 7 servings (125 calories per ½-cup serving).

PRO 4.7 / FAT 0.6 / CARB 26.8 / FIB 0.5 / CHOL 0 / SOD 310 / POT 209

COUSCOUS WITH VEGETABLES

¼ pound carrots, scraped and cut into
    julienne strips (about ¾ cup)
½ pound fresh asparagus, trimmed and
    cut into 1-inch pieces (about 1 cup)
¾ cup diagonally sliced zucchini
1 cup fresh snow peas
1 teaspoon unsalted margarine, melted
¼ cup golden raisins
½ teaspoon curry powder
¼ teaspoon ground cinnamon
¼ teaspoon dried whole thyme
¾ cup water
2 teaspoons unsalted margarine
¼ teaspoon salt
1 cup couscous, uncooked

Cook carrots in boiling water in a medium saucepan 8 minutes or until crisp-tender; drain and transfer to a large bowl. Cook asparagus in boiling water in saucepan 3 minutes or until crisp-tender; drain and transfer to bowl. Cook zucchini in boiling water in saucepan 2 minutes or until crisp-tender; drain and transfer to bowl. Cook snow peas in boiling water in saucepan 1 minute; drain and transfer to bowl. Toss vegetables with 1 teaspoon margarine, raisins, curry powder, cinnamon, and thyme; set aside, and keep warm.

Bring ¾ cup water, 2 teaspoons margarine, and salt to a boil in saucepan; remove from heat, and add couscous. Toss couscous 3 minutes or until water is absorbed.

Arrange couscous on a platter, and top with vegetable mixture. Yield: 8 servings (70 calories per serving).

PRO 2.4 / FAT 1.1 / CARB 13.7 / FIB 0.9 / CHOL 0 / SOD 83 / POT 276

BAKED CHEESE GRITS

2 cups water
¼ teaspoon salt
½ cup quick-cooking grits, uncooked
½ cup (2 ounces) shredded extra-sharp Cheddar
    cheese
1 egg, beaten
¼ cup skim milk
¼ teaspoon freshly ground black pepper
⅛ teaspoon Worcestershire sauce
Vegetable cooking spray

Bring water and salt to a boil in a saucepan. Stir in grits; cover and reduce heat to low. Cook 5 minutes or until done, stirring occasionally.

Combine grits with next 5 ingredients, mixing well; pour into a 1-quart baking dish coated with cooking spray. Bake at 350° for 40 to 50 minutes or until lightly browned. Yield: 6 servings (100 calories per ½-cup serving).

PRO 4.8 / FAT 4.2 / CARB 10.8 / FIB 0.1 / CHOL 56 / SOD 174 / POT 52

Pasta, in all its variety, packs a great complex-carbohydrate punch. Plus, it's high in protein and low in fat and sodium. It is an economical source of nutrition, particularly if a good commercial enriched pasta is used. And if you don't use pasta as an excuse to eat rich sauces, it is not especially fattening. Pasta is usually made from flour and water, but noodle products made with eggs also fall in this category. The flour that is most often used is Semolina, a high-protein variety that provides B vitamins and iron.

VEGETABLE BULGUR

1 (10¾-ounce) can chicken broth, undiluted
½ cup diced onion
½ cup diced leek
½ cup diced celery
1⅓ cups water
1 cup bulgur wheat, uncooked
⅛ teaspoon pepper

Combine first 4 ingredients in a 2-quart saucepan; cover and cook over medium heat 6 minutes. Add water, and bring to a boil. Add bulgur. Cover; reduce heat, and simmer 20 minutes. Uncover and simmer 3 to 5 minutes or until liquid is absorbed. Season with pepper, and spoon into serving bowl. Yield: 6 servings (120 calories per ½-cup serving).

PRO 4.6 / FAT 0.8 / CARB 24.2 / FIB 0.8 / CHOL 0 / SOD 173 / POT 174

RIGATONI WITH CURRIED VEGETABLES

½ (16-ounce) package rigatoni or other tubular pasta
1⅓ cups chopped green onion
1 medium carrot, scraped and coarsely grated
1 medium-size green pepper, seeded and cut into julienne strips
1 medium zucchini, coarsely grated
½ cup water
½ teaspoon chicken-flavored bouillon granules
2 cups cauliflower flowerets
1 cup broccoli flowerets
2 teaspoons curry powder
¾ cup plain low-fat yogurt
¼ cup sour cream
2 tablespoons minced fresh parsley or coriander
1 tablespoon lemon juice

Cook rigatoni according to package directions, omitting salt; drain well. Set aside, and keep warm.

Combine green onion, carrot, green pepper, zucchini, water, and bouillon granules in a Dutch oven; bring to a boil. Reduce heat, and cook, uncovered, 5 minutes, stirring occasionally. Add cauliflower and broccoli; simmer 5 minutes or until tender. Stir in curry powder; simmer 2 minutes. Stir in remaining ingredients,

and cook over medium-low heat until thoroughly heated, stirring occasionally. (Do not boil.) Serve over warm pasta. Yield: 8 side-dish servings (160 calories per serving).

PRO 6.4 / FAT 2.5 / CARB 28.8 / FIB 2.0 / CHOL 4 / SOD 55 / POT 383

SPAGHETTI WITH SPRING VEGETABLES

1 (16-ounce) package spaghetti
¼ pound fresh green beans
Vegetable cooking spray
1 medium onion, thinly sliced
1 clove garlic, minced
1 medium carrot, scraped and coarsely grated
1 medium-size red or green pepper, seeded and cut into julienne strips
½ cup water
½ teaspoon chicken-flavored bouillon granules
¼ pound fresh asparagus, cut into ¾-inch pieces
½ cup fresh English peas
½ cup plain low-fat yogurt
½ cup sour cream
2 tablespoons lemon juice
⅓ cup minced fresh parsley
1 tablespoon minced chives
¼ teaspoon dried whole tarragon or 1 tablespoon minced fresh tarragon
¼ teaspoon dried whole basil or 1 tablespoon minced fresh basil
⅛ teaspoon pepper

Cook spaghetti according to package directions, omitting salt; drain well. Set aside, and keep warm.

Remove strings from beans, and cut into ¾-inch pieces; set aside. Coat a large Dutch oven with cooking spray; place over medium heat until hot. Add onion and garlic, and sauté 5 minutes or until tender. Add carrot and red pepper; cook 2 minutes, stirring constantly. Add water, bouillon granules, asparagus, peas, and green beans; cook, covered, 8 minutes or until vegetables are crisp-tender. Add remaining ingredients; cook until thoroughly heated, stirring frequently. (Do not allow sauce to boil.) Serve over warm pasta. Yield: 16 side-dish servings (140 calories per serving).

PRO 5.0 / FAT 2.1 / CARB 25.4 / FIB 1.4 / CHOL 4 / SOD 29 / POT 179

Even if you're dieting, you can enjoy pasta and rice in a wide variety of sizes, shapes, and types.

WHOLE WHEAT FETTUCCINE WITH VEGETABLES

½ (16-ounce) package whole wheat fettuccine
4 cups broccoli flowerets
4 cups cauliflower flowerets
Vegetable cooking spray
2 cloves garlic, minced
1 medium onion, sliced
½ teaspoon crushed red pepper
½ teaspoon dried whole basil
¼ teaspoon dried whole oregano
½ cup dry white wine
½ cup water
½ teaspoon chicken-flavored bouillon granules
¼ cup pine nuts, toasted
2 tablespoons minced fresh parsley

Cook fettuccine according to package directions, omitting salt. Drain and keep warm.

Bring 4 inches of water to a boil in a large Dutch oven; add broccoli and cauliflower, and return to a boil. Drain and set aside.

Coat a large skillet with cooking spray; place over medium heat until hot. Add garlic, and sauté 30 seconds. Add onion, pepper, basil, and oregano. Cook until onion is golden, stirring occasionally. Add wine, water, and bouillon granules; boil 1 minute. Add broccoli and cauliflower; return to a boil. Cover; reduce heat, and simmer 5 minutes.

Combine vegetable mixture and warm noodles in a large bowl, tossing gently. Sprinkle with pine nuts and parsley. Serve warm. Yield: 8 side-dish servings (168 calories per serving).

PRO 6.8 / FAT 5.8 / CARB 26.1 / FIB 1.9 / CHOL 0 / SOD 46 / POT 515

VERMICELLI WITH TOMATO-BASIL SAUCE

½ (16-ounce) package vermicelli
Vegetable cooking spray
2 cloves garlic, minced
1 medium onion, thinly sliced
5 medium tomatoes, peeled and chopped
1 (8-ounce) can unsalted tomato sauce
1 tablespoon dried whole basil or ¼ cup
  minced fresh basil
⅛ teaspoon pepper
2 tablespoons grated Parmesan cheese

Cook vermicelli according to package directions, omitting salt; drain and set aside.

Coat a Dutch oven with cooking spray; place over medium heat until hot. Add garlic and onion; sauté 5 minutes or until tender. Stir in tomato, tomato sauce, basil, and pepper; simmer 15 minutes. Stir in vermicelli, and cook over low heat until thoroughly heated, stirring occasionally. Transfer to a large platter, and sprinkle with Parmesan cheese to serve. Yield: 8 side-dish servings (143 calories per serving).

PRO 5.4 / FAT 0.9 / CARB 28.5 / FIB 0.9 / CHOL 1 / SOD 33 / POT 264

LINGUINE WITH RED CLAM SAUCE

Vegetable cooking spray
1 cup chopped onion
1 clove garlic, minced
1 (6-ounce) can tomato paste
1 cup diced tomato
1 teaspoon dried whole basil
1 teaspoon dried whole oregano
⅛ teaspoon pepper
1 bay leaf
½ cup dry red wine
2 (6½-ounce) cans minced clams, rinsed
  and drained
½ (16-ounce) package linguine

Coat a medium skillet with cooking spray, and place over low heat until hot. Add onion and garlic; sauté 5 minutes. Add next 7 ingredients. Bring to a boil. Cover; reduce heat, and simmer 30 minutes. Add clams; cover and simmer 30 minutes. Discard bay leaf.

Cook linguine according to package directions, omitting salt and fat; drain.

Combine red clam sauce and linguine in a large bowl, tossing gently. Serve immediately. Yield: 4 main-dish servings (311 calories per serving).

PRO 15.4 / FAT 2.2 / CARB 58.4 / FIB 2.7 / CHOL 22 / SOD 78 / POT 760

ZITI SALAD WITH AVOCADO SAUCE

1 (16-ounce) package ziti
¾ cup plain low-fat yogurt
1 medium-size green chile pepper, seeded
  and minced
¼ cup minced fresh parsley or coriander
3 tablespoons lemon juice
1 clove garlic, minced
¼ teaspoon salt
⅛ teaspoon pepper
1 medium avocado, cubed and divided
1 medium-size red or green pepper, seeded
  and chopped
2 medium tomatoes, seeded and chopped
½ cup minced green onion

Cook ziti according to package directions, omitting salt; drain and set aside.

Combine yogurt, chile pepper, parsley, lemon juice, garlic, salt, pepper, and ½ cup avocado in container of an electric blender; process until pureed. Combine avocado sauce and ziti in a large bowl; add remaining avocado, red pepper, tomato, and green onion; toss gently. Cover and chill 1 to 2 hours. Yield: 8 main-dish servings (278 calories per serving).

PRO 9.3 / FAT 5.0 / CARB 49.6 / FIB 2.8 / CHOL 1 / SOD 97 / POT 452

Fish and shellfish have surged in popularity because of their low-fat benefits. With only 123 calories per serving, Spinach-Stuffed Flounder (page 126) is particularly appealing.

SESAME-BAKED BLUEFISH

2 tablespoons water
1½ teaspoons vegetable oil
1 teaspoon minced, peeled gingerroot
1 clove garlic
½ teaspoon lemon juice
½ teaspoon reduced-sodium soy sauce
¼ teaspoon crushed red pepper
1½ pounds bluefish fillets, skinned
¼ cup sesame seeds, toasted
Vegetable cooking spray
¼ teaspoon paprika
2 tablespoons minced fresh parsley

Combine first 7 ingredients in container of an electric blender, and process until smooth. Arrange bluefish fillets in a single layer in a large shallow dish; pour marinade over fillets, and turn to coat well. Cover and marinate in refrigerator at least 1 hour.

Remove fillets from marinade, and coat on both sides with sesame seeds. Arrange fillets in a single layer in a broiler pan coated with cooking spray; bake at 400° for 5 minutes. Turn oven to broil, and broil 3 to 4 inches from heat 3 to 5 minutes or until fillets flake easily when tested with a fork. Carefully transfer fish to a platter; sprinkle with paprika, and garnish with parsley before serving. Yield: 6 servings (180 calories per serving).

PRO 24.4 / FAT 8.0 / CARB 1.8 / FIB 0.3 / CHOL 62 / SOD 101 / POT 510

CREOLE CATFISH

6 medium catfish (about 3 pounds), cleaned and
    dressed
¼ cup water
2 tablespoons hot sauce
¼ cup self-rising cornmeal
¼ cup all-purpose flour
2 tablespoons unsalted margarine
Vegetable cooking spray

Place catfish in a large shallow baking dish. Combine water and hot sauce; pour over catfish. Cover and marinate in refrigerator at least 2 hours, turning fish over after 1 hour.

Combine cornmeal and flour in a medium mixing bowl. Remove catfish from marinade, discarding marinade. Dredge catfish in cornmeal mixture.

Melt margarine in a large skillet coated with cooking spray over medium-high heat. Add catfish, and cook until browned on both sides. Transfer to a large baking pan coated with cooking spray. Bake at 450° for 10 minutes or until catfish flakes easily when tested with a fork. Transfer to a platter to serve. Yield: 6 servings (307 calories per serving).

PRO 41.0 / FAT 11.0 / CARB 8.4 / FIB 0.5 / CHOL 0 / SOD 248 / POT 100

SPINACH-STUFFED FLOUNDER

1 (10-ounce) package frozen chopped spinach,
    thawed
Vegetable cooking spray
½ cup minced onion
1 clove garlic, minced
¼ teaspoon dried whole thyme
¼ teaspoon pepper
3 tablespoons sour cream
1½ pounds flounder or sole fillets
2 tablespoons dry white wine
Lemon wedges

Place spinach between paper towels, and squeeze until barely moist; set aside.

Coat a heavy saucepan with cooking spray; place over low heat until hot. Add onion and garlic; cover and cook over low heat 10 minutes or until soft, stirring occasionally. Add spinach, thyme, and pepper; cook over low heat until thoroughly heated, stirring constantly. Remove from heat, and let stand 10 minutes; stir in sour cream.

Place fillets, skin side up, on a cutting board; cut in half lengthwise. Flatten fillets slightly for uniform thickness, using a meat mallet or rolling pin. Spread 2 tablespoons spinach filling on one-third of each fillet. Starting at narrow end, roll up fillets jellyroll fashion; secure with wooden picks.

Place rolls in a baking dish coated with cooking spray; add wine. Cover and bake at 350° for 20 minutes or until fillets flake easily when tested with a fork. Garnish with lemon wedges. Yield: 6 servings (123 calories per serving).

PRO 20.8 / FAT 2.6 / CARB 3.7 / FIB 1.1 / CHOL 60 / SOD 128 / POT 581

DIJON-BROILED GROUPER

3 tablespoons Dijon mustard
1 tablespoon sliced green onion
¼ teaspoon coarsely ground black pepper
1½ pounds fresh or frozen grouper fillets
Vegetable cooking spray
1 tablespoon unsalted margarine, melted

Combine first 3 ingredients in a small bowl; set aside.

Thaw fillets if frozen; remove skin, and cut into serving size pieces. Place fillets on a broiler pan coated with cooking spray. Brush with margarine, and broil 4 inches from heat 8 minutes. Remove from oven, and turn fillets. Spread mustard mixture over fillets, and broil 3 minutes or until mixture is thoroughly heated and fillets flake easily when tested with a fork. Transfer to a platter to serve. Yield: 6 servings (125 calories per serving).

PRO 21.9 / FAT 2.9 / CARB 0.6 / FIB 0.0 / CHOL 62 / SOD 292 / POT 357

If you're weight conscious and concerned about fat, fish is an excellent food choice. Fish is low in cholesterol, fat, and calories, and, at the same time, is an optimum protein source.

Fish is classified as either lean (having a fat content of less than 5 percent) or fatty (having a fat content of more than 5 percent). Fatty fish will be slightly higher in calories than lean fish. But the good news is that the fat in all fish is largely polyunsaturated, a real bonus if you want to reduce the amount of saturated fat in your meals. Generally, fatty fish is darker than lean fish, and if you want to substitute the type of fish in a recipe, remember that the flavor of fatty fish is stronger than lean fish. Both types can be baked, broiled, poached, steamed, or grilled for lighter eating. Some favorites among the fatty fish are mackerel, lake trout, salmon, tuna, and herring. Lean favorites include cod, flounder, haddock, halibut, ocean perch, pompano, red snapper, scamp, and sole.

Try experimenting with lesser known varieties of fish, and you might be pleasantly surprised. Amberjack, orange roughy, redfish, and triggerfish will taste like those varieties that are more familiar to you, and some may be available at a lower price.

HALIBUT WITH VEGETABLE SAUCE

½ cup chopped green pepper
½ cup chopped onion
½ cup water
1 teaspoon chicken-flavored bouillon
   granules
½ cup chopped fresh parsley
½ teaspoon dried whole oregano
1 (16-ounce) can whole tomatoes,
   undrained and chopped
8 (4-ounce) halibut steaks, about ¾-inch thick

Place green pepper, onion, water, and bouillon granules in a saucepan; bring to a boil. Cover; reduce heat, and simmer 5 minutes or until vegetables are tender. Remove from heat; stir in parsley, oregano, and tomatoes.

Place halibut steaks in a single layer in a 13- x 9- x 2-inch baking dish; spoon vegetable mixture over halibut steaks. Bake, uncovered, at 350° for 30 minutes or until halibut steaks flake easily when tested with a fork. Yield: 8 servings (129 calories per serving).

PRO 23.3 / FAT 1.7 / CARB 4.2 / FIB 0.2 / CHOL 57 / SOD 318 / POT 692

LEMON-GRILLED ORANGE ROUGHY

½ teaspoon grated lemon rind
2 tablespoons lemon juice
1 tablespoon unsalted margarine,
   melted
½ teaspoon dried whole thyme
¼ teaspoon salt
¼ teaspoon paprika
Dash of garlic powder
4 (4-ounce) orange roughy fillets
4 slices lemon

Combine lemon rind, juice, margarine, thyme, salt, paprika, and garlic powder in a small bowl. Brush fillets with lemon mixture.

Grill fillets 4 to 6 inches from hot coals 5 minutes on each side or until fillets flake easily when tested with a fork. Baste often with lemon mixture. Transfer to a platter, and garnish with lemon slices. Yield: 4 servings (204 calories per serving).

PRO 21.5 / FAT 12.1 / CARB 0.9 / FIB 0.1 / CHOL 62 / SOD 206 / POT 354

GRILLED POMPANO

2 tablespoons unsalted margarine,
  melted
1 tablespoon lemon juice
½ teaspoon dried whole tarragon,
  crushed
¼ teaspoon pepper
1½ pounds pompano fillets
½ cup fine, dry breadcrumbs
Vegetable cooking spray

Combine first 4 ingredients in a bowl. Brush fillets with margarine mixture, and dredge in breadcrumbs. Arrange on rack in a broiler pan coated with cooking spray, and broil 4 to 6 inches from heat 8 minutes or until lightly browned and fillets flake easily when tested with a fork. Transfer to a platter to serve. Yield: 6 servings (255 calories per serving).

PRO 22.4 / FAT 14.9 / CARB 6.4 / FIB 0.0 / CHOL 63 / SOD 115 / POT 235

BROILED SALMON WITH ASPARAGUS

1 pound fresh asparagus, diagonally sliced
2 tablespoons unsalted margarine, melted
1 teaspoon lemon juice
6 (4-ounce) salmon steaks, about ¾-inch thick
Vegetable cooking spray
⅛ teaspoon salt
⅛ teaspoon pepper
2 tablespoons minced fresh chives or parsley
1 lemon, cut into wedges

Cook asparagus in boiling water 5 minutes or until crisp-tender; drain. Return to saucepan; keep warm. Combine margarine and lemon juice. Arrange steaks in a broiler pan coated with cooking spray. Brush with half of lemon mixture; sprinkle with salt and pepper. Broil 3 to 4 inches from heat 5 minutes or until fish flakes easily when tested with a fork.

Add remaining lemon mixture to asparagus; cook until thoroughly heated. Stir in chives, and spoon over salmon steaks. Garnish with lemon. Yield: 6 servings (261 calories per serving).

PRO 25.6 / FAT 16.3 / CARB 2.9 / FIB 0.8 / CHOL 37 / SOD 105 / POT 710

BAKED RED SNAPPER

1 (2½-pound) dressed red snapper, head
  and tail intact
2 cloves garlic, minced
1½ teaspoons minced, peeled gingerroot
1 teaspoon reduced-sodium soy sauce
½ teaspoon white wine vinegar
1 teaspoon sesame oil
Vegetable cooking spray
2 tablespoons minced fresh parsley

Make 3 deep diagonal slashes on both sides of snapper. Combine garlic, gingerroot, soy sauce, vinegar, and oil in a bowl; rub mixture on inside and outside of snapper.

Place snapper in a 15½- x 10½- x 1-inch jellyroll pan coated with cooking spray. Cover tail loosely with aluminum foil, and bake at 325° for 40 to 50 minutes or until snapper flakes easily when tested with a fork. Transfer snapper to a platter, and garnish with parsley. Yield: 8 servings (139 calories per serving).

PRO 22.6 / FAT 1.6 / CARB 0.4 / FIB 0.0 / CHOL 62 / SOD 43 / POT 371

SNAPPER CREOLE

Vegetable cooking spray
1 teaspoon vegetable oil
1½ cups thinly sliced onion
2 cloves garlic, minced
1 medium-size green or red pepper, seeded and cut into julienne strips
2 medium tomatoes, peeled and coarsely chopped
2 tablespoons dry white wine
½ teaspoon dried whole thyme
½ teaspoon paprika
½ teaspoon pepper
¼ teaspoon crushed red pepper
1½ pounds red snapper fillets, skinned
2 tablespoons minced fresh chives or parsley
1 teaspoon lemon juice

Coat a large skillet with cooking spray; add oil, and place over medium heat until hot. Add onion and garlic; sauté 6 minutes or until tender, stirring occasionally. Add green pepper, and sauté 2 minutes. Add next 6 ingredients, and cook over low heat 8 to 10 minutes or until tomato is softened, stirring often.

Push vegetables to one side of skillet; add fillets to skillet in a single layer. Spoon vegetable mixture over fillets. Cover and cook over low heat 8 minutes or until fillets flake easily when tested with a fork. Transfer to a serving platter; sprinkle with chives and lemon juice. Yield: 6 servings (139 calories per serving).

PRO 23.5 / FAT 2.1 / CARB 6.0 / FIB 0.9 / CHOL 62 / SOD 24 / POT 559

BAKED SOLE WITH MUSHROOM SAUCE

Vegetable cooking spray
2 teaspoons unsalted margarine
¾ cup minced onion
1 tablespoon all-purpose flour
1 pound fresh mushrooms, sliced
2 tablespoons water
3 tablespoons dry white wine, divided
¼ cup thinly sliced green onion
1½ pounds sole or flounder fillets, cut into serving-size pieces
⅛ teaspoon pepper

Coat a heavy skillet with cooking spray; add margarine, and place over low heat until melted. Add onion; cover and cook 8 minutes or until tender, stirring occasionally. Add flour, stirring until smooth. Cook 1 minute, stirring constantly. Add mushrooms, water, and 1 tablespoon wine; cook over medium heat 5 to 7 minutes or until mushrooms are tender, stirring constantly and adding additional water, if necessary, to prevent sticking. Stir in green onion. Cover; remove from heat, and set aside.

Place fillets between 2 sheets of waxed paper, and flatten slightly for uniform thickness, using a meat mallet or rolling pin. Arrange in a single layer in a 13- x 9- x 2-inch baking pan coated with cooking spray. Add remaining 2 tablespoons wine and pepper. Cover and bake at 400° for 10 to 12 minutes or until fillets flake easily when tested with a fork.

Transfer fillets to a platter; keep warm. Pour pan juices into skillet with mushroom mixture; bring to a boil. Spoon sauce over fillets. Yield: 6 servings (135 calories per serving).

PRO 21.0 / FAT 2.6 / CARB 6.8 / FIB 0.9 / CHOL 57 / SOD 93 / POT 719

WINE-BAKED SWORDFISH

½ cup sliced green onion
2 pounds fresh or frozen swordfish steaks, cut into serving-size pieces
Vegetable cooking spray
1½ cups sliced fresh mushrooms
1 medium tomato, chopped
1 (2-ounce) jar diced pimiento, drained
¼ cup chopped green pepper
½ cup dry white wine
2 tablespoons lemon juice
¼ teaspoon salt
⅛ teaspoon pepper

Sprinkle onion in a 12- x 8- x 2-inch baking dish coated with cooking spray; add swordfish. Combine next 4 ingredients; spoon over fish. Combine remaining ingredients; pour over vegetables. Cover and bake at 350° for 30 minutes or until fish flakes easily when tested with a fork. Yield: 8 servings (149 calories per serving).

PRO 22.4 / FAT 4.7 / CARB 3.4 / FIB 0.5 / CHOL 62 / SOD 139 / POT 647

BROILED SUNFLOWER TROUT

2 tablespoons unsalted margarine
2 tablespoons unsalted, shelled sunflower
  seeds
¾ teaspoon lemon juice
6 trout fillets (about 1½ pounds)
Vegetable cooking spray
¼ teaspoon salt
⅛ teaspoon pepper
1 lemon, cut into wedges

Melt margarine in a saucepan over low heat. Add sunflower seeds and lemon juice; cook 30 seconds, stirring constantly. Set aside.

Arrange fillets, skin side down, in a broiler pan coated with cooking spray; sprinkle with salt and pepper. Broil 3 to 4 inches from heat 3 to 5 minutes or until fillets flake easily when tested with a fork. Transfer to a platter; top with sunflower seed mixture. Garnish with lemon. Yield: 6 servings (241 calories per serving).

PRO 21.4 / FAT 16.6 / CARB 0.6 / FIB 0.1 / CHOL 62 / SOD 190 / POT 353

CLAM AND PORK DINNER

1 pound lean boneless pork loin
½ cup dry white wine
1 tablespoon paprika
1 bay leaf
2 whole cloves
1 teaspoon coriander seeds, crushed
Vegetable cooking spray
1 teaspoon vegetable oil
2 medium onions, chopped
1 (28-ounce) can whole tomatoes, drained and
  chopped
24 hard-shelled clams
2 tablespoons minced fresh parsley
3 cups hot cooked regular rice (cooked without salt
  or fat)
1 lemon, cut into wedges

Trim excess fat from pork; cut into 1-inch cubes, and set aside.

Combine next 5 ingredients in a large zip-top plastic bag. Add pork; seal bag, and shake to coat well. Marinate in refrigerator overnight. Drain pork, reserving marinade, and pat dry. Discard bay leaf and cloves.

Coat a large Dutch oven with cooking spray; add oil, and place over medium heat until hot. Add pork, and cook until browned on all sides. Transfer to a colander to drain. Add onion to Dutch oven; cook over low heat until tender. Add tomatoes and reserved marinade; bring to a boil, and add clams. Cover and steam 6 to 10 minutes or until clam shells open wide. Remove clams, discarding any unopened clams.

Return pork to Dutch oven; simmer 20 minutes. Add clams and parsley; cook until thoroughly heated. Serve over rice, and garnish with lemon. Yield: 6 servings (207 calories per serving plus 118 calories per ½-cup cooked rice).

PRO 22.8 / FAT 9.7 / CARB 35.7 / FIB 1.5 / CHOL 66 / SOD 396 / POT 401

CRAB PAELLA

Vegetable cooking spray
1 teaspoon vegetable oil
½ cup chopped onion
1 clove garlic, minced
1 pound boneless chicken breasts, skinned
  and cut into 1-inch pieces
2 cups water
1 cup regular rice, uncooked
1 teaspoon chicken-flavored bouillon granules
½ teaspoon dried whole oregano
¼ teaspoon pepper
⅛ teaspoon ground saffron
¾ cup frozen English peas, thawed and
  drained
1 medium tomato, diced
1 (2-ounce) jar diced pimiento, drained
1 pound lump crabmeat

Coat a large skillet with cooking spray; add oil, and place over medium heat until hot. Add onion and garlic; sauté until tender. Add chicken; cook until chicken is lightly browned. Add next 6 ingredients; bring to a boil. Cover; reduce heat, and simmer 20 minutes or until liquid is absorbed.

Add peas, tomato, and pimiento to skillet, stirring well. Cover and cook an additional 10 minutes. Add crabmeat; cook 5 minutes, stirring occasionally. Spoon onto a serving platter. Yield: 8 servings (230 calories per serving).

PRO 25.3 / FAT 3.4 / CARB 22.8 / FIB 1.4 / CHOL 92 / SOD 216 / POT 318

CRABMEAT SAUTÉ

½ pound fresh mushrooms, sliced
½ cup chopped green onion
⅓ cup cream sherry
1 pound lump crabmeat
¼ cup chopped fresh parsley
2 teaspoons lemon juice
2 cups hot cooked regular rice (cooked without salt or fat)

Combine mushrooms, onion, and sherry in a large skillet. Cook over medium heat, stirring constantly, until vegetables are tender. Stir in crabmeat and parsley; cook until thoroughly heated. Sprinkle with lemon juice, and serve over hot cooked rice. Yield: 4 servings (132 calories per serving plus 118 calories per ½ cup cooked rice).

PRO 23.3 / FAT 2.6 / CARB 32.3 / FIB 1.6 / CHOL 113 / SOD 245 / POT 511

BAKED OYSTERS WITH CABERNET SAUCE

1½ teaspoons cornstarch
1 tablespoon skim milk
Vegetable cooking spray
½ cup minced shallots
¼ pound fresh mushrooms, chopped
2 (12-ounce) containers Standard oysters, undrained
⅔ cup water
1 cup Cabernet Sauvignon or other dry red wine
1 teaspoon beef-flavored bouillon granules
¼ teaspoon pepper
⅛ teaspoon dried whole thyme
¼ cup soft whole wheat breadcrumbs
1 tablespoon plus 1 teaspoon grated Parmesan cheese
1 tablespoon minced fresh parsley
1 lemon, cut into wedges

Combine cornstarch and milk in a small bowl; set aside. Coat a saucepan with cooking spray; place over medium heat until hot. Add shallots and mushrooms; cook until tender and liquid evaporates, stirring constantly.

Drain oysters, reserving ½ cup liquid; set oysters aside. Add oyster liquid, water, wine, bouillon granules, pepper, and thyme to mushroom mixture; cook over medium heat 15 minutes or until mixture is reduced by half. Stir in cornstarch mixture; bring to a boil, and cook 1 minute or until thickened.

Place equal amounts of oysters in four (6-ounce) ramekins or custard cups. Spoon sauce over oysters; sprinkle with breadcrumbs and cheese. Bake at 450° for 10 minutes or until tops are golden and sauce is bubbly. Sprinkle with parsley, and serve with lemon wedges. Yield: 4 servings (170 calories per serving).

PRO 17.0 / FAT 4.1 / CARB 18.0 / FIB 0.9 / CHOL 87 / SOD 312 / POT 466

Many Americans display a ravenous appetite for meat — beef in particular. But there are signs that this love affair with red meat may be cooling. The USDA has determined that in 1984 Americans ate less red meat and more fish and poultry than in the past. One of the reasons for this shift may be that fish and shellfish are favorites with dieters because of their low-fat benefits — approximately 20 percent less fat than most red meats. The flesh of fish is also far easier to digest than any animal meat, and it is rich in protein and potassium. Recent studies are even indicating that more fish (not shellfish) in the diet may protect against coronary artery disease.

SCALLOP REMOULADE

¼ cup reduced-calorie salad dressing
1 tablespoon chopped green onion
1 to 1½ teaspoons dry mustard
1½ teaspoons prepared horseradish
1½ teaspoons vinegar
¼ teaspoon paprika
Dash of hot sauce (optional)
1 pound scallops, cooked
2 cups shredded lettuce

Combine first 7 ingredients in a bowl. Add scallops; toss to coat well. Cover; refrigerate 8 hours or overnight. Spoon scallop mixture onto individual lettuce-lined plates to serve. Yield: 4 servings (185 calories per serving).

PRO 18.0 / FAT 9.7 / CARB 5.5 / FIB 0.4 / CHOL 40 / SOD 466 / POT 516

SCALLOPS CREOLE

Vegetable cooking spray
2 teaspoons vegetable oil
1 cup minced onion
1 cup chopped green pepper
1 cup chopped celery
2 cloves garlic, minced
1 (6-ounce) can tomato paste
1 (8-ounce) can low-sodium tomato
  sauce
4 cups chopped fresh tomato
1 tablespoon chili powder
1 teaspoon sugar
½ teaspoon pepper
2 pounds scallops
4 cups hot cooked regular rice (cooked
  without salt or fat)

Coat a Dutch oven with cooking spray; add oil, and place over medium heat until hot. Add next 4 ingredients, and sauté 10 minutes or until tender. Stir in tomato paste, tomato sauce, chopped tomato, chili powder, sugar, and pepper. Bring to a boil. Cover; reduce heat, and simmer 15 minutes.

Rinse scallops thoroughly in cold water; drain. Add scallops to tomato mixture. Bring to a boil. Cover; reduce heat, and simmer 10 minutes or until scallops are done. Serve over rice. Yield: 8 servings (168 calories per serving plus 118 calories per ½ cup cooked rice).

PRO 19.9 / FAT 2.1 / CARB 18.4 / FIB 1.7 / CHOL 40 / SOD 340 / POT 1087

STIR-FRIED ORIENTAL SHRIMP

2 tablespoons dry white wine
1 tablespoon white wine vinegar
1 tablespoon reduced-sodium soy sauce
Vegetable cooking spray
2 teaspoons vegetable oil
⅔ cup minced green onion
2 tablespoons minced, peeled gingerroot
1 teaspoon minced garlic
2 pounds uncooked fresh shrimp, peeled
  and deveined
1 pound fresh asparagus, diagonally
  sliced
3 cups chopped Chinese cabbage

Combine first 3 ingredients in a small bowl; set aside. Coat a large skillet or wok with cooking spray; add oil, and place skillet over medium heat until hot. Add green onion, gingerroot, and garlic; stir-fry 1 minute. Add shrimp and asparagus; stir-fry 5 minutes. Add wine mixture and cabbage; stir-fry 5 minutes. Transfer to a platter to serve. Yield: 6 servings (147 calories per serving).

PRO 23.8 / FAT 2.7 / CARB 7.1 / FIB 1.3 / CHOL 170 / SOD 281 / POT 607

ORANGE-BARBECUED SHRIMP

½ cup unsweetened orange juice
⅓ cup reduced-calorie catsup
1 tablespoon brown sugar
2 tablespoons lemon juice
2 tablespoons minced onion
1 tablespoon reduced-sodium soy sauce
2 pounds uncooked, large fresh shrimp, peeled and
  deveined

Combine first 6 ingredients in a large zip-top plastic bag. Add shrimp. Seal and turn bag over to coat shrimp. Marinate shrimp in refrigerator 8 hours or overnight.

Thread shrimp onto 6 skewers, reserving marinade. Grill 4 to 5 inches from hot coals 10 minutes or until shrimp are done, basting frequently with marinade. Yield: 6 servings (129 calories per serving).

PRO 20.9 / FAT 0.9 / CARB 7.4 / FIB 0.0 / CHOL 170 / SOD 260 / POT 411

Including more meatless meals in your menu planning can be a healthy and frugal way to limit saturated fat in the diet. Vegetable-Cheddar Pita Sandwiches (page 138) contain one-third the amount of the fat in a cheeseburger and half the calories. Potatoes Stuffed with Vegetarian Chili (page 139) are high in carbohydrates and contain almost no fat.

HUEVOS RANCHEROS

Vegetable cooking spray
1 teaspoon vegetable oil
1 medium onion, chopped
2 medium-size green peppers, seeded and
chopped
1 clove garlic, minced
1 (28-ounce) can whole tomatoes, drained
and chopped
1 tablespoon minced fresh parsley
½ teaspoon minced green chiles
5 eggs
5 (8-inch) corn tortillas

Coat a skillet with cooking spray; add oil, and place over low heat until hot. Add onion, green pepper, and garlic; sauté until tender. Stir in tomatoes, parsley, and green chiles. Cover and simmer 15 minutes, stirring occasionally.

Make 5 depressions in tomato sauce with the back of a spoon. Break 1 egg into each depression. Cover; cook over medium heat 1 minute. Spoon sauce over egg whites; cook 4 minutes or until desired degree of doneness.

While eggs are cooking, place tortillas on a baking sheet. Bake at 350° for 10 minutes or until crisp and golden. Place tortillas on serving plates. Remove eggs with a spatula, placing 1 egg on each tortilla. Cover eggs with sauce. Yield: 5 servings (236 calories per serving).

PRO 10.8 / FAT 8.2 / CARB 31.8 / FIB 8.4 / CHOL 274 / SOD 277 / POT 428

OPEN-FACED VEGETABLE OMELET

1 medium onion, thinly sliced
1 medium-size green pepper, seeded and
thinly sliced
¼ teaspoon dried whole thyme
¼ teaspoon dried whole basil
¼ cup dry white wine
1 cup chopped tomato
4 eggs
4 egg whites or ½ cup frozen egg substitute,
thawed
¼ cup water
¼ teaspoon salt
⅛ teaspoon pepper
1½ teaspoons unsalted margarine
2 tablespoons minced fresh parsley

Combine first 5 ingredients in a saucepan. Bring to a boil. Cover; reduce heat, and simmer 10 minutes or until vegetables are tender, stirring occasionally. Stir in tomato; cook, uncovered, over medium heat until liquid evaporates, stirring frequently. Set aside, and keep warm.

Combine next 5 ingredients in a bowl, stirring with a wire whisk until well blended. Heat a 10-inch nonstick skillet over medium heat until hot enough to sizzle a drop of water. Add margarine, rotating skillet to coat bottom. Pour egg mixture into skillet. As mixture starts to cook, gently lift edges of omelet with a spatula, and tilt skillet, allowing uncooked portion to flow underneath. Cook until set but still moist. Spoon vegetable mixture over eggs, and fold in half. Sprinkle with parsley. Cut into wedges to serve. Yield: 6 servings (95 calories per serving).

PRO 7.2 / FAT 4.9 / CARB 5.7 / FIB 0.8 / CHOL 183 / SOD 182 / POT 242

BROCCOLI-RICE QUICHE

¼ cup chopped onion
1 (10-ounce) package frozen chopped broccoli
1½ cups cooked regular rice (cooked without
salt or fat)
¾ cup (3 ounces) shredded sharp Cheddar
cheese, divided
1 egg, lightly beaten
½ teaspoon salt, divided
Vegetable cooking spray
2 eggs, lightly beaten
¼ cup skim milk
1 (2.5-ounce) jar sliced mushrooms, drained
¼ teaspoon pepper

Cook onion with broccoli according to package directions; omit salt and fat. Drain. Combine rice, ½ cup cheese, 1 egg, and ¼ teaspoon salt. Press evenly over bottom and sides of a 9-inch pieplate coated with cooking spray.

Combine 2 eggs, milk, mushrooms, ¼ teaspoon salt, pepper, and broccoli mixture. Pour into prepared crust. Bake at 375° for 20 minutes. Remove from oven, and sprinkle with remaining ¼ cup cheese; bake an additional 10 minutes. Let stand 5 minutes before slicing. Yield: 6 servings (176 calories per serving).

PRO 9.7 / FAT 7.7 / CARB 17.1 / FIB 1.3 / CHOL 152 / SOD 382 / POT 214

BROCCOLI-CARROT FRITTATA

1 (10-ounce) package frozen chopped broccoli
½ cup diced carrot
¼ cup water
6 eggs
4 egg whites or ½ cup egg substitute, thawed
½ cup skim milk
1 tablespoon instant minced onion
2 teaspoons prepared mustard
1 teaspoon seasoned salt
⅛ teaspoon pepper
¾ cup (3 ounces) shredded Cheddar cheese
1 tablespoon unsalted margarine

Place frozen broccoli, carrot, and water in a 10-inch omelet pan or heavy skillet with oven-proof handle. Cover and cook 10 minutes or until carrots are crisp-tender. Drain well, and set vegetables aside.

Combine eggs, egg whites, milk, minced onion, mustard, seasoned salt, and pepper, beating well. Add cheese and reserved broccoli mixture, stirring until well combined.

Heat margarine in omelet pan over medium heat until bubbly. Pour egg mixture into pan. Cover and cook over low heat 10 minutes or until egg mixture is almost set. Broil frittata 6 inches from heat 3 minutes or until lightly browned and egg mixture is set. Cut into wedges, and serve immediately. Yield: 6 servings (192 calories per serving).

PRO 14.3 / FAT 12.4 / CARB 6.3 / FIB 1.0 / CHOL 289 / SOD 532 / POT 288

Surprise last minute guests with a bright and lively Broccoli-Carrot Frittata, a one-dish meal that's quick and nutritious.

CHEDDAR CHEESE SOUFFLÉ

3 tablespoons unsalted margarine
3 tablespoons all-purpose flour
1 cup skim milk
1 cup (4 ounces) shredded extra-sharp Cheddar
   cheese
¼ cup minced, seeded green chiles
⅛ teaspoon pepper
2 egg yolks, beaten
5 egg whites

Melt margarine in a heavy saucepan over low heat; add flour, stirring until smooth. Cook 1 minute, stirring constantly. Gradually add milk; cook over medium heat, stirring constantly, until mixture is thickened and bubbly.

Add cheese, chiles, and pepper to milk mixture; stir until cheese melts. Gradually stir one-fourth of hot mixture into yolks; add to remaining hot mixture, stirring constantly. Cool. Beat egg whites (at room temperature) until stiff but not dry; gently fold into cheese mixture.

Spoon into a lightly greased and floured 2½-quart soufflé dish; bake at 400° for 30 minutes or until puffed and golden. Serve immediately. Yield: 5 servings (230 calories per serving).

PRO 12.4 / FAT 16.6 / CARB 7.4 / FIB 0.2 / CHOL 134 / SOD 221 / POT 183

SPINACH-RICOTTA SOUFFLÉ

3 tablespoons unsalted margarine
3 tablespoons all-purpose flour
1 cup skim milk
3 egg yolks, beaten
⅓ cup frozen chopped spinach, thawed and
   squeezed dry
1 cup part-skim ricotta cheese
¼ teaspoon salt
⅛ teaspoon pepper
⅛ teaspoon ground nutmeg
5 egg whites

Grease and flour a 2-quart soufflé dish. Cut a piece of aluminum foil long enough to fit around soufflé dish, allowing a 1-inch overlap; fold lengthwise into thirds. Lightly oil one side of foil; wrap around outside of dish, oiled side against dish, allowing it to extend 3 inches above rim. Secure with string; set aside.

Melt margarine in a saucepan over low heat; add flour, stirring until smooth. Cook 1 minute, stirring constantly. Gradually add milk; cook over medium heat, stirring constantly, until mixture is thickened and bubbly. Remove from heat. Stir one-fourth of milk mixture into egg yolks; add to remaining milk mixture, and set aside. Combine spinach, cheese, salt, pepper, and nutmeg in container of an electric blender, and process until smooth. Combine with egg yolk mixture.

Beat egg whites (at room temperature) in a large bowl until stiff but not dry. Gently fold into spinach mixture. Spoon into prepared soufflé dish; bake at 400° for 45 to 50 minutes or until puffed and golden. Serve immediately. Yield: 5 servings (220 calories per serving).

PRO 13.1 / FAT 14.2 / CARB 9.7 / FIB 0.4 / CHOL 180 / SOD 267 / POT 237

BAKED MACARONI AND CHEESE

3 tablespoons cornstarch
3 cups skim milk
1 cup (4 ounces) shredded extra-sharp Cheddar
   cheese
¼ cup grated Parmesan cheese, divided
2 tablespoons grated onion
¾ teaspoon dry mustard
½ teaspoon salt
¼ teaspoon pepper
1 (16-ounce) package elbow macaroni or bowtie
   pasta (cooked al dente without salt or fat)
½ cup low-fat cottage cheese
Vegetable cooking spray
¼ teaspoon paprika

Combine cornstarch and milk in a Dutch oven; bring to a boil. Reduce heat, and cook, stirring constantly with a wire whisk, 5 minutes or until slightly thickened; remove from heat.

Add Cheddar cheese, 3 tablespoons Parmesan cheese, grated onion, mustard, salt, pepper, cooked macaroni, and cottage cheese to Dutch oven, mixing well.

Spoon mixture into a 13- x 9- x 2-inch baking dish coated with cooking spray. Sprinkle with 1 tablespoon Parmesan cheese and paprika. Bake at 350° for 30 minutes. Yield: 8 servings (337 calories per 1-cup serving).

PRO 16.9 / FAT 6.7 / CARB 51.0 / FIB 1.5 / CHOL 20 / SOD 387 / POT 305

Choose skim or low-fat milk and milk products to keep fat and calories low.

Milk, cheese, and eggs are staples in most kitchens, yet they present a problem for the cook who is intent on reducing saturated fat and cholesterol in her meal planning. Reading labels and becoming aware of the variety of choices that today's market offers will go a long way in helping you keep recipes that call for milk, cheese, or eggs more nutrient dense and calorie smart.

By choosing skim milk instead of whole milk, you can reduce the saturated fat and cholesterol in milk. What's more, you'll save over 70 calories per cup. Be wary of whole milk yogurt, too, as well as yogurt filled with fruit preserves. The added fruit and sugar can push calories per 8-ounce container up to 335 — that's compared to only 144 per 8 ounces of the plain low-fat kind.

On cottage cheese cartons, look for the "low-fat" label to save over 50 calories per cup.

Unlike low-fat cottage cheese, most natural cheeses are made from whole milk and are high in fat. By choosing strong-flavored cheeses, such as Swiss or extra-sharp Cheddar, you can cut back on the amount you use and still get plenty of cheese flavor. Some cheeses, such as mozzarella, may be made partially from skim milk and are lower in calories than most natural cheeses. Several diet cheeses on the market bear labels identifying them as "low-fat," "low-calorie," "low-cholesterol," and/or "low-sodium."

To reduce cholesterol in eggs, start using more of the whites, which contain no cholesterol, or try the no-cholesterol egg substitutes available on the market.

BROCCOLI-CHEESE CALZONE

1 package dry yeast
¼ cup warm water (105° to 115°)
¼ cup plus 1 tablespoon honey
¼ cup unsalted margarine
¾ cup water
1 egg
3 cups unbleached or all-purpose flour,
  divided
1 teaspoon salt
1½ cups whole wheat flour
Vegetable cooking spray
Broccoli-Cheese Filling

Dissolve yeast in ¼ cup warm water in a large bowl; let stand 10 minutes. Combine honey, margarine, and ¾ cup water in a saucepan, and cook over low heat to 105° to 115°; add honey mixture and egg to dissolved yeast, and beat well. Stir in 1 cup unbleached flour and salt; mix well. Combine remaining 2 cups unbleached flour and whole wheat flour; stir in enough flour mixture to make a stiff dough.

Turn dough out onto a lightly floured surface, and knead until smooth and elastic (about 8 to 10 minutes). Place in a bowl coated with cooking spray, turning to grease top. Cover and let rise in a warm place (85°), free from drafts, 1 hour or until doubled in bulk.

Punch dough down, and divide into 14 pieces. Roll each piece into a 5-inch circle. Spoon ¼ cup Broccoli-Cheese Filling onto each circle, leaving a ½-inch border. Moisten edges of circles with water; fold each circle in half, making sure edges are even. Press pastry edges firmly together, using a fork dipped in flour. Place calzones on 2 baking sheets coated with cooking spray, and bake at 400° for 15 to 20 minutes or until golden brown. Yield: 14 calzones (252 calories each).

Broccoli-Cheese Filling:

1 (10-ounce) package frozen chopped broccoli,
  cooked without salt or fat
1 (15-ounce) carton part-skim ricotta cheese
¼ cup grated Parmesan cheese
½ cup (2 ounces) shredded part-skim mozzarella
  cheese
½ teaspoon dried whole oregano

Place broccoli between paper towels; squeeze until barely moist. Combine broccoli and remaining ingredients in a bowl, mixing well. Yield: 3½ cups (64 calories per ¼ cup).

PRO 5.6 / FAT 3.5 / CARB 2.7 / FIB 0.4 / CHOL 13 / SOD 88 / POT 87

BROCCOLI-SWISS MELT

2 cups broccoli flowerets
Vegetable cooking spray
½ cup sliced fresh mushrooms
1 tablespoon plus 1 teaspoon coarse-grain mustard
2 whole wheat English muffins, split and toasted
1 tablespoon sliced green onion
4 ounces Swiss cheese, thinly sliced

Cook broccoli in a small amount of boiling water 2 minutes or until crisp-tender. Transfer to a colander to drain. Coat a skillet with cooking spray; place over medium heat until hot. Add mushrooms, and sauté until tender. Transfer to colander to drain. Keep vegetables warm.

Spread mustard on muffin halves, and top with broccoli and mushrooms. Sprinkle with green onion, and top with cheese. Broil 4 to 6 inches from heat until cheese is hot and bubbly. Serve immediately. Yield: 4 open-faced sandwiches (215 calories each).

PRO 9.6 / FAT 8.3 / CARB 4.1 / FIB 0.7 / CHOL 26 / SOD 235 / POT 216

VEGETABLE-CHEDDAR PITA
SANDWICHES

1 tablespoon plus 1 teaspoon reduced-calorie
  mayonnaise
½ teaspoon dry mustard
¼ teaspoon pepper
2 (6-inch) whole wheat pita bread rounds,
  halved
2 cups torn Romaine lettuce
½ cup (2 ounces) shredded Cheddar cheese
½ medium cucumber, thinly sliced
1 medium tomato, thinly sliced

Combine mayonnaise, mustard, and pepper; spread on inside of pita halves. Line pita with lettuce, and stuff with cheese, cucumber, and tomato. Yield: 2 sandwiches (301 calories each).

PRO 11.8 / FAT 13.7 / CARB 31.6 / FIB 1.4 / CHOL 33 / SOD 261 / POT 521

CHEESE ENCHILADAS

1 cup (4 ounces) shredded sharp Cheddar cheese
¼ cup minced, seeded green chiles
½ cup plus 2 tablespoons minced onion, divided
8 (8-inch) corn tortillas
Vegetable cooking spray
¾ cup diced red pepper
1 clove garlic, minced
1 cup chopped tomato
2 drops hot sauce

Combine cheese, green chiles, and 2 tablespoons onion in a bowl. Spoon mixture down centers of tortillas, and roll up. Arrange in an 8-inch square baking dish coated with cooking spray, and set aside.

Coat a skillet with cooking spray; place over medium heat until hot. Add red pepper, ½ cup onion, and garlic; sauté 2 to 3 minutes or until tender. Add tomato and hot sauce; cook 1 minute. Place mixture in container of an electric blender, and process until smooth. Return to skillet, and keep warm.

Cover and bake prepared enchiladas at 400° for 7 minutes or until cheese melts. To serve, top with warm tomato sauce. Yield: 4 servings (358 calories per 2-enchilada serving).

PRO 13.9 / FAT 12.1 / CARB 51.2 / FIB 1.6 / CHOL 30 / SOD 249 / POT 258

BEAN BURRITOS

Vegetable cooking spray
1 medium onion, chopped
1 clove garlic, minced
2 medium tomatoes, chopped
1 (15-ounce) can pinto beans, drained and rinsed
1 teaspoon ground cumin
½ to 1 teaspoon minced, pickled jalapeño peppers
10 (8-inch) whole wheat flour tortillas
½ medium avocado, peeled and chopped
2 tablespoons minced fresh coriander or 1½ teaspoons dried whole cilantro
¾ cup (3 ounces) shredded Monterey Jack cheese

Coat a large saucepan with cooking spray; place over medium heat until hot. Add onion and garlic; sauté until tender. Stir in tomatoes,

beans, cumin, and jalapeño peppers; simmer, uncovered, 30 minutes or until mixture is a thick paste, stirring and mashing beans with a wooden spoon. Set aside, and keep warm.

Wrap tortillas in aluminum foil, and bake at 350° for 10 to 15 minutes or until thoroughly heated. Spoon 2 tablespoons bean mixture onto each tortilla; top with remaining ingredients, and roll up. Place on a warm platter, and serve immediately. Yield: 5 servings (266 calories per 2-burrito serving).

PRO 11.7 / FAT 9.3 / CARB 37.3 / FIB 3.5 / CHOL 12 / SOD 229 / POT 419

POTATOES STUFFED WITH VEGETARIAN CHILI

8 (8-ounce) baking potatoes
Vegetable cooking spray
¼ pound fresh mushrooms, sliced
½ cup chopped onion
⅓ cup chopped green pepper
1 clove garlic, minced
1 (16-ounce) can red kidney beans, undrained
1 (14½-ounce) can stewed tomatoes, undrained
¼ teaspoon ground cumin
⅛ teaspoon hot sauce
⅛ teaspoon pepper
⅛ teaspoon ground red pepper
⅛ teaspoon dried whole oregano
½ cup (2 ounces) shredded Monterey Jack cheese
2 tablespoons sliced green onion

Prick potatoes with a fork, and bake at 400° for 1 hour or until tender. Wrap in aluminum foil, and keep warm.

Coat a large saucepan with cooking spray; place over medium heat until hot. Add mushrooms, onion, green pepper, and garlic; sauté 5 minutes or until tender. Stir in next 7 ingredients; cook over low heat just until thoroughly heated, stirring occasionally.

Remove foil from potatoes. Split tops lengthwise, and fluff pulp with a fork. Arrange in a 13- x 9- x 2-inch baking dish. Spoon chili mixture evenly over potatoes, and top with cheese. Bake at 400° for 5 to 7 minutes or until cheese melts. Garnish with green onion. Yield: 8 servings (282 calories per serving).

PRO 11.6 / FAT 2.8 / CARB 54.4 / FIB 8.4 / CHOL 6 / SOD 306 / POT 1632

WHOLE WHEAT PIZZA WITH EGGPLANT-MUSHROOM SAUCE

1 package dry yeast
1½ cups warm water (105° to 115°)
2 cups unbleached or all-purpose flour
2 cups whole wheat flour
1 teaspoon salt
2 teaspoons vegetable oil
Vegetable cooking spray
2 tablespoons cornmeal
Eggplant-Mushroom Sauce
1½ cups (6 ounces) shredded part-skim
    mozzarella cheese
½ cup grated Romano cheese

Dissolve yeast in warm water in a large bowl; let stand 10 minutes. Add next 4 ingredients, and stir until a stiff dough is formed.

Turn dough out onto a lightly floured surface, and knead until smooth and elastic (about 8 to 10 minutes). Place in a bowl coated with cooking spray, turning to grease top. Cover and let rise in a warm place (85°), free from drafts, 2 hours or until doubled in bulk.

Coat two 12-inch pizza pans with cooking spray, and sprinkle with cornmeal. Punch dough down, and divide in half. Coat hands with cooking spray; pat dough evenly into prepared pans. Spoon Eggplant-Mushroom Sauce evenly over dough, using a slotted spoon. Sprinkle equal amounts of mozzarella and Romano cheese over sauce. Bake at 400° for 10 minutes or until browned and bubbly. Cut each pizza into 8 slices to serve. Yield: 16 pizza slices (352 calories per 2-slice serving).

Eggplant-Mushroom Sauce:

Vegetable cooking spray
1 cup chopped onion
2 to 3 cloves garlic, minced
4 cups diced, peeled eggplant
2 cups sliced fresh mushrooms
2 cups diced tomato
2 teaspoons dried whole basil
2 teaspoons dried whole oregano
½ teaspoon salt
½ teaspoon pepper
½ cup dry red wine

Coat a Dutch oven with cooking spray; place over medium heat until hot. Add onion and garlic, and sauté 5 minutes. Add eggplant, mushrooms, and tomato, and cook 5 minutes. Add remaining ingredients, and simmer, uncovered, 10 minutes, stirring occasionally. Yield: 5 cups.

PRO 17.2 / FAT 7.7 / CARB 57.1 / FIB 4.8 / CHOL 20 / SOD 636 / POT 629

ITALIAN ZUCCHINI CASSEROLE

2¼ pounds zucchini, thinly sliced
    lengthwise
Vegetable cooking spray
1 (8-ounce) carton low-fat cottage cheese
2 tablespoons skim milk
2 eggs, lightly beaten
½ teaspoon pepper
¼ cup plus 2 tablespoons grated Parmesan
    cheese, divided
1 cup (4 ounces) shredded part-skim
    mozzarella cheese, divided
1 (28-ounce) can whole tomatoes, undrained
    and chopped
½ cup chopped green onion
1 clove garlic, minced
1 teaspoon dried whole basil

Arrange zucchini slices in a single layer on a broiler pan coated with cooking spray; broil 3 inches from heat 4 to 5 minutes or until golden, turning after 2 minutes. Set aside. Combine cottage cheese, milk, eggs, pepper, and ¼ cup Parmesan cheese in container of an electric blender, and process until smooth.

Line bottom of an 12- x 8- x 2-inch baking dish coated with cooking spray with one-third of zucchini. Top with half of cottage cheese mixture and ½ cup mozzarella cheese.

Add half of remaining zucchini, remaining cottage cheese mixture, and remaining mozzarella cheese. Top with remaining zucchini, and sprinkle with remaining 2 tablespoons Parmesan cheese. Bake at 375° for 30 minutes or until set and top is golden.

Combine remaining ingredients in a small saucepan; bring to a boil. Reduce heat; simmer 10 minutes, stirring occasionally. Serve sauce with casserole. Yield: 6 servings (227 calories per serving with ⅓ cup sauce per serving).

PRO 23.1 / FAT 8.6 / CARB 15.9 / FIB 1.2 / CHOL 115 / SOD 1018/POT 571

VEGETABLE LASAGNA

2 tablespoons chopped onion
1 clove garlic, minced
1 teaspoon olive oil
1½ cups diced, peeled tomato
2 cups diced, peeled eggplant
½ cup chopped green pepper
1 medium zucchini, diced
¼ pound fresh mushrooms, chopped
1 teaspoon dried whole oregano
1 bay leaf
¼ teaspoon salt
¼ teaspoon pepper
6 uncooked lasagna noodles
⅛ teaspoon salt
2 eggs, beaten
1 cup low-fat cottage cheese
1 tablespoon chopped fresh parsley
Vegetable cooking spray
½ cup (2 ounces) shredded mozzarella
  cheese
1 tablespoon grated Parmesan cheese

Sauté onion and garlic in oil in a large skillet. Stir in next 9 ingredients. Cover; reduce heat, and simmer 10 minutes. Remove bay leaf.

Cook lasagna according to package directions, reducing salt to ⅛ teaspoon. Drain noodles, and cut in half crosswise; set aside.

Coat an 8-inch square baking dish with cooking spray. Place 4 noodle halves in dish. Spoon half of cottage cheese mixture over noodles. Spread half of vegetable mixture over cottage cheese mixture; sprinkle with half of mozzarella cheese. Repeat layers, ending with noodles. Cover and bake at 350° for 20 minutes. Sprinkle with Parmesan cheese; cover and bake 5 minutes. Yield: 6 servings (224 calories per serving).

PRO 14.4 / FAT 6.3 / CARB 28.4 / FIB 2.1 / CHOL 102 / SOD 380 / POT 506

Vegetable proteins are a low-fat option to animal proteins, but they must be eaten in certain combinations to be considered complete protein sources. Legumes, when combined with seeds or grains (such as in Red Beans and Rice and Hoppin' John), make up complementary proteins which are good substitutes for meat and dairy products.

STIR-FRY TOFU AND VEGETABLES

½ pound tofu
1 egg white
2 tablespoons plus 1 teaspoon cornstarch,
  divided
1 teaspoon reduced-sodium soy sauce
2 tablespoons vegetable oil
½ teaspoon sesame oil
2 cloves garlic, minced
1 (6-ounce) package frozen snow peas,
  thawed and drained
2 cups sliced fresh mushrooms
1 (8-ounce) can sliced water chestnuts,
  drained
1 (8-ounce) can sliced bamboo shoots,
  drained
½ cup cold water
1 tablespoon reduced-sodium soy sauce
1 teaspoon chicken-flavored bouillon
  granules
½ teaspoon sugar
¼ teaspoon ground ginger
⅛ teaspoon oriental five-spice powder
2 cups hot cooked regular rice (cooked without
  salt or fat)
½ cup Chinese noodles

Wrap tofu with several layers of cheesecloth or paper towels; press lightly to remove excess liquid. Remove cheesecloth; cut tofu into ½-inch cubes, and set aside.

Combine egg white, 1 teaspoon cornstarch, and 1 teaspoon soy sauce in a bowl; add tofu, and toss. Chill 30 minutes.

Coat a wok or large skillet with cooking spray; add vegetable and sesame oil; heat at medium-high heat (325°) 2 minutes. Add garlic, and stir-fry 30 seconds. Add pea pods, and stir-fry 2 minutes. Add tofu mixture, mushrooms, water chestnuts, and bamboo shoots; stir-fry 2 minutes. Combine remaining 2 tablespoons cornstarch and ½ cup water; stir into wok with soy sauce, bouillon granules, sugar, ginger, and five-spice powder. Cook until thickened and bubbly. Serve over rice, and top each serving with 2 tablespoons Chinese noodles. Yield: 4 servings (213 calories per 1-cup serving plus 118 calories per ½ cup cooked rice).

PRO 11.6 / FAT 11.7 / CARB 46.5 / FIB 2.4 / CHOL 1 / SOD 371 / POT 515

TOFU STROGANOFF

1 pound tofu
1 tablespoon vegetable oil
3 cups sliced fresh mushrooms
1 clove garlic, crushed
2 tablespoons all-purpose flour
1½ teaspoons chicken-flavored bouillon
    granules
½ teaspoon dried whole chervil
¼ teaspoon pepper
¾ cup skim milk
1 (8-ounce) carton plain low-fat yogurt
3 cups hot cooked spinach noodles
½ medium tomato, sliced
½ hard-cooked egg, sliced
Fresh dill

Wrap tofu with several layers of cheesecloth or paper towels; press lightly to remove excess liquid. Remove cheesecloth, and cut tofu into ¾-inch cubes.

Sauté tofu in hot oil in a large skillet 3 to 4 minutes; remove tofu, and set aside. Add mushrooms and garlic to skillet; sauté 2 to 3 minutes. Remove from heat, and set aside.

Combine flour, bouillon granules, chervil, and pepper; gradually add milk, stirring until blended. Add milk mixture to skillet; bring to a boil. Cook 1 minute, stirring constantly. Stir yogurt into milk mixture. Add sautéed ingredients, and cook until thoroughly heated (do not boil). Serve over spinach noodles. Garnish with tomato slices, egg slices, and dill. Yield: 6 servings (213 calories per serving).

PRO 12.9 / FAT 8.4 / CARB 23.2 / FIB 1.4 / CHOL 26 / SOD 160 / POT 417

HOPPIN' JOHN

2 cups dried black-eyed peas
1½ quarts water
1 cup chopped onion
½ cup chopped celery
2 teaspoons chicken-flavored bouillon granules
¼ teaspoon salt
¼ teaspoon pepper
1 cup regular rice, uncooked
Hot sauce to taste (optional)

Sort and wash peas; place in a large Dutch oven. Add water, and let soak overnight.

Add next 5 ingredients, and bring to a boil. Cover, reduce heat to medium, and cook 35 to 45 minutes or until peas are almost tender. Add rice; cover and simmer 20 minutes. Add hot sauce before serving, if desired. Yield: 8 servings (140 calories per serving).

PRO 5.2 / FAT 0.6 / CARB 28.4 / FIB 1.5 / CHOL 0 / SOD 178 / POT 235

RED BEANS WITH RICE

Vegetable cooking spray
1 teaspoon vegetable oil
1 medium onion, chopped
½ cup chopped celery
1 clove garlic, minced
1 cup chopped zucchini
¼ teaspoon dried whole oregano
¼ teaspoon dried whole thyme
1 (16-ounce) can whole tomatoes, undrained
    and chopped
1 (15-ounce) can red kidney beans, drained
    and rinsed
⅛ teaspoon ground red pepper
2 cups hot cooked regular rice (cooked without
    salt or fat)

Coat a large skillet with cooking spray; add vegetable oil, and place over medium heat until hot. Add onion, celery, and garlic; sauté until just tender.

Stir in zucchini, oregano, and thyme; cook 5 minutes, stirring well. Add tomatoes, beans, and red pepper; simmer, uncovered, 20 minutes, stirring occasionally. Serve over rice. Yield: 4 servings (105 calories per serving plus 118 calories per ½ cup cooked rice).

PRO 7.8 / FAT 1.6 / CARB 44.7 / FIB 7.7 / CHOL 0 / SOD 622 / POT 215

Enjoy a wide variety of meats, but choose lean cuts and calorie-smart cooking methods: Beef Teriyaki over rice (page 146), Herbed Pork Roast (page 155), and Grilled Skewered Lamb (page 153).

BEEF SHIITAKE

1 ounce dried shiitake mushrooms (about 1 cup)
3 cups hot water
Vegetable cooking spray
1/8 teaspoon pepper
1 teaspoon chopped shallots
1 pound beef tenderloin
Vegetable cooking spray
1 teaspoon unsalted margarine
2/3 cup water
1/4 cup Madeira
3/4 teaspoon beef-flavored bouillon granules

Soak mushrooms in 3 cups hot water 30 minutes; drain. Remove stems; reserve for other uses. Cut caps into fourths; set aside. Coat a skillet with cooking spray; place over medium heat until hot. Add mushrooms, and sauté 3 minutes. Add pepper and shallots; sauté 30 seconds. Remove from skillet, and set aside.

Trim excess fat from tenderloin; cut into thin slices. Add margarine to skillet; place over medium heat until melted. Add tenderloin; cook 2 minutes on each side. Remove to a platter; keep warm. Add remaining ingredients to skillet; cook over medium-high heat 5 minutes or until liquid is reduced by half. Add beef and mushroom mixture to skillet; cook until hot. Yield: 4 servings (186 calories per serving).

PRO 27.0 / FAT 4.6 / CARB 6.7 / FIB 0.8 / CHOL 54 / SOD 138 / POT 432

STEAK DIANE

4 (5-ounce) boneless rib-eye steaks, 1/4-inch thick
Vegetable cooking spray
1 teaspoon unsalted margarine
1/2 cup dry sherry
1/4 cup brandy
2 tablespoons minced shallots
2 tablespoons minced fresh chives
1 teaspoon Worcestershire sauce
1/2 cup water
1/2 teaspoon beef-flavored bouillon granules
1/8 teaspoon pepper
2 tablespoons minced fresh parsley

Trim excess fat from steaks; place steaks between two sheets of waxed paper, and pound to 1/8-inch thickness, using a meat mallet or a rolling pin. Set aside. Coat a skillet with cooking spray; add margarine, and place over high heat until melted. Add steaks, and cook 2 minutes on each side (for medium-rare meat). Transfer to a platter, and keep warm.

Pour off pan drippings from skillet. Add sherry and brandy to skillet, and heat just until warm (do not boil). Ignite mixture with a long-handled match, and allow to burn. When flames die, add next 5 ingredients. Cook over medium-high heat 5 minutes.

Remove from heat, and stir in pepper. Spoon sauce over steaks, and sprinkle with parsley. Yield: 4 servings (254 calories per serving).

PRO 34.0 / FAT 6.7 / CARB 3.6 / FIB 0.1 / CHOL 69 / SOD 136 / POT 459

FLANK STEAK WITH MUSHROOM SAUCE

1 1/2 pounds flank steak
1 clove garlic, minced
1/4 teaspoon pepper
1/3 cup dry red wine
2 tablespoons minced shallots
1 cup finely chopped fresh mushrooms
1 teaspoon cornstarch
1/2 cup water
1 teaspoon Worcestershire sauce

Trim excess fat from steak. Score steak with 1/8-inch-deep diagonal cuts on both sides. Rub steak with garlic and pepper. Broil steak 4 to 5 inches from heat for 5 to 7 minutes on each side or until desired degree of doneness.

Transfer steak to a serving platter; cover and keep warm.

Combine wine and shallots in a small saucepan, and cook over medium heat until most of liquid evaporates. Add mushrooms, and cook 2 minutes or until tender, stirring well. Combine cornstarch, water, Worchestershire sauce, and any juices that have accumulated on steak platter in a small bowl; gradually add to mushroom mixture. Cook, stirring constantly, until thickened and bubbly.

Cut steak in thin slices across grain, and serve with mushroom sauce. Yield: 6 servings (166 calories per serving with 2 1/2 tablespoons sauce per serving).

PRO 27.4 / FAT 4.6 / CARB 2.4 / FIB 0.1 / CHOL 55 / SOD 61 / POT 391

MARINATED FLANK STEAK

1½ pounds flank steak
½ cup sliced green onion
1 tablespoon sugar
2 tablespoons sliced, peeled gingerroot
2 tablespoons reduced-sodium soy sauce
2 tablespoons dry sherry
2 cloves garlic, minced

Trim excess fat from steak. Score steak with ⅛-inch-deep diagonal cuts on both sides. Combine remaining ingredients in a large, shallow dish; add steak, turning to coat well with marinade. Cover and marinate in refrigerator 4 hours or overnight, turning occasionally.

Remove steak from marinade, and scrape off seasonings. Broil steak 4 to 5 inches from heat 5 to 7 minutes on each side or until desired degree of doneness. Transfer steak to a cutting board; cut in thin slices across grain. Yield: 6 servings (180 calories per serving).

PRO 27.6 / FAT 4.5 / CARB 4.0 / FIB 0.3 / CHOL 55 / SOD 246 / POT 349

BEEF BURGUNDY

Vegetable cooking spray
1 medium onion, thinly sliced
¼ pound fresh mushrooms, quartered
1 pound boneless round steak
1 tablespoon plus 1½ teaspoons all-purpose flour
1 cup Burgundy or other dry red wine
¼ cup water
1 teaspoon beef-flavored bouillon granules
½ teaspoon dried whole marjoram
¼ teaspoon freshly ground black pepper
2 cups hot cooked whole wheat noodles (cooked without salt or fat)

Coat a large skillet with cooking spray; place over medium-high heat, and add onion and mushrooms. Sauté 5 minutes or until tender; remove from skillet, and set aside.

Trim excess fat from steak; cut steak into 1-inch strips. Add steak to skillet, and sauté until browned. Stir in flour; add next 5 ingredients. Bring to a boil. Cover; reduce heat, and simmer 1 hour and 15 minutes or until tender. Add onion and mushrooms, cook until thoroughly heated. Serve over noodles. Yield: 4 servings (250 calories per serving plus 76 calories per ½ cup cooked noodles).

PRO 41.8 / FAT 7.9 / CARB 20.4 / FIB 0.9 / CHOL 134 / SOD 418 / POT 676

BEEF STROGANOFF

1 pound boneless sirloin
Vegetable cooking spray
1 cup chopped onion
2 cups sliced fresh mushrooms
2 tablespoons unsalted margarine
2 tablespoons all-purpose flour
1 cup water
1 teaspoon beef-flavored bouillon granules
½ cup plain low-fat yogurt
¼ cup dry red wine
¼ cup sour cream
½ teaspoon pepper
½ (12-ounce) package egg noodles

Trim excess fat from sirloin; cut sirloin into thin strips. Set aside. Coat a Dutch oven with cooking spray, and place over medium-high heat until hot. Add sirloin, onion, and mushrooms; sauté 10 minutes. Remove from heat, and drain well.

Melt margarine in a saucepan over low heat; add flour, stirring until smooth. Cook 1 minute, stirring constantly. Gradually add water; add bouillon granules, and cook over medium heat until thickened and bubbly, stirring constantly. Stir in yogurt, wine, sour cream, pepper, and sirloin mixture. Cook over low heat 5 minutes or until thoroughly heated. (Do not boil.)

Cook noodles according to package directions, omitting salt and fat; drain. Serve sirloin mixture over noodles. Yield: 6 servings (233 calories per serving plus 110 calories per ½ cup cooked noodles).

PRO 30.0 / FAT 11.6 / CARB 28.0 / FIB 0.6 / CHOL 81 / SOD 144 / POT 523

BEEF TERIYAKI

¼ cup reduced-sodium soy sauce
¼ cup water
2 tablespoons light molasses
2 teaspoons minced garlic
½ teaspoon ground ginger
1½ pounds boneless sirloin
Vegetable cooking spray
1 teaspoon vegetable oil
1 medium-size red pepper, seeded and sliced
1 medium-size green pepper, seeded and sliced
½ cup sliced onion
1 cup sliced fresh mushrooms
4 cups hot cooked regular rice (cooked without salt or fat)

Combine first 5 ingredients in a shallow dish; set aside. Trim excess fat from beef; cut into thin strips. Add sirloin to marinade, tossing to coat. Cover and marinate in refrigerator 1 hour.

Coat a skillet or wok with cooking spray; add oil, and place over medium-high heat until hot. Add sirloin, pepper, and onion; stir-fry 5 minutes. Add mushrooms; stir-fry 5 minutes or until sirloin is done. Serve over rice. Yield: 8 servings (207 calories per serving plus 118 calories per ½ cup cooked rice).

PRO 30.4 / FAT 5.4 / CARB 33.2 / FIB 1.3 / CHOL 55 / SOD 346 / POT 526

CHILI CON CARNE

2¾ pounds lean boneless chuck roast
Vegetable cooking spray
2 medium onions, chopped
4 cloves garlic or to taste, minced
1 (28-ounce) can crushed tomatoes, undrained
2 cups water
1 tablespoon plus 1 teaspoon ground cumin
¾ teaspoon crushed red pepper
½ teaspoon dried whole oregano
1 bay leaf
¼ teaspoon salt

Trim excess fat from roast; cut roast into ¼-inch cubes. Coat a large Dutch oven with cooking spray; place over medium-high heat until hot. Add meat, and cook until browned; drain in a colander.

Add onion and garlic to Dutch oven; cook over medium-low heat until tender, stirring frequently. Add meat and remaining ingredients; bring to a boil. Reduce heat; simmer, uncovered, 1 hour and 45 minutes or until meat is very tender and mixture is thickened, stirring occasionally. Add additional water, if necessary. Discard bay leaf. Ladle into bowls to serve. Yield: 8 servings (231 calories per serving).

PRO 34.8 / FAT 6.1 / CARB 8.0 / FIB 0.9 / CHOL 68 / SOD 268 / POT 298

PICCADILLO

Vegetable cooking spray
1½ pounds lean ground chuck
1 medium onion, finely chopped
1 medium tomato, peeled, seeded, and finely chopped
⅓ cup raisins
½ cup chopped green pepper
1 clove garlic, minced
¼ teaspoon dried whole oregano
1 bay leaf
12 pimiento-stuffed olives, thinly sliced
¼ cup dry red wine
¼ cup water
3 tablespoons low-sodium tomato sauce
¼ teaspoon salt
⅛ teaspoon grated nutmeg
2 to 3 drops hot sauce
3 cups hot cooked regular rice (cooked without salt or fat)
1 medium tomato, chopped

Coat a large deep skillet with cooking spray, and place over medium heat until hot. Add ground chuck, and cook 5 minutes or until browned, stirring to crumble; transfer to a colander to drain. Return ground chuck to skillet; add next 7 ingredients. Cover and cook 10 minutes, stirring occasionally.

Add olives, wine, water, tomato sauce, salt, nutmeg, and hot sauce; bring to a boil. Cover; reduce heat to low, and simmer 30 minutes. Uncover and simmer until mixture is thickened and liquid evaporates. Discard bay leaf.

Spoon over rice; garnish with chopped tomato. Yield: 6 servings (251 calories per serving plus 118 calories per ½ cup cooked rice).

PRO 24.6 / FAT 11.5 / CARB 12.2 / FIB 1.5 / CHOL 80 / SOD 460 / POT 655

BEEF AND SPINACH LOAF

2 pounds lean ground chuck
½ cup chopped onion
2 slices whole-grain bread, crumbled
1 egg, lightly beaten
1 teaspoon Worcestershire sauce
1 teaspoon Dijon mustard
¼ teaspoon dried whole thyme
¼ cup minced fresh parsley
⅛ teaspoon pepper
1 (10-ounce) package frozen chopped spinach, thawed
1 egg, lightly beaten
⅛ teaspoon pepper
1 tablespoon grated Parmesan cheese
2 tablespoons low-fat cottage cheese

Combine first 9 ingredients in a large bowl, and set aside.

Place spinach between paper towels, and squeeze until barely moist. Combine spinach, 1 egg, ⅛ teaspoon pepper, Parmesan cheese, and cottage cheese in a medium bowl.

Shape half of ground chuck mixture into an 8- x 5-inch rectangle; spread with spinach filling, leaving a 1-inch border on all sides. Shape remaining beef into an 8- x 5-inch rectangle, and place on top of spinach filling. Pinch edges to seal; place loaf on a rack in a roasting pan.

Cover loaf loosely with aluminum foil, and bake at 375° for 50 minutes. Remove foil, and bake an additional 25 minutes. Let stand 10 minutes, and cut into 1-inch slices to serve. Yield: 8 servings (249 calories per serving).

PRO 27.8 / FAT 11.9 / CARB 6.8 / FIB 1.1 / CHOL 149 / SOD 153 / POT 554

A healthier way of eating does not mean that you have to give up red meat. It does mean learning to choose smaller and leaner portions of meat and then flavoring them with herbs, spices, and wine.

A general rule to remember when shopping for meat is that the tenderest cuts usually carry the most fat. That extra fat is what makes the calorie count per ounce of rib-eye steak, t-bone steak, rib roast, and ground beef higher than the leaner cuts, such as round steak, flank steak, tip roast, and ground chuck.

BEEF-STUFFED PEPPERS

1 cup frozen whole kernel corn
5 medium-size green peppers
Vegetable cooking spray
1 pound lean ground chuck
¼ cup chopped onion
½ cup (2 ounces) shredded extra-sharp Cheddar cheese
⅓ cup reduced-calorie catsup
1 teaspoon chili powder
1 teaspoon Worcestershire sauce

Cook corn according to package directions, omitting salt and fat; drain and set aside.

Cut tops off green peppers; remove seeds. Chop tops; set aside. Cook peppers in boiling water to cover 5 minutes; drain and set aside.

Coat a skillet with cooking spray; place over medium heat until hot. Add ground chuck, onion, and chopped pepper; cook until ground chuck is browned. Drain. Stir in corn, cheese, catsup, chili powder, and Worcestershire sauce; spoon mixture into peppers. Place in a shallow baking dish. Bake at 350° for 30 to 40 minutes. Yield: 5 servings (269 calories per serving).

PRO 23.7 / FAT 12.4 / CARB 16.2 / FIB 2.3 / CHOL 76 / SOD 126 / POT 794

BEEF LIVER IN TOMATO SAUCE

Vegetable cooking spray
1 cup sliced fresh mushrooms
½ cup chopped onion
1½ pounds thinly sliced calf liver
1 (8-ounce) can low-sodium tomato sauce
¼ to ½ teaspoon dried whole oregano
¼ teaspoon freshly ground black pepper
¼ teaspoon dried whole thyme
1 bay leaf

Coat a large skillet with cooking spray; place over medium heat until hot. Add mushrooms and onion. Sauté until tender; remove from skillet, and set aside. Cook liver in skillet over medium heat 5 minutes on each side or until browned; add sautéed mixture and remaining ingredients. Simmer over low heat 5 minutes. Remove bay leaf; transfer to a platter to serve. Yield: 6 servings (181 calories per serving).

PRO 22.6 / FAT 5.4 / CARB 9.5 / FIB 0.3 / CHOL 340 / SOD 92 / POT 546

VEAL PAILLARDS WITH LEMON

2 teaspoons unsalted margarine, melted
1 teaspoon lemon juice
½ teaspoon Dijon mustard
¼ teaspoon pepper
1 pound veal cutlets
Vegetable cooking spray
1 tablespoon minced fresh parsley
1 lemon, thinly sliced

Combine first 4 ingredients; set aside. Trim excess fat from veal cutlets. Place cutlets between 2 sheets of waxed paper, and flatten to ⅛-inch thickness. Brush veal with lemon mixture.

Place a nonstick skillet coated with cooking spray over medium-high heat until hot. Add veal cutlets and cook 1 minute on each side or until done. Transfer to a platter. Sprinkle with parsley; garnish with lemon. Yield: 4 servings (217 calories per serving).

PRO 22.5 / FAT 13.3 / CARB 0.3 / FIB 0.0 / CHOL 86 / SOD 87 / POT 434

WIENER SCHNITZEL

1 pound veal cutlets
¼ cup all-purpose flour
⅛ teaspoon pepper
2 eggs, beaten
¾ cup fine, dry breadcrumbs
Vegetable cooking spray
2 teaspoons unsalted margarine
1 lemon, cut into wedges
1 teaspoon capers (optional)

Trim excess fat from veal cutlets. Place cutlets between 2 sheets of waxed paper; flatten to ⅛-inch thickness, using a meat mallet or rolling pin. Combine flour and pepper in a shallow dish. Dredge cutlets in flour mixture; dip veal in egg, and dredge in breadcrumbs.

Coat a large nonstick skillet with cooking spray; add margarine, and place over medium heat until margarine melts. Add veal cutlets, and cook 4 to 5 minutes on each side or until browned. Transfer to a platter; garnish with lemon wedges and capers, if desired. Yield: 4 servings (338 calories per serving).

PRO 28.7 / FAT 14.7 / CARB 20.6 / FIB 0.3 / CHOL 218 / SOD 275 / POT 433

VEAL IN MUSHROOM-WINE SAUCE

1 pound veal cutlets
Vegetable cooking spray
2 tablespoons unsalted margarine
¼ teaspoon pepper
¼ pound fresh mushrooms, sliced
2 tablespoons all-purpose flour
¾ cup dry white wine
½ cup water
1 teaspoon chicken-flavored bouillon granules
¼ cup (1 ounce) shredded part-skim mozzarella cheese
2 tablespoons grated Parmesan cheese

Trim excess fat from veal cutlets; place cutlets between 2 sheets of waxed paper, and flatten to ⅛-inch thickness, using a meat mallet or rolling pin.

Coat a large skillet with cooking spray; add margarine, and place over medium-high heat until margarine melts. Add veal cutlets, and cook 1 to 2 minutes on each side or until lightly browned. Drain on paper towels; place in a 10- x 6- x 2-inch baking dish coated with cooking spray, overlapping edges. Sprinkle with pepper.

Sauté mushrooms in skillet until tender; remove from skillet, reserving pan drippings in skillet. Sprinkle mushrooms over veal cutlets.

Add flour to skillet; stir until smooth. Cook over low heat 1 minute; stir constantly. Gradually add wine, water, and bouillon granules; cook over medium heat, stirring constantly, until thickened and bubbly. Spoon over veal cutlets. Top with cheese. Bake at 425° for 10 to 12 minutes. Yield: 4 servings (289 calories per serving).

PRO 25.9 / FAT 17.3 / CARB 6.8 / FIB 0.4 / CHOL 88 / SOD 274 / POT 524

Veal is tender and juicy even though it comes from very young animals that do not have excessive marbling (streaks of fat). Its neutral flavor presents an ideal meat for a variety of sauces, such as that in Veal in Mushroom Wine Sauce. And, yet, it is just as flavorful when grilled or sautéed with mustard and lemon juice, as in Veal Paillards with Lemon.

So when you want to add variety to your low-calorie meals, choose veal cutlets or lean veal chops, and flavor them imaginatively.

A classic entrée, Veal Cordon Bleu can be lightened and still retain its flavor and texture.

VEAL CORDON BLEU

8 veal cutlets (1 pound)
2 (¾-ounce) slices Swiss cheese
2 (½-ounce) slices lean cooked ham
½ teaspoon pepper
1 egg, lightly beaten
2 tablespoons all-purpose flour
1 egg, lightly beaten
½ cup fine, dry breadcrumbs
1½ teaspoons unsalted margarine, melted
1½ teaspoons vegetable oil
Vegetable cooking spray
Fresh parsley sprigs (optional)
Lemon slices (optional)

Trim excess fat from cutlets. Place cutlets between 2 sheets of waxed paper, and flatten to ⅛-inch thickness. Cut cheese and ham slices in half. Sprinkle 4 cutlets with pepper, and brush edges with 1 egg; top each with ½ slice of cheese and ham. Cover with remaining 4 cutlets; pound edges to seal.

Dredge sealed cutlets in flour; dip in 1 egg, and coat with breadcrumbs. Cook in hot margarine and oil in a nonstick skillet over medium-high heat 2 minutes on each side or until browned. Arrange in a 12- x 8- x 2-inch baking dish coated with cooking spray. Bake at 375° for 20 minutes. Transfer to a serving platter. Garnish with parsley sprigs and lemon slices, if desired. Yield: 4 servings (358 calories per serving).

PRO 31.9 / FAT 18.9 / CARB 13.3 / FIB 0.2 / CHOL 231 / SOD 358 / POT 458

SHERRIED VEAL

½ pound veal cutlets
⅛ teaspoon pepper
Vegetable cooking spray
1 teaspoon olive oil
1 tablespoon minced shallot
1 clove garlic, minced
3 tablespoons dry sherry or Madeira
1 teaspoon minced fresh chives or parsley

Trim excess fat from veal cutlets. Place cutlets between 2 sheets of waxed paper, and flatten to ¼-inch thickness, using a meat mallet or rolling pin; sprinkle with pepper. Coat a heavy skillet with cooking spray; add oil, and place over medium-high heat until hot. Add veal cutlets; cook 2 minutes on each side or until browned. Transfer to a platter; keep warm.

Add shallot, garlic, and sherry to skillet; simmer 5 minutes. Return veal to skillet; cover and cook 2 minutes or until cutlets are done. Transfer to platter, and sprinkle with chives. Yield: 2 servings (210 calories per serving).

PRO 22.6 / FAT 11.3 / CARB 3.2 / FIB 0.1 / CHOL 81 / SOD 104 / POT 405

VEAL PARMIGIANA

Vegetable cooking spray
½ cup chopped onion
2 teaspoons minced garlic
2 cups chopped, peeled tomato
1 (6-ounce) can tomato paste
1 (8-ounce) can tomato sauce
¼ cup dry red wine
½ teaspoon dried whole oregano
1½ pounds veal cutlets
½ cup fine, dry breadcrumbs
2 tablespoons grated Parmesan cheese
1 egg, beaten
1 teaspoon olive oil
1 cup (4 ounces) shredded part-skim mozzarella cheese

Coat a Dutch oven with cooking spray; place over medium heat until hot. Add onion and garlic, and sauté 5 minutes. Add tomato, and cook 10 minutes. Stir in tomato paste, tomato sauce, wine, and oregano; simmer, uncovered, 30 minutes. Remove from heat, and set aside.

Trim excess fat from veal cutlets. Place cutlets between 2 sheets of waxed paper, and flatten to ¼-inch thickness, using a meat mallet or rolling pin. Combine breadcrumbs and Parmesan cheese in a shallow dish. Dip cutlets in egg, and dredge in breadcrumb mixture. Let stand on waxed paper 15 minutes.

Coat a skillet with cooking spray; add oil, and place over medium heat until hot. Add cutlets, and cook 4 to 5 minutes on each side or until lightly browned.

Spoon ¼ cup tomato sauce into a 13- x 9- x 2-inch baking dish coated with cooking spray. Place cutlets in dish, and top with remaining sauce. Cover and bake at 350° for 25 minutes. Remove from oven, and top with mozzarella cheese. Bake, uncovered, an additional 8 minutes or until cheese is bubbly. Yield: 6 servings (338 calories per serving).

PRO 32.1 / FAT 15.0 / CARB 18.5 / FIB 0.4 / CHOL 139 / SOD 481 / POT 965

VEAL ROLLS WITH POLENTA

3 cups plus 1 tablespoon water, divided
½ cup cornmeal
2 tablespoons grated Parmesan cheese
½ teaspoon dried whole sage
1 pound veal cutlets
3 tablespoons all-purpose flour
Vegetable cooking spray
2 teaspoons vegetable oil
½ cup dry vermouth
1 teaspoon chicken-flavored bouillon granules
1 teaspoon cornstarch

Bring 2 cups water to a boil in a large saucepan. Add cornmeal, a little at a time, stirring constantly. (Procedure should take 20 minutes.) Remove from heat, and stir in Parmesan cheese and sage; set aside.

Trim excess fat from veal cutlets. Place cutlets between 2 sheets of waxed paper; flatten to ¼- to ⅛-inch thickness, using a meat mallet or rolling pin. Dredge cutlets in flour, and set aside. Coat a skillet with cooking spray; add oil, and place over medium heat until hot. Add cutlets; cook 2 minutes on each side. Transfer to a plate. Add vermouth to skillet; cook over medium-high heat until reduced to 2 tablespoons. Add 1 cup water and bouillon granules.

Place 2 tablespoons cornmeal mixture in center of each veal cutlet. Roll up cutlets, and secure with wooden picks. Add to skillet; bring to a boil. Cover; reduce heat, and simmer 2 minutes; transfer veal rolls to a platter.

Combine cornstarch and 1 tablespoon water; stir into skillet, and cook until thickened and bubbly. Spoon sauce over veal rolls to serve. Yield: 4 servings (377 calories per serving).

PRO 33.2 / FAT 19.0 / CARB 15.8 / FIB 2.5 / CHOL 117 / SOD 234 / POT 650

SAVORY VEAL

½ (12-ounce) package corkscrew pasta
1 pound veal cutlets
¼ teaspoon freshly ground black pepper
1 clove garlic, crushed
2 teaspoons unsalted margarine, melted
1 medium onion, cut into strips
2 green peppers, seeded and cut into strips
½ cup dry white wine
½ cup water
1 teaspoon beef-flavored bouillon granules
½ teaspoon dried whole basil
¼ teaspoon dried whole oregano
1½ teaspoons cornstarch
2 tablespoons water
12 cherry tomatoes, halved

Cook pasta according to package directions, omitting salt; drain and set aside.

Trim excess fat from veal cutlets; cut into 1-inch strips. Sprinkle with pepper.

Sauté garlic in margarine in a large skillet over medium-high heat until tender. Add cutlets, and cook until browned. Stir in next 7 ingredients, and bring to a boil. Cover; reduce heat, and simmer 5 minutes or until vegetables are crisp-tender.

Combine cornstarch and 2 tablespoons water, stirring until blended; stir into veal mixture. Bring to a boil, and cook 1 minute or until slightly thickened. Stir in tomatoes. Serve over corkscrew pasta. Yield: 6 servings (163 calories per serving plus 105 calories per ½ cup pasta).

PRO 19.5 / FAT 8.1 / CARB 28.8 / FIB 1.7 / CHOL 54 / SOD 151 / POT 523

White wine enhances the flavor of Savory Veal.

VEAL CHOPS WITH SHALLOT SAUCE

2 (5-ounce) loin veal chops, ¾-inch thick
Vegetable cooking spray
1 teaspoon unsalted margarine
½ cup dry white wine
¼ cup minced shallot
¼ cup chicken broth
¼ teaspoon dried whole rosemary, crushed
1 tablespoon minced fresh parsley

Trim excess fat from veal chops. Coat a large skillet with cooking spray. Add margarine, and place over medium-high heat until margarine melts. Add veal chops, and cook 4 minutes on each side; transfer to a platter.

Add wine to skillet. Add shallot, and cook over medium-high heat until mixture is reduced by half. Add chicken broth, rosemary, and veal.

Cover and simmer 20 to 25 minutes or until tender. Transfer veal chops to platter; keep warm. Cook remaining pan juices over medium-high heat until reduced by half. Spoon sauce over veal chops; garnish with parsley. Yield: 2 servings (224 calories per serving).

PRO 23.6 / FAT 11.2 / CARB 6.2 / FIB 0.2 / CHOL 81 / SOD 205 / POT 522

BRAISED VEAL SHANKS

6 (5-ounce) veal shanks
Vegetable cooking spray
1 cup dry white wine
½ cup water
1 cup sliced carrots
½ cup diced onion
½ cup diced, peeled tomato
1 tablespoon minced garlic
½ teaspoon dried whole thyme
½ teaspoon chicken-flavored bouillon granules

Trim excess fat from veal shanks. Coat a large skillet with cooking spray; place over medium-high heat until hot. Add shanks; cook 3 minutes on each side or until browned. Drain; transfer to a 4-quart casserole. Add remaining ingredients. Cover and bake at 325° for 1½ hours. Yield: 6 servings (201 calories per serving).

PRO 24.1 / FAT 8.7 / CARB 5.5 / FIB 0.4 / CHOL 83 / SOD 107 / POT 555

LAMB STEAKS WITH MINT SAUCE

6 (4-ounce) lamb steaks with bone, ¼-inch thick
1 cup red wine vinegar
2 medium-size red onions, sliced
3 tablespoons minced fresh mint
½ teaspoon pepper
Vegetable cooking spray
2 tablespoons sugar
¾ cup chicken broth

Combine steaks and vinegar in a large shallow dish; top with onion, mint, and pepper. Cover and marinate in refrigerator 1 hour.
Drain steaks and onion, reserving marinade. Place steaks and onion on a rack in a broiler pan coated with cooking spray; broil 4 inches from heat 4 minutes on each side or until desired degree of doneness. Transfer to a platter; cover and keep warm.
Combine reserved marinade with sugar in a small saucepan, and bring to a boil; reduce heat, and simmer until mixture is reduced by half. Add broth, and cook until sauce is reduced by half. Drizzle sauce over steaks to serve. Yield: 6 servings (201 calories per serving with 1 tablespoon plus 1½ teaspoons sauce per serving).

PRO 25.6 / FAT 6.3 / CARB 7.8 / FIB 0.4 / CHOL 85 / SOD 160 / POT 375

Out of the over 20 minerals the body needs for overall mental and physical functioning, iron is one of the most valuable. Every cell relies on iron for giving oxygen. Most of the iron in the body is a part of the proteins hemoglobin and myoglobin. Hemoglobin is the oxygen carrier in the red blood cells, and myoglobin carries the oxygen in the muscle cells.

Almost 80 percent of the iron in the body is in the blood, so iron losses are greatest whenever blood is lost. Thus, women, due to menstruation, need 18 milligrams of iron per day, and men only 10. Iron deficiency can sometimes be a problem with athletes because heavy, continuous sweating may increase iron loss by 1 milligram per day. Other groups prone to iron deficiency are dieters and vegetarians.

Iron-rich foods include liver (also high in cholesterol), lean red meats, dark meat of poultry, seafood (notably tuna and salmon), legumes, tofu, and enriched breads, cereals and pasta.

It is important to remember that iron does not work alone. Vitamin C eaten in combination with any iron source helps the body absorb the maximum amount of iron. And drinking tea while eating iron-rich foods will cut iron absorption by about 50 percent.

ORANGE LAMB CHOPS

6 (5-ounce) lamb chops, ¾-inch thick
Vegetable cooking spray
½ cup sliced onion
½ cup unsweetened orange juice
2 tablespoons dry white wine
1 teaspoon reduced-sodium soy sauce
¼ teaspoon ground ginger
⅛ teaspoon pepper or to taste
1 tablespoon orange rind

Trim excess fat from lamb chops; set lamb chops aside. Coat a large nonstick skillet with cooking spray; place over medium heat until hot. Add lamb chops, and cook 3 to 4 minutes on each side or until lightly browned. Add next 6 ingredients; bring to a boil. Cover; reduce heat, and simmer 15 to 20 minutes or until lamb chops are tender. Transfer to a platter, and garnish with grated orange rind. Yield: 6 servings (183 calories per serving).

PRO 24.6 / FAT 7.2 / CARB 3.3 / FIB 0.1 / CHOL 85 / SOD 124 / POT 419

GRILLED SKEWERED LAMB

1 pound lean boneless lamb
4 fresh mushrooms, halved
4 pearl onions
1 medium-size green or yellow pepper, seeded and cut into 1-inch pieces
1 tablespoon minced garlic
⅛ teaspoon salt
⅛ teaspoon pepper
⅛ teaspoon dried whole thyme
⅛ teaspoon dried whole savory
½ cup red wine

Trim excess fat from lamb; cut into 1-inch cubes. Combine lamb and remaining ingredients in a large shallow dish; stir to coat. Cover and marinate in refrigerator overnight.

Thread lamb, mushrooms, onions, and green pepper onto 4 metal skewers. Broil 4 to 6 inches from heat 12 to 16 minutes or until browned, turning and basting frequently with marinade. Yield: 4 servings (188 calories per serving).

PRO 25.1 / FAT 6.7 / CARB 6.2 / FIB 0.7 / CHOL 85 / SOD 137 / POT 441

GRILLED LEG OF LAMB

1 cup red wine vinegar
3 tablespoons Worcestershire sauce
1 tablespoon Dijon mustard
3 cloves garlic, minced
1½ teaspoons dried whole thyme
1 teaspoon pepper
1 (3-pound) boned and butterflied leg of lamb

Combine first 6 ingredients in a large shallow dish, mixing well. Trim excess fat from leg of lamb; add lamb to marinade, turning to coat.

Cover and marinate in refrigerator 2 hours.

Drain lamb, reserving marinade. Grill over medium-hot coals 25 to 30 minutes on each side or until meat thermometer registers 140° for medium-rare meat; 160° for medium meat; or 170° for well-done meat. Baste frequently with reserved marinade during grilling. Let stand 10 minutes, and carve into thin slices to serve. Yield: 12 servings (167 calories per serving).

PRO 24.6 / FAT 6.1 / CARB 1.2 / FIB 0.1 / CHOL 85 / SOD 135 / POT 298

SPICED LAMB AND RICE

1 pound lean boneless lamb
Vegetable cooking spray
2 cups thinly sliced onion
2 teaspoons minced garlic
1 teaspoon vegetable oil
1½ cups chicken broth
¾ cup water
⅓ cup raisins
1 tablespoon minced, peeled gingerroot
1 teaspoon grated lemon rind
1½ teaspoons ground cumin
½ teaspoon ground cinnamon
½ teaspoon ground mace
¼ teaspoon crushed red pepper
¼ teaspoon ground turmeric
1 cup regular rice, uncooked

Trim excess fat from lamb; cut lamb into 1-inch strips, and set aside. Coat a skillet with cooking spray; place over medium heat until hot. Add onion and garlic, and sauté until tender. Remove from skillet, and set aside.

Add oil to skillet, and place over medium-high heat until hot. Add lamb, and cook until browned; transfer meat to a colander to drain.

Combine broth and water in a small saucepan; bring to a boil. Add raisins. Remove from heat; let stand 5 minutes. Add gingerroot, lemon rind, cumin, cinnamon, mace, red pepper, and turmeric, mixing well.

Place rice in a 10- x 6- x 2-inch baking dish coated with cooking spray; top with lamb, onion mixture, and broth mixture. Cover and bake at 350° for 30 minutes; uncover and bake an additional 15 to 20 minutes. Yield: 8 servings (208 calories per serving).

PRO 15.1 / FAT 4.3 / CARB 26.4 / FIB 1.3 / CHOL 43 / SOD 180 / POT 292

ORIENTAL STIR-FRIED LAMB

½ cup water
¼ cup reduced-sodium soy sauce
2 teaspoons cornstarch
¼ teaspoon ground ginger
1 pound boneless leg of lamb
Vegetable cooking spray
1 cup sliced onion
2 small red or green peppers, seeded and
   cut into julienne strips
½ cup sliced green onion
¼ cup coarsely chopped walnuts
2 cups hot cooked regular rice (cooked without salt
   or fat)

Combine first 4 ingredients in a bowl; set aside. Trim excess fat from lamb; cut lamb into thin strips, and set aside. Coat a large skillet with cooking spray; place over high heat until hot. Add lamb; stir-fry 5 minutes. Add onion; stir-fry 2 minutes. Add red peppers; stir-fry 1 minute.

Add soy sauce mixture; bring to a boil, stirring constantly. Stir in green onion and walnuts. Serve over rice. Yield: 4 servings (242 calories per serving plus 118 calories per ½-cup rice).

PRO 26.7 / FAT 10.5 / CARB 10.0 / FIB 1.8 / CHOL 79 / SOD 670 / POT 561

LAMB SHOULDER PROVENÇAL

2½ pounds lamb shoulder with bone
½ teaspoon pepper
Vegetable cooking spray
2 cups chopped onion
2 cloves garlic, minced
1 (10¾-ounce) can chicken broth, undiluted
¾ cup water
½ cup dry white wine
3 tablespoons tomato paste
½ teaspoon dried whole basil
½ teaspoon dried whole thyme
1 tablespoon cornstarch
1 tablespoon water
3 cups diced eggplant
1 cup diced green pepper
1½ cups diced tomato

Trim excess fat from lamb shoulder; cut lamb into 16 pieces, and discard bone. Sprinkle lamb with pepper. Coat a large heavy Dutch oven with cooking spray; place over medium-high heat until hot. Add lamb, and cook 2 to 3 minutes on each side or until browned.

Add next 8 ingredients to Dutch oven; bring to a boil. Cover; reduce heat, and simmer 1 hour or until tender. Skim fat from broth.

Combine cornstarch and 1 tablespoon water in a small bowl; set aside. Coat a large skillet with cooking spray; place over medium heat until hot. Add eggplant and green pepper; cook 3 minutes or until eggplant is slightly softened, stirring constantly. Add tomato, and cook 1 minute. Stir dissolved cornstarch and eggplant mixture into lamb mixture in Dutch oven, and cook over low heat 15 minutes or until thickened, stirring occasionally. Yield: 8 servings (238 calories per serving).

PRO 26.6 / FAT 9.6 / CARB 10.8 / FIB 1.4 / CHOL 90 / SOD 195 / POT 613

MOUSSAKA

1 pound eggplant, cut into ¼-inch slices
Vegetable cooking spray
1 pound coarsely ground lean lamb
1 cup chopped onion
1 teaspoon minced garlic
1 cup chopped tomato
2 tablespoons tomato paste
½ teaspoon ground cinnamon
¼ teaspoon dried whole oregano
2 eggs
¼ cup all-purpose flour
1 cup skim milk
¼ teaspoon ground nutmeg
2 tablespoons grated Parmesan cheese

Place eggplant on a baking sheet coated with cooking spray; bake at 350° for 5 to 7 minutes. Turn eggplant slices, and bake an additional 5 to 7 minutes.

Coat a skillet with cooking spray; place over medium-high heat until hot. Add ground lamb, and cook 5 minutes or until browned; transfer to a colander to drain, and return to skillet. Stir in onion and garlic; cook 2 minutes. Add next 4 ingredients; reduce heat to low, and cook 5 minutes.

Arrange half of lamb mixture in an 8-inch square baking dish coated with cooking spray; top with half of eggplant. Repeat with remaining lamb mixture and eggplant.

Combine eggs and flour in a bowl, stirring with a wire whisk until smooth; set aside. Place milk in a saucepan, and bring to a boil; reduce heat to low. Gradually add ¼ cup of milk to flour mixture, stirring with a wire whisk; stir flour mixture into remaining milk. Cook over low heat 2 to 3 minutes or until thickened, stirring with a wire whisk. Stir in nutmeg. Pour sauce over eggplant and lamb mixture.

Sprinkle with Parmesan cheese, and bake at 350° for 1 hour or until top is browned. Yield: 6 servings (184 calories per serving).

PRO 17.7 / FAT 5.6 / CARB 16.1 / FIB 1.9 / CHOL 133 / SOD 128 / POT 591

STUFFED PORK LOIN

Vegetable cooking spray
½ cup finely chopped onion
1 clove garlic, minced
1 slice whole-grain bread, crumbled
1 egg, lightly beaten
4 pitted prunes, minced
2 tablespoons minced fresh parsley
½ teaspoon grated lemon rind
¼ teaspoon dried whole rosemary, crushed
¼ teaspoon pepper
1 (2½-pound) boneless pork loin roast, rolled and tied
½ teaspoon dried whole rosemary, crushed
¼ teaspoon dried whole thyme
⅛ teaspoon pepper

Coat a medium skillet with cooking spray; place over medium heat until hot. Add onion and garlic; sauté until tender. Remove from heat, and add next 7 ingredients, mixing well.

Untie roast, and trim excess fat. Stuff roast with bread mixture, and retie. Sprinkle roast with ½ teaspoon rosemary, thyme, and ⅛ teaspoon pepper. Place roast on a rack in a roasting pan, and insert meat thermometer, if desired. Place roast in oven at 450°. Reduce heat to 350°, and bake 2 hours or until meat thermometer registers 170°.

Transfer roast to a cutting board; let stand 10 minutes. Remove string; cut into ½-inch slices. Yield: 10 servings (233 calories per serving).

PRO 24.1 / FAT 12.6 / CARB 4.7 / FIB 0.3 / CHOL 104 / SOD 73 / POT 365

HERBED PORK ROAST

1 (3½-pound) boneless pork loin roast
2 cloves garlic, minced
½ teaspoon dried whole thyme or 1½ teaspoons fresh thyme
¼ teaspoon dried whole oregano or ¾ teaspoon fresh oregano
¼ teaspoon pepper
⅛ teaspoon dried whole sage or ¼ teaspoon fresh sage

Trim excess fat from roast; roll, tie, and set aside. Combine remaining ingredients in a small bowl; rub herb mixture over surface of roast. Place roast on a rack in a roasting pan, and insert a meat thermometer, if desired. Bake, uncovered, at 350° for 2 hours or until meat thermometer registers 170°. Let roast stand 10 minutes; remove string, and cut into thin slices. Yield: 12 servings (239 calories per serving).

PRO 26.7 / FAT 13.8 / CARB 0.3 / FIB 0.0 / CHOL 89 / SOD 69 / POT 368

BRAISED PORK WITH APPLES

1½ pounds boneless pork loin
Vegetable cooking spray
½ cup unsweetened apple cider
1 tablespoon brown sugar
¼ teaspoon ground cinnamon
⅛ teaspoon pepper
3 medium Granny Smith apples, cored and sliced into rings
1 tablespoon cornstarch
2 tablespoons water

Trim excess fat from roast; cut into ¾-inch-thick pieces, and set aside. Coat a Dutch oven with cooking spray; place over medium heat until hot. Add roast; brown on all sides. Add next 4 ingredients; bring to a boil. Cover; reduce heat, and simmer 10 minutes, stirring occasionally. Add apples; cook 10 minutes or until roast and apples are tender. Transfer to a serving dish, using a slotted spoon; keep warm.

Combine cornstarch and water; stir into Dutch oven. Cook over medium heat until thickened; stir constantly. Serve over roast and apples. Yield: 6 servings (264 calories per serving).

PRO 23.0 / FAT 12.1 / CARB 15.2 / FIB 1.4 / CHOL 77 / SOD 60 / POT 419

OVEN-BARBECUED PORK CHOPS

1 (10½-ounce) can low-sodium tomato soup
  with tomato pieces
½ cup chopped onion
¼ cup cider vinegar
1 tablespoon minced green pepper
1 tablespoon barbecue spice
2 teaspoons brown sugar
1 teaspoon dry mustard
¼ teaspoon pepper
⅛ teaspoon ground red pepper
¾ teaspoon hot sauce
6 (6-ounce) center loin pork chops, ¾-inch thick

Combine first 10 ingredients in a saucepan; bring mixture to a boil. Cover; reduce heat, and simmer 45 minutes, stirring occasionally. Set mixture aside.

Trim excess fat from pork chops. Arrange chops in a single layer in a 12- x 8- x 2-inch baking dish; top with reserved sauce. Cover and bake at 350° for 45 minutes to 1 hour or until pork chops are done. Yield: 6 servings (253 calories per serving).

PRO 25.3 / FAT 12.5 / CARB 9.1 / FIB 0.5 / CHOL 77 / SOD 73 / POT 455

ORANGE-PINEAPPLE PORK CHOPS

4 (6-ounce) center loin pork chops, ½-inch thick
Vegetable cooking spray
¼ teaspoon salt
¼ teaspoon pepper
1 cup unsweetened pineapple juice, divided
1 teaspoon cornstarch
⅛ teaspoon ground allspice
1 medium orange, peeled, sectioned, and seeded

Trim excess fat from pork chops; set aside. Coat a large skillet with cooking spray; place over medium-high heat until hot. Add chops, and brown on each side. Season with salt and pepper. Add ¾ cup pineapple juice, and bring to a boil. Cover; reduce heat, and simmer 45 minutes or until pork chops are tender.

Combine cornstarch, remaining ¼ cup pineapple juice, and allspice in a small bowl; stir into skillet, and cook until thickened and bubbly, stirring constantly. Add orange sections, and cook until thoroughly heated. Yield: 4 servings (260 calories per serving).

PRO 24.9 / FAT 11.3 / CARB 13.8 / FIB 0.8 / CHOL 77 / SOD 206 / POT 479

SWEET-AND-SOUR PORK

1½ pounds boneless pork loin
Vegetable cooking spray
1 (8-ounce) can tomato sauce
¼ cup cider vinegar
2 tablespoons brown sugar
2 teaspoons reduced-sodium soy sauce
⅛ teaspoon garlic powder
⅛ teaspoon pepper
1 (20-ounce) can unsweetened pineapple chunks, undrained
1 medium-size green pepper, seeded and cut into 1-inch pieces
½ cup thinly sliced onion
2 tablespoons cornstarch
4 cups hot cooked regular rice (cooked without salt or fat)

Trim excess fat from roast; cut roast into ½-inch pieces, and set aside. Coat a skillet with cooking spray; place over medium heat until hot. Add pork; cook 10 minutes or until browned, stirring well. Remove pork; drain.

Combine pork and next 6 ingredients in skillet. Bring to a boil. Cover; reduce heat, and simmer 15 to 20 minutes or until pork is tender.

Drain pineapple, reserving ½ cup juice. Add pineapple, green pepper, and onion to skillet; cover and simmer 5 minutes or until vegetables are crisp-tender. Combine cornstarch and reserved ½ cup pineapple juice; stir into pork mixture. Cook, stirring constantly, until thickened and bubbly. Serve over rice. Yield: 8 servings (214 calories per serving plus 118 calories per ½-cup cooked rice).

PRO 20.4 / FAT 9.1 / CARB 41.2 / FIB 1.2 / CHOL 57 / SOD 221 / POT 518

Stir-frying seals in nutrients and saves color and crunch in Pork and Vegetable Stir-Fry.

PORK AND VEGETABLE STIR-FRY

1 pound lean boneless pork
¾ pound fresh mushrooms
1 (1-pound) bunch fresh broccoli
Vegetable cooking spray
1 teaspoon vegetable oil
5 carrots, sliced diagonally
¼ cup reduced-sodium soy sauce
2 tablespoons cornstarch
1½ teaspoons chicken-flavored bouillon granules
½ teaspoon salt
1½ cups water
2 cups hot cooked regular pasta (cooked without salt or fat)

Partially freeze pork; trim excess fat from pork. Slice across grain into 2- x ¼-inch strips, and set aside. Wipe mushrooms with a damp paper towel; remove stems, and reserve for another use. Slice caps, and set aside.

Wash broccoli, and remove flowerets; reserve stalks for another use. Cut flowerets into small pieces; set aside.

Coat a wok or large skillet with cooking spray; add oil, and place over high heat until hot. Add pork; stir-fry 4 minutes or until lightly browned. Add mushroom caps, carrots, and soy sauce. Cover; reduce heat to low, and cook 8 minutes. Add broccoli; cover and cook 3 minutes or until broccoli is crisp-tender.

Combine cornstarch, bouillon granules, salt, and water; mix well. Pour over pork and vegetables, stirring well. Cook, stirring constantly, until sauce is slightly thickened. Serve over pasta. Yield: 4 servings (312 calories per serving plus 105 calories per ½-cup cooked pasta).

PRO 35.9 / FAT 10.8 / CARB 45.6 / FIB 4.3 / CHOL 71 / SOD 1158/POT 1444

PORK BREAKFAST PATTIES

1 pound ground pork shoulder
½ teaspoon salt
1 teaspoon fennel seeds
1 teaspoon minced garlic
¾ teaspoon dried whole thyme
Vegetable cooking spray

Combine first 5 ingredients in a bowl, mixing just until combined. Cover and chill at least 1 hour or overnight. Shape pork mixture into 8 (½-inch-thick) patties.

Coat a large skillet with cooking spray; place over medium heat until hot. Add pork patties to skillet, and cook 7 to 8 minutes on each side or until lightly browned. Yield: 8 servings (106 calories per serving).

PRO 10.9 / FAT 6.4 / CARB 0.3 / FIB 0.1 / CHOL 41 / SOD 179 / POT 156

CURRIED HAM LOAF

1 (8-ounce) can unsweetened sliced pineapple, undrained
1 pound ground fresh lean ham
½ pound ground lean pork
1 egg, slightly beaten
1 medium-size green pepper, finely chopped
1 cup soft whole wheat breadcrumbs
¼ cup skim milk
1 tablespoon prepared mustard
½ teaspoon curry powder
¼ teaspoon pepper
Vegetable cooking spray

Drain pineapple, reserving juice; set pineapple aside. Combine pineapple juice, ground ham and pork, egg, green pepper, breadcrumbs, milk, mustard, curry powder, and pepper in a large bowl; mix well.

Coat a 9- x 5- x 3-inch loafpan with cooking spray. Cut pineapple slices in half, and arrange in bottom of loafpan. Spoon ham mixture into loafpan, packing lightly; bake at 350° for 1 hour or until done. Pour off pan drippings; let stand 10 minutes before unmolding. Transfer to a serving platter, and cut into slices. Yield: 8 servings (240 calories per serving).

PRO 24.5 / FAT 10.3 / CARB 11.8 / FIB 0.8 / CHOL 107 / SOD 155 / POT 373

APRICOT-GLAZED HAM

⅓ cup reduced-calorie apricot spread
2 tablespoons spicy hot mustard
1 teaspoon reduced-sodium soy sauce
1 (3½-pound) boneless, fully-cooked ham

Combine spread, mustard, and soy sauce in a small bowl. Place ham on a rack in a roasting pan. Bake at 325° for 1 hour, basting with apricot glaze every 10 minutes during last 30 minutes of cooking. Transfer ham to a cutting board, and carve into thin slices to serve. Yield: 14 servings (220 calories per serving).

PRO 20.1 / FAT 12.1 / CARB 6.5 / FIB 0.0 / CHOL 65 / SOD 1534 / POT 388

HAM AND LEEK GRATIN

1 pound leeks, chopped
2 tablespoons all-purpose flour
1 cup skim milk
⅛ teaspoon ground nutmeg
⅛ teaspoon pepper
½ cup (2 ounces) shredded Gruyère cheese
¼ pound cooked lean ham, diced

Cook leeks in a small amount of boiling water 5 minutes or until tender; drain.

Place flour in a small saucepan; gradually add milk, stirring with a wire whisk until smooth. Add nutmeg and pepper, and bring to a boil over medium heat. Cook 2 minutes; remove from heat, and add cheese.

Layer cheese sauce, leeks, and ham in a 9-inch gratin dish, beginning and ending with cheese sauce. Bake at 400° for 15 minutes or until thoroughly heated. Yield: 4 servings (206 calories per serving).

PRO 14.4 / FAT 6.7 / CARB 22.8 / FIB 1.5 / CHOL 32 / SOD 443 / POT 404

Poultry, a preferred source of animal protein, never lacks for interest in its presentation. Clockwise from front: Chicken Paillards (page 160), Phyllo Chicken Potpie (page 165), and Cold Fruited Chicken (page 166).

BARBECUED CHICKEN

Vegetable cooking spray
1 medium onion, finely chopped
2 cloves garlic, minced
½ cup water
½ cup reduced-calorie catsup
¼ cup red wine vinegar
1 tablespoon sugar
2 tablespoons lemon juice
⅛ teaspoon ground red pepper
1 tablespoon Dijon mustard
1 tablespoon Worcestershire sauce
1 (3-pound) broiler-fryer, cut into serving-size
    pieces and skinned

Coat a saucepan with cooking spray; place over medium heat until hot. Add onion and garlic, and sauté until tender. Add next 6 ingredients, and bring to a boil; reduce heat, and simmer 15 minutes or until sauce is slightly thickened, stirring occasionally. Stir in mustard and Worcestershire sauce.

Arrange chicken on a rack in a baking pan coated with cooking spray; brush with sauce. Bake at 350° for 50 to 60 minutes, brushing with sauce every 10 minutes. Yield: 4 servings (253 calories per serving).

PRO 32.3 / FAT 8.4 / CARB 9.6 / FIB 0.3 / CHOL 96 / SOD 247 / POT 399

HERB BAKED CHICKEN

½ cup fine, dry breadcrumbs
¼ cup grated Parmesan cheese
½ teaspoon dried whole oregano
¼ teaspoon dried whole basil
¼ teaspoon pepper
6 (6½-ounce) chicken breast halves, skinned
½ cup buttermilk
Vegetable cooking spray

Combine first 5 ingredients in a shallow dish. Dip chicken in buttermilk, and dredge in breadcrumb mixture. Arrange chicken, bone side down, in a 13- x 9- x 2-inch baking dish coated with cooking spray; cover and refrigerate 1 hour. Bake, uncovered, at 350° for 1 hour, turning after 30 minutes. Yield: 6 servings (201 calories per serving).

PRO 30.2 / FAT 4.7 / CARB 7.4 / FIB 0.1 / CHOL 78 / SOD 210 / POT 275

GRILLED SESAME CHICKEN BREASTS

½ cup white grape juice
¼ cup reduced-sodium soy sauce
¼ cup dry white wine
1 tablespoon sesame seeds
2 tablespoons vegetable oil
¼ teaspoon garlic powder
¼ teaspoon ground ginger
4 (4-ounce) boneless chicken breast halves, skinned

Combine first 7 ingredients in a shallow dish; mix well. Add chicken, turning to coat; cover and marinate in the refrigerator at least 2 hours.

Remove chicken from marinade, reserving marinade. Grill 4 to 5 inches from medium-hot coals 15 minutes, turning and basting frequently with reserved marinade. Yield: 4 servings (254 calories per serving).

PRO 27.6 / FAT 11.0 / CARB 7.2 / FIB 0.1 / CHOL 70 / SOD 645 / POT 277

CHICKEN PAILLARDS

4 (4-ounce) boneless chicken breast halves, skinned
2 tablespoons rum
2 tablespoons reduced-sodium soy sauce
3 tablespoons lime juice
1 tablespoon plus 1½ teaspoons brown sugar
1 tablespoon Worcestershire sauce
1 tablespoon vegetable oil
⅛ teaspoon pepper
Vegetable cooking spray
1 tablespoon minced fresh parsley
1 lime, cut into 4 wedges

Place chicken between 2 sheets of waxed paper; flatten to ¼-inch thickness, using a meat mallet or rolling pin; set aside. Combine next 7 ingredients in a shallow dish; mixing well. Add chicken to marinade, turning to coat well; cover and marinate in refrigerator 30 minutes.

Coat a nonstick skillet or ridged grill pan with cooking spray, and place over medium heat until hot. Remove chicken from marinade, and place in skillet; cook 4 minutes on each side or until tender. Transfer chicken to a platter, and garnish with parsley. Squeeze lime over chicken before serving. Yield: 4 servings (193 calories per serving).

PRO 26.4 / FAT 6.4 / CARB 5.9 / FIB 0.0 / CHOL 70 / SOD 390 / POT 267

CHICKEN PICCATA

4 (4-ounce) boneless chicken breast halves,
  skinned
¼ cup all-purpose flour
¼ teaspoon salt
¼ teaspoon pepper
Vegetable cooking spray
2 tablespoons unsalted margarine
¼ cup lemon juice
½ lemon, thinly sliced
2 tablespoons chopped fresh
  parsley

Place chicken between 2 sheets of waxed paper; flatten to ¼-inch thickness, using a meat mallet or rolling pin. Cut each breast in 2 to 3 pieces, if desired. Combine flour, salt, and pepper; dredge chicken in flour mixture.

Coat a large skillet with cooking spray; add margarine, and place over medium heat until margarine melts. Add chicken, and cook 3 to 4 minutes on each side or until golden brown. Remove chicken, and drain on paper towels; transfer to a platter, and keep warm.

Add lemon juice to pan drippings in skillet; cook until thoroughly heated, stirring occasionally. Pour lemon mixture over chicken, and garnish with lemon slices and chopped parsley. Yield: 4 servings (222 calories per serving).

PRO 26.7 / FAT 8.7 / CARB 8.0 / FIB 0.3 / CHOL 70 / SOD 209 / POT 251

Next to seafood, poultry is a cook's best bet for limiting saturated fat. You can add to the low-fat benefits of poultry in the way you prepare it. Since birds carry most of their fat under the skin and near the tail, skinning and removing the excess fat before cooking reduces the calories by about 50 percent. And poultry lends itself to the calorie-smart cooking methods: stewing, roasting, braising, grilling, and stir-frying. A 3-pound chicken that is fried with the skin intact contains 1,769 calories and 98.1 grams of fat. Compare that with a chicken of the same size that has been skinned and roasted, and you will have only 922 calories and 32 grams of fat. If never being able to eat chicken skin again sounds unbearable, try our Herb Baked Chicken. The delicious coating keeps the chicken so moist you'll never miss the skin.

CHICKEN WITH SHIITAKE MUSHROOM SAUCE

2 teaspoons chicken-flavored bouillon
  granules
2 cups water
1 ounce dried shiitake mushrooms (about 1 cup)
2 teaspoons cornstarch
1 tablespoon Madeira or dry sherry
4 (4-ounce) boneless chicken breast halves, skinned
3 tablespoons all-purpose flour
¼ teaspoon pepper
Vegetable cooking spray
2 teaspoons unsalted margarine
¼ cup minced shallots
½ teaspoon dried whole thyme
½ teaspoon peppercorns, crushed
¼ cup dry white wine
1 clove garlic, minced
1 tablespoon minced fresh parsley

Combine bouillon granules and water in a saucepan; bring to a boil. Remove from heat, and add mushrooms. Let stand 30 minutes. Drain, reserving broth. Remove stems from mushrooms, and reserve for other uses; cut caps into fourths, and set aside. Combine cornstarch and Madeira in a small bowl, and set aside.

Place chicken between 2 sheets of waxed paper; flatten to ¼-inch thickness, using a meat mallet or rolling pin. Dredge chicken in flour, and sprinkle with pepper. Coat a large skillet with cooking spray; add margarine, and place over medium heat until margarine melts. Add chicken, and cook 2 to 3 minutes on each side or until lightly browned; transfer to a platter. Add shallots to skillet, and cook 1 minute. Stir in reserved mushrooms, thyme, and crushed peppercorns; cook 3 minutes, tossing gently. Add wine, and cook until mixture is reduced by half. Add reserved broth and garlic; cover and simmer 10 minutes. Add chicken, and simmer 5 minutes.

Transfer chicken to a serving platter. Cook sauce until reduced to 1¼ cups; stir in cornstarch mixture. Bring to a boil. Cook 1 minute or until sauce is slightly thickened, stirring constantly. Spoon over chicken; garnish with parsley. Yield: 4 servings (225 calories per serving).

PRO 27.5 / FAT 5.2 / CARB 14.7 / FIB 1.2 / CHOL 70 / SOD 256 / POT 394

CHICKEN WITH APPLEJACK

1 pound medium Granny Smith apples,
  sliced
Vegetable cooking spray
2 cups sliced onion
4 (4-ounce) boneless chicken breast
  halves, skinned
2 teaspoons unsalted margarine
¼ cup applejack or apple brandy
1¼ cups water
1 teaspoon chicken-flavored bouillon
  granules

Cook apples in a skillet coated with cooking spray over medium heat 3 minutes; transfer to a bowl. Cook onion in a skillet coated with cooking spray over medium heat 7 minutes or until tender. Transfer to a bowl with apples.

Cook chicken in margarine in a skillet coated with cooking spray over medium-high heat 2 minutes on each side. Transfer chicken to a plate, and set aside. Add apples, onion, applejack, water, and bouillon granules to skillet, and cook over medium-high heat until mixture is reduced by half. Add chicken, and cook 1 minute or until done. Transfer to a serving platter. Yield: 4 servings (245 calories per serving).

PRO 26.7 / FAT 5.8 / CARB 22.1 / FIB 3.2 / CHOL 70 / SOD 159 / POT 447

CHICKEN AND BARLEY DINNER

Vegetable cooking spray
1 cup diced onion
⅔ cup diced leek
½ teaspoon dried whole thyme
1 cup barley, uncooked
¼ teaspoon salt
⅛ teaspoon pepper
1 (10¾-ounce) can chicken broth, undiluted
¼ cup water
⅔ cup coarsely chopped carrot
6 (4-ounce) boneless chicken breast halves, skinned
3 tablespoons all-purpose flour
2 teaspoons unsalted margarine, melted

Coat a 2½-quart shallow, ovenproof ceramic casserole with cooking spray; place over medium heat until hot. Add onion, and sauté 2 to 3 minutes or until translucent. Add leek and thyme; cook 1 minute, stirring constantly. Stir in barley, salt, pepper, broth, and water; bring to a boil. Remove from heat. Cover; transfer to oven. Bake at 350° for 30 minutes. Add carrot and additional water, if needed. Return to oven; bake 20 to 30 minutes or until barley is tender and liquid is absorbed.

Dredge chicken in flour, and cook in margarine in a nonstick skillet over medium heat 5 to 6 minutes or until golden brown. Spoon barley onto a platter, and top with chicken. Yield: 6 servings (310 calories per serving).

PRO 30.5 / FAT 5.0 / CARB 34.7 / FIB 2.9 / CHOL 70 / SOD 329 / POT 418

STIR-FRIED CHICKEN AND VEGETABLES

2 teaspoons cornstarch
¼ cup plus 1 tablespoon water, divided
Vegetable cooking spray
2 teaspoons sesame oil
1½ pounds boneless chicken breast halves, skinned
  and cut into ¼-inch strips
1 tablespoon minced, peeled gingerroot
3 cups julienne yellow squash
3 cups julienne zucchini
1 cup diagonally sliced green onion
¼ teaspoon chicken-flavored bouillon granules
1 teaspoon reduced-sodium soy sauce
1½ teaspoons dried whole basil or 2 tablespoons
  minced fresh basil
¼ teaspoon salt
⅛ teaspoon crushed red pepper
⅛ teaspoon ground red pepper

Combine cornstarch in 1 tablespoon water in a small bowl, and set aside. Coat a large heavy skillet or wok with cooking spray; add oil, and place over high heat until hot. Add chicken strips and gingerroot; stir-fry 4 to 5 minutes or until chicken is done.

Add yellow squash, zucchini, and green onion; stir-fry 2 minutes. Add remaining ¼ cup water, bouillon granules, soy sauce, and cornstarch mixture; bring to a boil, and cook 1 minute or until thickened, stirring constantly. Stir in remaining ingredients. Serve immediately. Yield: 6 servings (184 calories per serving).

PRO 27.6 / FAT 4.8 / CARB 7.3 / FIB 1.6 / CHOL 70 / SOD 212 / POT 549

ORIENTAL CHICKEN STIR-FRY

¼ pound fresh snow peas
1 pound fresh broccoli
2 tablespoons cornstarch
1 cup plus 3 tablespoons water, divided
1½ pounds boneless chicken breast halves, skinned and cut into ½-inch strips
2 tablespoons reduced-sodium soy sauce
2 tablespoons lemon juice
Vegetable cooking spray
1½ teaspoons peanut oil
1 tablespoon minced garlic
1 tablespoon minced, peeled gingerroot
1 cup chopped green onion
1 teaspoon chicken-flavored bouillon granules
1 tablespoon Worcestershire sauce

Remove strings from snow peas. Set peas aside. Remove flowerets from broccoli; slice stems thin, and set flowerets and stems aside.

Combine cornstarch in 3 tablespoons water in a small bowl. Set aside.

Combine chicken, soy sauce, and lemon juice in a bowl, tossing to coat; cover and marinate in refrigerator 1 hour.

Drain chicken, reserving marinade. Coat a wok with cooking spray; add oil, and heat at medium-high (325°) until very hot. Add garlic and gingerroot; stir-fry 30 seconds. Add chicken; stir-fry 1 minute. Add green onion and broccoli; stir-fry 1 minute. Add reserved marinade, remaining 1 cup water, bouillon granules, and Worcestershire sauce; bring to a boil. Cover and cook 2 minutes.

Add cornstarch mixture and snow peas to wok. Bring to a boil, stirring constantly. Cook 1 minute or until sauce thickens, stirring constantly. Serve hot. Yield: 6 servings (204 calories per serving).

PRO 29.4 / FAT 4.5 / CARB 11.3 / FIB 2.5 / CHOL 70 / SOD 358 / POT 515

BOURBON-MARINATED CHICKEN ROLLS

4 (4-ounce) boneless chicken breast halves, skinned
1¼ teaspoons chicken-flavored bouillon granules
1¼ cups water
⅓ cup minced green onion
¼ cup bourbon (80 proof)
2 tablespoons brown sugar
2 tablespoons white wine vinegar
2 tablespoons Dijon mustard
2 teaspoons reduced-sodium soy sauce
⅛ teaspoon dried whole thyme
1 clove garlic, minced
1 bay leaf
2 slices bacon, halved
Vegetable cooking spray
2 teaspoons cornstarch
1 tablespoon water
1 teaspoon Dijon mustard
1 tablespoon minced green onion tops

Place chicken between 2 sheets of waxed paper, and flatten to ¼-inch thickness, using a meat mallet or rolling pin; set aside.

Combine next 11 ingredients in a large shallow dish, mixing well. Add chicken, turning to coat. Cover and marinate in refrigerator at least 2 hours. Transfer chicken to paper towels. Strain marinade into a saucepan; set aside.

Roll up chicken breasts, beginning with a long side; wrap ½ slice bacon around each, and secure with wooden picks. Arrange rolls on a broiler pan coated with cooking spray. Broil 4 to 6 inches from heat 3 to 5 minutes on each side or until bacon is crisp and chicken is done. Transfer rolls to a platter; remove and discard wooden picks. Cover and keep warm.

Bring marinade to a boil. Reduce heat; simmer 5 minutes. Combine cornstarch and 1 tablespoon water in a bowl; add to marinade, and simmer until slightly thickened, stirring constantly. Stir in 1 teaspoon mustard. Spoon sauce over chicken; garnish with green onion. Yield: 4 servings (257 calories per serving).

PRO 28.9 / FAT 12.2 / CARB 7.7 / FIB 0.3 / CHOL 80 / SOD 761 / POT 352

CITRUS CHICKEN AND VEGETABLES

3 tablespoons unsalted margarine, softened
1 tablespoon minced fresh mint leaves
1 tablespoon minced fresh parsley
1 teaspoon finely grated lemon rind
1 teaspoon finely grated orange rind
1 teaspoon lemon juice
1 clove garlic, minced
4 (4-ounce) boneless chicken breast halves, skinned
2 medium carrots, thinly sliced
½ cup frozen whole kernel corn, thawed
¼ cup chopped green onion

Combine first 7 ingredients in a bowl. Place each chicken breast on a 12-inch square of aluminum foil; spread each piece with one-fourth of margarine mixture. Top each with equal amounts of vegetables. Seal edges of foil tightly; place in a baking pan. Bake at 400° for 20 minutes or until chicken is done. Yield: 4 servings (249 calories per serving).

PRO 26.9 / FAT 11.6 / CARB 9.2 / FIB 1.2 / CHOL 70 / SOD 76 / POT 402

CHICKEN-VEGETABLE KABOBS

1 pound boneless chicken breast halves, skinned
2 tablespoons vegetable oil
1 to 2 cloves garlic, minced
½ teaspoon ground ginger
1 green onion, minced
¼ cup water
¼ teaspoon chicken-flavored bouillon granules
2 medium zucchini, cut into ¾-inch pieces
1 (8-ounce) package fresh mushrooms
12 cherry tomatoes

Cut chicken breasts into 1½-inch pieces; place in a shallow container, and set aside.

One way to enjoy chicken to the fullest: Chicken-Vegetable Kabobs.

Combine next 6 ingredients in a jar; cover tightly, and shake vigorously. Pour over chicken; cover and marinate in refrigerator 2 hours.

Parboil zucchini 2 minutes; drain well. Clean mushrooms with damp paper towels.

Remove chicken from marinade; reserve marinade. Alternate chicken and vegetables on skewers. Broil 6 inches from heat 8 minutes or until chicken is tender, turning and basting often with marinade. Yield: 4 servings (231 calories per serving).

PRO 28.0 / FAT 10.2 / CARB 6.8 / FIB 1.2 / CHOL 70 / SOD 93 / POT 665

CURRIED CHICKEN AND RICE

2 stalks celery, chopped
1 medium onion, chopped
1 medium apple, cored and chopped
1 clove garlic, minced
1 teaspoon vegetable oil
Vegetable cooking spray
1 pound boneless chicken breast halves, skinned and cut into 1-inch pieces
1 cup regular rice, uncooked
1 cup chopped tomato
¼ cup raisins
1½ teaspoons chicken-flavored bouillon granules
2 teaspoons curry powder
2 cups water
2 tablespoons minced fresh parsley
⅛ teaspoon ground red pepper

Cook first 5 ingredients in an ovenproof ceramic casserole coated with cooking spray over medium heat until softened. Stir in chicken, rice, tomato, raisins, bouillon granules, curry powder, and water; bring to a boil. Remove from heat and cover. Transfer to oven, and bake at 350° for 25 to 30 minutes or until broth is absorbed. Stir in parsley and red pepper. Yield: 6 servings (261 calories per serving).

PRO 20.2 / FAT 3.3 / CARB 37.1 / FIB 2.3 / CHOL 47 / SOD 155 / POT 400

PHYLLO CHICKEN POTPIE

2 pounds chicken thighs, skinned, boned,
  and trimmed of fat
1 medium onion, chopped
1 medium-size tart apple, peeled
  and chopped
2 medium carrots, chopped
1½ cups chopped celery
1 medium-size red or green pepper,
  chopped
1 cup chopped green onion
¼ teaspoon ground nutmeg
⅛ teaspoon dried whole thyme
⅛ teaspoon pepper
1 cup chicken broth
2 tablespoons cornstarch
2 tablespoons water
1 tablespoon Worcestershire sauce
3 tablespoons minced fresh parsley
Vegetable cooking spray
2 tablespoons unsalted margarine,
  melted
1 tablespoon lemon juice
8 sheets frozen phyllo or strudel dough,
  thawed
Additional sheet frozen phyllo or strudel dough,
  thawed (optional)

Cut chicken into 1-inch pieces; combine with next 10 ingredients in a large Dutch oven. Cook over medium heat 1 hour or until chicken pieces are tender, stirring frequently.

Combine cornstarch, water, and Worcestershire sauce in a small bowl, stirring until blended; stir into chicken mixture. Add parsley, and bring to a boil. Reduce heat, and simmer until sauce thickens, stirring constantly; remove from heat. Transfer mixture to a 10-inch pie-plate coated with cooking spray.

Combine margarine and lemon juice in a bowl. Place 1 phyllo sheet on a flat surface; brush lightly with a small amount of margarine mixture. Repeat procedure with remaining 7 phyllo sheets, arranging sheets on top of each other to form a stack. Cut phyllo stack into a 10-inch round, and place over chicken mixture, pressing dough to edge of pieplate to seal. Cut slits in phyllo. Use additional phyllo sheet to decorate top, if desired. Brush top with remaining margarine mixture. Bake at 350° for 45 minutes or until top of pie is golden brown. Yield: 8 servings (275 calories per serving).

PRO 15.1 / FAT 17.0 / CARB 15.1 / FIB 1.6 / CHOL 50 / SOD 207 / POT 094

CHICKEN DIVAN

1 pound fresh broccoli
2 tablespoons unsalted margarine
3 tablespoons all-purpose flour
1 cup water
1 teaspoon chicken-flavored bouillon
  granules
1 cup skim milk
¼ cup dry white wine
¼ cup plus 2 tablespoons grated Parmesan
  cheese, divided
Vegetable cooking spray
2 cups coarsely chopped, cooked chicken breasts

Trim off large leaves from broccoli. Remove tough ends of stalks, and wash broccoli thoroughly; separate into spears. Arrange broccoli in steaming rack, with stalks to center of rack. Place over boiling water; cover and steam 10 minutes or just until tender.

Melt margarine in a saucepan over low heat; add flour, and stir until smooth. Combine water and bouillon granules, stirring until dissolved; add milk. Gradually add broth mixture to saucepan; cook over medium heat, stirring constantly, until mixture is thickened and bubbly. Gradually add wine and ¼ cup Parmesan cheese, stirring well. Cook over low heat 5 minutes.

Arrange broccoli in a 13- x 9- x 2-inch baking dish coated with cooking spray; top with chicken, and pour sauce over chicken. Sprinkle with 2 tablespoons Parmesan cheese, and bake, uncovered, at 350° for 30 minutes or until top is golden brown. Yield: 6 servings (180 calories per serving).

PRO 20.1 / FAT 6.9 / CARB 9.9 / FIB 1.7 / CHOL 43 / SOD 195 / POT 395

COLD CURRIED CHICKEN

2¾ cups broccoli flowerets
½ cup plain low-fat yogurt
2 tablespoons reduced-calorie mayonnaise
1 teaspoon curry powder
1 teaspoon lemon juice
¼ teaspoon pepper
2 cups coarsely chopped, cooked chicken or turkey breast
⅓ cup sliced green onion
¼ teaspoon salt

Cook broccoli flowerets in a small amount of boiling water 3 minutes or until crisp-tender; drain and set aside. Combine yogurt, mayonnaise, curry powder, lemon juice, and pepper in a large bowl; add broccoli, chicken, green onion, and salt, mixing well. Cover and chill. Yield: 4 servings (179 calories per serving).

PRO 25.7 / FAT 5.3 / CARB 7.5 / FIB 1.8 / CHOL 64 / SOD 286 / POT 453

COLD FRUITED CHICKEN

¼ cup dried apricot halves, quartered
¼ cup chopped red onion
2 tablespoons dry white wine
2 tablespoons unsweetened orange juice
1½ teaspoons red wine vinegar
2 cups chopped, cooked chicken or turkey breast
½ cup coarsely chopped orange segments
½ cup seedless red or green grapes
¼ cup sliced almonds, toasted
¼ cup chopped fresh parsley
¼ teaspoon pepper
⅛ teaspoon salt
Dash of crushed red pepper
4 leaves red leaf lettuce

Combine first 5 ingredients in a saucepan, and bring to a boil. Set aside to cool.
Combine apricot mixture with chicken, orange, grapes, almonds, parsley, pepper, salt, and crushed red pepper in a large bowl; cover and chill 1 to 2 hours. Spoon chicken mixture onto a lettuce-lined platter to serve. Yield: 4 servings (229 calories per serving).

PRO 24.5 / FAT 6.3 / CARB 19.7 / FIB 1.7 / CHOL 59 / SOD 132 / POT 616

CHICKEN LIVERS CREOLE

Vegetable cooking spray
1 teaspoon vegetable oil
1½ pounds chicken livers
1 medium onion, chopped
1 stalk celery, chopped
2 medium-size green peppers, seeded and sliced
1 tablespoon all-purpose flour
1 cup chopped tomato
¼ teaspoon dried whole sage
1 cup water
1 tablespoon minced fresh celery leaves
1 teaspoon Worcestershire sauce
1 teaspoon Dijon mustard
½ teaspoon chicken-flavored bouillon granules
⅛ teaspoon ground red pepper
3 cups hot cooked regular rice (cooked without salt or fat)

Coat a large skillet with cooking spray; add oil, and place over medium-high heat until hot. Add chicken livers, and cook 2 to 3 minutes or until browned, stirring well. Transfer livers to a bowl, using a slotted spoon.
Cook onion, celery, and green pepper in skillet over medium-low heat until softened, stirring often. Stir in flour, and cook 3 minutes, stirring constantly. Stir in tomato, sage, and water; bring to a boil. Reduce heat, and simmer, stirring constantly, until thickened and bubbly. Stir in chicken livers and next 5 ingredients; cook until thoroughly heated. Serve over rice. Yield: 6 servings (144 calories per serving plus 118 calories per ½-cup cooked rice).

PRO 19.9 / FAT 5.0 / CARB 33.0 / FIB 1.7 / CHOL 429 / SOD 111 / POT 317

The Massachusetts Institute of Technology found that high-carbohydrate, low-protein lunches may produce a 2:00 p.m. slump; they release more insulin than their counterpart — high-protein, low-carbohydrate lunches. Insulin alters some amino acids, the building blocks of proteins. The result is increased blood levels of a particular amino acid called tryptophan, which may increase drowsiness. Avoid the afternoon slump by eating high-protein lunches that are low in carbohydrates; try Cold Curried Chicken or Quick Turkey Marsala.

CHICKEN LIVERS IN WINE

1½ pounds chicken livers
½ cup dry white wine
3 tablespoons lemon juice
¼ teaspoon salt
½ teaspoon pepper
Vegetable cooking spray
¼ pound fresh mushrooms, sliced

Combine chicken livers, wine, lemon juice, salt, and pepper in a bowl; cover and marinate in refrigerator 30 minutes.

Coat a large skillet with cooking spray; place over medium heat until hot. Add chicken livers and mushrooms, and sauté 5 minutes or until livers are done. Yield: 4 servings (190 calories per serving).

PRO 25.6 / FAT 5.7 / CARB 3.6 / FIB 0.2 / CHOL 644 / SOD 201 / POT 283

QUICK TURKEY MARSALA

2 (4-ounce) turkey breast slices
Vegetable cooking spray
1 tablespoon unsalted margarine
6 fresh mushrooms, sliced
½ cup Marsala wine
¼ teaspoon salt
Dash of pepper
1 teaspoon lemon juice
2 teaspoons chopped fresh parsley

Place each slice of turkey breast between 2 sheets of waxed paper, and flatten to ¼-inch thickness, using a meat mallet or rolling pin. Set turkey aside.

Coat a medium skillet with cooking spray, and add margarine; place over medium heat until margarine melts. Add turkey, and cook over low heat 4 minutes on each side. Remove turkey to a serving platter, and keep warm. Add mushrooms, wine, salt, pepper, and lemon juice to skillet; cook until mushrooms are tender. Pour wine mixture over turkey, and sprinkle with chopped parsley. Yield: 2 servings (216 calories per serving).

Note: ½ cup white wine plus 2 teaspoons brandy may be substituted for the Marsala wine.

PRO 26.7 / FAT 8.6 / CARB 7.4 / FIB 0.4 / CHOL 59 / SOD 353 / POT 514

BRAISED TURKEY BREAST WITH VEGETABLES

1 cup water
1 teaspoon chicken-flavored bouillon granules
1 cup dry white wine
1 (5-pound) turkey breast, skinned and boned
1 cup chopped carrots
½ cup chopped celery
1 cup sliced fresh mushrooms
1 cup sliced onion
2 cups sliced new potatoes

Combine water, bouillon granules, and wine. Arrange turkey in a roasting pan, and surround with remaining ingredients. Insert meat thermometer, if desired. Pour broth mixture over top. Bake at 325° for 2 hours or until meat thermometer registers 185°, basting every 30 minutes with pan juices. Transfer to a platter; carve into thin slices to serve. Yield: 14 servings (192 calories per serving).

PRO 28.4 / FAT 3.0 / CARB 11.5 / FIB 0.7 / CHOL 62 / SOD 96 / POT 634

ROAST TURKEY WITH ZUCCHINI-RICE STUFFING

2 cups cooked brown rice (cooked without fat or salt)
1 medium zucchini, diced
½ cup sliced fresh mushrooms
¼ cup chopped onion
1 egg
½ teaspoon dried whole sage
1 (5-pound) turkey breast, skinned and boned
½ cup water
½ teaspoon chicken-flavored bouillon granules

Combine first 6 ingredients in a bowl, and mix well. Stuff turkey breast cavity with rice mixture, and secure with string; insert meat thermometer, if desired. Place turkey in a browning bag. Pour water over turkey, and sprinkle with bouillon granules. Bake at 325° for 2 hours or until a meat thermometer registers 185°. Yield: 14 servings (174 calories per serving).

PRO 28.0 / FAT 3.5 / CARB 5.9 / FIB 0.6 / CHOL 81 / SOD 135 / POT 328

CORNISH HENS VÉRONIQUE

4 (1¼-pound) Cornish hens, skinned
⅛ teaspoon dried whole thyme
⅛ teaspoon pepper
1 tablespoon cornstarch
1 (10¾-ounce) can chicken broth, diluted
1½ cups dry white wine
¾ pound seedless green grapes

Remove giblets from hens; reserve for another use. Rinse hens with cold water; pat dry. Sprinkle with thyme and pepper; arrange in a large roasting pan. Bake at 350° for 1 hour and 15 minutes or until done. Transfer to a platter; keep warm. Transfer pan drippings to a saucepan.

Combine cornstarch and broth in a bowl; set aside. Add wine to saucepan, and cook over high heat until mixture is reduced by half, stirring constantly. Add broth mixture and grapes, and simmer 6 minutes or until thickened.

Press one-third of grapes through a sieve, discarding skins; add pulp to sauce, mixing well. Split each hen in half lengthwise, and arrange on individual plates. Spoon sauce over hens. Yield: 8 servings (243 calories per serving with 3 tablespoons sauce per serving).

PRO 30.8 / FAT 8.1 / CARB 10.6 / FIB 0.7 / CHOL 90 / SOD 308 / POT 424

CORNISH HENS WITH SPRING VEGETABLES

¾ pound new potatoes, quartered
2 tablespoons lemon juice
1 clove garlic, minced
½ teaspoon pepper
¼ teaspoon dried whole rosemary
¼ teaspoon dried whole thyme
2 (1¼-pound) Cornish hens, skinned
Vegetable cooking spray
1 clove garlic, minced
½ teaspoon pepper
3 cups sliced leek, cut into 1-inch pieces
1 cup sliced carrots
½ cup sliced green onion
¼ cup dry white wine
¼ cup water
¼ teaspoon salt
¼ pound fresh asparagus, cut into 1-inch pieces

Cook potatoes in boiling water to cover 5 minutes; drain and set aside. Combine lemon juice, 1 clove garlic, ½ teaspoon pepper, rosemary, and thyme in a small bowl. Brush inside and outside of hens with mixture.

Spread next 8 ingredients in a 10- x 6- x 2-inch baking dish coated with cooking spray; top with hens. Cover with aluminum foil; bake at 350° for 45 minutes. Uncover; baste with pan juices. Bake an additional 40 minutes or until done.

Cook asparagus in boiling water in a saucepan 3 to 4 minutes or until crisp-tender; drain. Split each hen in half lengthwise, and arrange on individual plates. Divide asparagus and baked vegetables evenly among plates. Yield: 4 servings (333 calories per serving).

PRO 33.7 / FAT 8.0 / CARB 32.2 / FIB 2.8 / CHOL 90 / SOD 267 / POT 1059

TANGY BARBECUE SAUCE

Vegetable cooking spray
½ cup minced celery
¼ cup minced onion
1 cup reduced-calorie catsup
2 tablespoons vinegar
2 tablespoons lemon juice
1 tablespoon Worcestershire sauce
1 tablespoon honey
1 teaspoon dry mustard
¼ teaspoon pepper

Coat a medium saucepan with cooking spray; place over medium heat until hot. Add onion and celery, and sauté 5 minutes or until tender. Add remaining ingredients, and cook over low heat 20 minutes, stirring occasionally. Use as a basting sauce for chicken. Yield: 1½ cups (10 calories per tablespoon).

PRO 0.1 / FAT 0.1 / CARB 2.1 / FIB 0.0 / CHOL 0 / SOD 11 / POT 98

Salads offer ideas for more than one course. Serve Tomato-Mozzarella Salad (page 174) to complement the main course. Fruit salads, such as Four Berry Salad (page 171), can make a naturally sweet dessert, and Steak Salad with Blue Cheese Dressing (page 177) is hearty enough for the main course.

Salads & Salad Dressings

The sprightly flavor mix in the Mandarin-Bibb Salad makes it a tasty accompaniment to any entrée.

WALDORF-GRAPE SALAD

3 medium-size Red Delicious apples, cored and cubed
1 cup seedless green grapes, halved
¾ cup chopped celery
⅓ cup reduced-calorie salad dressing
2 teaspoons lemon juice
8 lettuce leaves

Combine first 5 ingredients in a bowl; mix well. Cover and chill at least 1 hour. Serve on lettuce leaves. Yield: 8 servings (62 calories per ½-cup serving).

PRO 0.6 / FAT 1.7 / CARB 12.5 / FIB 1.7 / CHOL 5 / SOD 24 / POT 160

TANGERINE-BELGIAN ENDIVE SALAD

⅓ cup unsweetened tangerine juice or orange juice
½ teaspoon cornstarch
4 tangerines, peeled, sectioned, and seeded
½ pound Belgian endive, cut into julienne strips
1 cup watercress leaves
1½ cups sliced fresh mushrooms
4 lettuce leaves
Freshly ground black pepper (optional)

Combine tangerine juice and cornstarch in a small saucepan; bring to a boil. Reduce heat, and simmer until thickened, stirring frequently. Cool; set aside.
Combine tangerines, endive, watercress, and mushrooms in a large bowl. Pour dressing over salad, and toss gently. Chill. Spoon onto lettuce leaves; sprinkle with pepper, if desired. Yield: 4 servings (68 calories per 1-cup serving).

PRO 2.3 / FAT 0.5 / CARB 15.7 / FIB 1.3 / CHOL 0 / SOD 20 / POT 506

MANDARIN-BIBB SALAD

1 medium head Bibb lettuce
1 (11-ounce) can unsweetened mandarin oranges, chilled and drained
3 tablespoons pecan halves, toasted
2 green onions, thinly sliced
¼ cup Italian reduced-calorie salad dressing

Arrange lettuce, oranges, pecan halves, and onion on individual serving plates. Spoon salad dressing over salads. Yield: 4 servings (74 calories per 1-cup serving).

PRO 1.2 / FAT 5.0 / CARB 9.1 / FIB 1.0 / CHOL 1 / SOD 128 / POT 282

KUMQUAT SALAD

¼ pound fresh snow peas
2 cups torn spinach leaves
¼ pound curly endive, torn into pieces (about 3 cups)
12 medium-size fresh kumquats, halved
2 tablespoons unsweetened orange juice or kumquat juice
1 teaspoon sesame oil
2 teaspoons vegetable oil

Remove strings from snow peas. Blanch peas in boiling water 1 minute; drain. Combine peas, spinach, endive, and kumquats in a large bowl. Combine remaining ingredients in a small bowl, and stir with a wire whisk until blended. Pour over salad, and toss. Yield: 8 servings (46 calories per 1-cup serving).

PRO 1.2 / FAT 1.8 / CARB 7.1 / FIB 1.8 / CHOL 0 / SOD 16 / POT 221

FOUR BERRY SALAD

1 cup fresh blueberries, sliced
1 cup fresh raspberries
1 cup fresh blackberries or dewberries
1 cup sliced fresh strawberries
2 tablespoons slivered almonds,
   toasted
¼ cup sour cream
½ cup plain low-fat yogurt
1 tablespoon plus 1 teaspoon honey
1 tablespoon cream sherry
1 tablespoon lemon juice

Arrange berries in a large serving bowl, and sprinkle with almonds; set aside. Combine sour cream, yogurt, honey, sherry, and lemon juice in a small bowl. Spoon berries into individual serving bowls, and top with yogurt mixture. Yield: 8 servings (84 calories per ½-cup serving).

PRO 1.9 / FAT 3.1 / CARB 13.1 / FIB 2.5 / CHOL 4 / SOD 16 / POT 171

HERBED ASPARAGUS SALAD

1 pound fresh asparagus
½ cup water
⅓ cup white wine vinegar
⅓ cup water
2 tablespoons chopped green onion
1 tablespoon plus 1½ teaspoons Dijon
   mustard
½ teaspoon dried whole tarragon
¼ teaspoon freshly ground black
   pepper
1 head Bibb lettuce

Snap off tough ends of asparagus. Remove scales from stalks, using a knife or vegetable peeler, if desired.

Arrange spears in a large skillet; add ½ cup water, and bring to a boil. Cover; reduce heat, and steam 7 minutes or until crisp-tender. Drain and place in a shallow dish.

Combine vinegar, ⅓ cup water, green onion, mustard, tarragon, and pepper, and mix well. Pour over asparagus; cover and chill. Arrange asparagus on lettuce leaves, reserving marinade. Spoon marinade over salad, if desired. Yield: 4 servings (44 calories per serving).

PRO 4.3 / FAT 0.8 / CARB 6.3 / FIB 1.6 / CHOL 0 / SOD 174 / POT 512

BROCCOLI AND CHEDDAR SALAD

1¼ pounds fresh broccoli
¼ pound Cheddar cheese, cut into
   julienne strips
1 cup sliced celery
¼ cup minced green onion
2 tablespoons grated Parmesan
   cheese
2 tablespoons minced fresh parsley
2 tablespoons plain low-fat yogurt
1 tablespoon olive oil
1 tablespoon Dijon mustard
1 teaspoon white wine vinegar
¼ teaspoon pepper
¼ teaspoon celery seeds

Trim off large leaves of broccoli; remove tough ends of lower stalks. Wash broccoli thoroughly, and separate into spears. Cook broccoli in boiling water in a saucepan 1 minute; drain and cool. Combine broccoli with Cheddar cheese, celery, and green onion in a large bowl; set aside.

Combine remaining ingredients in a small bowl; pour over salad, and toss gently. Yield: 4 servings (213 calories per 1-cup serving).

PRO 13.1 / FAT 14.5 / CARB 10.5 / FIB 2.5 / CHOL 32 / SOD 405 / POT 626

QUICK COLESLAW

½ cup reduced-calorie mayonnaise
¼ cup sour cream
1 tablespoon sugar
2 tablespoons cider vinegar
1 teaspoon celery seeds
1 teaspoon Dijon mustard
¼ teaspoon salt
¼ teaspoon dried whole tarragon
⅛ teaspoon freshly ground black
   pepper
1 (2-pound) cabbage, shredded
2 medium carrots, shredded

Combine first 9 ingredients, stirring with a whisk until smooth. Pour mixture over cabbage and carrots in a large bowl, tossing well. Cover and chill. Yield: 16 servings (50 calories per ½-cup serving).

PRO 1.0 / FAT 2.9 / CARB 5.6 / FIB 0.8 / CHOL 4 / SOD 117 / POT 180

RED CABBAGE AND APPLE SLAW

1 cup chopped Granny Smith apple
2 cups chopped or shredded red cabbage
2 tablespoons chopped walnuts, toasted
2 tablespoons raisins
½ cup plain low-fat yogurt
¼ cup unsweetened apple juice
1 tablespoon honey
½ teaspoon ground cinnamon
1 teaspoon poppy seeds

Combine first 4 ingredients in a large bowl; set aside. Combine yogurt, apple juice, honey, and cinnamon in a small bowl, mixing well. Pour dressing over salad, and toss well. Sprinkle with poppy seeds; cover and chill. Yield: 7 servings (61 calories per ½-cup serving).

PRO 1.9 / FAT 1.9 / CARB 10.4 / FIB 1.0 / CHOL 1 / SOD 15 / POT 142

CORN SALAD

2 cups frozen whole kernel corn
1 (4-ounce) jar diced pimiento, drained
½ cup chopped green pepper
¼ cup chopped green onion
1 tablespoon sugar
2 tablespoons cider vinegar
1 tablespoon vegetable oil
1 teaspoon celery seeds
¼ teaspoon salt

Cook corn according to package directions, omitting salt. Drain and cool. Combine corn and remaining ingredients; cover and chill. Yield: 4 servings (133 calories per ½-cup serving).

PRO 3.0 / FAT 4.4 / CARB 23.5 / FIB 2.3 / CHOL 0 / SOD 155 / POT 279

MINTED CUCUMBER SALAD

2 medium cucumbers, thinly sliced
1 tablespoon chopped fresh mint or ¾ teaspoon dried mint
1½ teaspoons dried whole basil or 2 tablespoons chopped fresh basil
1 tablespoon vegetable oil
1 tablespoon lemon juice
⅛ teaspoon salt
⅛ teaspoon pepper

Combine all ingredients in a bowl; toss well. Cover and chill at least 2 hours. Yield: 8 servings (24 calories per ½-cup serving).

PRO 0.4 / FAT 1.8 / CARB 2.0 / FIB 0.3 / CHOL 0 / SOD 38 / POT 97

CARROT-ORANGE SALAD

3 tablespoons golden raisins
2 tablespoons cider vinegar
3 cups shredded carrot
1 (11-ounce) can unsweetened mandarin oranges, undrained
⅛ teaspoon ground cinnamon

Combine raisins and vinegar in a small bowl; let stand 30 minutes. Drain, reserving vinegar. Place raisins in a medium bowl; add carrot, and set aside.

Drain oranges, reserving ¼ cup juice; add oranges to raisin-carrot mixture. Combine reserved juice, reserved vinegar, and cinnamon; pour over carrot mixture, and toss well. Cover and chill. Yield: 8 servings (42 calories per ½-cup serving).

PRO 0.6 / FAT 0.1 / CARB 10.3 / FIB 0.8 / CHOL 0 / SOD 18 / POT 216

Most Americans are aware of the importance of exercise, but are they doing anything about it? Not the majority. According to the Department of Health and Human Services, 80 to 90 percent of Americans still don't get sufficient exercise.

The Public Health Service definition of "sufficient" exercise is anything that raises heart and lung performance to 60 percent or more of its capacity at least 3 times a week for at least 20 minutes each session.

Children were included in the HHS study, too. They appear to be more overweight than the children of the '60s, spending only an average of 13 hours a week exercising and 3 to 4 times that many hours watching television and playing video games.

All this despite the fact that consumers purchased 1.2 million Jane Fonda tapes and 1 billion dollars worth of home exercise equipment last year. Enthusiasm for improving fitness seems to be largely limited to affluent college graduates.

RED LEAF LETTUCE-MUSHROOM SALAD

1 (1-pound) head red leaf lettuce, torn into pieces
2 medium cucumbers, peeled and sliced
½ pound fresh mushrooms, sliced
½ cup minced onion
1 medium-size green pepper, seeded and chopped
¼ cup water
2 tablespoons sugar
2 tablespoons lemon juice
2 tablespoons white wine vinegar
1 tablespoon vegetable oil
1 clove garlic, minced
¼ teaspoon pepper

Combine lettuce, cucumber, mushrooms, onion, and green pepper in a large bowl, tossing well. Combine remaining ingredients in a jar; cover tightly, and shake vigorously. Pour dressing over salad, and toss. Yield: 12 servings (39 calories per serving).

Note: For additional flavor, marinate cucumber, mushrooms, onion, and green pepper in dressing 1 to 2 hours. Add vegetables to lettuce; toss and serve.

PRO 1.3 / FAT 1.4 / CARB 6.3 / FIB 1.2 / CHOL 0 / SOD 6 / POT 261

MUSTARD POTATO SALAD

½ cup reduced-calorie salad dressing
2 tablespoons Dijon mustard
2 tablespoons sweet pickle relish
1 tablespoon white wine vinegar
¼ teaspoon salt
⅛ teaspoon pepper
5 cups cooked, sliced new potatoes
¼ cup minced fresh chives or parsley

Combine first 6 ingredients in a large bowl. Add potatoes, and toss to coat. Cover and chill overnight. Garnish with chives. Yield: 10 servings (92 calories per ½-cup serving).

PRO 1.5 / FAT 1.9 / CARB 17.5 / FIB 0.4 / CHOL 6 / SOD 188 / POT 270

SPAGHETTI SQUASH SALAD

1 (3-pound) spaghetti squash
Vegetable cooking spray
1 cup thinly sliced onion
1 cup shredded carrots
3 tablespoons lemon juice
2 tablespoons golden raisins
¼ teaspoon salt

Cut squash in half, and discard seeds. Place squash, cut side down, in a Dutch oven; add 2 inches of water. Bring water to a boil. Cover; reduce heat, and cook 20 to 25 minutes or until tender. Drain squash, and cool. Using a fork, remove spaghetti-like strands; transfer to a bowl, and set aside.

Coat a skillet with cooking spray, and place over medium heat until hot. Add onion, and cook 10 to 12 minutes or until tender. Remove from heat, and let cool. Combine onion, carrots, lemon juice, raisins, salt, and reserved squash; toss gently. Cover and refrigerate 2 hours or overnight. Yield: 12 servings (46 calories per ½ cup serving).

PRO 1.0 / FAT 0.3 / CARB 10.7 / FIB 1.8 / CHOL 0 / SOD 73 / POT 195

TOMATO SALAD

3 medium tomatoes
1 medium cucumber, thinly sliced
4 green onions, sliced
1 small yellow squash, thinly sliced
½ cup water
½ cup tarragon vinegar
1 tablespoon sugar
¼ teaspoon freshly ground black pepper
⅛ teaspoon paprika
Lettuce leaves

Cut tomatoes into ¼-inch-thick slices. Combine tomato slices, cucumber, green onions, and squash in a shallow dish; set aside. Combine water, vinegar, sugar, pepper, and paprika, and mix well. Pour dressing over vegetables; cover and chill 2 to 3 hours. Serve on lettuce leaves. Yield: 6 servings (38 calories per 1-cup serving).

PRO 1.5 / FAT 0.3 / CARB 8.8 / FIB 1.5 / CHOL 0 / SOD 9 / POT 340

TOMATO-MOZZARELLA SALAD

4 medium tomatoes, cut into ¼-inch-thick
   slices
½ medium-size red onion, thinly
   sliced
2 tablespoons olive oil
2 tablespoons white wine vinegar
¼ teaspoon pepper
20 fresh basil leaves
½ pound part-skim mozzarella cheese,
   cut into ⅛-inch-thick slices

Arrange tomato and onion slices in a shallow baking dish. Combine oil, vinegar, and pepper; spoon over tomatoes and onion. Cover and chill 1 hour or until serving time.

Place basil leaves on a serving platter. Arrange tomato, onion, and cheese slices on basil leaves. Spoon any remaining oil and vinegar mixture over tomatoes. Yield: 4 servings (207 calories per serving).

PRO 15.3 / FAT 12.8 / CARB 9.0 / FIB 1.4 / CHOL 33 / SOD 275 / POT 379

Buying low-sodium canned goods is a smart way to shop — especially since sodium has been linked to hypertension. The only catch is that sometimes these products are unavailable or expensive.

One alternative to buying low-sodium canned foods is to rinse regular canned foods before using them. Duke University conducted a study to determine whether or not rinsing certain foods would significantly reduce their sodium content. They found, for example, that rinsing tuna for 1 minute in a strainer under cold tap water and letting it drain for 1 minute lowered the sodium content by almost 80 percent. The same rinsing and draining procedure was applied to canned green beans; the results were not so dramatic, but the sodium was still reduced by 41 percent.

Effect of Water Rinsing Canned Foods

FOOD	Sodium Content per 100 grams UNRINSED (mg)	RINSED (mg)
Tuna	418	86
Green Beans	308	184

The low-sodium versions are still best, but rinsing can make a significant difference.

MARINATED CRAB SALAD

1 pound fresh crabmeat, drained and
   flaked
½ cup chopped onion
2 tablespoons cider vinegar
2 teaspoons Dijon mustard
½ teaspoon minced garlic
½ teaspoon dried whole basil
½ teaspoon lemon juice
¼ teaspoon freshly ground black
   pepper
4 lettuce leaves

Combine crabmeat and onion in a bowl. Combine next 6 ingredients in a small bowl, and pour over crabmeat mixture. Toss gently to mix well; cover and chill overnight. Spoon onto lettuce leaves to serve. Yield: 4 servings (121 calories per serving).

PRO 20.1 / FAT 2.4 / CARB 3.5 / FIB 0.4 / CHOL 113 / SOD 315 / POT 286

TUNA-CHILE SALAD

2 (6½-ounce) cans water-packed tuna
½ cup sliced onion
½ cup chopped red or green pepper
¼ cup chopped canned green chiles,
   rinsed and drained
1 clove garlic, minced
¼ teaspoon ground cumin
⅛ teaspoon pepper
Dash of crushed red pepper
2 tablespoons reduced-calorie mayonnaise
1 tablespoon lime juice
4 cups shredded lettuce
1 cup diced tomato
1 tablespoon lime juice

Place tuna in a colander, and rinse under cold tap water 1 minute; set colander aside to let tuna drain 1 minute.

Combine tuna and next 9 ingredients in a large bowl, mixing until well combined. Cover and chill 1 hour. Arrange lettuce on a serving platter, and mound tuna mixture in center. Garnish salad with tomato, and sprinkle with lime juice. Yield: 4 servings (133 calories per ½-cup serving).

PRO 19.3 / FAT 2.9 / CARB 7.2 / FIB 1.4 / CHOL 43 / SOD 107 / POT 454

Shrimp Salad in Tomato Cups would be center attraction at any luncheon, formal or informal.

SHRIMP SALAD IN TOMATO CUPS

1½ pounds fresh medium shrimp
2 tablespoons olive oil
¼ cup dry white wine
1 teaspoon lemon juice
1 (0.6-ounce) envelope Italian salad dressing mix
Dash of pepper
1 cup frozen English peas, cooked and drained
3 tablespoons sliced green onion
6 medium tomatoes

Add shrimp to boiling water, and reduce heat. Simmer 3 minutes. Drain well, and chill. Peel and devein shrimp; set aside.

Combine oil, wine, lemon juice, salad dressing mix, and pepper in a jar. Cover tightly, and shake vigorously.

Combine shrimp, peas, and green onion. Pour dressing over shrimp mixture; toss to coat well. Cover and chill at least 2 hours.

Cut tops from tomatoes; scoop out pulp, leaving shells intact. Reserve pulp for use in another recipe. Invert tomato shells on paper towels, and allow to drain.

Drain shrimp mixture, and spoon into tomato cups. Yield: 6 servings (161 calories per serving).

Note: Frozen shrimp may be substituted for fresh shrimp.

PRO 17.6 / FAT 5.4 / CARB 9.8 / FIB 0.7 / CHOL 128 / SOD 511 / POT 367

SIMPLE CHICKEN SALAD

2½ cups diced, cooked chicken breast
½ cup diced celery
½ cup diced green pepper
¼ teaspoon salt
2 tablespoons unsweetened orange juice
1 tablespoon minced onion
¼ cup reduced-calorie salad dressing
6 lettuce leaves

Combine first 7 ingredients in a bowl, mixing well. Cover and chill thoroughly. Serve on lettuce leaves. Yield: 6 servings (121 calories per ½-cup serving).

PRO 18.6 / FAT 3.5 / CARB 2.6 / FIB 0.5 / CHOL 55 / SOD 164 / POT 247

LIME CHICKEN SALAD

1 cup fresh parsley sprigs
¼ cup plus 1 tablespoon lime juice
2 tablespoons vegetable oil
1 tablespoon water
2 cloves garlic
1 teaspoon ground cumin
½ teaspoon pepper
2 cups chopped, cooked chicken or turkey breasts
1 medium-size green pepper, seeded and cut into thin strips
1 cup thinly sliced red onion
1 cup canned garbanzo beans, rinsed and drained
½ cup diced, peeled avocado

Combine first 7 ingredients in container of an electric blender, and process until smooth; set aside. Combine chicken, green pepper, onion, and garbanzo beans in a bowl; add dressing, and mix well. Add avocado, and toss gently. Chill. Yield: 6 servings (192 calories per 1-cup serving).

PRO 17.7 / FAT 8.2 / CARB 12.3 / FIB 3.5 / CHOL 40 / SOD 207 / POT 495

APPLE-CHICKEN SALAD

2 cups chopped, cooked chicken or turkey breast
1 medium Granny Smith apple, chopped
½ cup chopped celery
⅓ cup thinly sliced green onion
¼ cup plain low-fat yogurt
¼ cup reduced-calorie mayonnaise
2 tablespoons coarsely chopped pecans, toasted
2 tablespoons chopped fresh parsley
2 teaspoons lemon juice
½ teaspoon pepper
¼ teaspoon salt
4 lettuce leaves

Combine all ingredients, except lettuce leaves, in a large bowl, and mix well. Cover and chill. Serve over lettuce leaves. Yield: 4 servings (219 calories per 1-cup serving).

PRO 23.5 / FAT 9.4 / CARB 9.9 / FIB 1.4 / CHOL 65 / SOD 336 / POT 380

CHICKEN AND ORANGE SALAD

4 (4-ounce) boneless chicken breast halves, skinned
1 cup chicken broth
½ cup water
6 whole peppercorns
2 whole cloves
1 bay leaf
3 tablespoons vegetable oil
1 teaspoon grated orange rind
3 tablespoons unsweetened orange juice
2 tablespoons cider vinegar
1 tablespoon lemon juice
1 tablespoon Dijon mustard
¼ teaspoon pepper
½ cup thinly sliced green onion
½ cup minced celery
1 medium apple, diced
6 escarole leaves
1 orange, peeled, sliced, and seeded
2 tablespoons julienne orange rind

Combine first 6 ingredients in a saucepan; bring to a boil. Cover; reduce heat, and simmer 30 minutes or until chicken is tender. Drain and chill. Cut into ¼-inch-thick strips. Set aside.

Combine oil, grated orange rind, orange juice, vinegar, lemon juice, mustard, and pepper in container of an electric blender, and process until smooth.

Combine chicken, green onion, celery, and apple in a large bowl. Add dressing, and toss well. Line a platter with escarole; spoon salad into center, and surround with orange slices. Garnish with julienne orange rind. Yield: 4 servings (296 calories per serving).

PRO 28.1 / FAT 14.1 / CARB 14.9 / FIB 2.1 / CHOL 70 / SOD 387 / POT 566

SPICY CHICKEN SALAD

½ teaspoon pepper
¼ teaspoon paprika
⅛ teaspoon dried whole thyme
⅛ teaspoon celery seeds
Dash of crushed red pepper
6 (4-ounce) boneless chicken breast halves, skinned
Vegetable cooking spray
2 teaspoons vegetable oil
¾ cup chicken broth
¼ cup dry white wine
½ cup thinly sliced green onion
½ cup diced red or green pepper
1 tablespoon plus 1 teaspoon lemon juice
3 cups torn red leaf lettuce
3 cups torn Boston lettuce
3 cups torn spinach leaves
1 cup torn endive

Combine first 5 ingredients; sprinkle over chicken breasts, and set aside. Coat a heavy skillet with cooking spray; add oil, and place over medium heat until hot. Add chicken, and cook until browned. Add broth and wine, and bring to a boil. Cover; reduce heat to low, and cook 25 minutes or until chicken is done. Transfer chicken to a plate. Cover; set aside, and keep warm.

Pour pan juices into a large bowl. Stir in green onion, red pepper, and lemon juice; add greens, and toss well.

Divide Boston lettuce, spinach, and endive among individual serving plates. Slice chicken breasts into ¼-inch-thick strips, and arrange over greens. Spoon any remaining dressing over chicken. Serve warm. Yield: 6 servings (134 calories per serving).

PRO 19.7 / FAT 4.0 / CARB 4.9 / FIB 1.8 / CHOL 47 / SOD 166 / POT 554

DILLED CHICKEN PASTA SALAD

½ (12-ounce) package seashell pasta, cooked al
  dente without salt or fat
2 cups cooked chicken or turkey breast,
  cut into strips
2 cups chopped tomato
½ cup diced celery
¼ cup minced red onion
¼ cup chopped fresh parsley
1 tablespoon vegetable oil
1½ teaspoons dried whole dillweed
1 tablespoon plus 2 teaspoons red
  wine vinegar
2 teaspoons grated Parmesan cheese
2 cloves garlic, minced
½ teaspoon pepper
¼ teaspoon salt

Combine pasta, chicken, tomato, celery,
onion, and parsley in a large bowl; set aside.

Combine remaining ingredients in a small
bowl, mixing well. Pour dressing over pasta mixture, and toss gently. Cover and chill 1 to 2
hours to blend flavors. Yield: 8 servings (171 calories per 1-cup serving).

PRO 14.3 / FAT 3.8 / CARB 19.2 / FIB 1.1 / CHOL 30 / SOD 120 / POT 275

FRUITED PORK SALAD

1 tablespoon plus 1 teaspoon lime
  juice
2 teaspoons honey
2 teaspoons olive oil
1 teaspoon water
¼ teaspoon pepper
¼ teaspoon ground coriander
2 cups sliced seedless red grapes
1½ cups cubed roast pork
⅓ cup sliced green onion
4 lettuce leaves

Combine lime juice, honey, olive oil, water,
pepper, and coriander in a small bowl.

Combine grapes, pork, and green onion in a
large bowl; add dressing, and toss gently. Cover
and chill thoroughly to blend flavors. Serve over
lettuce leaves. Yield: 4 servings (223 calories per
serving).

PRO 14.2 / FAT 10.7 / CARB 18.8 / FIB 1.8 / CHOL 51 / SOD 44 / POT 394

STEAK SALAD WITH
BLUE CHEESE DRESSING

4 cups watercress leaves
⅓ cup sliced red onion
2 tablespoons chopped fresh parsley
1 tablespoon olive oil
1 tablespoon water
1 tablespoon red wine vinegar
1 clove garlic, minced
⅛ teaspoon pepper
¾ pound lean broiled steak, cut across
  grain into 2-inch strips
¾ cup sliced radishes
½ cup coarsely crumbled blue cheese

Line a large serving bowl with watercress.
Combine next 7 ingredients in a bowl. Add
steak and radishes; toss well. Spoon salad over
watercress. Sprinkle with blue cheese. Yield: 4
servings (249 calories per serving).

PRO 31.1 / FAT 12.1 / CARB 2.7 / FIB 0.5 / CHOL 66 / SOD 269 / POT 545

CHEF'S SALAD

3 tablespoons water
2 tablespoons red wine vinegar
2 tablespoons vegetable oil
1 tablespoon lemon juice
1 to 2 teaspoons minced fresh chives
1 teaspoon Dijon mustard
½ teaspoon reduced-sodium soy sauce
¼ teaspoon pepper
¼ teaspoon chicken-flavored bouillon
  granules
⅛ teaspoon dried whole thyme
2 cups torn leaf lettuce
2 cups watercress leaves
¼ pound cooked lean ham, cubed
1 cup chopped cooked chicken breast
½ cup (2 ounces) shredded Cheddar cheese
1 medium tomato, chopped

Combine first 10 ingredients in a small bowl;
mix well. Divide lettuce, watercress, ham,
chicken, cheese, and tomato among 4 serving
plates; spoon dressing over salads. Yield: 4 servings (245 calories per serving).

PRO 20.6 / FAT 16.1 / CARB 4.2 / FIB 0.8 / CHOL 61 / SOD 585 / POT 388

LENTIL AND BROWN RICE SALAD

1 cup dry lentils
5 cups water, divided
½ cup brown rice
¼ pound cherry tomatoes, halved
¼ cup chopped green onion
3 tablespoons cider vinegar
2 tablespoons peanut oil
2 teaspoons honey
½ teaspoon dried whole oregano

Soak lentils in water to cover in a bowl over-night. Drain. Combine lentils and 4 cups water in a large saucepan; bring to a boil. Cover; re-duce heat, and simmer 30 minutes. Drain well, and cool.

Combine brown rice and 1 cup water in a saucepan; bring to a boil. Cover; reduce heat, and simmer 50 minutes or until liquid is ab-sorbed. Remove from heat, and cool.

Combine lentils, rice, and remaining ingre-dients in a large bowl. Cover and chill. Yield: 4 servings (325 calories per serving).

PRO 13.8 / FAT 7.8 / CARB 51.9 / FIB 4.0 / CHOL 0 / SOD 19 / POT 514

BLUE CHEESE SALAD DRESSING

1 cup low-fat cottage cheese
1 cup buttermilk
½ cup crumbled blue cheese
2 tablespoons thinly sliced green onion
2 tablespoons chopped fresh parsley
¼ teaspoon freshly ground black pepper

Combine cottage cheese and buttermilk in container of an electric blender, and process until smooth. Transfer to a bowl, and stir in re-maining ingredients. Cover and chill. Yield: 2 cups (16 calories per 1-tablespoon serving).

PRO 1.6 / FAT 0.7 / CARB 0.7 / FIB 0.0 / CHOL 2 / SOD 62 / POT 25

ORANGE-POPPY SEED SALAD DRESSING

1 teaspoon unflavored gelatin
2 cups unsweetened orange juice
1 tablespoon plus 1 teaspoon poppy seeds
2 teaspoons grated orange rind

Combine gelatin and orange juice in a sauce-pan; let stand 1 minute. Cook over medium heat, stirring constantly, 2 to 3 minutes or until gelatin dissolves. Stir in remaining ingredients; chill overnight. Serve over fruit salads. Yield: 2 cups (9 calories per 1-tablespoon serving).

PRO 0.3 / FAT 0.2 / CARB 1.8 / FIB 0.0 / CHOL 0 / SOD 0 / POT 32

THOUSAND ISLAND SALAD DRESSING

1 cup reduced-calorie salad dressing
⅔ cup spicy tomato juice
¼ cup minced dill pickle
1½ tablespoons minced green onion
1½ tablespoons minced green pepper

Combine salad dressing and tomato juice, stir-ring with a wire whisk until smooth. Stir in re-maining ingredients. Cover and refrigerate. Serve over salad greens. Yield: 2 cups (12 calo-ries per 1-tablespoon serving).

PRO 0.1 / FAT 1.0 / CARB 0.7 / FIB 0.1 / CHOL 4 / SOD 53 / POT 24

YOGURT-CUCUMBER SALAD DRESSING

1 medium cucumber, peeled, seeded, and finely chopped
⅛ teaspoon salt
1 (16-ounce) carton plain low-fat yogurt
¼ cup thinly sliced green onion
¼ cup chopped green pepper
1 clove garlic, minced
⅛ teaspoon crushed red pepper

Toss cucumber in a bowl with salt. Cover; chill 30 minutes. Rinse and drain cucumber; squeeze out excess moisture with paper towels. Combine cucumber and remaining ingredients in a bowl, mixing well. Cover and refrigerate. Serve over salad greens. Yield: 2¾ cups (8 calories per 1-ta-blespoon serving).

PRO 0.6 / FAT 0.2 / CARB 1.0 / FIB 0.1 / CHOL 1 / SOD 8 / POT 36

Cold Gazpacho (page 180), Asparagus Vichyssoise (page 180), or Apple-Beet Soup (page 180) makes an excellent appetizer for dinner, or serve one of these chilled soups alongside a salad or sandwich for lunch.

APPLE-BEET SOUP

2 (16-ounce) cans sliced beets, undrained
1 tablespoon unsalted margarine
1 medium onion, chopped
2 cloves garlic, minced
2 medium Granny Smith apples, peeled and chopped
1 medium potato, peeled and diced
1 medium carrot, chopped
1 quart water
2 teaspoons chicken-flavored bouillon granules
1 tablespoon lemon juice
⅛ teaspoon pepper
½ cup plain low-fat yogurt
1 tablespoon prepared horseradish, drained
1 tablespoon minced fresh parsley

Drain beets, reserving juice; set aside.

Melt margarine in a large Dutch oven over medium heat; add next 5 ingredients, and cook 10 minutes, stirring occasionally. Add water and bouillon granules; bring to a boil. Cover; reduce heat, and simmer 20 minutes or until potato is very tender. Add beets, and simmer 5 minutes.

Place one-fourth of mixture in container of an electric blender, and process until smooth. Repeat with remaining mixture. Pour vegetable mixture into a large bowl; stir in reserved beet juice, lemon juice, and pepper. Cover and chill thoroughly.

Combine yogurt, horseradish, and parsley in a small bowl. Ladle soup into soup bowls; spoon yogurt mixture on top, and serve immediately. Yield: 8 cups (113 calories per 1-cup serving with 1 tablespoon yogurt mixture).

PRO 2.7 / FAT 1.9 / CARB 23.2 / FIB 1.2 / CHOL 1 / SOD 430 / POT 485

ASPARAGUS VICHYSSOISE

2 pounds fresh asparagus
1 medium leek
2 cups diced, peeled potato
3 cups water
2 teaspoons chicken-flavored bouillon granules
¾ cup skim milk
¼ teaspoon salt
⅛ teaspoon white pepper
3 dashes hot sauce
Lemon rind strips

Snap off tough ends of asparagus. Remove scales from stalks with a knife or vegetable peeler, if desired. Cut asparagus into 1-inch pieces, reserving tips; set pieces aside. Cook asparagus tips in boiling water in a small saucepan 6 to 8 minutes or until tender; drain and chill thoroughly.

Cut white part of leek into ¼-inch-thick slices, and set aside; reserve green top for another use. Combine asparagus pieces, leek slices, potato, water, and bouillon granules in a large saucepan. Bring to a boil over medium-high heat. Cover; reduce heat, and simmer 25 minutes or until vegetables are tender. Place mixture in container of an electric blender; process until smooth. Pour mixture into a large bowl; stir in next 4 ingredients. Chill thoroughly.

Ladle pureed mixture into chilled soup bowls; garnish with asparagus tips and lemon rind, and serve immediately. Yield: 5 cups (116 calories per 1-cup serving).

PRO 8.5 / FAT 0.8 / CARB 22.6 / FIB 2.4 / CHOL 1 / SOD 301 / POT 980

Sipping soup may be more satisfying than you think. A one-year study done by Baylor College of Medicine showed that soup makes an effective behavior modification tool — it provides something low in calories that is filling and, therefore, helps control eating.

COLD GAZPACHO

1 quart tomato juice
2 tomatoes, peeled and cut into ½-inch cubes
1 green pepper, seeded and finely chopped
1 cucumber, finely chopped
1 cup chopped celery
¼ cup finely chopped onion
2 tablespoons lemon juice
¼ teaspoon pepper
⅛ to ¼ teaspoon hot sauce

Combine all ingredients in a medium bowl, stirring well. Cover and chill at least 3 hours. Ladle into chilled soup bowls to serve. Yield: 8 cups (40 calories per 1-cup serving).

PRO 1.7 / FAT 0.3 / CARB 9.6 / FIB 1.5 / CHOL 0 / SOD 459 / POT 640

GARBANZO BEAN SOUP

1 (1¼-pound) acorn squash, halved and
  seeded
1¾ cups water
1 (28-ounce) can crushed tomatoes, undrained
1 medium onion, chopped
1 medium carrot, chopped
1 medium stalk celery, chopped
1 teaspoon beef-flavored bouillon granules
½ teaspoon ground cumin
½ teaspoon caraway seeds, crushed
¼ teaspoon red pepper
1 bay leaf
1 (15-ounce) can garbanzo beans, drained
1 medium zucchini, cut into 1-inch slices

Peel acorn squash, and cut into ¾-inch pieces.
Combine acorn squash and next 10 ingredients in a large Dutch oven; bring to a boil. Cover; reduce heat, and simmer 15 minutes. Add garbanzo beans and zucchini; simmer 10 minutes or until zucchini is tender. Discard bay leaf. Ladle into soup bowls to serve. Yield: 9 cups (86 calories per 1-cup serving).

PRO 3.5 / FAT 0.9 / CARB 17.7 / FIB 3.5 / CHOL 0 / SOD 294 / POT 637

BLACK BEAN SOUP

1 (16-ounce) package dried black beans
3 quarts water
2 medium onions, chopped
1 (7-ounce) jar roasted red peppers,
  drained and chopped
2 cloves garlic, minced
1 teaspoon salt
1 bay leaf
¼ cup dry sherry
2 tablespoons red wine vinegar
1 teaspoon ground cumin
½ teaspoon dried whole oregano
¼ teaspoon red pepper
3 tablespoons plus 1 teaspoon plain low-fat yogurt
3 tablespoons plus 1 teaspoon minced fresh parsley

Sort and wash beans; place in a large Dutch oven. Cover with water 2 inches above beans; let soak overnight. Drain beans, and return to Dutch oven. Add next 6 ingredients; bring to a boil. Reduce heat to low; cook, uncovered, 2

hours or until beans are tender, stirring occasionally. Discard bay leaf.

Place half of bean mixture in container of an electric blender, and process until pureed. Repeat procedure with remaining bean mixture. Return puree to Dutch oven, and stir in next 5 ingredients. Simmer 10 minutes or until thoroughly heated, stirring occasionally. Ladle into soup bowls, and garnish each serving with 1 teaspoon yogurt and 1 teaspoon parsley. Yield: 10 cups (176 calories per 1-cup serving).

PRO 10.9 / FAT 1.0 / CARB 32.0 / FIB 11.8 / CHOL 0 / SOD 252 / POT 573

MUSHROOM SOUP

Vegetable cooking spray
2 teaspoons unsalted margarine
¾ pound fresh mushrooms, sliced
2 cups minced onion
½ stalk celery, sliced
1 clove garlic, minced
6 sprigs fresh parsley
½ teaspoon dried whole thyme
⅛ teaspoon pepper
¼ cup dry white wine
1 bay leaf
1 quart water
1 tablespoon chicken-flavored bouillon granules
½ cup plain low-fat yogurt
2 teaspoons cornstarch
¼ teaspoon lemon juice

Coat a saucepan with cooking spray; add margarine, and place over low heat until melted. Add next 7 ingredients, and cook 1 minute, stirring constantly. Add wine and bay leaf, and bring to a boil. Cover; reduce heat, and simmer 5 minutes, stirring occasionally. Add water and bouillon granules, and bring to a boil. Cover partially, and simmer 30 minutes. Remove from heat, and discard bay leaf and parsley sprigs.

Combine yogurt and cornstarch in a small bowl; set aside. Place mushroom mixture in container of an electric blender; process until smooth. Return to saucepan; stir in yogurt mixture, and cook over low heat until hot. Stir in lemon juice. Ladle into soup bowls. Yield: 7 cups (53 calories per 1-cup serving.)

PRO 2.6 / FAT 1.8 / CARB 8.0 / FIB 0.8 / CHOL 1 / SOD 169 / POT 303

MUSHROOM-BARLEY SOUP

1½ quarts water, divided
1 tablespoon beef-flavored bouillon granules
½ cup barley, uncooked
Vegetable cooking spray
1 cup chopped onion
2 cloves garlic, minced
1 cup sliced leek
¾ cup sliced carrot
½ cup sliced celery
4 cups sliced fresh mushrooms
1 teaspoon dried whole dillweed or 1 tablespoon chopped fresh dill
1 tablespoon lemon juice
½ teaspoon freshly ground black pepper

Combine 3 cups water, bouillon granules, and barley in a saucepan, and bring to a boil. Cover; reduce heat, and simmer 35 to 45 minutes or until softened.

Coat a large Dutch oven with cooking spray; place over medium heat until hot. Add onion and garlic, and sauté until tender. Stir in leek, carrot, celery, and remaining 3 cups water; bring to a boil. Cover; reduce heat, and simmer 10 minutes.

Add mushrooms and barley mixture; bring to a boil. Cover; reduce heat, and simmer 10 minutes. Remove from heat; stir in dillweed, lemon juice, and pepper. Ladle into soup bowls. Yield: 8 cups (77 calories per 1-cup serving).

PRO 2.4 / FAT 0.6 / CARB 16.7 / FIB 1.7 / CHOL 0 / SOD 188 / POT 277

FRENCH ONION SOUP

1 clove garlic, crushed
1 cup sliced carrot
1 tablespoon beef-flavored bouillon granules
1 quart water
Vegetable cooking spray
2 teaspoons unsalted margarine
3 medium-size yellow onions, thinly sliced
4 (½-inch) slices French bread
½ cup (2 ounces) shredded Gruyère cheese

Combine first 4 ingredients in a large Dutch oven, and simmer 20 minutes. Strain stock, discarding carrot; return stock to saucepan, and set aside.

Coat a large skillet with cooking spray; add margarine, and place over medium heat until hot. Add onion, and cook 30 minutes or until tender and lightly browned, stirring occasionally. Combine onion and stock in Dutch oven; bring to a boil. Reduce heat, and simmer 1 minute or until thoroughly heated.

Place bread slices on baking sheet; bake at 350° for 5 minutes or until lightly toasted. Sprinkle with cheese; bake an additional 3 minutes or until cheese melts.

To serve, spoon soup into individual serving bowls, and top each with cheese toasts. Yield: 4 cups (211 calories per 1-cup serving).

PRO 8.6 / FAT 8.1 / CARB 26.7 / FIB 2.0 / CHOL 16 / SOD 545 / POT 310

RED PEPPER-ONION SOUP

Vegetable cooking spray
1 teaspoon unsalted margarine
4 medium onions, thinly sliced
1 quart water
3 medium-size red peppers, seeded and thinly sliced
1 medium carrot, sliced
2 tablespoons regular rice, uncooked
2 teaspoons chicken-flavored bouillon granules
¼ teaspoon dried whole thyme
1 bay leaf
5 (2-inch) strips orange rind
2 tablespoons lemon juice
Dash of red pepper
2 tablespoons grated orange rind

Coat a large saucepan with cooking spray; add margarine, and place over medium heat until margarine melts. Add onion, and sauté until golden brown. Add next 8 ingredients, and bring to a boil. Cover; reduce heat, and simmer 25 minutes. Discard bay leaf and orange rind strips.

Place mixture in container of an electric blender, and process until coarsely pureed. Return to pan, and cook over low heat until thoroughly heated. Season with lemon juice and red pepper. Ladle into soup bowls, and garnish with grated orange rind. Yield: 6 cups (72 calories per 1-cup serving).

PRO 2.0 / FAT 1.3 / CARB 14.8 / FIB 1.6 / CHOL 0 / SOD 135 / POT 295

DILLED POTATO SOUP

3 medium-size baking potatoes, peeled and diced
2 medium parsnips, chopped
1 medium onion, chopped
1 medium carrot, chopped
5 cups water
1 tablespoon chicken-flavored bouillon granules
⅛ teaspoon pepper
1 cup frozen English peas, thawed
1 tablespoon lemon juice
¾ teaspoon dried whole dillweed or 1 tablespoon
  minced fresh dill

Combine first 7 ingredients in a large Dutch oven; bring to a boil. Cover; reduce heat, and simmer 30 to 35 minutes or until tender.

Place 1 cup vegetable mixture in container of an electric blender, and process until pureed. Return puree to Dutch oven with remaining vegetable mixture; stir in peas. Bring to a boil; reduce heat, and simmer 5 to 7 minutes or until peas are tender, stirring frequently. Stir in lemon juice and dillweed. Ladle into soup bowls, and serve immediately. Yield: 9 cups (103 calories per 1-cup serving).

PRO 3.4 / FAT 0.4 / CARB 22.1 / FIB 1.6 / CHOL 0 / SOD 157 / POT 655

POTATO-TURNIP SOUP

2 medium-size baking potatoes (about ⅔ pound),
  peeled and thinly sliced
½ cup thinly sliced onion
1 medium turnip, peeled and thinly sliced
2 medium stalks celery, thinly sliced
¼ teaspoon salt
⅛ teaspoon freshly ground black pepper
1 cup water
1 cup skim milk

Combine first 7 ingredients in a 2-quart saucepan. Bring to a boil. Cover; reduce heat, and simmer 30 minutes or until tender. Drain, discarding cooking liquid.

Combine vegetables and milk in container of an electric blender; process until smooth. Return to saucepan, and cook over low heat until thoroughly heated. Ladle into soup bowls to serve. Yield: 4 cups (84 calories per 1-cup serving).

PRO 4.7 / FAT 0.3 / CARB 16.6 / FIB 2.0 / CHOL 1 / SOD 229 / POT 565

The unadorned potato tuber makes a terrific health food. A 5-ounce potato contains approximately 100 calories, 3 grams of protein, 23 grams of carbohydrates, and a miniscule amount of fat. Potatoes are high in fiber, if the skin is kept intact, and naturally low in sodium. There's more — the vitamin C content of the potato supplies more than half the daily RDA and as an additional bonus contains a number of other vitamins and minerals essential to good health.

ORIENTAL TOFU-VEGETABLE SOUP

¼ pound snow peas
1 tablespoon cornstarch
2 tablespoons water
2 teaspoons minced garlic
2 teaspoons minced, peeled gingerroot
⅔ cup minced green onion
2 teaspoons vegetable oil
5 cups water
1 tablespoon chicken-flavored bouillon granules
3 medium carrots, thinly sliced
½ cup frozen whole kernel corn, thawed
1 cup shredded spinach leaves
½ cup thinly sliced fresh mushrooms
¼ cup minced green pepper
1 teaspoon reduced-sodium soy sauce
1 teaspoon Dijon mustard
4 ounces tofu, drained and cubed
1 tablespoon minced fresh parsley

Remove strings from snow peas, and split peas lengthwise in half; set aside. Dissolve cornstarch in 2 tablespoons water in a small bowl, and set aside.

Cook garlic, gingerroot, and green onion in hot oil in a large saucepan over medium heat 5 minutes. Add 5 cups water and bouillon granules; bring to a boil. Add carrots, and simmer 2 minutes. Add corn, and simmer 3 minutes. Add snow peas, spinach, mushrooms, and green pepper, and simmer 1 minute. Add cornstarch mixture, soy sauce, and mustard; bring to a boil, and cook 1 minute. Divide tofu among soup bowls, and ladle soup over tofu to serve. Garnish with parsley. Yield: 7 cups (80 calories per 1-cup serving).

PRO 3.5 / FAT 2.8 / CARB 12.2 / FIB 2.5 / CHOL 0 / SOD 245 / POT 305

VEGETABLE-SPLIT PEA SOUP

1½ cups dried split peas
7½ cups water
½ cup dry white wine
1 (16-ounce) can whole tomatoes, undrained
2 medium carrots, sliced
2 cups finely chopped onion
1 medium stalk celery, sliced
2 cloves garlic, minced
1 bay leaf
1 tablespoon beef-flavored bouillon granules
1 teaspoon dried whole thyme
½ teaspoon dried whole basil
½ teaspoon fennel seeds, crushed
¼ teaspoon pepper

Combine all ingredients in a Dutch oven, and bring to a boil. Cover; reduce heat, and simmer 2 hours. Discard bay leaf. Ladle into soup bowls to serve. Yield: 12 cups (114 calories per 1-cup serving).

PRO 6.9 / FAT 0.5 / CARB 21.5 / FIB 3.5 / CHOL 0 / SOD 272 / POT 418

CHICKEN-NOODLE SOUP

1 (5-pound) stewing hen, skinned
1 bay leaf
8 sprigs fresh parsley
2 medium onions, halved
3 stalks celery, halved
3 medium carrots, halved
1 gallon water
2 teaspoons salt
½ cup sliced carrot
½ cup sliced celery
¼ teaspoon ground marjoram
½ (8-ounce) package spaghetti, broken into
   2-inch pieces
¼ teaspoon pepper

Combine first 8 ingredients in a large Dutch oven, and bring to a boil. Cover; reduce heat, and simmer 3 hours. Strain stock, reserving chicken. Let chicken cool to touch; bone and cut meat into cubes. Refrigerate stock and chicken in separate containers overnight.

Remove fat from top of stock, and discard; strain stock through cheesecloth. Combine stock, sliced carrot, sliced celery, and marjoram in Dutch oven, and bring to a boil. Cover; reduce heat, and simmer 5 minutes. Add spaghetti, and simmer 12 minutes. Add chicken and pepper, and cook until thoroughly heated. Ladle into soup bowls, and serve immediately. Yield: 12 cups (172 calories per 1-cup serving).

PRO 18.5 / FAT 6.9 / CARB 7.8 / FIB 0.5 / CHOL 47 / SOD 441 / POT 163

CHICKEN-TORTILLA SOUP

2 (8-inch) corn tortillas, cut into strips
Vegetable cooking spray
1 medium onion, chopped
1 cup diced tomato
1 clove garlic
¼ teaspoon dried whole oregano
1 quart water
2 teaspoons chicken-flavored bouillon
   granules
¾ pound chicken breast halves, skinned
1 cup diced tomato
½ medium avocado, peeled and
   cubed
½ cup (2 ounces) shredded sharp Cheddar
   cheese
2 teaspoons minced hot chile pepper

Place tortilla strips on a baking sheet coated with cooking spray, and bake at 350° for 10 to 15 minutes or until golden and crisp. Set aside.

Place onion, 1 cup tomato, garlic, and oregano in container of an electric blender, and process until pureed. Transfer puree to a large saucepan, and simmer 5 minutes, stirring constantly. Stir in water and bouillon granules, and bring to a boil. Reduce heat, and add chicken breasts; simmer 15 to 20 minutes or until chicken is done.

Remove chicken from soup, keeping soup warm. Let chicken cool to touch; bone and cut meat into cubes. Return chicken to soup. Cook over low heat until thoroughly heated.

Ladle soup into soup bowls. Divide tortilla strips, 1 cup tomato, avocado, cheese, and chile pepper among bowls, and serve immediately. Yield: 7 cups (135 calories per 1-cup serving).

PRO 10.8 / FAT 6.2 / CARB 9.7 / FIB 1.0 / CHOL 28 / SOD 189 / POT 300

SHRIMP AND SCALLOP SOUP

½ pound fresh shrimp
4 cups fish stock (recipe on page 188)
Vegetable cooking spray
1 cup chopped canned tomatoes
1 medium onion, chopped
1 medium stalk celery, chopped
1 medium potato, peeled and diced
1 medium parsnip, chopped
1 medium-size red or green pepper, seeded and chopped
½ pound fresh scallops, coarsely chopped
½ cup skim milk
¾ teaspoon salt
½ teaspoon paprika
⅛ teaspoon red pepper
1 tablespoon lemon juice

Peel and devein shrimp, reserving shells. Chop shrimp, and set aside. Combine shrimp shells and fish stock in a large saucepan; bring to a boil, and cook until mixture is reduced to 3 cups; set aside.

Coat a Dutch oven with cooking spray; place over low heat until hot. Add next 6 ingredients; cover and cook 10 minutes or until softened, stirring occasionally.

Strain shrimp stock through a fine sieve into Dutch oven; bring to a boil. Cover; reduce heat, and simmer 15 minutes. Stir in scallops and shrimp, and simmer 2 minutes or until seafood is done, stirring occasionally.

Place 1 cup mixture in container of an electric blender; add milk, salt, and paprika, and process until pureed. Stir puree into soup, and season with red pepper and lemon juice. Ladle into soup bowls, and serve immediately. Yield: 8 cups (116 calories per 1-cup serving).

SMOKED TURKEY-VEGETABLE SOUP

Vegetable cooking spray
½ cup diced onion
¼ cup sliced celery
1 small green pepper, seeded and cut into julienne strips
3 cups water
2 cups sliced okra
2 cups chopped tomato
¼ cup regular rice, uncooked
1 teaspoon chicken-flavored bouillon granules
½ teaspoon Worcestershire sauce
⅛ teaspoon dried whole thyme
⅛ teaspoon freshly ground black pepper
⅛ teaspoon hot sauce
1¼ cups cubed, cooked, smoked turkey or chicken breast

Coat a large saucepan with cooking spray; place over medium heat until hot. Add onion and celery, and sauté 3 minutes. Add green pepper, and sauté 3 minutes. Add next 9 ingredients, and bring to a boil. Cover; reduce heat, and simmer 30 minutes, stirring occasionally. Add turkey, and cook until thoroughly heated. Ladle into soup bowls to serve. Yield: 6 cups (123 calories per 1-cup serving).

PRO 13.4 / FAT 1.6 / CARB 13.7 / FIB 1.4 / CHOL 26 / SOD 106 / POT 426

PRO 10.1 / FAT 0.5 / CARB 12.8 / FIB 3.1 / CHOL 42 / SOD 387 / POT 540

CARROT AND PARSNIP CHOWDER

4 medium carrots, diced
3 medium parsnips, diced
1 medium onion, chopped
1 medium potato, peeled and diced
3½ cups water
1 teaspoon chicken-flavored bouillon granules
¾ teaspoon dried whole dillweed or 1 tablespoon chopped fresh dill
⅛ teaspoon pepper

Combine first 6 ingredients in a large saucepan; bring to a boil. Cover; reduce heat, and simmer 40 minutes or until vegetables are very tender. Place 2 cups vegetable mixture in container of an electric blender; add dillweed and pepper, and process until smooth. Return pureed mixture to saucepan with remaining vegetable mixture, and cook over low heat until thoroughly heated. Ladle into individual soup bowls to serve. Yield: 4 cups (146 calories per 1-cup serving).

PRO 3.7 / FAT 0.8 / CARB 33.2 / FIB 5.0 / CHOL 0 / SOD 135 / POT 1006

CURRIED CORN CHOWDER

2 cups water
2 cups diced, peeled potato
1 medium onion, chopped
½ cup chopped celery
1½ teaspoons curry powder
1 bay leaf
¼ teaspoon salt
1 (10-ounce) package frozen whole kernel corn
1 tablespoon unsalted margarine
2 tablespoons all-purpose flour
1½ cups skim milk
Dash of red pepper
2 tablespoons minced fresh parsley

Combine first 7 ingredients in a saucepan. Bring to a boil. Cover; reduce heat, and simmer 25 minutes or until potato is tender. Add corn; simmer 5 minutes. Discard bay leaf.

Place ½ cup vegetable mixture in container of an electric blender; process until smooth. Return pureed mixture to pan, and set aside.

Melt margarine in a small saucepan over low heat; add flour, and cook 1 minute, stirring constantly. Gradually add milk, and cook until thickened and bubbly. Add milk mixture to corn mixture, and cook over low heat until thoroughly heated, stirring frequently. (Do not allow soup to boil.) Season with red pepper, and ladle into soup bowls to serve. Garnish with parsley. Yield: 6 cups (141 calories per 1-cup serving).

PRO 5.3 / FAT 2.6 / CARB 26.5 / FIB 1.7 / CHOL 1 / SOD 144 / POT 555

RED SNAPPER CHOWDER

1½ quarts water
½ cup dry white wine
3 leeks, chopped
2 medium stalks celery, chopped
6 sprigs fresh parsley
6 whole peppercorns
1 bay leaf
¼ teaspoon dried whole thyme
1 (2¼-pound) dressed red snapper, head and tail intact
2 medium potatoes, peeled and diced
1 medium onion, chopped
1 medium carrot, diced
1 (28-ounce) can whole tomatoes, undrained and chopped
2 tablespoons minced fresh parsley
¼ teaspoon freshly ground black pepper
⅛ teaspoon crushed red pepper

Combine first 8 ingredients in a large Dutch oven; bring to a boil, and add snapper. Cover; reduce heat, and cook at a bare simmer 30 minutes or until fish flakes easily with a fork. Transfer snapper to a platter, using a large metal spatula. Discard skin; remove fish from bones. Cover fish; set aside in refrigerator. Return head, tail, and bones to Dutch oven.

Cook stock over high heat until mixture is reduced to 3 cups. Strain stock well through a double layer of cheesecloth.

Combine stock, potatoes, onion, carrot, and tomatoes in Dutch oven; bring to a boil. Cover; reduce heat, and simmer 30 minutes or until vegetables are tender. Add fish, parsley, and pepper; cook over medium heat until hot. Ladle into soup bowls to serve. Yield: 10 cups (143 calories per 1-cup serving).

PRO 17.6 / FAT 0.9 / CARB 15.8 / FIB 0.6 / CHOL 44 / SOD 319 / POT 605

BOUILLABAISSE

1 pound fresh medium shrimp
Vegetable cooking spray
1 teaspoon olive oil
1 cup dry white wine
12 small hard-shelled clams
3 cups fish stock (recipe on page 188)
2 medium onions, chopped
2 cloves garlic, minced
2 medium stalks celery, chopped
2 medium-size green peppers, seeded and
  chopped
½ pound fennel, sliced
1 (28-ounce) can whole tomatoes, undrained
  and chopped
1 tablespoon tomato paste
1 pound fresh scallops
1 pound red snapper fillets, cut into 1-inch pieces
¾ pound cooked lobster meat, diced
2 tablespoons minced fresh parsley
Mediterranean Pepper Sauce

Peel and devein shrimp, reserving shells. Set shrimp aside in refrigerator. Coat a large Dutch oven with cooking spray; add oil, and place over medium heat until hot. Add shrimp shells, and cook 3 minutes, stirring constantly. Add wine and clams; cover and cook over high heat 5 minutes or until clams open, shaking pan occasionally. Remove from heat, and discard any unopened clams. Shuck clams, discarding shells; set clam meat aside in refrigerator.

Add fish stock to cooking liquid in Dutch oven; bring to a boil, and cook until stock is reduced to 2 cups. Strain stock through a double layer of cheesecloth; repeat straining, if necessary. (Reserve 3 tablespoons stock for Mediterranean Pepper Sauce.) Combine remaining stock and next 5 ingredients in Dutch oven; cover and cook over medium heat 10 minutes. Stir in tomatoes and tomato paste; bring to a boil. Cover; reduce heat, and simmer 15 minutes.

Add shrimp, scallops, and snapper; simmer 5 minutes or just until seafood is done, stirring often. Stir in clams, lobster, and parsley. Cook over low heat until thoroughly heated. Ladle into individual soup bowls, and serve with Mediterranean Pepper Sauce. Yield: 8 cups (248 calories per 1-cup serving with 1 teaspoon sauce per serving).

Mediterranean Pepper Sauce:

1 tablespoon pimiento, chopped
1 clove garlic, minced
½ teaspoon olive oil
¼ teaspoon red pepper
3 tablespoons reserved Bouillabaisse stock

Combine all ingredients in container of an electric blender, and process until smooth. Yield: ¼ cup (3 calories per teaspoon).

PRO 38.8 / FAT 3.2 / CARB 15.3 / FIB 0.9 / CHOL 205 / SOD 693 / POT 1115

SEAFOOD GUMBO

1¼ pounds chicken thighs, skinned
2 medium onions, sliced
1 medium-size green pepper, seeded and diced
1 teaspoon minced garlic
1 tablespoon vegetable oil
2 tablespoons all-purpose flour
7 cups water
1 (28-ounce) can whole tomatoes, undrained and
  chopped
1 pound fresh okra, sliced
2 tablespoons chopped fresh parsley
1 bay leaf
1 teaspoon salt
1 teaspoon vinegar
½ teaspoon pepper
¼ teaspoon red pepper
¼ teaspoon dried whole thyme
1 pound fresh crabmeat
1 pound fresh medium shrimp, peeled and
  deveined

Trim excess fat from chicken thighs. Place in a saucepan with water to cover, and bring to a boil. Cover; reduce heat, and cook 30 minutes. Drain chicken, and let cool to touch. Remove chicken from bone; chop meat, and set aside.

Sauté onion, green pepper, and garlic in oil in a large Dutch oven; add flour, and cook 1 minute, stirring constantly. Add chicken and next 10 ingredients; bring mixture to a boil. Reduce heat, and simmer, uncovered, 40 to 45 minutes. Stir in crabmeat and shrimp; cook 8 minutes. Remove bay leaf. Yield: 14 cups (144 calories per 1-cup serving).

PRO 16.3 / FAT 4.8 / CARB 8.6 / FIB 0.6 / CHOL 86 / SOD 496 / POT 428

FISH STOCK

3½ pounds fish bones and trimmings, chopped
2 medium stalks celery, chopped
1 medium carrot, chopped
1 medium onion, sliced
1 medium parsnip, chopped
6 sprigs fresh parsley
1 bay leaf
½ teaspoon dried whole thyme
6 whole peppercorns
1 cup dry white wine
2 quarts water

Combine all ingredients in a large Dutch oven, and bring to a boil. Cover; reduce heat, and simmer 30 minutes. Strain fish stock through a double layer of cheesecloth; repeat straining, if necessary. Cool. Store in refrigerator or freezer. Yield: 8 cups (5 calories per cup).

PRO 0.0 / FAT 0.0 / CARB 1.2 / FIB 0.0 / CHOL 0 / SOD 1 / POT 27

SPICY INDONESIAN FISH STEW

Vegetable cooking spray
1 tablespoon unsalted margarine
2 medium potatoes, peeled and diced
1 medium-size green pepper, chopped
1 medium carrot, chopped
1 medium onion, chopped
3 cloves garlic, minced
1 tablespoon minced, peeled gingerroot
2 tablespoons all-purpose flour
1½ teaspoons curry powder
1 teaspoon ground cumin
¼ teaspoon salt
⅛ teaspoon pepper
4 cups fish stock (see above)
1 bay leaf
1 pound cod fillets, cut into 1-inch pieces
⅓ cup minced green onion
¼ cup minced fresh parsley
1 fresh green chile pepper, seeded and minced
2 tablespoons lemon juice or to taste

Coat a Dutch oven with cooking spray; add margarine, and place over medium heat until margarine is melted. Add next 6 ingredients; cover and cook 10 minutes or until tender, stirring occasionally. Reduce heat to low, and stir in flour, curry powder, cumin, salt, and pepper; cook 3 minutes, stirring constantly. Add fish stock and bay leaf, and bring to a boil, stirring well. Cover; reduce heat, and simmer 25 minutes. Discard bay leaf.

Place 1 cup vegetable mixture in container of an electric blender, and process until pureed. Stir puree into soup; add cod, and simmer 5 minutes or until cod flakes easily when tested with a fork. Stir in remaining ingredients, and cook until thoroughly heated. Ladle into soup bowls, and serve immediately. Yield: 8 cups (160 calories per 1-cup serving).

PRO 12.4 / FAT 2.0 / CARB 18.8 / FIB 1.5 / CHOL 28 / SOD 129 / POT 807

SEAFOOD STEW

Vegetable cooking spray
1 teaspoon vegetable oil
¼ cup finely chopped green pepper
2 tablespoons chopped onion
1 clove garlic, minced
1 (16-ounce) can tomatoes, undrained
1 (8-ounce) can tomato sauce
½ cup Burgundy or other dry red wine
3 tablespoons chopped fresh parsley
¼ teaspoon salt
¼ teaspoon dried whole oregano
¼ teaspoon dried whole basil
Dash of pepper
1 (16-ounce) package frozen perch fillets
1 (4½-ounce) can shrimp, rinsed and drained
1 (6½-ounce) can minced clams, undrained

Coat a large Dutch oven with cooking spray; add oil, and place over medium heat until hot. Add green pepper, onion, and garlic; sauté until tender. Add tomatoes, tomato sauce, wine, parsley, salt, oregano, basil, and pepper; bring mixture to a boil. Cover; reduce heat, and simmer 20 minutes, stirring occasionally.

Cook perch according to package directions; cut into small pieces. Add perch, shrimp, and clams to tomato mixture; cover and simmer an additional 3 minutes. Yield: 6 cups (169 calories per 1-cup serving).

PRO 23.3 / FAT 4.3 / CARB 8.9 / FIB 0.4 / CHOL 82 / SOD 846 / POT 0

TURKEY-VEGETABLE STEW

Vegetable cooking spray
1 pound sweet Italian sausage, crumbled
1 cup chopped onion
1 clove garlic, minced
1 (3-pound) turkey breast, skinned, boned, and cut into 2-inch pieces
4 cups chopped tomato
3 cups chopped green pepper
2 cups sliced yellow squash
2 cups sliced fresh mushrooms
1 cup sliced zucchini
1 cup dry white wine
1 teaspoon dried whole basil
1 teaspoon dried whole oregano

Coat a Dutch oven with cooking spray; place over medium heat until hot. Add sausage, onion, and garlic; cook until lightly browned. Drain in a colander. Add turkey to Dutch oven, and cook over medium heat 10 minutes or until golden brown; stir often.

Add sausage mixture and remaining ingredients to turkey in Dutch oven; bring to a boil. Cover; reduce heat, and simmer 1 hour. Ladle into soup bowls to serve. Yield: 10 cups (273 calories per 1-cup serving).

PRO 31.3 / FAT 11.6 / CARB 10.6 / FIB 1.7 / CHOL 78 / SOD 368 / POT 757

BEEF STEW

2 pounds lean boneless round steak
Vegetable cooking spray
5 cups water
1 medium onion, sliced
1 clove garlic, minced
2 teaspoons beef-flavored bouillon granules
1 teaspoon Worcestershire sauce
½ teaspoon salt
½ teaspoon dried whole thyme
1 bay leaf
6 small onions (about 1½ pounds), quartered
5 medium carrots, cut into 1-inch pieces
4 medium potatoes, cubed
3 stalks celery, cut into 1-inch pieces
2 tablespoons all-purpose flour
¼ cup water

Trim excess fat from steak; cut steak into 1-inch pieces. Coat a large Dutch oven with cooking spray; place over medium heat until hot. Add beef; cook until browned. Stir in next 8 ingredients. Cover; reduce heat, and simmer 1 hour. Add quartered onions, carrots, potatoes, and celery; cover and cook over low heat 30 minutes or until tender. Remove bay leaf.

Combine flour and ¼ cup water; stir into stew. Bring to a boil; cook 1 minute, stirring constantly. Ladle into soup bowls to serve. Yield: 16 cups (166 calories per 1-cup serving).

PRO 19.8 / FAT 3.3 / CARB 13.7 / FIB 1.2 / CHOL 37 / SOD 186 / POT 586

Major crises may not cause the most stress. It could be the cumulative effect of all the minor irritations encountered each day. Because these hassles are chronic problems (getting stuck in traffic, family arguments, juggling the checkbook) and not isolated events, they exert long-term pressure. If you use bank lines to catch up on your reading, you've developed a coping mechanism, the key to dealing with minor problems.

MIXED VEGETABLE STEW

1½ pounds lean ground chuck
1 (16-ounce) package frozen mixed vegetables
1 (16-ounce) can whole tomatoes, undrained and cut into quarters
1 (4-ounce) can mushroom stems and pieces, undrained
2 cups tomato juice
2 tablespoons instant minced onion
1 teaspoon dried whole basil
½ teaspoon dried whole oregano
½ teaspoon pepper

Cook ground chuck in a Dutch oven until browned, stirring to crumble; drain meat in a colander, and pat dry with a paper towel. Wipe pan drippings from Dutch oven.

Return meat to Dutch oven; stir in remaining ingredients. Bring to a boil. Cover; reduce heat, and simmer 30 minutes. Yield: 8 cups (209 calories per 1-cup serving).

PRO 20.8 / FAT 7.6 / CARB 14.4 / FIB 1.1 / CHOL 60 / SOD 544 / POT 0

LAMB STEW WITH BARLEY

2 pounds boneless leg of lamb
Vegetable cooking spray
1 quart water
¼ pound pearl onions
2 cloves garlic, minced
½ teaspoon salt
½ teaspoon dried whole thyme
½ teaspoon dried whole rosemary
⅛ teaspoon pepper
1 cup barley, uncooked
1½ cups sliced carrot

Trim excess fat from leg of lamb, and cut meat into bite-size pieces. Coat a Dutch oven with vegetable cooking spray, and place over medium heat until hot. Add lamb pieces, and cook 4 minutes or until lamb is browned, stirring occasionally. Drain lamb well on paper towels, and return to Dutch oven.

Add water, onions, garlic, salt, thyme, rosemary, and pepper to Dutch oven; bring mixture to a boil. Add barley. Cover; reduce heat, and simmer 45 minutes. Add sliced carrot, and simmer, uncovered, 30 minutes. Ladle into soup bowls to serve. Yield: 6 cups (295 calories per 1-cup serving).

PRO 27.7 / FAT 6.4 / CARB 30.9 / FIB 2.8 / CHOL 85 / SOD 266 / POT 425

GREEN AND YELLOW SPLIT PEA STEW

1 cup dried green split peas
1 cup dried yellow split peas
9 cups water
1 clove garlic, minced
1 teaspoon chicken-flavored bouillon
    granules
1 bay leaf
½ teaspoon dried whole thyme
1 medium potato, diced
2 cups diced zucchini
1½ cups diced carrot
1 cup diced celery
1 cup chopped onion
½ cup diced, peeled turnip
2 teaspoons lemon juice
½ teaspoon salt
½ teaspoon pepper

Sort and wash peas; place in a large Dutch oven. Cover with water 2 inches above peas; let soak overnight.

Drain peas, and return to Dutch oven. Add 9 cups water, garlic, bouillon granules, bay leaf, and thyme; bring to a boil. Cover; reduce heat to low, and cook 1½ hours or until peas are tender, stirring occasionally.

Add potato, zucchini, carrot, celery, onion, and turnip; bring to a boil. Cover; reduce heat, and simmer 15 minutes or until potato is tender. Remove and discard bay leaf.

Add lemon juice, salt, and pepper, stirring well. Ladle into soup bowls to serve. Yield: 12 cups (150 calories per 1-cup serving).

PRO 9.3 / FAT 0.5 / CARB 28.4 / FIB 4.7 / CHOL 0 / SOD 162 / POT 568

LENTIL STEW

1 quart water
1 cup chopped onion
1 cup diced potato
1 cup chopped carrot
1 cup sliced fresh mushrooms
½ cup chopped celery
½ cup chopped tomato
½ cup dried lentils
¼ cup brown rice, uncooked
2 vegetable-flavored bouillon cubes
½ teaspoon dried whole tarragon
½ teaspoon dried whole oregano

Combine all ingredients in a large Dutch oven, and bring to a boil. Cover; reduce heat to low, and simmer 1½ hours. Ladle into soup bowls to serve. Yield: 4 cups (195 calories per 1-cup serving).

PRO 9.6 / FAT 0.9 / CARB 38.8 / FIB 3.3 / CHOL 2 / SOD 517 / POT 747

Fruits and vegetables lend variety to any meal. Stuffed Pattypan Squash (page 200) is filled with grated zucchini and yellow squash. Broiled Pineapple (page 204) has a honey glaze to enhance its tangy sweet flavor, and Orange Beets (page 193) are simmered in a sweet-and-sour orange sauce.

Vegetables & Fruits

BRAISED ARTICHOKE HEARTS

2 (9-ounce) packages frozen artichoke hearts
1 medium onion, thinly sliced
1 cup water
1 bay leaf
½ teaspoon dried whole rosemary
¼ cup grated Parmesan cheese
½ teaspoon grated lemon rind
2 tablespoons lemon juice
2 teaspoons unsalted margarine
¼ teaspoon pepper

Combine first 5 ingredients in a large skillet; bring to a boil, separating artichoke hearts with a fork. Cover; reduce heat, and simmer 20 minutes or until artichoke hearts are tender. Drain; discard bay leaf. Transfer to a serving bowl, and toss vegetables with cheese, lemon rind and juice, margarine, and pepper. Yield: 6 servings (68 calories per serving).

PRO 3.9 / FAT 2.7 / CARB 9.0 / FIB 0.9 / CHOL 3 / SOD 103 / POT 260

VEGETABLE-STUFFED ARTICHOKES

6 medium artichokes
Vegetable cooking spray
1 teaspoon vegetable oil
1 (10-ounce) package frozen English peas, thawed and drained
1 (8-ounce) can sliced water chestnuts, drained
2 tablespoons dry white wine
1 tablespoon reduced-sodium soy sauce
¼ teaspoon ground ginger

Wash artichokes by plunging up and down in cold water. Cut off stem end, and trim ½-inch from top of each artichoke. Remove any loose bottom leaves. With scissors, trim away one-fourth of each outer leaf. Rub top and edges of leaves with a lemon wedge to prevent discoloration.

Place artichokes in a large Dutch oven with 1 inch of water. Cover and bring to a boil; reduce heat, and simmer 30 minutes or until leaves pull out easily. Spread leaves apart; scrape out the fuzzy thistle center (choke), using a spoon. Keep artichokes warm.

Coat a skillet or wok with cooking spray; add oil, and place over medium heat until hot. Add peas, water chestnuts, wine, soy sauce, and ginger, and stir-fry 5 minutes or until crisp-tender. Divide among artichoke cavities; transfer to a platter, and serve immediately. Yield: 6 servings (135 calories per serving).

PRO 6.5 / FAT 1.0 / CARB 27.1 / FIB 3.4 / CHOL 0 / SOD 259 / POT 563

LEMON GREEN BEANS

1 pound fresh green beans
½ cup sliced red pepper
½ teaspoon dried whole basil
2 tablespoons lemon juice
2 teaspoons sesame seeds, toasted
2 tablespoons julienne lemon rind

Remove strings from green beans; wash and cut into 2-inch pieces, if desired. Place beans, red pepper, and basil in a saucepan with a small amount of water; cover and cook 12 minutes or until tender. Drain; transfer to a serving bowl, and add lemon juice and sesame seeds, tossing well. Garnish with lemon rind. Yield: 4 servings (48 calories per serving).

PRO 2.6 / FAT 1.0 / CARB 10.2 / FIB 2.6 / CHOL 0 / SOD 8 / POT 280

MINTED GREEN BEANS

1 pound fresh green beans
3 tablespoons cider vinegar
1 tablespoon plus 1 teaspoon unsalted margarine
1 tablespoon mint jelly
Dash of dried whole rosemary or ¾ teaspoon minced fresh rosemary
Lemon twist (optional)
Additional fresh rosemary (optional)

Remove strings from beans; wash thoroughly. Cover and cook beans in a small amount of boiling water 12 minutes or just until tender; drain.

Add next 4 ingredients to beans; cook until thoroughly heated, stirring gently to coat beans. Arrange beans on a serving platter; garnish with a lemon twist and fresh rosemary, if desired. Yield: 4 servings (83 calories per serving).

PRO 2.1 / FAT 3.9 / CARB 12.1 / FIB 2.4 / CHOL 0 / SOD 8 / POT 252

GREEN BEANS WITH GINGERROOT

1½ pounds fresh green beans
1 cup water
½ cup minced onion
1 tablespoon minced, peeled gingerroot
½ teaspoon chicken-flavored bouillon granules
½ teaspoon fennel seeds, crushed
2 tablespoons minced fresh parsley

Remove strings from beans; wash and cut into 2-inch pieces. Combine beans and next 5 ingredients in a saucepan; bring to a boil. Cover; reduce heat, and simmer 12 minutes or until tender. Transfer bean mixture to a serving bowl, and toss with parsley. Yield: 6 servings (42 calories per serving).

PRO 2.3 / FAT 0.2 / CARB 9.5 / FIB 2.5 / CHOL 0 / SOD 40 / POT 273

Cooked fresh vegetables can add nutrition as well as flavor, color, and texture to your meals. Add variety and interest to your vegetable dishes by serving them whole or halved or use some of the new garnishing tools to create more unusual shapes.

ORANGE BEETS

2 pounds fresh beets
1 tablespoon cornstarch
2 tablespoons water
⅓ cup unsweetened orange juice
1 tablespoon brown sugar
1 tablespoon cider vinegar
Dash of ground cinnamon
Dash of ground allspice
1 tablespoon grated orange rind

Leave root and 1-inch of stem on beets; scrub with a brush. Place beets in a large saucepan, and add water to cover; bring to a boil. Cover; reduce heat, and simmer 40 minutes or until tender. Drain, reserving ⅔ cup cooking liquid. Peel beets, and cut into ¼-inch slices; set aside. Combine cornstarch and water in a small bowl, stirring to blend; set aside.

Combine reserved cooking liquid, orange juice, brown sugar, and vinegar in saucepan, and bring to a boil; reduce heat, and cook, stirring constantly, until sugar dissolves. Stir in cornstarch mixture; add beets, cinnamon, allspice, and orange rind. Cook over low heat 10 minutes, stirring occasionally. Transfer to a bowl, and serve immediately. Yield: 8 servings (63 calories per serving).

PRO 1.8 / FAT 0.2 / CARB 14.7 / FIB 1.1 / CHOL 0 / SOD 82 / POT 394

Spices add a natural, no-calorie zip to these vegetables: Minted Green Beans (page 192), Vegetable-Stuffed Squash (page 199), and Herbed Zucchini (page 200).

BROCCOLI STIR-FRY

1½ teaspoons cornstarch
1½ teaspoons sugar
¼ teaspoon ground ginger
⅛ teaspoon pepper
½ cup water
1 tablespoon lemon juice
1½ pounds fresh broccoli
Vegetable cooking spray
2 teaspoons vegetable oil
½ cup thinly sliced onion
1 cup diagonally sliced carrots
1 cup coarsely shredded cabbage

Combine cornstarch, sugar, ginger, and pepper; stir in water and lemon juice, mixing well. Set aside.

Trim off large leaves of broccoli. Remove tough ends of lower stalks; wash broccoli thoroughly. Remove flowerets from stems, and set aside. Cut stems in thin slices; set aside.

Coat a wok with cooking spray. Pour oil around top of preheated wok; allow to heat 10 minutes. Add onion to wok, and stir-fry 2 minutes. Add broccoli and carrots; stir-fry 4 to 5 minutes or until crisp-tender. Add cabbage; stir-fry 2 minutes. Add cornstarch mixture to wok, and cook, stirring constantly, until thickened. Transfer to a serving bowl. Yield: 8 servings (53 calories per serving).

PRO 3.1 / FAT 1.5 / CARB 8.9 / FIB 2.3 / CHOL 0 / SOD 23 / POT 318

BROCCOLI-CAULIFLOWER GRATIN

3 cups cauliflower flowerets (about 1 pound)
1 cup water
1 teaspoon chicken-flavored bouillon granules
1 pound fresh broccoli, broken into flowerets
1 tablespoon unsalted margarine
2 tablespoons all-purpose flour
1 cup skim milk
2 slices low-fat process Cheddar cheese, torn into pieces
¼ teaspoon white pepper
1 tablespoon minced fresh parsley
1 tablespoon grated Parmesan cheese

Combine cauliflower, water, and bouillon granules in a large saucepan; bring to a boil.

Cover; reduce heat, and cook 12 minutes or until tender. Transfer to a 13- x 9- x 2-inch baking dish, using a slotted spoon. Add broccoli to pan, and bring to a boil. Cover; reduce heat, and cook 8 minutes or until tender. Drain and transfer to baking dish.

Melt margarine in a small skillet over low heat. Add flour, stirring until smooth (mixture will be dry). Cook 1 minute, stirring constantly. Gradually add milk, stirring with a wire whisk; cook over medium heat, stirring until thickened and bubbly. Add Cheddar cheese and pepper; stir until cheese melts. Spoon sauce over vegetables. Sprinkle with parsley and Parmesan cheese. Broil 4 to 6 inches from heat 1 to 2 minutes or until top is browned. Yield: 8 servings (74 calories per serving).

PRO 5.7 / FAT 2.4 / CARB 9.2 / FIB 1.3 / CHOL 1 / SOD 182 / POT 446

Cook vegetables for as short a time as possible to obtain a nutrient-filled product that is also delicious. The desired end product is vegetables that are crisp-tender.

BRUSSELS SPROUTS IN ORANGE SAUCE

1 pound fresh brussels sprouts
1¼ cups water
½ teaspoon dried whole dillweed
1½ teaspoons cornstarch
¼ cup unsweetened orange juice
1 medium orange, peeled, sectioned, and seeded

Remove any discolored leaves from brussels sprouts. Cut off stem ends, and wash sprouts thoroughly. Cut a small cross in the base of each sprout. Combine sprouts, water, and dillweed in a saucepan; bring to a boil. Cover; reduce heat, and simmer 20 minutes or until tender. Drain; return sprouts to saucepan.

Combine cornstarch and orange juice; mix well. Stir cornstarch mixture into saucepan. Cook over low heat, stirring constantly, until thickened and bubbly. Add orange sections, and cook until thoroughly heated, stirring occasionally. Transfer to a serving bowl. Yield: 6 servings (41 calories per serving).

PRO 2.7 / FAT 0.2 / CARB 8.9 / FIB 2.2 / CHOL 0 / SOD 19 / POT 209

SWEET-AND-SOUR RED CABBAGE

2½ pounds red cabbage, shredded
1 medium onion, thinly sliced
1 cup unsweetened apple juice
½ cup red wine vinegar
½ cup dry red wine
¼ cup sugar
¼ teaspoon pepper
1 bay leaf
1 teaspoon grated lemon rind
2 tablespoons lemon juice

Combine first 8 ingredients in a Dutch oven; bring to a boil. Cover, reduce heat, and cook 15 to 20 minutes or until onion and cabbage are tender, stirring occasionally.

Discard bay leaf, and stir in lemon rind and juice. Transfer to a serving bowl. Yield: 8 servings (88 calories per serving).

PRO 2.2 / FAT 0.5 / CARB 20.8 / FIB 1.8 / CHOL 0 / SOD 19 / POT 386

COLCANNON

Vegetable cooking spray
1 teaspoon unsalted margarine
1 cup sliced onion
1 clove garlic, minced
3 cups coarsely chopped cabbage
2½ cups diced potato
½ cup water
½ teaspoon chicken-flavored bouillon granules
¼ teaspoon salt
¼ teaspoon pepper
⅛ teaspoon paprika

Coat a large Dutch oven with cooking spray; add margarine, and place over low heat until melted. Add onion and garlic, and cook 8 to 10 minutes or until lightly browned. Add cabbage, and cook 5 minutes or until wilted, stirring frequently. Add potato, water, and bouillon granules, and bring to a boil. Cover; reduce heat, and simmer 20 minutes or until potato is tender. Season with salt and pepper, and mash lightly with a potato masher. Transfer to a serving bowl, and sprinkle with paprika. Yield: 7 servings (69 calories per ½-cup serving).

PRO 2.1 / FAT 0.8 / CARB 14.5 / FIB 1.1 / CHOL 0 / SOD 126 / POT 479

CAULIFLOWER WITH CHEESE SAUCE

3½ cups cauliflower flowerets (about 1¼ pounds)
Vegetable cooking spray
1 tablespoon cornstarch
1½ cups skim milk
½ cup (2 ounces) coarsely shredded sharp Cheddar cheese
2 tablespoons grated Parmesan cheese, divided
⅛ teaspoon dry mustard
⅛ teaspoon pepper
Dash of ground nutmeg
1 tablespoon fine, dry breadcrumbs

Cook cauliflower in boiling water in a saucepan 8 minutes or until crisp-tender; drain. Transfer to a 10- x 6- x 2-inch baking dish coated with cooking spray, and set aside.

Combine cornstarch and milk in a small heavy saucepan; cook over medium heat, stirring constantly, until thickened and bubbly. Stir in Cheddar cheese, 1 tablespoon Parmesan, mustard, pepper, and nutmeg. Cook over low heat, stirring constantly, until cheese melts.

Pour cheese sauce over cauliflower in baking dish. Sprinkle with remaining Parmesan and breadcrumbs; broil 3 to 4 inches from heat 6 minutes or until brown and bubbly. Yield: 6 servings (91 calories per serving).

PRO 6.5 / FAT 3.9 / CARB 8.0 / FIB 0.5 / CHOL 13 / SOD 138 / POT 323

LEMON CARROTS

6 medium carrots, scraped and cut into julienne strips
2 tablespoons lemon juice
2 teaspoons unsalted margarine, melted
1 teaspoon sugar
⅛ teaspoon ground ginger
1 tablespoon minced fresh parsley

Cook carrots in a vegetable steamer over boiling water 8 to 10 minutes or until crisp-tender. Drain carrots and transfer to a serving bowl; set aside, and keep warm. Combine remaining ingredients; pour over carrots, and toss well. Yield: 5 servings (56 calories per ½-cup serving).

PRO 0.9 / FAT 1.7 / CARB 10.2 / FIB 1.3 / CHOL 0 / SOD 31 / POT 291

Low in fat and calories, but high in nutrient value, vegetables are food gems adding color, flavor, and texture to any meal.

MARINATED BABY CARROTS

¾ pound baby carrots, scraped
⅓ cup sliced green onion
1 tablespoon olive oil
1 tablespoon water
2 teaspoons cider vinegar
2 teaspoons lemon juice
⅛ teaspoon celery seeds
⅛ teaspoon dillseeds

Cook carrots in a small amount of boiling water 10 minutes or until crisp-tender. Drain and transfer to a large bowl. Add remaining ingredients; toss to coat. Cover and chill overnight. Yield: 4 servings (71 calories per serving).

PRO 1.0 / FAT 3.6 / CARB 9.7 / FIB 1.6 / CHOL 0 / SOD 30 / POT 301

SAUTÉED MUSHROOMS

Vegetable cooking spray
3 green onions, sliced
1 pound fresh mushrooms, sliced
2 tablespoons dry sherry
¼ teaspoon freshly ground black pepper
2 teaspoons Worcestershire sauce

Coat a skillet with cooking spray; place over medium heat until hot. Add green onion, and sauté 5 minutes or until tender. Stir in remaining ingredients; cover and cook over low heat 10 minutes or until mushrooms are tender. Transfer to a bowl to serve. Yield: 4 servings (43 calories per serving).

PRO 2.6 / FAT 0.5 / CARB 6.8 / FIB 1.2 / CHOL 0 / SOD 30 / POT 471

PARMESAN CELERY

4 cups diagonally sliced celery
½ cup water
Vegetable cooking spray
1 medium onion, chopped
¼ cup grated Parmesan cheese
2 tablespoons chopped fresh parsley
1 (2-ounce) jar diced pimiento, drained
¼ teaspoon pepper

Combine celery and water in a medium saucepan; bring to a boil. Cover; reduce heat, and simmer 5 minutes or until crisp-tender. Drain and set aside.

Coat a large skillet with cooking spray; place over medium heat until hot. Add onion, and sauté until tender. Stir in celery, and cook until thoroughly heated. Remove from heat, and stir in remaining ingredients. Transfer to a serving bowl. Yield: 6 servings (39 calories per serving).

PRO 2.3 / FAT 1.2 / CARB 5.5 / FIB 1.0 / CHOL 3 / SOD 136 / POT 297

STEWED OKRA AND TOMATOES

Vegetable cooking spray
1 teaspoon unsalted margarine
½ cup minced onion
1 stalk celery, minced
¾ pound okra, sliced
2 medium tomatoes, seeded and chopped
1 clove garlic, minced
½ teaspoon dried whole thyme
½ teaspoon dried whole basil
1 bay leaf
⅛ teaspoon ground red pepper
⅛ teaspoon salt
⅓ cup dry white wine

Coat a large skillet with cooking spray; add margarine, and place over medium heat until margarine melts. Add onion and celery; sauté until tender. Stir in remaining ingredients, and bring to a boil. Cover; reduce heat, and simmer 15 minutes or until okra is tender, stirring occasionally. Discard bay leaf. Transfer to a serving bowl. Yield: 6 servings (45 calories per serving).

PRO 1.8 / FAT 0.8 / CARB 8.5 / FIB 1.1 / CHOL 0 / SOD 64 / POT 328

ONIONS STUFFED WITH BROCCOLI

6 medium onions
1 (10-ounce) package frozen chopped broccoli
2 slices low-fat process American cheese, torn into pieces
¼ teaspoon pepper
1 tablespoon grated Parmesan cheese
¼ cup dry white wine
¼ cup water

Peel onions; cut a slice from top of each. Place onions in a Dutch oven; add water to cover. Bring to a boil. Cover; reduce heat, and simmer 20 minutes or until tender. Drain and let cool to touch. Scoop out centers, leaving ¼-inch-thick shells. Chop centers, reserving ½ cup

Cook broccoli in a small amount of boiling water 8 minutes or until tender; drain. Combine broccoli, chopped onion, American cheese, and pepper; spoon into onion shells. Sprinkle tops with Parmesan; place in a shallow baking dish. Pour wine and water around onions. Cover; bake at 350° for 20 minutes. Yield: 6 servings (77 calories per serving).

PRO 4.9 / FAT 1.2 / CARB 13.4 / FIB 2.0 / CHOL 1 / SOD 121 / POT 335

ENGLISH PEAS AND PEARL ONIONS

2 pounds fresh English peas
1 cup pearl onions
3 cups water
Vegetable cooking spray
½ pound fresh mushrooms, sliced
1 (2-ounce) jar sliced pimiento, drained
¼ teaspoon salt
¼ teaspoon ground savory
⅛ teaspoon freshly ground black pepper

Shell and wash peas. Place peas, onions, and water in a Dutch oven; bring to a boil. Cover; reduce heat, and simmer 12 to 15 minutes or until peas are tender. Drain.

Coat a large skillet with cooking spray; add mushrooms, and sauté until tender. Stir in peas and onions and remaining ingredients; cook, stirring constantly, until thoroughly heated. Yield: 6 servings (60 calories per serving).

PRO 3.8 / FAT 0.5 / CARB 11.3 / FIB 2.2 / CHOL 0 / SOD 104 / POT 317

SEASONED BLACK-EYED PEAS

2½ cups shelled fresh or frozen black-eyed peas
1 medium onion, chopped
⅓ cup chopped celery
1 teaspoon beef-flavored bouillon granules
¼ teaspoon dried whole savory
¼ teaspoon freshly ground black pepper
2 cups water

Combine all ingredients in a medium saucepan; bring to a boil. Cover; reduce heat, and simmer 1 hour or until peas are tender. Yield: 6 servings (87 calories per serving).

PRO 5.8 / FAT 0.6 / CARB 15.2 / FIB 1.4 / CHOL 0 / SOD 86 / POT 321

PEPPER-ONION SAUTÉ

Vegetable cooking spray
1 teaspoon unsalted margarine
1 medium-size green pepper, seeded and
cut into ¼-inch strips
1 medium-size red pepper, seeded and
cut into ¼-inch strips
1 cup sliced fresh mushrooms
6 green onions, cut into 1-inch pieces
1 clove garlic, minced
¼ teaspoon salt
⅛ teaspoon white pepper
⅛ teaspoon celery seeds

Coat a large skillet with cooking spray; add margarine, and place over medium heat until melted. Add green and red pepper, mushrooms, onion, and garlic; sauté 5 to 10 minutes or until crisp-tender. Stir in salt, white pepper, and celery seeds, and cook 1 minute. Yield: 4 servings (45 calories per serving).

PRO 1.6 / FAT 1.4 / CARB 8.0 / FIB 2.2 / CHOL 0 / SOD 151 / POT 290

POTATOES ROASTED WITH ONIONS

7 pearl onions
1 clove garlic, minced
1 teaspoon vegetable oil
9 new potatoes (about 1½ pounds)
2 teaspoons unsalted margarine, cut into bits
⅛ teaspoon pepper

Sauté onions and garlic in hot oil in a nonstick skillet over medium high heat until onions are golden brown; transfer to a 13- x 9- x 2-inch baking dish. Cut potatoes in half, and place, cut side up, in baking dish. Dot with margarine, and sprinkle with pepper. Cover and bake at 400° for 50 minutes. Yield: 6 servings (117 calories per serving).

PRO 3.0 / FAT 2.2 / CARB 22.0 / FIB 1.3 / CHOL 0 / SOD 9 / POT 645

Bone up on your calcium requirements. The National Institute of Health recommends that women have more than 1,000 milligrams of calcium per day well before menopause and 1,500 thereafter. Men need 800 milligrams. If you think you need to include more calcium-rich foods in your diet or take a calcium supplement, keep these points in mind:
*Milk and milk products and dark green vegetables are rich sources of calcium.
*Calcium carbonate usually supplies the most pure calcium per tablet for the least cost. One 500 milligram tablet contains 200 milligrams of pure calcium (40 percent).
*Sodium-free antacid tablets that contain calcium carbonate make a good inexpensive calcium supplement.
*If you have ever had kidney stones, check with your doctor before taking calcium supplements.

EASY BAKED SWEET POTATOES

2 pounds sweet potatoes, peeled and cut
into ¼-inch slices
2 tablespoons grated orange rind
¼ cup lemon juice
2 teaspoons unsalted margarine

Place sweet potatoes in a single layer on a sheet of aluminum foil. Sprinkle with orange rind and lemon juice, and dot with margarine. Fold foil over potatoes, and crimp edges together. Tuck ends of foil under to make an airtight package. Place on a baking sheet, and bake at 400° for 40 minutes or until tender. Yield: 8 servings (129 calories per serving).

PRO 1.9 / FAT 1.3 / CARB 28.6 / FIB 2.4 / CHOL 0 / SOD 15 / POT 244

ORANGE SWEET POTATOES AND APPLES

Vegetable cooking spray
2 medium sweet potatoes, peeled and
　cut into ½-inch slices
2 medium apples, cored and cut into rings
¼ teaspoon ground cinnamon
1 tablespoon cornstarch
1 tablespoon brown sugar
1 cup unsweetened orange juice

Coat a 10- x 6- x 2-inch baking dish with cooking spray. Arrange half of sweet potato slices in baking dish; top with half of apple rings and half of cinnamon. Repeat layers with remaining sweet potato slices, apple, and cinnamon.

Combine cornstarch, sugar, and orange juice in a small saucepan, stirring to blend. Bring to a boil; reduce heat to low, and cook 1 minute or until mixture is thickened and bubbly, stirring constantly.

Pour over sweet potato mixture. Cover and bake at 350° for 1 hour or until sweet potatoes are tender. Yield: 6 servings (118 calories per serving).

PRO 1.4 / FAT 0.4 / CARB 28.4 / FIB 2.2 / CHOL 0 / SOD 9 / POT 256

SESAME SPINACH

1 pound spinach
Vegetable cooking spray
1 teaspoon vegetable oil
1 tablespoon sesame seeds, toasted
¼ teaspoon salt

Remove stems from spinach; wash leaves well in lukewarm water, and pat dry with paper towels. Set leaves aside.

Coat a Dutch oven with cooking spray; add oil, and place over medium heat until hot. Add half of spinach; cook until spinach begins to wilt, stirring occasionally. Add remaining spinach, and cook 1 minute or until wilted, stirring constantly. Remove from heat, and stir in sesame seeds and salt. Transfer to a serving bowl, and serve immediately. Yield: 4 servings (49 calories per serving).

PRO 3.9 / FAT 2.8 / CARB 4.2 / FIB 3.7 / CHOL 0 / SOD 237 / POT 642

YELLOW SQUASH CASSEROLE

½ cup plain low-fat yogurt
½ cup low-fat cottage cheese
¼ cup grated Parmesan cheese
¼ teaspoon dried whole thyme
2 eggs, beaten
Vegetable cooking spray
1 cup sliced onion
3 cups sliced yellow squash
¼ cup soft whole wheat breadcrumbs, divided

Combine first 5 ingredients in a bowl; set aside. Coat a skillet with cooking spray; place over medium heat until hot. Add onion, and sauté until tender; drain and set aside.

Place 1 cup squash in a 2-quart casserole coated with cooking spray. Top with one-third of onion and one-third of yogurt mixture. Repeat procedure with remaining squash, onion, and yogurt mixture. Sprinkle with breadcrumbs; cover and bake at 350° for 25 minutes. Uncover and bake until top is browned. Yield: 6 servings (100 calories per serving.)

PRO 8.5 / FAT 3.8 / CARB 8.6 / FIB 1.1 / CHOL 97 / SOD 198 / POT 256

VEGETABLE-STUFFED SQUASH

4 small yellow squash
2 bay leaves
½ cup finely chopped tomato
2 tablespoons finely chopped green onion
⅛ teaspoon celery seeds
⅛ teaspoon freshly ground black pepper

Wash squash, and place in a large saucepan with bay leaves. Cover with water; bring to a boil. Cover; reduce heat, and simmer 5 minutes or until tender but still firm. Drain and let cool to touch. Discard bay leaves.

Cut squash in half lengthwise; gently scoop out pulp, leaving firm shells. Drain and chop squash pulp; combine pulp and remaining ingredients. Place squash shells in a 10- x 6- x 2-inch baking dish; spoon vegetable mixture into shells. Cover and bake at 350° for 15 to 20 minutes or until thoroughly heated. Yield: 4 servings (19 calories per serving).

PRO 1.0 / FAT 0.2 / CARB 4.1 / FIB 1.0 / CHOL 0 / SOD 3 / POT 169

STUFFED PATTYPAN SQUASH

1 cup coarsely grated zucchini
1 cup coarsely grated yellow squash
⅛ teaspoon salt
6 small pattypan squash
Vegetable cooking spray
⅛ teaspoon dried whole basil
⅛ teaspoon pepper
1 tablespoon grated Parmesan cheese

Toss zucchini and yellow squash with salt in a colander. Cover and set aside to drain 30 minutes. Press gently to remove as much moisture as possible.

Cover and cook pattypan squash in boiling water in a large saucepan 10 to 15 minutes or just until tender. Drain and let cool to touch. Cut a ½-inch slice off stem end of each squash. Scoop out squash seeds, leaving shells intact; discard seeds. Set squash shells aside.

Coat a nonstick skillet with cooking spray; place over medium heat until hot. Add zucchini and yellow squash, basil, and pepper, and cook 2 minutes. Divide mixture among pattypan squash shells, and sprinkle with Parmesan; place in a large baking pan coated with cooking spray. Bake at 400° for 10 minutes or until thoroughly heated and cheese is browned. Yield: 6 servings (42 calories per serving).

PRO 2.6 / FAT 0.6 / CARB 8.2 / FIB 2.0 / CHOL 1 / SOD 68 / POT 393

Vegetable-Stuffed Zucchini, topped with cheese.

HERBED ZUCCHINI

3 medium zucchini
½ cup water
1 teaspoon minced fresh parsley
1 teaspoon chopped fresh chives
¼ teaspoon dried whole basil or 1 teaspoon minced fresh basil
¼ teaspoon dried whole rosemary or 1 teaspoon minced fresh rosemary
¼ teaspoon dried whole dillweed or 1 teaspoon minced fresh dillweed
Freshly ground black pepper to taste

Cut zucchini in half lengthwise. Place water in a large skillet; arrange zucchini, cut sides up, in skillet. Combine herbs and pepper; sprinkle over zucchini.

Bring water to a boil. Cover; reduce heat, and simmer 4 to 6 minutes or until zucchini is crisp-tender. Carefully transfer to a serving platter. Yield: 6 servings (8 calories per serving).

PRO 0.7 / FAT 0.1 / CARB 1.7 / FIB 0.3 / CHOL 0 / SOD 2 / POT 146

VEGETABLE-STUFFED ZUCCHINI

4 medium zucchini
¾ cup chopped tomato
⅓ cup chopped green pepper
¼ cup chopped onion
¼ teaspoon salt
¼ teaspoon dried whole basil
⅓ cup shredded extra sharp Cheddar cheese

Wash squash thoroughly; place in a saucepan with water to cover, and bring to a boil. Cover; reduce heat, and simmer 8 minutes or until tender but still firm. Drain and cool to touch. Cut squash in half lengthwise; remove and reserve pulp, leaving a firm shell.

Chop pulp; combine pulp and next 5 ingredients. Place squash shells in a 12- x 8- x 2-inch baking dish. Spoon vegetable mixture into shells. Bake at 400° for 15 minutes. Sprinkle with cheese, and bake an additional 5 minutes. Transfer to a serving platter. Yield: 8 servings (34 calories per serving).

PRO 2.1 / FAT 1.7 / CARB 3.2 / FIB 0.5 / CHOL 5 / SOD 106 / POT 202

HERBED SPAGHETTI SQUASH

1 (3-pound) spaghetti squash
1 tablespoon minced fresh parsley
2 teaspoons unsalted margarine
½ teaspoon dried whole basil
¼ teaspoon salt
⅛ teaspoon pepper
Dash of dried whole sage

Cut squash in half, and discard seeds. Place squash, cut side down, in a large Dutch oven; add 2 inches of water. Bring water to a boil. Cover; reduce heat, and cook 20 to 25 minutes or until tender.

Drain squash. Using a fork, remove spaghetti-like strands; discard shells. Place squash in a bowl; add remaining ingredients, and toss gently. Serve warm. Yield: 4 servings (92 calories per serving).

PRO 1.7 / FAT 2.6 / CARB 16.9 / FIB 3.7 / CHOL 0 / SOD 193 / POT 311

TURNIP GREENS WITH MUSTARD SAUCE

2 pounds turnip greens
½ pound diced, peeled turnips
⅛ teaspoon salt
⅛ teaspoon pepper
Vegetable cooking spray
¼ cup chopped shallots
2 tablespoons all-purpose flour
½ cup plus 2 tablespoons skim milk
1 bay leaf
⅛ teaspoon salt
⅛ teaspoon pepper
1 tablespoon white wine
1 teaspoon Dijon mustard

Wash turnip greens thoroughly; drain. Tear into bite-size pieces.

Place greens in a large Dutch oven; cover with water, and bring to a boil. Cover; reduce heat, and simmer 20 minutes. Stir in turnips and ⅛ teaspoon salt. Cover and cook an additional 30 minutes or until turnips are tender. Drain. Transfer to a serving dish; sprinkle with ⅛ teaspoon pepper, and keep warm.

Coat a saucepan with cooking spray; place over medium heat until hot. Add shallots, and sauté until tender. Remove from heat, and set aside. Combine flour and milk in a small bowl, stirring with a wire whisk until smooth. Add milk mixture, bay leaf, ⅛ teaspoon salt, and ⅛ teaspoon pepper to shallots in saucepan. Cook over medium heat until thickened, stirring constantly (do not boil); discard bay leaf. Stir in wine and mustard. Serve sauce separately with greens. Yield: 4 servings (116 calories per ½-cup serving with 3 tablespoons of sauce per serving).

PRO 5.9 / FAT 1.0 / CARB 23.7 / FIB 2.5 / CHOL 1 / SOD 352 / POT 888

GLAZED TURNIPS

1 pound turnips, peeled and cut into wedges
1 cup water
1 tablespoon minced fresh parsley
1 tablespoon unsalted margarine
2 teaspoons sugar
⅛ teaspoon salt
⅛ teaspoon pepper

Combine all ingredients in a saucepan; bring to a boil. Cover; reduce heat to medium, and cook 8 to 10 minutes or until crisp-tender. Uncover; cook over high heat until liquid is reduced to ¼ cup and turnips are tender, stirring constantly. Transfer to a bowl, and serve hot. Yield: 4 servings (64 calories per serving).

PRO 1.0 / FAT 2.9 / CARB 9.2 / FIB 1.0 / CHOL 0 / SOD 150 / POT 223

SPICED RUTABAGAS

1 medium rutabaga, peeled and cubed
2 cups water
½ teaspoon ground cinnamon
¼ teaspoon ground nutmeg
⅛ teaspoon pepper
1 tablespoon sugar
1 tablespoon chopped fresh parsley

Combine first 5 ingredients in a saucepan. Bring to a boil. Cover; reduce heat, and simmer 30 minutes. Add sugar, and cook, uncovered, an additional 10 minutes or until rutabaga is tender. Drain. Transfer to a serving dish; sprinkle with parsley. Yield: 6 servings (52 calories per ½-cup serving).

PRO 1.1 / FAT 0.1 / CARB 12.6 / FIB 2.3 / CHOL 0 / SOD 5 / POT 228

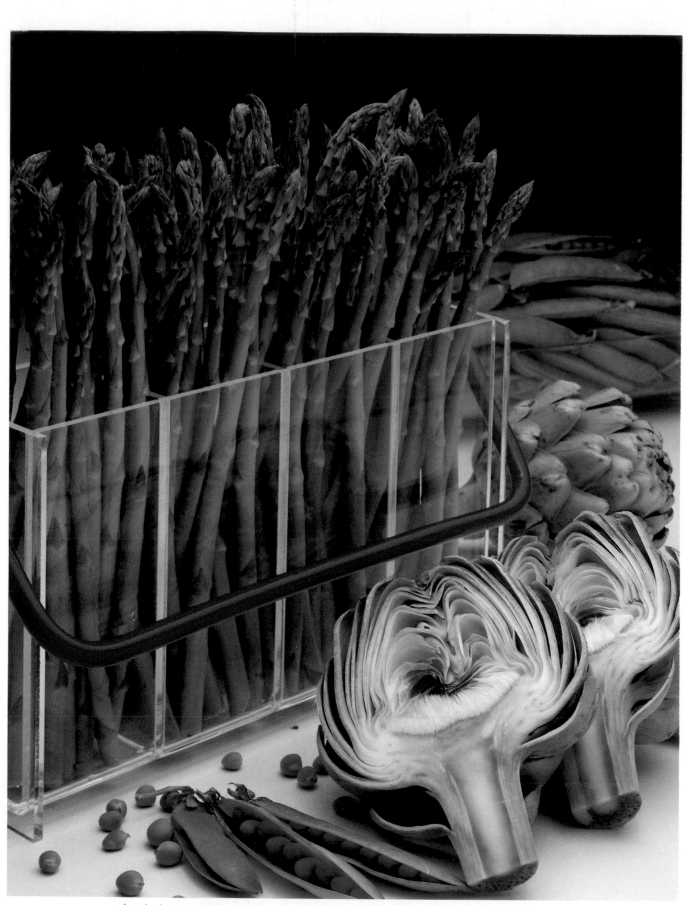

Artichokes, asparagus, and green peas are examples of the wide variety of vegetables available.

SAUTÉED VEGETABLE MEDLEY

½ pound fresh snow peas
Vegetable cooking spray
2 cups thinly sliced onion
1 teaspoon unsalted margarine
1 cup julienne zucchini
1 cup shelled fresh English peas
¼ teaspoon dried whole thyme
⅛ teaspoon pepper

Remove strings from snow peas, and set aside. Coat a skillet with cooking spray; place over medium heat until hot. Add onion, and sauté 5 minutes or until golden brown. Add margarine, zucchini, and English peas, and sauté 2 to 3 minutes or until zucchini is tender. Add snow peas, thyme, and pepper, and sauté 2 minutes or until tender and bright green. Transfer to a serving bowl. Yield: 6 servings (43 calories per ⅔-cup serving).

PRO 2.3 / FAT 0.7 / CARB 7.4 / FIB 1.5 / CHOL 0 / SOD 3 / POT 187

MIXED VEGETABLE STIR-FRY

1 large cucumber, peeled
1 tablespoon cornstarch
2 tablespoons sherry
2 teaspoons reduced-sodium soy sauce
1 teaspoon peanut oil
Vegetable cooking spray
1 cup sliced carrots
¼ pound fresh mushrooms, quartered
1 clove garlic, minced
2 cups fresh snow peas
½ cup sliced water chestnuts
⅔ cup water
½ teaspoon chicken-flavored bouillon granules

Cut cucumber in half lengthwise; remove seeds. Cut cucumber into strips; set aside.

Combine cornstarch, sherry, and soy sauce; set aside. Heat oil in a large skillet or wok coated with cooking spray over medium heat until hot. Add carrot, mushrooms, and garlic. Sauté 3 minutes or until crisp-tender. Push vegetables to side of skillet. Add cucumber, snow peas, and water chestnuts. Cook 3 minutes or until crisp-tender, stirring constantly.

Stir in cornstarch mixture, water, and bouillon granules. Bring to a boil, and cook 1 minute or until thickened, stirring constantly. Yield: 6 servings (73 calories per serving).

PRO 2.6 / FAT 1.1 / CARB 12.6 / FIB 2.3 / CHOL 0 / SOD 111 / POT 388

RATATOUILLE CASSEROLE

2 cloves garlic, minced
1 tablespoon dried whole basil or ¼ cup minced fresh basil
1 tablespoon minced fresh parsley
¼ teaspoon salt
Vegetable cooking spray
2 medium onions, thinly sliced
2 medium-size green peppers, seeded and cut into julienne strips
2 teaspoons olive oil
1 (¾-pound) eggplant, peeled and cut into 1/4-inch-thick slices
2 medium tomatoes, peeled and cut into 1/4-inch-thick slices
2 medium zucchini, halved lengthwise and cut into ¼-inch-thick slices
2 tablespoons grated Parmesan cheese

Combine first 4 ingredients in a small bowl; set aside. Coat a large skillet with cooking spray; place over medium heat until hot. Add onion, and sauté 20 minutes or until golden. Add green pepper, and cook 10 minutes; remove onion and pepper from skillet, and set aside. Recoat skillet with cooking spray; add oil, and place over medium heat until hot. Add eggplant, and cook until lightly browned on both sides. Remove from skillet, and set aside.

Spread one-third of onion mixture in a 9-inch-square baking dish coated with cooking spray; top with one-third of herb mixture, one-third of tomatoes, and all of eggplant. Top with one-third of onion mixture, one-third of herb mixture, one-third of tomatoes, and all of zucchini. Top with remaining onion mixture, tomatoes, and herb mixture.

Cover and bake at 350° for 45 minutes. Sprinkle with Parmesan; cook, uncovered, 5 minutes. Yield: 10 servings (45 calories per serving).

PRO 1.9 / FAT 1.5 / CARB 7.2 / FIB 1.1 / CHOL 1 / SOD 81 / POT 276

APPLE AND CHEDDAR GRATIN

1½ pounds cooking apples, cored and sliced
2 tablespoons lemon juice
Vegetable cooking spray
1 tablespoon brown sugar
½ teaspoon ground cinnamon
¼ teaspoon ground nutmeg
⅛ teaspoon ground allspice
½ cup (2 ounces) shredded Cheddar cheese
½ cup soft breadcrumbs

Combine apples and lemon juice in a skillet coated with cooking spray. Cover and cook over medium heat 5 minutes or just until apples are tender, stirring frequently. Transfer to a 10- x 6- x 2-inch baking dish coated with cooking spray. Combine sugar and spices; sprinkle over apples.

Combine cheese and breadcrumbs; sprinkle evenly over apples. Bake at 400° for 10 minutes or until golden brown and bubbly. Yield: 8 servings (109 calories per serving).

PRO 2.7 / FAT 3.0 / CARB 19.2 / FIB 1.8 / CHOL 8 / SOD 90 / POT 124

BROILED GRAPEFRUIT

3 medium grapefruit, halved
2 tablespoons brown sugar, divided
2 tablespoons cherry brandy, divided

Remove seeds, and loosen sections of grapefruit halves. Sprinkle each half with 1 teaspoon sugar and 1 teaspoon brandy.

Place grapefruit halves in a baking pan; broil 6 inches from heat 6 minutes or until sugar melts and grapefruit is thoroughly heated. Serve immediately. Yield: 6 servings (63 calories per serving).

PRO 0.8 / FAT 0.1 / CARB 14.4 / FIB 0.2 / CHOL 0 / SOD 1 / POT 177

BROILED PINEAPPLE

¼ cup unsweetened orange juice
2 tablespoons honey
½ to ¾ teaspoon ground ginger
2 cups fresh pineapple chunks
Vegetable cooking spray

Combine first 3 ingredients in a small bowl. Thread pineapple chunks onto 4 skewers, and brush with glaze. Place skewered pineapple on a broiler pan coated with cooking spray. Broil 4 to 6 inches from heat 8 minutes or until golden brown, turning and brushing pineapple with remaining glaze after 4 minutes. Yield: 4 servings (78 calories per serving).

PRO 0.5 / FAT 0.4 / CARB 20.2 / FIB 1.2 / CHOL 0 / SOD 2 / POT 125

Fruits bring vitamins, minerals, and fiber to frozen desserts, a refreshing alternative to rich, creamy fare. Clockwise from front: Orange Ice (page 211), Apple-Grape Sorbet (page 211), Frozen Peach Yogurt (page 213), and Strawberry-Lemon Granita (213) have fewer than 130 calories per serving.

DOUBLE RASPBERRY YOGURT PARFAIT

1 (16-ounce) carton plain low-fat yogurt
2 cups fresh raspberries, divided
2 tablespoons sugar
1 tablespoon raspberry liqueur

Line a colander with a double layer of cheesecloth that has been rinsed out and squeezed dry, letting it overlap at the sides. Stir yogurt until smooth, and pour into colander; fold edges of cheesecloth over to cover yogurt. Drain 1 hour.

Combine 1 cup raspberries, sugar, and liqueur in container of an electric blender, and process until smooth. Transfer to a bowl; stir in yogurt. Fold in remaining raspberries. Spoon into wine glasses, and chill thoroughly. Yield: 4 servings (131 calories per serving).

PRO 6.5 / FAT 2.1 / CARB 21.6 / FIB 2.9 / CHOL 7 / SOD 80 / POT 362

CHOCOLATE MOUSSE PUDDING

¼ cup evaporated skim milk
1 tablespoon sugar
2 tablespoons strong brewed coffee
⅓ cup Dutch process or unsweetened cocoa
2 egg yolks, beaten
2 tablespoons unsalted margarine
3 egg whites
3 tablespoons sugar
1 teaspoon vanilla extract

Combine milk, 1 tablespoon sugar, and coffee in a saucepan, and bring to a simmer. Remove from heat, and add cocoa, beating until smooth. Beat in egg yolks, 1 at a time; add margarine, beating until smooth. Transfer to a large bowl, and cool completely.

Beat egg whites (at room temperature) in a bowl until foamy. Gradually add 3 tablespoons sugar, 1 tablespoon at a time, and beat until stiff peaks form. Beat in vanilla. Stir one-fourth of whites into chocolate mixture; fold in remaining whites gently but thoroughly.

Spoon mixture into 6 (4-ounce) ramekins or custard cups, and chill 2 hours. Yield: 6 servings (119 calories per serving).

PRO 4.2 / FAT 6.8 / CARB 12.1 / FIB 0.2 / CHOL 91 / SOD 75 / POT 96

A good way to reduce calories and saturated fat in a chocolate recipe is to use cocoa powder instead of chocolate squares. For each 1-ounce square of chocolate, use ¼ cup of cocoa plus 2 teaspoons of margarine or oil. Plain cocoa is the lowest in fat, but Dutch process cocoa produces a more mellow flavor, darker color, and better dispersion.

CHOCOLATE-ORANGE PARFAITS

4 eggs, separated
½ cup sugar
2 cups evaporated skim milk
1⅓ cups skim milk
1 envelope unflavored gelatin
3 tablespoons water
2 teaspoons lemon juice
2 tablespoons plus 2 teaspoons Dutch process or unsweetened cocoa
1¼ teaspoons almond extract
1 tablespoon plus 1 teaspoon undiluted frozen orange juice concentrate, thawed
2 teaspoons grated orange rind

Beat egg yolks and sugar in a bowl until light and lemon colored; set aside. Combine evaporated milk and skim milk in a saucepan; bring to a simmer over low heat. Gradually stir one-fourth of hot milk into yolk mixture. Add to remaining hot milk, stirring constantly. Cook over low heat until thickened, stirring constantly.

Soften gelatin in cold water; let stand 1 minute. Add softened gelatin and lemon juice to hot milk mixture, stirring until gelatin dissolves. Divide milk mixture between 2 bowls. Add cocoa and almond extract to one bowl, beating well; set aside. Add orange concentrate and orange rind to other bowl, beating well. Chill both mixtures until the consistency of unbeaten egg white.

Beat egg whites (at room temperature) in a large bowl until stiff but not dry. Fold half of whites into chocolate mixture and half into orange mixture.

Layer spoonfuls of chocolate and orange mixtures alternately in parfait glasses, and chill until firm. Yield: 8 servings (165 calories per serving).

PRO 10.3 / FAT 3.3 / CARB 23.8 / FIB 0.1 / CHOL 140 / SOD 133 / POT 340

RICE PUDDING

1 envelope unflavored gelatin
2 cups skim milk, divided
2 eggs, beaten
⅓ cup sugar
1 teaspoon grated lemon rind
¼ cup raisins
½ cup cooked regular rice (cooked without salt or fat)
1 tablespoon vanilla extract
¼ teaspoon ground cinnamon or nutmeg

Combine gelatin and ½ cup milk in a medium saucepan; let stand 1 minute. Cook over low heat, stirring constantly, 5 minutes or until gelatin dissolves; set aside.

Combine eggs and sugar in a large heavy saucepan, and beat well. Add remaining milk

and lemon rind, mixing well; stir in raisins. Add gelatin mixture to saucepan, and cook over low heat 4 minutes or until slightly thickened, stirring constantly. Remove from heat, and transfer mixture to a bowl. Chill to consistency of unbeaten egg white. Stir in rice and vanilla; cover and chill at least 2 hours. Spoon into dessert dishes; sprinkle with cinnamon. Yield: 6 servings (147 calories per serving).

PRO 6.4 / FAT 2.0 / CARB 25.1 / FIB 0.6 / CHOL 93 / SOD 69 / POT 210

A light and refreshing dessert: Cold Orange Soufflé.

COLD ORANGE SOUFFLÉ

Vegetable cooking spray
6 eggs, separated
1 tablespoon grated orange rind
1 cup orange juice
1 envelope unflavored gelatin
½ cup sugar
¾ teaspoon cream of tartar
1 (5⅓-ounce) can evaporated skim milk, chilled
Orange slices, halved
Fresh mint leaves (optional)

Cut a piece of aluminum foil or waxed paper to fit around a 1½-quart soufflé dish, allowing a 1-inch overlap; fold lengthwise into thirds. Coat one side of foil with cooking spray; wrap around outside of dish, oiled side against dish, allowing it to extend 3 inches above rim to form a collar. Secure with freezer tape.

Beat egg yolks; combine yolks and next 3 ingredients in a large saucepan, stirring well. Cook over medium heat, stirring constantly, until mixture begins to boil. Remove from heat; stir in sugar until dissolved. Cool.

Beat egg whites (at room temperature) until foamy; add cream of tartar, and beat until stiff peaks form. Set aside.

Beat chilled milk at high speed of an electric mixer until stiff peaks form. Fold egg whites and whipped milk into yolk mixture.

Place orange slices around outer edge of the bottom of soufflé dish. Gently spoon soufflé into prepared dish, and chill until firm. Remove collar from dish. Garnish with mint leaves, if desired. Yield: 8 servings (139 calories per serving).

PRO 7.1 / FAT 4.3 / CARB 18.6 / FIB 0.0 / CHOL 206 / SOD 94 / POT 181

GINGERED CANTALOUPE

3 cups cantaloupe balls
1 tablespoon plus 1 teaspoon sugar
1 teaspoon grated lemon rind
2 teaspoons lemon juice
½ teaspoon ground ginger

Combine all ingredients in a bowl. Cover and chill 1 hour. Spoon into dessert dishes to serve. Yield: 6 servings (40 calories per serving).

PRO 0.7 / FAT 0.2 / CARB 9.8 / FIB 0.3 / CHOL 0 / SOD 7 / POT 252

SHERRIED FIGS

2 pounds fresh figs, peeled and quartered
3 tablespoons cream sherry
1 teaspoon lemon juice

Combine all ingredients in a bowl; cover and chill at least 2 hours. Yield: 6 servings (122 calories per serving).

PRO 1.2 / FAT 0.5 / CARB 30.5 / FIB 1.8 / CHOL 0 / SOD 2 / POT 360

STRAWBERRIES À L'ORANGE

2¼ cups fresh strawberries, halved
1 tablespoon Cointreau or other orange-flavored liqueur
1 teaspoon sugar
2 to 3 teaspoons grated fresh orange rind
2 tablespoons unsweetened orange juice

Combine all ingredients in a bowl. Cover; chill at least 2 hours. Spoon into individual dishes. Yield: 4 servings (51 calories per serving).

PRO 0.7 / FAT 0.4 / CARB 10.3 / FIB 1.6 / CHOL 0 / SOD 1 / POT 154

Strawberries are more than just a pretty face — they're a nutritional stronghold. One-half cup has only 27 calories, but it provides 100 percent of your daily vitamin C needs and contains more fiber than a slice of whole wheat bread.
Leave the green caps intact when storing strawberries so that they retain their vitamin C.

BRANDIED HONEYDEW AND BERRIES

3 cups honeydew balls
1½ cups quartered fresh strawberries
3 tablespoons brandy
1 tablespoon honey
1 tablespoon unsweetened orange juice

Combine honeydew and strawberries in a bowl; set aside. Combine brandy, honey, and orange juice in a small bowl, and pour over fruit. Chill 1 hour. Yield: 8 servings (53 calories per ½-cup serving).

PRO 0.7 / FAT 0.3 / CARB 9.6 / FIB 0.9 / CHOL 0 / SOD 8 / POT 211

LYCHEE-MANDARIN DESSERT

2 (11-ounce) cans unsweetened mandarin oranges, drained
1 (15-ounce) can whole seedless lychees, drained
¼ cup unsweetened orange juice
1 tablespoon lemon juice
2 tablespoons fresh grated coconut

Combine first 4 ingredients in a bowl, and toss gently. Cover and chill at least 1 hour. Spoon into 6 individual serving bowls, and garnish each with 1 teaspoon coconut. Yield: 6 servings (94 calories per serving).

PRO 0.8 / FAT 1.3 / CARB 20.7 / FIB 0.6 / CHOL 0 / SOD 12 / POT 286

TROPICAL FRUIT DESSERT

1 medium papaya, halved and seeded
1 cup diced nectarine
2 tablespoons fresh grated coconut, toasted
1 kiwi, peeled and sliced
1 tablespoon sliced almonds, toasted

Scoop out pulp from papaya halves, leaving ¼-inch-thick shells. Dice pulp, and combine with nectarine and coconut in a small bowl. Spoon fruit mixture into shells; arrange kiwi slices on top. Sprinkle with almonds. Yield: 2 servings (154 calories per serving).

PRO 2.9 / FAT 5.8 / CARB 25.9 / FIB 2.1 / CHOL 0 / SOD 6 / POT 614

SUMMER FRUIT IN SPARKLING CIDER

2 cups cubed fresh pineapple
2 cups sliced nectarines
1½ cups pitted fresh cherries
1½ cups seedless green grapes
1 cup sliced plums
2 cups sparkling apple cider, chilled

Combine fruit in a large glass bowl, and freeze 1 hour or until partially frozen. To serve, pour cider over fruit, and serve immediately. Yield: 8 servings (116 calories per serving).

PRO 1.0 / FAT 0.6 / CARB 29.0 / FIB 2.7 / CHOL 0 / SOD 4 / POT 362

SPIKED FRUIT BOWL

1 cup water
½ cup cream sherry
2 tablespoons sugar
2 cups fresh strawberries
2 cups watermelon balls
1½ cups honeydew balls
1½ cups cantaloupe balls
1 medium pear, thinly sliced
1 cup quartered plums
1 cup fresh pineapple chunks

Combine water, sherry, and sugar in a saucepan, and bring to a boil over medium heat. Reduce heat, and simmer 5 minutes. Remove from heat, and set aside to cool completely.

Combine remaining ingredients in a large glass bowl. Pour sherry mixture over fruit; cover and chill at least 2 hours. Yield: 10 servings (80 calories per serving).

PRO 1.1 / FAT 0.6 / CARB 19.6 / FIB 2.2 / CHOL 0 / SOD 7 / POT 323

BANANA-STRAWBERRY YOGURT

1 cup sliced ripe banana
1 teaspoon sugar
1 teaspoon vanilla extract
½ teaspoon lemon juice
1 (8-ounce) carton plain low-fat
   yogurt
1 cup sliced fresh strawberries

Combine sliced banana, sugar, vanilla, and lemon juice in container of an electric blender, and process until smooth. Transfer mixture to a bowl, and stir in yogurt and strawberries, mixing well. Chill. Spoon into individual serving dishes, and serve immediately. Yield: 4 servings (92 calories per serving).

PRO 3.6 / FAT 1.2 / CARB 17.4 / FIB 1.2 / CHOL 3 / SOD 40 / POT 343

LEMON-BLUEBERRY SNOW

4 (8-ounce) cartons lemon low-fat
   yogurt
1 tablespoon grated orange rind
2 teaspoons grated lemon rind
½ cup unsweetened orange juice
1 tablespoon lemon juice
2 envelopes unflavored gelatin
1 cup fresh blueberries
Vegetable cooking spray

Combine yogurt, orange rind, and lemon rind in a large bowl, stirring with a wire whisk until smooth; set mixture aside.

Combine orange juice, lemon juice, and gelatin in a small saucepan; let stand 1 minute. Cook over low heat 5 minutes or until gelatin completely dissolves, stirring constantly. Remove from heat, and add to reserved yogurt mixture, stirring well. Fold in blueberries.

Pour lemon-blueberry mixture into a 4-cup mold coated with cooking spray. Cover and refrigerate at least 3 hours or until set. Unmold onto a serving platter. Yield: 8 servings (95 calories per serving).

Note: 1 cup frozen blueberries, thawed and drained, may be substituted for 1 cup fresh blueberries.

PRO 7.7 / FAT 1.8 / CARB 12.6 / FIB 0.6 / CHOL 7 / SOD 83 / POT 315

COCONUT BAVARIAN MOLD

2 egg yolks
3 tablespoons sugar
2 tablespoons all-purpose flour
1 cup skim milk
1 envelope unflavored gelatin
3 tablespoons cold water
1 teaspoon vanilla extract
1 teaspoon coconut extract
¼ teaspoon almond extract
½ cup unsweetened grated coconut
3 egg whites
Vegetable cooking spray
1 (11-ounce) can unsweetened mandarin oranges, drained

Beat egg yolks in top of a double boiler until thick and lemon colored. Gradually add sugar; beat well. Add flour; beat until smooth. Add milk; beat well. Cook over boiling water, stirring constantly, until mixture coats a spoon.

Soften gelatin in cold water; let stand 1 minute. Add to hot milk mixture, stirring until gelatin dissolves. Remove from heat, and transfer to a large mixing bowl; cool to room temperature. Stir in flavorings and coconut; chill to consistency of unbeaten egg white.

Beat egg whites (at room temperature) until stiff but not dry. Fold into milk mixture; spoon into a 3½-cup mold coated with cooking spray. Chill until firm. Unmold onto a serving platter; garnish with mandarin orange sections. Yield: 6 servings (139 calories per serving).

PRO 5.8 / FAT 6.3 / CARB 14.6 / FIB 0.5 / CHOL 92 / SOD 56 / POT 174

CHOCOLATE-MINT CHIFFON PIE

12 zwieback toast slices, finely crushed
3 tablespoons unsalted margarine, melted
2 tablespoons sugar
⅓ cup Dutch process or unsweetened cocoa
¼ cup sugar
1½ cups skim milk
3 egg yolks
3 tablespoons sugar
1 envelope unflavored gelatin
2 tablespoons cold water
¼ teaspoon peppermint extract
4 egg whites

Combine zwieback crumbs, margarine, and 2 tablespoons sugar in a bowl. Press mixture into a 9-inch pieplate, and bake at 350° for 10 minutes. Cool.

Combine cocoa and ¼ cup sugar in a saucepan. Add milk, stirring with a whisk until smooth. Bring to a simmer over low heat, stirring constantly. Remove from heat; set aside.

Beat egg yolks in a bowl until foamy. Add 3 tablespoons sugar, and beat until light and lemon colored. Gradually add egg yolk mixture to chocolate mixture, beating well. Cook over low heat until thickened, stirring constantly.

Soften gelatin in cold water; let stand 1 minute. Add softened gelatin to saucepan, stirring until gelatin dissolves. Transfer to a large bowl, and add peppermint extract; chill until consistency of unbeaten egg white.

Beat egg whites (at room temperature) until stiff but not dry. Stir one-fourth of whites into chocolate mixture; fold in remaining whites gently but thoroughly. Spoon filling into crust, and chill overnight. Yield: 8 servings (198 calories per serving).

PRO 6.8 / FAT 8.2 / CARB 25.9 / FIB 0.2 / CHOL 104 / SOD 105 / POT 144

STRAWBERRY CHEESECAKE

1 teaspoon unsalted margarine
¼ cup finely ground almonds, toasted
4 (8-ounce) packages Neufchâtel cheese, softened
½ cup skim milk
1 cup sugar
4 eggs, lightly beaten
1 teaspoon vanilla extract
2 tablespoons grated orange rind
1 tablespoon grated lemon rind
2 cups strawberries, caps and stems removed

Grease an 8-inch round cakepan, 3 inches deep, with margarine. Sprinkle pan with ground almonds; set aside.

Combine cheese, milk, and sugar in a bowl; beat at medium speed of an electric mixer until smooth. Add eggs, beating well. Stir in vanilla and rind; pour into prepared pan.

Place cakepan in a 13- x 9- x 2-inch baking pan. Pour hot water into baking pan, filling two-thirds full. Bake at 325° for 2 hours or until firm, adding more boiling water to baking pan, if necessary. Turn off oven, and open oven door. Allow cheesecake to cool to room temperature in oven.

Invert cheesecake onto a plate; chill thoroughly. Arrange strawberries on top of cheesecake before serving. Yield: 16 servings (240 calories per serving).

PRO 8.0 / FAT 16.1 / CARB 17.0 / FIB 0.5 / CHOL 112 / SOD 248 / POT 142

APPLE-GRAPE SORBET

2 pounds Golden Delicious apples, peeled, cored, and quartered
¼ cup lemon juice
2 cups unsweetened white grape juice

Combine apple and lemon juice in container of an electric blender, and process until pureed. Add grape juice, and process 10 seconds or until well combined. Pour mixture into freezer can of a 1-gallon hand-turned or electric freezer. Freeze according to manufacturer's instructions. Yield: 5½ cups (76 calories per ½-cup serving).

PRO 0.4 / FAT 0.2 / CARB 19.7 / FIB 2.0 / CHOL 0 / SOD 2 / POT 156

MANGO-PINEAPPLE ICE

2½ pounds ripe mangos, peeled and cut into pieces (about 3 mangos)
2 cups unsweetened pineapple juice
¼ cup sugar
3 tablespoons lime juice

Place mango in container of an electric blender, and process until pureed. Add pineapple juice, sugar, and lime juice, and process until combined.

Pour mixture into an 8-inch square baking pan. Freeze several hours, stirring 2 to 3 times during freezing process, until mixture reaches consistency of a sherbet. Spoon into sherbet dishes; serve immediately. Yield: 5 cups (122 calories per ½-cup serving).

PRO 0.8 / FAT 0.4 / CARB 31.4 / FIB 1.3 / CHOL 0 / SOD 3 / POT 257

ORANGE ICE

7½ cups unsweetened orange juice
2 tablespoons grated orange rind

Combine orange juice and orange rind in bowl, and pour into freezer can of a 1-gallon hand-turned or electric freezer. Freeze according to manufacturer's instructions. Yield: 9 cups (47 calories per ½-cup serving).

PRO 0.7 / FAT 0.1 / CARB 11.3 / FIB 0.0 / CHOL 0 / SOD 1 / POT 194

STRAWBERRY ICE

4 cups fresh strawberries
½ cup unsweetened orange juice
3 tablespoons honey

Combine all ingredients in container of an electric blender; process until smooth. Pour mixture into an 8-inch square baking pan; cover and freeze until slushy. Spoon mixture into container of electric blender; process until smooth. Freeze until firm. Yield: 4 servings (117 calories per serving).

PRO 1.3 / FAT 0.8 / CARB 28.9 / FIB 2.8 / CHOL 0 / SOD 3 / POT 310

Kiwi Ice is one dessert that won't interrupt your efforts at losing weight. One serving contains only 26 calories.

KIWI ICE

4 kiwi, peeled and cubed
2 cups unsweetened apple juice
1 tablespoon lemon juice
½ teaspoon grated orange rind
Orange slices (optional)

Combine kiwi, apple juice, and lemon juice in container of an electric blender; process until smooth. Stir in orange rind. Pour mixture into an 8-inch square baking pan, and freeze until almost firm.

Spoon frozen mixture into a mixing bowl; beat with an electric mixer until fluffy. Return to pan, and freeze until firm. Let stand at room temperature 10 minute before serving. Garnish with orange slices, if desired. Yield: 4 cups (26 calories per ½-cup serving).

PRO 0.3 / FAT 0.2 / CARB 6.1 / FIB 0.3 / CHOL 0 / SOD 1 / POT 100

BANANA-VANILLA GRANITA

1½ cups water
¼ cup sugar
1 vanilla bean, finely chopped
4 medium bananas
¼ cup lemon juice

Combine water, sugar, and vanilla bean in a small saucepan; bring to a rolling boil. Remove from heat, and set aside.

Cut bananas into pieces; place banana and lemon juice in container of a food processor or an electric blender. Process until smooth, scraping down sides as needed. Transfer mixture to a 1-quart bowl, and stir in sugar mixture. Freeze 6 hours, stirring vigorously with a fork every 2 hours. Spoon into sherbet dishes to serve. Yield: 2 cups (169 calories per ½-cup serving).

PRO 1.3 / FAT 0.6 / CARB 42.4 / FIB 1.7 / CHOL 0 / SOD 1 / POT 491

STRAWBERRY-LEMON GRANITA

⅓ cup sugar
1½ cups water
4 cups fresh strawberries, caps and stems removed
1 teaspoon grated lemon rind
¼ cup lemon juice

Combine sugar and water in a saucepan, and bring to a boil. Boil 1 minute. Remove from heat; cool to room temperature.

Place strawberries in container of an electric blender, and process until pureed. Add syrup, lemon rind, and juice; process 15 seconds or until combined. Pour mixture into a bowl. Freeze 5 hours, stirring vigorously with a fork every 1½ hours. Spoon into individual sherbet dishes; serve immediately. Yield: 4 cups (62 calories per ½-cup serving).

PRO 0.6 / FAT 0.4 / CARB 15.2 / FIB 1.4 / CHOL 0 / SOD 1 / POT 132

CHOCOLATE FREEZE

½ cup sugar
⅓ cup Dutch process or unsweetened cocoa
3 cups skim milk
1 (3-inch) stick cinnamon, broken into pieces
2 teaspoons vanilla extract

Combine sugar and cocoa in a small saucepan, mixing well. Add milk, stirring until blended; add cinnamon. Cook over medium heat until hot, stirring constantly. Remove from heat, and cool; add vanilla.

Strain cocoa mixture into a large metal baking pan, discarding cinnamon. Freeze several hours, stirring 2 to 3 times during freezing process, until mixture reaches the consistency of a sherbet. Yield: 6 servings (126 calories per ½-cup serving).

PRO 5.0 / FAT 1.4 / CARB 25.2 / FIB 0.2 / CHOL 2 / SOD 98 / POT 235

BANANA ICE MILK

1 envelope unflavored gelatin
½ cup unsweetened orange juice
4 medium bananas, sliced
3 tablespoons lemon juice
2 teaspoons vanilla extract
2 eggs
¼ cup plus 2 tablespoons sugar
3½ cups skim milk

Sprinkle gelatin over orange juice in a medium saucepan, and let stand 1 minute. Cook over medium heat, stirring constantly, 1 minute or until gelatin is completely dissolved. Set aside, and cool completely.

Combine bananas, lemon juice, and vanilla in container of an electric blender; process until pureed. Set aside. Beat eggs in a large bowl until foamy; gradually add sugar, 1 tablespoon at a time, beating until thick and lemon colored. Stir in banana mixture, gelatin mixture, and milk, mixing well.

Pour mixture into a large metal baking pan. Freeze several hours, stirring every 30 minutes until frozen. Yield: 7 cups (93 calories per ½-cup serving).

PRO 3.8 / FAT 1.1 / CARB 17.8 / FIB 0.5 / CHOL 40 / SOD 43 / POT 266

FROZEN PEACH YOGURT

4 medium-size ripe peaches
1 tablespoon ascorbic-citric powder
½ cup plain low-fat yogurt
¼ cup superfine sugar
2 teaspoons lemon juice

Peel and slice peaches; toss with ascorbic-citric powder. Arrange peaches in a single layer on a baking sheet, and freeze.

Process peaches in container of an electric blender until finely chopped. Add yogurt, sugar, and lemon juice, and process until smooth. Freeze until firm. Spoon into dessert dishes, and serve immediately. Yield: 4 servings (126 calories per serving).

PRO 2.2 / FAT 0.6 / CARB 29.9 / FIB 2.9 / CHOL 2 / SOD 21 / POT 323

CARROT-DATE SQUARES

1¼ cups all-purpose flour
1½ teaspoons baking powder
¼ teaspoon salt
2 teaspoons ground cinnamon
½ cup vegetable oil
½ cup honey
2 eggs, beaten
2 teaspoons vanilla extract
1 cup grated carrots
½ cup chopped dates
Vegetable cooking spray

Combine first 4 ingredients in a large bowl, and beat in oil, honey, eggs, and vanilla. Stir in carrots and dates. Pour batter into a 8-inch-square baking pan coated with cooking spray. Bake at 325° for 35 minutes or until a wooden pick inserted in center comes out clean. Cut into 2-inch squares. Yield: 16 servings (162 calories per serving).

PRO 2.1 / FAT 7.7 / CARB 22.2 / FIB 0.8 / CHOL 34 / SOD 77 / POT 84

DARK GINGERBREAD

1½ cups unbleached or all-purpose flour
2 teaspoons baking soda
½ teaspoon ground cinnamon
½ teaspoon ground cloves
½ teaspoon ground ginger
½ cup wheat germ
½ cup regular oats, uncooked
1 egg, beaten
¾ cup unsweetened apple juice
¼ cup light molasses
¼ cup unsalted margarine, melted
2 tablespoons brown sugar
Vegetable cooking spray
2 tablespoons sifted powdered
  sugar

Combine first 7 ingredients in a bowl, and set aside.

Combine egg, apple juice, molasses, margarine, and brown sugar in a large bowl; beat at medium speed of an electric mixer until mixture is smooth. Stir in reserved flour mixture, and beat well.

Pour batter into an 8-inch-square baking pan coated with cooking spray. Bake at 350° for 25 minutes or until a wooden pick inserted in center comes out clean. Remove from oven, and cool in pan on a wire rack; sprinkle with powdered sugar. Cut into 2-inch squares. Yield: 16 servings (115 calories per serving).

PRO 3.0 / FAT 3.9 / CARB 18.2 / FIB 0.7 / CHOL 17 / SOD 50 / POT 118

CHOCOLATE-ALMOND CUPCAKES

3 tablespoons unsalted margarine
⅓ cup sugar
1 egg
¼ cup sour cream
2 tablespoons sugar
2 tablespoons Dutch process or unsweetened
  cocoa
¼ cup boiling water
1 teaspoon vanilla extract
½ teaspoon almond extract
⅔ cup all-purpose flour
2 tablespoons cornstarch
½ teaspoon baking powder
¼ teaspoon baking soda
⅛ teaspoon salt
¼ cup finely ground almonds
1 tablespoon sifted powdered sugar

Cream margarine in a bowl; gradually add ⅓ cup sugar, beating with an electric mixer until light and fluffy. Add egg, beating well. Add sour cream, and mix until blended.

Combine 2 tablespoons sugar, cocoa, and water in a small bowl, and beat until smooth. Add to egg mixture, stirring until combined. Stir in flavorings.

Combine flour, cornstarch, baking powder, soda, and salt. Add to chocolate mixture, stirring by hand just until combined. Stir in almonds.

Line 8 muffin tins with paper baking cups; spoon in batter, filling two-thirds full. Bake at 350° for 20 minutes or until a wooden pick inserted in center comes out clean. Cool in pan 10 minutes; remove to wire rack to cool completely. Sprinkle with powdered sugar. Yield: 8 cupcakes (176 calories per serving).

PRO 2.8 / FAT 7.8 / CARB 24.4 / FIB 0.5 / CHOL 37 / SOD 89 / POT 52

ANGEL CAKE WITH
PINEAPPLE-ORANGE SAUCE

1 (14.5-ounce) package white angel
　food cake mix
½ teaspoon ground cardamom
¼ teaspoon ground nutmeg
Pineapple-Orange Sauce
Orange twists (optional)

Prepare cake mix according to package directions, adding cardamom and nutmeg to batter; bake according to package directions. Invert pan on funnel or bottle until cake is completely cooled (approximately 2 hours).

Loosen cake from sides of pan, using a small metal spatula. Remove from pan. Serve with ¼ cup of Pineapple-Orange Sauce; garnish with orange twists, if desired. Yield: 12 servings (178 calories per serving).

Pineapple-Orange Sauce:

1 (15¼-ounce) can unsweetened pineapple chunks
1 teaspoon grated orange rind
¾ cup unsweetened orange juice
¼ cup Cointreau or other orange-flavored liqueur
1 tablespoon plus 1 teaspoon cornstarch
¼ teaspoon ground cardamom
1 (11-ounce) can unsweetened mandarin oranges,
　drained

Drain pineapple, reserving juice. Combine juice and next 5 ingredients in a saucepan. Cook over medium heat, stirring constantly, until clear and thickened. Stir in pineapple and oranges; cook until hot. Yield: 3 cups.

PRO 3.1 / FAT 0.1 / CARB 39.1 / FIB 0.1 / CHOL 0 / SOD 67 / POT 125

Cointreau adds a special touch to the sauce for Angel Cake with Pineapple Orange Sauce.

HAZELNUT ANGEL FOOD CAKE

1 cup sifted all-purpose flour
⅓ cup superfine sugar
¼ teaspoon salt
1½ cups egg whites (about 11 egg whites)
1 teaspoon cream of tartar
¾ cup superfine sugar, divided
1½ teaspoons vanilla extract
¼ cup (1 ounce) finely ground, lightly toasted hazelnuts
Vegetable cooking spray

Sift together flour, ⅓ cup sugar, and salt in a bowl; set aside.

Combine egg whites (at room temperature) and cream of tartar in a large bowl; beat until foamy. Gradually add ¼ cup sugar, 1 tablespoon at a time, and beat until soft peaks form. Beat in vanilla.

Gently fold one-third of flour mixture into egg white mixture. Repeat folding procedure with remaining flour mixture, adding one-third of mixture at a time. Fold in toasted hazelnuts in 2 portions. Fold in remaining ½ cup sugar in 3 portions.

Spoon batter into a 10-inch tube pan coated with cooking spray. Bake at 300° for 1 hour or until cake springs back when lightly touched. Remove from oven. Invert pan on funnel or bottle until cake is completely cooled (approximately 2 hours).

Loosen cake from sides of pan, using a small metal spatula. Remove cake from pan, and place on a serving platter. Slice cake with a serrated knife. Yield: 12 servings (136 calories per serving).

PRO 4.4 / FAT 1.6 / CARB 26.2 / FIB 0.4 / CHOL 0 / SOD 112 / POT 70

CHOCOLATE MARBLE CAKE

¼ cup plus 2 tablespoons unsalted margarine
½ cup sugar
3 eggs
1¾ cups all-purpose flour
1½ teaspoons baking powder
½ teaspoon baking soda
⅛ teaspoon salt
⅓ cup Dutch process or unsweetened cocoa
¼ cup sugar
¼ cup water
¾ cup buttermilk
Vegetable cooking spray
2 tablespoons sifted powdered sugar

Cream margarine in a large bowl. Gradually add ½ cup sugar, beating with an electric mixer until light and fluffy. Add eggs, 1 at a time, beating after each addition.

Combine flour, baking powder, soda, and salt; set aside. Combine cocoa and ¼ cup sugar in a medium bowl. Add water, beating until smooth. Set aside.

Add flour mixture to creamed mixture alternately with buttermilk, beginning and ending with flour mixture. Stir 1 cup batter into chocolate mixture, and blend well.

Spoon plain batter into a 6½-cup Bundt pan coated with cooking spray. Drizzle with chocolate batter, and swirl batters together with a fork. Bake at 350° for 30 minutes or until a wooden pick inserted in center comes out clean. Cool cake in pan 5 minutes; turn cake out onto a wire rack to cool completely. Transfer cake to a serving platter, and sprinkle with powdered sugar. Yield: 16 servings (157 calories per serving).

PRO 3.4 / FAT 5.9 / CARB 23.2 / FIB 0.5 / CHOL 52 / SOD 96 / POT 56

You can easily adapt recipes so that they will not compete with your health goals. These tips will help get you started:
*Try using one-third less sugar than the recipe calls for; then add spices and flavorings to enhance the taste.
*Use low-fat dairy products, reduced-calorie mayonnaise, and less oil, margarine, and butter, using vegetable cooking spray when possible.

*Reduce the amount of salt you use. Start by removing the salt shaker from the table, and then cut the salt in every recipe by half or more.
*Try to limit protein to 4-ounce servings, and put greater emphasis on the healthier vegetable proteins and less on the high-fat animal proteins.
*And remember to exercise — a good workout allows you to enjoy more foods without gaining weight.

THIN APPLE TART

¾ cup unbleached or all-purpose flour
Dash of salt
3 tablespoons unsalted margarine
2 to 3 tablespoons cold water
¼ teaspoon vanilla extract
Vegetable cooking spray
2 medium-size Golden Delicious apples, peeled and
   thinly sliced
1 tablespoon lemon juice
½ teaspoon vanilla extract
1 tablespoon plus 1 teaspoon sugar, divided

Combine flour and salt in a bowl; cut in margarine with a pastry blender until mixture resembles coarse meal. Sprinkle with water and ¼ teaspoon vanilla, and stir with a fork until all dry ingredients are moistened.

Shape dough into a ball, and place on a baking sheet coated with cooking spray. Roll into a 12-inch round; set aside.

Combine apples, lemon juice, and ½ teaspoon vanilla, tossing well. Arrange apples in concentric circles on dough, starting 1 inch from edge. Sprinkle with 2 teaspoons sugar. Bake at 400° for 25 minutes or until golden and crisp. Sprinkle with remaining 2 teaspoons sugar. Broil 4 to 6 inches from heat 2 to 3 minutes or until golden brown. Cool. Yield: 8 servings (103 calories per serving).

PRO 1.2 / FAT 4.4 / CARB 15.2 / FIB 0.7 / CHOL 0 / SOD 19 / POT 52

FRESH APPLE PIE

1 cup all-purpose flour
¼ teaspoon salt
¼ cup vegetable shortening
3 to 4 tablespoons cold water
1 tablespoon cornstarch
2 tablespoons unsweetened apple juice
5 cups diced, peeled apple
½ cup unsweetened apple juice
1 tablespoon brown sugar
½ teaspoon pumpkin pie spice
1 medium apple, thinly sliced
Lemon juice

Combine flour and salt in a medium bowl; cut in shortening with a pastry blender until mixture

resembles coarse meal. Sprinkle cold water, 1 tablespoon at a time, evenly over surface; stir with a fork until all dry ingredients are moistened. Shape dough into a ball.

Roll pastry to ⅛-inch thickness on a lightly floured surface. Place pastry in a 9-inch pieplate; trim and flute edges. Prick bottom and sides of pastry shell with a fork. Bake at 425° for 12 minutes or until golden brown. Set aside to cool.

Combine cornstarch and 2 tablespoons apple juice, mixing well; set aside.

Combine next 4 ingredients in a large saucepan. Bring to a boil. Cover; reduce heat, and simmer 3 to 4 minutes or just until apples are tender. Stir in cornstarch mixture; cook, stirring constantly, until mixture is clear and thickened. Cool; spoon into pastry shell. Dip apple slices in lemon juice; drain. Garnish top of pie with apple slices. Yield: 8 servings (170 calories per serving).

PRO 2.0 / FAT 5.8 / CARB 28.6 / FIB 2.4 / CHOL 0 / SOD 75 / POT 132

CHERRY CLAFOUTI

3 cups pitted fresh black cherries
2 tablespoons sugar
2 tablespoons Cognac
2 teaspoons lemon juice
1 cup skim milk
2 eggs
½ cup all-purpose flour
3 tablespoons sugar
1 teaspoon vanilla extract
½ teaspoon almond extract
⅛ teaspoon salt
Vegetable cooking spray

Combine cherries, 2 tablespoons sugar, Cognac, and lemon juice in a bowl, and let stand 30 minutes.

Combine milk, eggs, flour, sugar, flavorings, and salt in container of an electric blender, and process until smooth. Spoon cherry mixture into a 12- x 8- x 2-inch baking dish coated with cooking spray. Pour milk mixture evenly over top of cherry mixture. Bake at 350° for 1 hour or until top is golden. Yield: 6 servings (172 calories per serving).

PRO 5.1 / FAT 2.2 / CARB 30.2 / FIB 1.5 / CHOL 92 / SOD 95 / POT 239

Lighten calories in fruit pies and cobblers; leave off the top or bottom crust. Fresh Apple Pie (page 217), Peach Cobbler (page 219), and Fresh Cherry Cobbler (front to back) are examples of how that's done.

FRESH CHERRY COBBLER

2 tablespoons cornstarch
2 tablespoons sugar
⅛ teaspoon ground allspice
1 cup unsweetened white grape juice
4 cups pitted fresh sweet cherries
½ teaspoon almond extract
Vegetable cooking spray
¼ cup whole wheat flour
¼ cup all-purpose flour
⅛ teaspoon salt
⅛ teaspoon ground cinnamon
2 tablespoons plus 1½ teaspoons vegetable shortening
1 to 1½ tablespoons cold water

Combine cornstarch, sugar, and allspice in a saucepan; stir in grape juice until blended. Cook over medium heat, stirring constantly, until clear and thickened. Remove from heat; stir in cherries and almond extract. Spoon mixture into a 1½-quart casserole coated with cooking spray; set aside.

Combine flour, salt, and cinnamon in a mixing bowl; cut in shortening with a pastry blender until mixture resembles coarse meal. Sprinkle cold water evenly over surface; stir with a fork until all dry ingredients are moistened. Shape dough into a ball. Roll pastry to ⅛-inch thickness on a lightly floured surface; cut into decorative shapes.

Place pastry cutouts on top of cherry mixture; bake at 425° for 20 minutes or until lightly browned and filling is bubbly. Yield: 6 servings (187 calories per serving).

PRO 2.3 / FAT 4.8 / CARB 34.8 / FIB 2.2 / CHOL 0 / SOD 53 / POT 263

PEACH COBBLER

1 tablespoon cornstarch
2 tablespoons unsweetened apple juice
4 cups sliced, peeled fresh peaches
½ cup unsweetened apple juice
¼ teaspoon ground nutmeg
½ teaspoon almond extract
½ cup all-purpose flour
⅛ teaspoon salt
⅛ teaspoon ground nutmeg
2 tablespoons vegetable shortening
1 to 1½ tablespoons cold water
Vegetable cooking spray

Combine cornstarch and 2 tablespoons apple juice, mixing well. Combine peaches, ½ cup apple juice, and ¼ teaspoon nutmeg in a saucepan. Bring to a boil. Cover; reduce heat, and simmer 10 minutes. Stir in cornstarch mixture; cook, stirring constantly, until clear and thickened. Remove from heat, and stir in almond extract. Cool.

Combine flour, salt, and ⅛ teaspoon nutmeg; cut in shortening with pastry blender until mixture resembles coarse meal. Sprinkle water over surface; stir until dry ingredients are moistened. Shape into a ball. Roll pastry to ⅛-inch thickness on a floured surface; cut into 8- x ½-inch strips.

Spoon cooled peach mixture into an 8-inch square baking dish coated with cooking spray. Arrange pastry strips over peaches. Bake at 425° for 20 minutes or until lightly browned. Yield: 6 servings (134 calories per serving).

PRO 1.9 / FAT 3.8 / CARB 23.9 / FIB 3.0 / CHOL 0 / SOD 51 / POT 271

STRAWBERRY-RHUBARB COBBLER

3 cups sliced fresh strawberries
1½ cups sliced fresh rhubarb
½ cup sugar
3 tablespoons cornstarch
2 tablespoons lemon juice
½ teaspoon ground cinnamon
Dash of ground cloves
Vegetable cooking spray
Biscuit Crust Dough
1 egg
1 tablespoon water

Combine first 7 ingredients in a large bowl; toss well, and let stand 15 minutes. Spread mixture in a 10- x 6- x 2-inch baking dish coated with cooking spray.

Roll Biscuit Crust Dough on a lightly floured surface into a 10- x 6-inch rectangle. Place over fruit mixture in dish. Cut 4-inch slits crosswise at 1-inch intervals.

Combine egg and water in a small bowl, mixing well; brush over dough. Bake at 425° for 10 minutes. Reduce heat to 350°, and bake 25 minutes or until crust is golden and filling is bubbly. Yield: 8 servings (192 calories per serving).

Biscuit Crust Dough:

1 cup all-purpose flour
2 teaspoons sugar
1 teaspoon baking powder
¼ teaspoon salt
2 tablespoons unsalted margarine
4 to 5 tablespoons skim milk

Combine first 4 ingredients in a bowl. Cut in margarine with a pastry blender until mixture resembles coarse meal. Sprinkle milk over surface; stir until dry ingredients are moistened. Shape into a ball. Yield: crust for one 10- x 6-inch cobbler.

PRO 3.5 / FAT 4.0 / CARB 36.3 / FIB 1.8 / CHOL 34 / SOD 126 / POT 204

 It may take a while to "get into" your second wind each time you start your workout. For the first few minutes of exercise, the cardiovascular system cannot pump as much oxygen as the muscles need, so the body must function anaerobically (without oxygen) until the system catches up.

The better shape you are in, the less time this takes. A 5 to 10 minute warm-up period gives your body the leeway it needs to start functioning at peak efficiency.

The cool-down phase is just as important. The adrenalin level continues to rise for 3 minutes after exercising because of the sudden drop in blood pressure. Slowing down gradually after a workout lets your blood pressure return to normal by degrees and avoids that extra spurt of adrenalin that puts stress on your heart.

ALMOND TUILLES

⅓ cup whole blanched almonds
3 tablespoons unsalted margarine
⅓ cup sugar
2 egg whites
1 teaspoon vanilla extract
¼ teaspoon almond extract
¼ cup unbleached or all-purpose flour
Vegetable cooking spray

Place almonds in container of an electric blender, and process until finely ground. Cream margarine; gradually add sugar, beating with an electric mixer until light and fluffy. Add egg whites (at room temperature) and flavorings, and beat just until combined. Fold in flour and ground almonds.

Drop batter by rounded teaspoonfuls 4 inches apart onto baking sheets coated with cooking spray; spread into rounds with the back of a spoon. Bake at 400° for 6 to 8 minutes or until golden brown around the edges.

Loosen cookies from baking sheets with a metal spatula, and curl around a rolling pin coated with cooking spray. Cool until cookies hold their shape. Transfer to wire racks to cool completely. (If cookies become too hard to curl, return to oven for a few seconds to soften.) Store in an airtight container. Yield: 2 dozen (41 calories each).

PRO 0.8 / FAT 2.5 / CARB 4.1 / FIB 0.0 / CHOL 0 / SOD 4 / POT 20

COCONUT MERINGUES

½ cup sugar
2 egg whites
⅛ teaspoon cream of tartar
1 teaspoon vanilla extract
½ cup grated fresh coconut, toasted lightly
Vegetable cooking spray

Place sugar in container of an electric blender, and process until finely ground. Beat egg whites (at room temperature) and cream of tartar until foamy. Gradually add sugar, 1 tablespoon at a time, and beat until stiff peaks form. Beat in vanilla, and fold in coconut.

Drop batter by heaping teaspoonfuls 1 inch apart onto baking sheets coated with cooking

spray. Bake at 350° for 12 to 15 minutes or until firm and cream colored. Turn oven off; let cookies cool in oven with door closed 2 hours. Remove from baking sheets; store in an airtight container. Yield: 2½ dozen (23 calories each).

PRO 0.3 / FAT 0.9 / CARB 3.7 / FIB 0.1 / CHOL 0 / SOD 5 / POT 11

MOLASSES COOKIES

¼ cup unsalted margarine
3 tablespoons sugar
1 egg
⅓ cup light molasses
2¼ cups unbleached or all-purpose flour
¾ teaspoon baking soda
1 teaspoon ground cinnamon
½ teaspoon ground ginger
¼ teaspoon ground cloves
Vegetable cooking spray

Cream margarine; gradually add sugar, beating until light and fluffy. Add egg, and beat well. Add molasses, and beat until smooth.

Combine next 5 ingredients in a bowl; stir into molasses mixture, mixing to form a stiff dough. Chill at least 2 hours or overnight.

Divide dough into four equal portions. Roll each portion to ⅛-inch thickness on a lightly floured surface. Cut into rounds with a decorative 2-inch cookie cutter. Repeat procedure with remaining dough.

Place cookies on baking sheets coated with cooking spray. Bake at 350° for 12 minutes or until firm. Transfer to wire racks to cool. Yield: 4 dozen (38 calories each).

PRO 0.7 / FAT 1.1 / CARB 6.4 / FIB 0 / CHOL 6 / SOD 8 / POT 30

PEANUT BUTTER COOKIES

¼ cup unsalted margarine
¼ cup sugar
¼ cup firmly packed brown sugar
1 egg
⅓ cup peanut butter (without added sugar or salt)
½ teaspoon vanilla extract
1 cup unbleached or all-purpose flour
½ teaspoon baking soda

Cream margarine; gradually add sugar, beating until light and fluffy. Add egg, and beat well. Add peanut butter and vanilla, and beat until mixture is smooth. Combine flour and soda; add to peanut butter mixture, mixing until well blended.

Shape dough into 1-inch balls, and place 1 inch apart on ungreased baking sheets. Flatten into 2-inch rounds with a fork in a crosshatch pattern. Bake at 350° for 8 to 10 minutes or until firm. Transfer to wire racks to cool. Yield: 2½ dozen (57 calories each).

PRO 1.4 / FAT 3.2 / CARB 6.2 / FIB 0.1 / CHOL 9 / SOD 9 / POT 31

SPICE COOKIES

2½ cups unbleached flour
1 teaspoon baking soda
½ teaspoon ground allspice
½ teaspoon ground cinnamon
¼ teaspoon ground cloves
¼ teaspoon ground ginger
½ cup unsalted margarine, softened
½ cup light molasses
1 egg, beaten
½ cup wheat germ
Vegetable cooking spray

Combine first 6 ingredients, and set aside. Cream margarine; add molasses and egg, beating well. Add flour mixture, mixing until blended. Cover and chill 1 hour. Shape dough into 1-inch balls, and roll in wheat germ. Place 1 inch apart on baking sheets coated with cooking spray; flatten with bottom of a glass. Bake at 375° for 8 to 10 minutes or until browned. Transfer to wire racks to cool. Yield: 5 dozen (41 calories each).

PRO 0.9 / FAT 1.8 / CARB 5.8 / FIB 0.1 / CHOL 5 / SOD 8 / POT 39

COFFEE YOGURT DESSERT SAUCE

1 tablespoon plus 1 teaspoon Kahlúa or other coffee-flavored liqueur
1 tablespoon plus 1 teaspoon sugar
1 teaspoon instant coffee granules
1 (16-ounce) carton plain low-fat yogurt

Combine liqueur, sugar, and coffee in a bowl; stir until sugar and coffee dissolve. Add yogurt, stirring with a wire whisk until smooth. Serve over vanilla ice milk or fruit. Yield: 2 cups (13 calories per 1-tablespoon serving).

PRO 0.7 / FAT 0.2 / CARB 1.7 / FIB 0.0 / CHOL 1 / SOD 10 / POT 34

BLUEBERRY-CINNAMON SAUCE

2 tablespoons sugar
1 tablespoon cornstarch
½ cup water
1 (3-inch) stick cinnamon
1 teaspoon grated lemon rind
1 tablespoon lemon juice
2 cups fresh blueberries

Combine sugar and cornstarch in a small saucepan; stir in water, mixing until smooth. Add remaining ingredients, and bring to a boil. Reduce heat, and simmer 2 minutes or until mixture is clear and thickened, stirring constantly. Remove from heat, and let stand 15 minutes; discard cinnamon stick. Serve warm sauce over angel food cake, vanilla yogurt, or vanilla ice milk. Yield: 1½ cups (49 calories per ¼-cup serving).

PRO 0.3 / FAT 0.2 / CARB 12.4 / FIB 1.5 / CHOL 0 / SOD 3 / POT 47

SUMMER FRUIT DESSERT TOPPING

1¼ cups unsweetened apple juice
1 tablespoon honey
3 fresh peaches, peeled and sliced
2 bananas, sliced
1 cup fresh cherries, pitted and halved

Combine apple juice and honey in a medium saucepan; bring to a boil. Reduce heat, and simmer, uncovered, until mixture is reduced by one-third, stirring occasionally. Stir in fruit; simmer 5 minutes or until fruit is thoroughly heated. Serve warm sauce over vanilla ice milk or angel food cake. Yield: 3 cups (58 calories per ¼-cup serving).

PRO 0.6 / FAT 0.2 / CARB 14.4 / FIB 1.1 / CHOL 0 / SOD 3 / POT 211

What's New In The Marketplace?

Like hairstyles and hemlines, trends in food and fitness come and go. But today's trend toward eating light and staying fit can yield health benefits long after the newness has worn off.

Many studies have demonstrated the nutritional superiority of fresh food — it's high in fiber, low in cholesterol and has more nutrients than processed foods.

The current trend toward freshness has created a demand for a wider variety of tastes and textures. Nowhere is that concept more obvious than in the supermarket produce section, where you'll find a bountiful crop of unusual fruits and vegetables. Many of these exotic-sounding newcomers are closely related to foods you're accustomed to buying, and most can be used with, or instead of,
more familiar items to add variety and adventure to your meals.

Americans who have embraced the idea of regular exercise have discovered its ability to relieve stress as it improves cardiovascular efficiency and burns excess calories. The joggers of the '70s are "working out" in the '80s, seeking total body fitness that can't be achieved with running alone. Americans spent $1 billion on home exercise equipment last year, buying bikes, rowing machines, and other devices to help them fit exercise into their schedules.

On the following pages, you'll find tips on choosing from these new options in food and exercise equipment. Use the information to add variety and adventure to your own quest for health and fitness.

New Wave Produce

There are twice as many kinds of fruit and vegetables in the supermarket today as were there 10 years ago. As consumers have become more inventive with their cooking, retailers have started stocking their shelves with a wider variety of foods.

Some old favorites have taken on a new look: yellow cherry tomatoes, golden bell peppers, even yellow-fleshed watermelons. Baby vegetables — tiny carrots, squashes, turnips, corn, artichokes —
first appeared in trendy restaurants, but many supermarkets now offer them in their produce sections. Like their full-sized counterparts, baby vegetables retain more nutrients and flavor when steamed until crisp-tender and can be used as attractive low-calorie appetizers and garnishes, too.

TROPICAL FRUITS
Carambola (ca-ram-BOWL-uh) is a bright yellow

The kiwifruit (center) among other fruits to be found at the marketplace.

fruit with a crisp, sweet-tart flesh. Rich in vitamins A and C and potassium, carambola has 35 calories per 3½ ounces. It is also called star fruit because it resembles a star when sliced crosswise.

Cherimoya (cheh-ree-MOY-uh) looks like a fat green pine cone and has a white pulp with a sweet-tart flavor that resembles a combination of strawberry, pineapple, and banana. Cut into halves or quarters and eat with a spoon for a vitamin C-rich dessert that has only 27 calories per ounce, or remove seeds and use in fruit cups and salads.

Kiwifruit (KEE-wee-froot), the delicious egg-shaped fruit with fuzzy brown skin, was originally called a "Chinese gooseberry." Ten years ago the fruit was imported to the United States from New Zealand and renamed "kiwifruit" for that country's native flightless bird. The fruit's fuzzy brown exterior resembles that of the kiwi bird and may explain

the name association. Today, 98 percent of the kiwifruit found in North America's marketplace is produced in California, where more than 6,000 acres are devoted to the crop.

Kiwifruit is an excellent source of vitamin C and is high in fiber and potassium. It is naturally sweet and low in sodium and fat. Try *Cooking Light's* Kiwi Ice for a scrumptious yet nutritious ending to one of your meals.

Lychee nuts (LEE-chee), also spelled litchi, lichee or lichi, are a delicious fruit that have a pearly white, jellylike pulp with a flavor that resembles a cherry. Often sold by the pound, lychee nuts have about 64 calories per 3½ ounces, are high in vitamin C, and can be served by themselves as a dessert or in a fruit salad.

Ugli fruit, named for its rough, knobby peel, is about the size of a grapefruit and has a nearly

Spaghetti squash has flesh that can be fluffed up into strands.

seedless pulp that closely resembles an orange. The light green blemishes on the skin will turn orange as the fruit ripens. Use like other citrus fruit in salads, or peel and eat out of the hand.

VEGETABLES

Cactus leaves, also called "nopales," are delicious and somewhat similar in taste to green beans. The thorns or "eyes" must be removed with a knife or potato peeler, and the leaves can then be sliced or diced and served raw in green salads or cooked in egg dishes or vegetable casseroles.

Chayote (chai-YOH-tay) is also known as a vegetable pear or mango squash. A cousin to the squash, its skin and flesh range from creamy white to dark green. Prepare as you would any summer squash for a vegetable dish that's low in sodium, high in vitamins A and C and potassium, and has about 15 calories per ½ cup.

Elephant garlic, also called Tahiti garlic, has larger cloves, a darker color, and a more delicate flavor than the more familiar Creole or Italian types. It contains ajoene, which has been credited, by a recent State University of New York study, with helping keep blood pressure down. Use it like other types of garlic.

Jicama (HEE-cama), which is high in vitamin A and fiber, looks like a turnip and is also called the Mexican potato. Those large in size tend to be woody, so choose small, firm ones. Wash well, peel, and cut into thin slices to serve raw with dip, or use like water chestnuts in casseroles.

Kohlrabi (Coal-RAH-bee) is related to the cabbage and the brussels sprout. This cruciferous vegetable tastes like a turnip, has only 24 calories per 3½ ounces, and is a fair source of calcium, phosphorus, potassium, and vitamin C. Light green or purple kohlrabi has a bulbous stem topped with leaves that resemble turnip greens. Wash, peel, and slice the bulb for steaming, or serve raw with a dip. Cook the leaves like spinach.

Mexican bell peppers are a cross between a bell pepper and a chile pepper. They are mildly hot peppers that don't need to be roasted or peeled. Try using the Mexi bells with eggs, in salads, in stir-fry, or as a topping for spicy pizza.

Radish sprouts add a crunchy, tart taste to salads and sandwiches as well as providing important enzymes and amino acids. Actually a crossbreed of radishes and alfalfa sprouts, they are low in calories (about 20 calories per ½ cup) and should be rinsed in cold water before serving. For extra crunch, chill in ice water for 30 minutes; then drain well.

Spaghetti squash is lower in calories and higher in fiber than regular spaghetti. This vegetable can be baked in the oven, steamed on top of the range, or microwaved at high for 8 to 10 minutes. When cooked, the flesh of the spaghetti squash can be fluffed up into strands and removed with a fork. It is best served as a side dish, tossed lightly with margarine and herbs.

Tamarillos (tam-a-REE-yos), strikingly deep-red tree tomatoes from New Zealand, are similar to standard tomatoes but tarter in taste.

Yellow Finnish potatoes and yellow rose potatoes already have a buttery taste so there is no need to add butter. Use these potatoes exactly as you would a russet — they are great for baking, boiling, mashing, or in salads.

MUSHROOMS

Chanterelles (shant-uh-RELS) have flared, tulip-shaped yellowish or beige tops, are slightly peppery and can be sautéed or braised.

Enoki-dakes (eh-NO-kee-DAH-kees) have long stalks and tiny heads, use in stir-fry dishes.

Shiitakes (shee-TAH-kees), also called Golden Oaks, have beige marbling over their dark brown caps. Because they absorb other flavors as they cook, they're ideal for meat recipes.

Largely composed of water, a pound of mushrooms (about 30 medium) has only 135 calories. Dried mushrooms have a much more intense flavor than fresh and will regain their texture when soaked in several changes of water. Buy fresh instead of canned whenever possible, since sodium may be added during processing.

Working Out At Home

While 9 million Americans headed for health clubs last year, more than 31 million chose the privacy and convenience of working out at home. The most basic home gym might include a jump rope, a mat, and some hand weights at a total cost of about $50. A more elaborate set-up might include an exercise bike, a rowing machine, or a weight machine, ranging in price from $200 to $2,000. Consumer experts advise buying the sturdiest you can afford and trying the equipment before you buy to ensure its comfort and quality.

And whether you spend a little or a lot of money, remember that your workout should include aerobic, flexibility, and strength exercises. (For more on exercise, see pages 14 through 19.)

EXERCISE BICYCLES

The stationary bike, the most popular at-home exercise machine, can be as good for your heart and lungs as swimming or running. Since the seat supports your weight, pedaling is less stressful to your leg joints. Bikes are good for beginners because you can start at any level and increase the resistance as you progress.

Stationary bicycles are designated either as standard or ergometric. Both have one heavy metal flywheel at the front that turns as you pedal, and on both types, the resistance can be increased by tightening or loosening a knob on the seat shaft. Ergometers have indicators that calculate your output in watts or in calories burned, letting you keep track of the amount of work you're doing. You can eliminate the need (and the expense) for these indicators by monitoring your heart rate (see page 19) at intervals throughout the workout.

Most stationary bikes do not exercise the upper body, but some new models have movable handlebars that work the arm and shoulder muscles.

If you already own a 10-speed bike, there's a less expensive option. You can buy an adapter that will convert your bike to a stationary cycle. Another adapter called a wind-load simulator duplicates the wind resistance of outdoor bicycling, thus building leg strength and endurance.

Mountain bicycles — shorter, sturdier and heavier than regular bikes — have 15 to 18 gears and are designed for people who want to get their exercise outdoors. They are equipped with larger tires for extra traction and adjustable seat shafts for various terrains.

Never buy an exercise bike without a test ride. Check for toe clips to keep your feet from sliding off the pedals; make sure the seat is adjustable; and look for seat and handlebar pads for comfort.

Start your workout with little or no resistance and a moderate pedaling rate. Gradually increase the tension and pedaling rate. Pedaling at a faster rate with less resistance reduces premature fatigue and knee injury.

ROWING MACHINES

If you buy one piece of equipment, it should probably be a rowing machine. Rowing exercises the whole body: the sliding seat allows the leg muscles to move back and forth without the pounding that accompanies running, and the oars strengthen the arms, chest, shoulders, back, and abdominal muscles.

There are three types of rowing machines:

Piston, which has two arms attached to the frame close to the seat track. Resistance is provided by hydraulic pistons that can be adjusted to increase the workload.

Oarlock, which has two arms that pivot in brackets at the sides, with resistance supplied by friction or a hydraulic device. Oarlock rowing requires more concentration because the arm movement is less controlled.

Flywheel, which uses a single bar attached to a wheel rather than two arms. It gives a smoother ride than the other types, and resistance is provided by gears on the wheel.

All rowing machines have a sliding seat, and the best ones move on ball bearings. The lighter the machine, the rougher the ride, because your weight can affect the seat's motion. Footrests should be flexible, since the fixed rests on some models can strain the tendons.

Consult your doctor before undertaking a rowing program if you have had knee or back trouble. As with all exercise, warm up before you row, and start with a few slow repetitions at moderate tension until you find a comfortable resistance. Sitting erect, start each stroke with your legs and finish by pulling with your arms.

HOME GYMS

Weight machines and bench-and-frame gyms are designed to exercise the entire body with adjustable weights, positions, and movements.

A weight-stack machine has a sliding column of weights that move when you pull on a bar, cuff, or handgrip attached to a pulley. The amount of weight is adjusted by slipping a pin into the stack.

Bench-and-frame models are usually freestanding, using a padded flat or slanted bench and an overhead bar or tow to work the legs and upper body. Some use springs for resistance; others use pivoting bars or large flexible bands.

Do you need a home gym? Try it out before you buy, and make sure the bench, bars, and grips can be adjusted to your height. It's a good idea to get some help from a qualified exercise specialist — otherwise, you could injure yourself.

Free weights are less costly than home gyms or club memberships; however, if you get into weightlifting, safety requires that you work out with a partner.

Calorie/Nutrient Chart

FOOD	APPROXIMATE MEASURE	FOOD ENERGY (CALORIES)	PROTEIN (GRAMS)	FAT (GRAMS)	CARBOHYDRATES (GRAMS)	SODIUM (MILLIGRAMS)
Apple						
Fresh	1 medium	96	.3	1.0	24.0	2
Fresh	1 small	61	.2	.6	15.3	1
Dried rings, uncooked	½ cup	117	.5	.7	30.5	2
Juice, unsweetened	1 cup	117	.2	Tr	29.5	2
Applesauce, unsweetened	½ cup	50	.3	.3	13.2	3
Apricot						
Fresh	3 medium	55	1.1	.2	13.7	1
Canned, unsweetened	½ cup	47	.9	.1	11.8	1
Canned, in syrup	½ cup	111	.8	.2	28.4	2
Dried, uncooked	5 medium halves	46	.9	.1	11.6	5
Artichokes, fresh, boiled	1 medium	51	2.8	.2	9.9	30
Asparagus						
Fresh, cooked	4 medium spears	12	1.3	.1	2.2	1
Canned, regular pack	½ cup	22	2.3	.4	3.6	288
Avocado	1 medium	378	4.8	37.1	14.3	9
Bacon, fried and drained						
Cured, sliced	1 medium slice	43	1.9	3.9	.3	77
Canadian-style	1 (⅔-ounce) slice	58	5.7	3.7	.1	537
Bamboo shoots, raw	1 cup	41	3.9	.5	7.9	-
Banana						
Whole	1 medium	101	1.3	.2	26.4	1
Mashed	1 cup	191	2.5	.5	50.0	2
Beans						
Baked, canned with pork and tomato sauce	½ cup	156	7.8	3.3	24.3	591
Garbanzo, cooked	½ cup	169	10.0	2.3	30.5	13
Great Northern, dry, cooked	½ cup	106	7.0	.6	19.1	7
Green, fresh, cooked	½ cup	16	1.0	.2	3.4	3
Green, canned, regular pack	½ cup	22	1.2	.1	5.0	282
Kidney, canned	½ cup	114	7.8	.4	19.9	418
Kidney, dry, cooked	½ cup	109	7.2	.5	19.8	3
Lima, canned, regular pack	½ cup	88	5.1	.4	16.6	293
Lima, immature seeds, cooked	½ cup	95	6.5	.5	16.8	1
Lima, mature seeds, cooked	½ cup	131	7.8	.6	24.3	2
Yellow or wax, fresh, cooked	½ cup	14	.9	.2	2.9	2
Yellow or wax, canned, regular pack	½ cup	23	1.2	.3	5.0	282
Bean sprouts, mung, raw	1 cup	37	4.0	.2	6.9	5
Beef, trimmed of excess fat						
Chuck roast (arm and round bone cuts), braised and drained	3 ounces	152	25.9	6.0	0	45
Flank steak, braised and drained	3 ounces	162	25.9	6.2	0	45

Tr = Trace amount of nutrient   Dash (-) indicates insufficient data available

FOOD	APPROXIMATE MEASURE	FOOD ENERGY (CALORIES)	PROTEIN (GRAMS)	FAT (GRAMS)	CARBOHYDRATES (GRAMS)	SODIUM (MILLIGRAMS)
Beef (continued)						
Round steak, broiled	3 ounces	161	26.6	5.2	0	65
Rump roast, roasted	3 ounces	162	24.7	7.9	0	61
Sirloin, broiled	3 ounces	178	27.4	6.5	0	67
Beef, corned, canned	3 ounces	198	23.2	11.0	0	-
Beef, dried	1 ounce	58	9.7	1.8	0	1,219
Beef, ground						
10% fat, broiled	3 ounces	186	23.3	9.6	0	57
21% fat, broiled	3 ounces	243	19.8	16.6	0	49
Beet greens, cooked	½ cup	13	1.3	.2	2.4	55
Beets						
Fresh, diced, cooked	½ cup	27	1.0	.1	6.1	37
Canned, regular pack	½ cup	42	1.1	.1	9.7	291
Beverages, alcoholic						
Beer	1 ounce	13	.1	0	1.1	2
Beer, light	1 ounce	8	.1	0	1.1	2
Champagne	1 ounce	22	.1	0	.4	1
Cognac brandy	1 ounce	72	-	-	-	-
Crème de ménthe liqueur	1 ounce	99	-	-	8.9	-
Curaçao liqueur	1 ounce	92	0	0	8.4	-
Gin, rum, vodka, whiskey (90-proof)	1 ounce	74	-	-	Tr	Tr
Sherry, dry	1 ounce	34	.1	0	.4	3
Sherry, sweet	1 ounce	40	.1	0	2.0	4
Vermouth, dry	1 ounce	35	0	0	1.6	5
Vermouth, sweet	1 ounce	45	0	0	4.7	8
Wine, dessert	1 ounce	41	Tr	0	2.3	1
Wine, dessert, after cooking	1 ounce	9	0	0	2.3	1
Wine, table	1 ounce	25	Tr	0	1.2	1
Wine, table, after cooking	1 ounce	5	0	0	1.2	1
Beverages, non-alcoholic						
Carbonated, artificially sweetened dietary drinks	1 ounce	-	0	0	-	-
Carbonated, cola-type, sweetened	1 ounce	12	0	0	3.1	-
Carbonated, Ginger ale	1 ounce	9	0	0	2.4	-
Carbonated, unsweetened (club soda)	1 ounce	0	0	0	0	-
Biscuit, 2-inch diameter	1 biscuit	103	2.1	4.8	12.8	175
Blackberries, fresh	½ cup	42	.9	.7	9.3	Tr
Blueberries, fresh	½ cup	45	.5	.4	11.1	Tr
Bouillon						
Beef-flavored granules	1 teaspoon	5	0	.5	0	461
Chicken-flavored granules	1 teaspoon	5	.2	.5	.2	381
Instant	1 cube	5	.8	.1	.2	960
Bran						
Oat	½ cup	185	9.2	4.6	26.2	4
Wheat, raw	½ cup	59	4.0	1.3	7.5	3
Bread, cut into approximately 1-ounce slices						
French or Vienna	1 slice	88	2.8	1.0	16.6	174
Italian	1 slice	83	2.7	.2	16.9	176
Pumpernickel	1 slice	69	2.5	.4	14.8	158
Raisin	1 slice	74	1.9	.8	15.0	102
Rye	1 slice	68	2.6	.3	14.6	156
White	1 slice	76	2.4	.9	14.1	142
Whole wheat	1 slice	68	2.9	.8	13.3	148

Tr = Trace amount of nutrient   Dash (-) indicates insufficient data available

FOOD	APPROXIMATE MEASURE	FOOD ENERGY (CALORIES)	PROTEIN (GRAMS)	FAT (GRAMS)	CARBOHYDRATES (GRAMS)	SODIUM (MILLIGRAMS)
Breadcrumbs, dry	1 cup	392	12.6	4.6	73.4	736
Broccoli, fresh, cooked, chopped	½ cup	20	2.4	.3	3.5	8
Brussels sprouts, fresh, cooked	½ cup	28	3.3	.3	4.9	8
Bulgur, dry	1 cup	628	15.2	2.5	139.1	-
Butter						
Regular type	1 tablespoon	102	.1	11.5	.1	140
Unsalted	1 tablespoon	102	.1	11.5	0	2
Whipped type	1 tablespoon	67	.1	7.6	Tr	93
Cabbage, common varieties						
Bok choy	1 cup	9	1.1	.1	1.5	46
Raw, shredded	1 cup	17	.9	.1	3.8	14
Cooked	½ cup	15	.8	.2	3.1	10
Cake						
Angel food, tube cake, cut into 12 slices	1 (2-ounce) slice	161	4.3	.1	36.1	170
Chocolate (2 layers) with chocolate icing, cut into 12 slices	1 slice	365	4.5	16.2	55.2	233
Pound, cut into 3½- x 3- x ½-inch slices	1 (1-ounce) slice	142	1.7	8.9	14.1	33
Sponge, tube cake, cut into 12 slices	1 slice	131	3.3	2.5	23.8	73
Candy						
Caramels	1 ounce	113	1.1	2.9	21.7	64
Chocolate, milk	1 ounce	147	2.2	9.2	16.1	27
Fudge, chocolate	1 (1-inch) cube	84	.6	2.6	15.8	40
Gum drops	1 ounce	98	Tr	.2	24.8	10
Hard	1 ounce	109	0	.3	27.6	9
Jellybeans	1 ounce	104	Tr	.1	26.4	3
Marshmallows, regular-size	1 marshmallow	23	.1	Tr	5.8	3
Cantaloupe, diced	1 cup	48	1.1	.2	12.0	19
Carrot						
Raw	1 medium	30	.8	.1	7.0	34
Fresh, sliced, cooked	½ cup	24	.7	.2	5.5	26
Canned, regular pack	½ cup	35	.8	.3	8.0	291
Catsup						
No salt added	1 tablespoon	15	0	0	4	6
Regular type	1 tablespoon	16	.3	.1	3.8	156
Cauliflower						
Raw, sliced	1 cup	23	2.3	.2	4.4	11
Fresh, sliced, cooked	½ cup	14	1.5	.2	2.6	6
Celery, raw, diced	½ cup	10	.6	Tr	2.4	76
Cereal						
Bran, whole	1 cup	129	6.2	1.1	40.0	567
Bran flakes	1 cup	106	3.6	.6	28.2	207
Corn flakes	1 cup	84	1.5	0	19.1	216
Granola	½ cup	240	6.0	8.0	38.0	80
Shredded wheat	1 biscuit	89	2.5	.5	20.0	1
Wheat, puffed	1 cup	53	2.2	.2	10.7	1
Chard, Swiss, cooked	½ cup	13	1.3	.2	2.4	63
Cheese, natural						
American Lite-Line	1 ounce	50	6.9	2.0	1.0	407
Blue or Roquefort	1 ounce	104	6.1	8.6	.6	-
Brie	1 ounce	95	5.9	7.8	.1	178

FOOD	APPROXIMATE MEASURE	FOOD ENERGY (CALORIES)	PROTEIN (GRAMS)	FAT (GRAMS)	CARBOHYDRATES (GRAMS)	SODIUM (MILLIGRAMS)
Cheese (*continued*)						
Camembert	1 ounce	85	5.0	7.0	.5	-
Cheddar	1 ounce	113	7.1	9.1	.6	198
Cottage (4% milk fat)	½ cup	120	15.3	4.8	3.3	258
Cottage (0.3% milk fat)	½ cup	63	12.4	.2	2.0	211
Cream	1 ounce	106	2.3	10.7	.6	71
Farmer's, dry curd	1 ounce	24	4.9	.1	.5	4
Farmer's, no salt added	1 ounce	40	4.0	3.0	1.0	2
Gruyere	1 ounce	117	8.5	9.2	.1	95
Monterey Jack	1 ounce	106	6.9	8.6	.2	152
Mozzarella, part-skim	1 ounce	72	6.9	4.5	.8	132
Muenster	1 ounce	104	6.6	8.5	.3	178
Neufchâtel	1 ounce	73	2.8	6.6	.8	112
Parmesan, grated	1 tablespoon	23	2.1	1.5	.2	44
Ricotta, part skim	½ cup	170	14.0	9.7	6.3	154
Romano	1 ounce	110	9.0	7.6	1.0	340
Swiss	1 ounce	105	7.8	7.9	.5	201
Cheese, process American	1 ounce	105	6.6	8.5	.5	322
Cherries, pitted						
Fresh, sour	½ cup	45	1.0	.3	11.1	2
Fresh, sweet	½ cup	51	1.0	.2	12.6	2
Sweet, canned, unsweetened	½ cup	60	1.1	.2	14.8	1
Sweet, canned in syrup	½ cup	104	1.2	.2	26.3	1
Candied	10 cherries	119	.2	.1	30.3	-
Chicken, skinned and roasted						
Dark meat	3 ounces	147	23.5	5.3	0	71
Light meat	3 ounces	140	26.6	2.9	0	53
Chili, with beans	1 cup	339	19.1	15.6	31.1	1,354
Chocolate						
Semisweet	1 (1-ounce) square	144	1.2	10.1	16.2	1
Sweet	1 (1-ounce) square	150	1.2	10.0	16.4	9
Unsweetened	1 (1-ounce) square	143	3.0	15.0	8.2	1
Chocolate syrup	1 tablespoon	62	1.0	2.6	10.2	17
Clams						
Raw, hard-shelled	5 large	80	11.1	.9	5.9	205
Raw, soft-shelled	4 large	82	14.0	1.9	1.3	36
Canned, drained	½ cup	98	15.8	2.5	1.9	-
Cocoa						
Dutch process	1 tablespoon	16	.9	1.3	2.4	39
Regular type	1 tablespoon	24	1.6	.7	2.6	0
Coconut, fresh, grated	1 cup, packed	450	4.6	45.9	12.2	30
Coffee, prepared as beverage	1 cup	2	Tr	Tr	Tr	2
Collards, fresh, cooked	½ cup	32	3.4	.7	4.9	-
Cookies						
Chocolate chip	1 (2¼-inch diameter)	50	.6	2.2	7.3	42
Oatmeal	1 (2½-inch diameter)	60	.8	2.0	9.5	21

Tr = Trace amount of nutrient   Dash (-) indicates insufficient data available

FOOD	APPROXIMATE MEASURE	FOOD ENERGY (CALORIES)	PROTEIN (GRAMS)	FAT (GRAMS)	CARBOHYDRATES (GRAMS)	SODIUM (MILLIGRAMS)
Cookies (*continued*)						
Sandwich type	1 (1¾-inch diameter)	50	.5	2.2	6.9	48
Vanilla wafers	1 cookie	14	.2	.5	2.2	8
Corn						
Fresh, kernels, cooked	½ cup	68	2.7	.9	15.5	Tr
Canned, cream-style, regular pack	½ cup	105	2.7	.8	25.6	302
Cornmeal						
Enriched, dry	1 cup	502	10.9	1.7	108.2	1
Self-rising, dry	1 cup	491	10.9	1.6	105.9	1,946
Cornstarch	1 tablespoon	29	Tr	Tr	7.0	Tr
Crab						
Fresh, steamed	3 ounces	78	14.5	1.6	.4	-
Canned, drained, flaked	½ cup	86	14.8	2.1	.9	850
Crackers						
Animal	1 cracker	11	.2	.2	2.1	8
Butter (1⅞-inch rounds)	1 cracker	15	.2	.6	2.2	36
Graham (2½-inch squares)	1 square	28	.6	.7	5.2	48
Saltines	1 cracker	12	.3	.3	2.0	31
Cranberries, fresh	½ cup	22	.2	.4	5.2	1
Cranberry sauce, canned	¼ cup	101	.1	.2	25.9	1
Cream						
Half-and-half	1 cup	324	7.7	28.3	11.1	111
Sour	1 tablespoon	26	.4	2.5	.5	6
Whipping	1 cup	838	5.2	89.5	7.4	76
Cucumber, raw						
Whole	1 large	45	2.7	.3	10.2	18
Sliced	1 cup	16	.9	.1	3.6	6
Currants	1 tablespoon	7	.2	0	1.8	0
Dates, pitted	5 medium	110	.9	.2	29.2	Tr
Doughnut, plain	1 doughnut	176	2.7	11.3	16.0	99
Egg						
Substitute	¼ cup	30	6.0	0	1.0	90
Whole	1 large	82	6.5	5.8	.5	61
White	1 white	17	3.6	Tr	.3	48
Yolk	1 yolk	59	2.7	5.2	.1	9
Eggplant, cooked without salt	½ cup	19	1.0	.2	4.1	1
Extracts						
Almond	1 teaspoon	10	-	-	-	-
Coconut	1 teaspoon	6	-	-	-	-
Vanilla	1 teaspoon	15	0	0	1.5	0
Farina, enriched, cooked without salt	1 cup	103	3.2	.2	21.3	Tr
Fig, raw	1 medium	40	.6	.2	10.2	1
Fish						
Bass, broiled	3 ounces	191	17.0	10.8	6.8	50
Cod, broiled	3 ounces	143	23.0	4.4	0	92
Flounder, baked	3 ounces	170	25.2	6.9	0	199
Haddock, broiled	3 ounces	118	16.9	5.5	.3	60

FOOD	APPROXIMATE MEASURE	FOOD ENERGY (CALORIES)	PROTEIN (GRAMS)	FAT (GRAMS)	CARBOHYDRATES (GRAMS)	SODIUM (MILLIGRAMS)
Fish (*continued*)						
Halibut, broiled	3 ounces	143	21.1	5.9	0	113
Mackerel, broiled	3 ounces	200	18.9	13.7	0	-
Salmon, broiled	3 ounces	153	22.7	6.2	0	97
Salmon, canned	1 (7¾-ounce) can	376	44.7	20.5	0	1,148
Sardines, canned in oil	1 (½-ounce) fish	24	2.9	1.3	-	99
Trout, cooked	3 ounces	165	19.7	9.4	.3	-
Tuna, canned in oil	1 (7-ounce) can	570	47.9	40.6	0	1,584
Tuna, canned in water	1 (6½ ounce) can	234	51.5	1.5	0	1,610
Flour						
All-purpose, sifted	1 cup	419	12.1	1.2	87.5	2
Rye, sifted	1 cup	314	8.3	.9	68.6	1
Unbleached	1 cup	401	12.0	1.0	86.3	5
Whole wheat, stirred	1 cup	400	16.0	2.4	85.2	4
Frankfurter	1 frankfurter	170	6.9	15.2	.9	-
Fruit cocktail						
Canned, unsweetened	½ cup	46	.5	.1	11.9	6
Canned, in syrup	½ cup	97	.5	.2	25.1	7
Garlic	1 clove	4	.2	Tr	.9	1
Gelatin						
Unflavored, dry	1 envelope	23	6.0	Tr	0	-
Flavored, prepared with water	½ cup	71	1.8	0	16.9	61
Grapefruit						
Fresh	½ grapefruit	40	.5	.1	10.3	1
Juice, unsweetened	1 cup	96	1.2	.2	22.6	.2
Grapes						
Green	10 grapes	34	.3	.2	8.7	2
Juice, unsweetened	1 cup	167	.5	Tr	42.0	5
Grits, cooked without salt	½ cup	63	1.5	.1	13.5	Tr
Honey	1 tablespoon	64	.1	0	17.3	1
Honeydew, diced	1 cup	56	1.4	.5	13.1	20
Horseradish, prepared	1 tablespoon	6	.2	Tr	1.4	14
Ice cream, vanilla, 10% fat	½ cup	128	3.0	7.1	13.9	42
Ice milk, vanilla	½ cup	100	3.2	3.4	14.7	45
Jams and Jellies	1 tablespoon	54	.1	Tr	14.0	2
Kale, cooked	½ cup	22	2.5	.4	3.4	24
Kiwi	1 medium	46	1.1	.5	9.6	0
Kohlrabi, raw, diced	1 cup	41	2.8	.1	9.2	11

Tr = Trace amount of nutrient   Dash (-) indicates insufficient data available

FOOD	APPROXIMATE MEASURE	FOOD ENERGY (CALORIES)	PROTEIN (GRAMS)	FAT (GRAMS)	CARBOHYDRATES (GRAMS)	SODIUM (MILLIGRAMS)
Lamb, trimmed of excess fat						
Leg, roasted	3 ounces	156	24.4	6.0	0	60
Loin chop, broiled and drained	2.3 ounces	120	18.3	4.9	0	45
Lard	1 tablespoon	117	0	13.0	0	0
Leeks, leaf portion, raw	½ cup	32	.8	.2	7.4	10
Lemon						
Fresh	1 medium	20	.8	.2	6.0	1
Juice	1 tablespoon	4	.1	Tr	1.2	Tr
Lemonade, frozen, sweetened, reconstituted	1 cup	107	.1	Tr	28.3	1
Lentils, cooked	½ cup	106	7.8	Tr	19.3	-
Lettuce						
Boston or Bibb, chopped	1 cup	8	.7	.1	1.4	5
Chicory	1 cup	18	1.2	.3	3.4	8
Endive or Escarole	1 cup	9	.6	.1	1.7	11
Iceberg, chopped	1 cup	10	.7	.1	2.2	.7
Romaine, chopped	1 cup	10	.7	.2	1.9	5
Lime	1 medium	19	.5	.1	6.4	1
Liver						
Beef, fried	3 ounces	195	22.4	9.0	4.5	156
Chicken, simmered	3 ounces	137	22.2	3.7	2.7	50
Lobster, cooked, meat only	3 ounces	81	15.3	1.2	.3	172
Luncheon meats						
Bologna	1 ounce	86	3.4	7.8	.3	369
Deviled ham	¼ cup	184	7.2	16.8	0	-
Salami	1 ounce	128	6.7	10.8	.3	-
Lychees, raw	1 each	18	.3	.1	4.6	1
Macaroni, cooked tender without salt	½ cup	78	2.4	.3	16.1	Tr
Mango, raw, diced	½ cup	55	.6	.4	13.9	6
Margarine						
Regular type	1 tablespoon	102	.1	11.5	.1	140
Unsalted	1 tablespoon	99	0	11.2	0	0
Mayonnaise						
Reduced-calorie	1 tablespoon	40	.1	4.0	1.0	111
Regular type	1 tablespoon	99	.2	11.0	.3	82
Milk						
Buttermilk	1 cup	88	8.8	.2	12.5	319
Skim	1 cup	88	8.8	.2	12.5	127
Low-fat (2% fat)	1 cup	122	8.1	4.7	11.7	122
Whole	1 cup	159	8.5	8.5	12.0	122
Evaporated	1 cup	345	17.6	19.9	24.4	297
Evaporated skim	1 cup	184	18.4	Tr	27.2	280
Sweetened condensed	1 cup	982	24.8	26.6	166.2	343
Instant nonfat dry milk	1 cup powder	244	24.3	.5	35.1	358
Molasses, cane	1 tablespoon	50	0	0	13.0	3
Mushrooms, fresh	1 cup	20	1.9	.2	3.1	11
Mustard, prepared	1 teaspoon	4	.2	.2	.3	63
Mustard greens, cooked	½ cup	16	1.6	.3	2.8	13
Nectarine, fresh	1 medium	88	.8	Tr	23.6	8

FOOD	APPROXIMATE MEASURE	FOOD ENERGY (CALORIES)	PROTEIN (GRAMS)	FAT (GRAMS)	CARBOHYDRATES (GRAMS)	SODIUM (MILLIGRAMS)
Noodles, chow mein	½ cup	110	2.9	5.3	13.1	-
Oatmeal, cooked without salt	1 cup	132	4.8	2.4	23.3	1
Oil, vegetable	1 tablespoon	120	0	13.6	0	0
Okra						
Cooked	½ cup	23	1.6	.3	4.8	2
Raw	½	19	1.0	0	3.8	4
Olives						
Green	10 small	33	.4	3.6	.4	686
Ripe	10 small	61	.5	6.5	1.2	385
Onions						
Mature, raw, chopped	½ cup	33	1.3	.1	7.4	9
Mature, cooked	½ cup	31	1.3	.1	6.9	8
Green, chopped	1 tablespoon	2	.1	Tr	.5	Tr
Orange						
Fresh	1 medium	64	1.3	.3	16.0	1
Juice, unsweetened	1 cup	112	1.7	.5	25.8	2
Oysters, raw	1 cup	158	20.2	4.3	8.2	175
Papaya, fresh, cubed	½ cup	28	.4	Tr	7.0	2
Parsley, fresh, chopped	1 tablespoon	2	.1	Tr	.3	2
Parsnip, diced, cooked	½ cup	51	1.2	.4	11.6	6
Pasta						
Egg type, cooked, without salt	½ cup	55	1.8	.6	10.2	0
Plain type, cooked without salt	½ cup	100	3.3	1.2	18.7	2
Peach						
Fresh	1 medium	58	.9	.2	14.8	2
Canned, unsweetened	½ cup	38	.5	.1	9.9	3
Canned, in syrup	½ cup	100	.5	.2	25.8	3
Dried	5 halves	171	2.0	.5	44.4	11
Peanuts, chopped, unsalted	1 tablespoon	52	2.4	4.4	1.9	Tr
Peanut butter	1 tablespoon	94	4.0	8.1	3.0	97
Pear						
Fresh	1 medium	100	1.1	.7	25.1	3
Canned, unsweetened	½ cup	39	.3	.3	10.2	1
Canned, in syrup	½ cup	97	.3	.3	25.0	2
Dried	5 halves	235	2.7	1.6	58.9	6
Peas						
Black-eyed, fresh, cooked	½ cup	89	6.7	.7	15	1
Black-eyed, canned, regular pack	½ cup	90	6.4	.4	15.8	301
English, fresh, cooked	½ cup	57	4.3	.3	9.7	1
English, canned, regular pack	½ cup	82	4.4	.4	15.6	294
Split, dry, cooked	½ cup	115	8.0	.3	20.8	13
Pecans, chopped	1 tablespoon	52	.7	5.3	1.1	Tr
Peppers						
Chili, hot	1 medium	6	.2	0	1.6	3
Green, sweet, raw	1 medium	23	.8	.5	4.9	3
Jalapeña	1 medium	6	.2	0	1.6	3
Red, sweet, raw	1 medium	23	.8	.4	4.9	3

Tr = Trace amount of nutrient   Dash (-) indicates insufficient data available

FOOD	APPROXIMATE MEASURE	FOOD ENERGY (CALORIES)	PROTEIN (GRAMS)	FAT (GRAMS)	CARBOHYDRATES (GRAMS)	SODIUM (MILLIGRAMS)
Pickle						
Dill, whole	1 pickle (4 inches long)	15	.9	.3	3.0	1,928
Dill, sliced	¼ cup	4	.3	.1	.9	553
Sweet, whole	1 pickle (3 inches long)	51	.2	.1	12.8	-
Sweet, chopped	¼ cup	59	.3	.1	14.6	-
Pie, baked, 9-inch diameter, cut into 8 slices						
Apple	1 slice	302	2.6	13.1	45.0	355
Chocolate meringue	1 slice	287	5.5	13.7	38.2	292
Pecan	1 slice	431	5.3	23.6	52.8	228
Pumpkin	1 slice	241	4.6	12.8	27.9	244
Pimiento	1 (4-ounce) jar	31	1.0	.6	6.6	-
Pineapple						
Fresh, diced	½ cup	41	.3	.2	10.6	1
Canned, unsweetened	½ cup	48	.4	.1	12.6	1
Canned, in syrup	½ cup	95	.4	.2	24.8	2
Juice, unsweetened	1 cup	138	1.0	.3	33.8	3
Plum, fresh	1 medium	32	.3	.1	8.1	1
Popcorn						
Unpopped	1 cup	742	24.4	9.6	147.8	6
Popped, plain without fat or salt	1 cup	23	.8	.3	4.6	Tr
Pork, trimmed of excess fat						
Ham, fresh, baked	3 ounces	187	25.2	8.5	0	55
Loin chop, broiled and drained	2 ounces	146	17.1	8.6	0	42
Picnic, cured, simmered	3 ounces	133	21.3	4.7	0	1128
Spareribs, braised	3 ounces	338	18.0	33.6	0	31
Potato						
Whole (about 3 per pound), baked	1 potato	103	2.8	.1	23.1	4
Diced, boiled	½ cup	59	1.7	.1	13.3	3
Potato chips	10 chips	114	1.1	8.0	10.0	-
Pretzels, thin sticks	10 pretzels	23	.6	.3	4.6	101
Prunes						
Dried, pitted	5 medium	130	1.1	.3	34.4	4
Juice	1 cup	197	1.0	.3	48.6	5
Pumpkin	½ cup	41	1.3	.4	9.7	3
Radishes, raw, sliced	½ cup	10	.6	Tr	2.1	11
Raisins, seedless	1 tablespoon	26	.2	Tr	7.0	2
Raspberries, fresh						
Black	½ cup	49	1.0	1.0	10.5	Tr
Red	½ cup	35	.8	.3	8.4	Tr
Rhubarb						
cooked, added sugar	½ cup	190	.7	.1	48.6	3
raw, diced	½ cup	10	.4	Tr	2.3	1
Rice						
Brown, cooked without salt	½ cup	116	2.5	.6	24.9	2
White, cooked, no added salt	½ cup	118	2.2	.1	26.1	1
White, parboiled, cooked without salt	½ cup	90	1.9	.1	20.4	2
Roll						
Bun, frankfurter or hamburger	1 bun	120	3.3	2.2	21.2	202
Hard	1 (1-ounce) roll	78	2.5	.8	14.9	156
Plain, brown-and-serve	1 (1-ounce) roll	84	2.2	1.9	14.2	136

FOOD	APPROXIMATE MEASURE	FOOD ENERGY (CALORIES)	PROTEIN (GRAMS)	FAT (GRAMS)	CARBOHYDRATES (GRAMS)	SODIUM (MILLIGRAMS)
Rutabaga, cubed, cooked	½ cup	30	.8	.1	6.9	4
Salad dressing, commercial						
Blue cheese	1 tablespoon	76	.7	7.8	1.1	164
French	1 tablespoon	66	.1	6.2	2.8	219
Italian	1 tablespoon	83	Tr	9.0	1.0	314
Russian	1 tablespoon	74	.2	7.6	1.6	130
Thousand Island	1 tablespoon	80	.1	8.0	2.5	112
Salt	1 teaspoon	.2	0	0	0	2,132
Sauerkraut	½ cup	21	1.2	.3	4.7	878
Sausage, pork, cooked						
Links	1 ounce	144	5.6	12.8	1.0	-
Patty	1 ounce	146	5.7	13.0	.9	-
Scallops, steamed	3 ounces	95	20.0	1.2	-	228
Sesame seeds	1 tablespoon	47	1.5	4.3	1.4	-
Shallot, bulbs, raw, chopped	½ cup	58	2.0	.1	13.4	10
Sherbet, orange	½ cup	129	.9	1.2	29.7	10
Shortening	1 tablespoon	111	0	12.5	0	0
Shrimp, fresh, raw	½ pound	207	42.8	1.8	3.5	319
Shrimp, canned, drained	½ cup	74	15.5	.7	.5	-
Soups, condensed, prepared with equal amount of water						
Beef broth or boullion	1 cup	31	5.0	0	2.6	782
Chicken, cream of	1 cup	94	2.9	5.8	7.9	970
Chicken Noodle	1 cup	62	3.4	1.9	7.9	979
Mushroom, cream of	1 cup	134	2.4	9.6	10.1	955
Tomato	1 cup	88	2.0	2.5	15.7	970
Vegetable	1 cup	78	2.7	1.7	13.5	845
Soy sauce						
Reduced-sodium	1 tablespoon	14	1.2	0	1.6	582
Regular type	1 tablespoon	12	1.0	.2	1.7	1,319
Soybeans, cooked	½ cup	117	9.9	5.2	9.7	2
Spaghetti, cooked without salt	½ cup	90	3.0	.3	18.3	Tr
Spinach						
Raw, chopped	1 cup	14	1.8	.2	2.4	39
Fresh, cooked	½ cup	21	2.7	.3	3.3	45
Canned, regular pack	½ cup	22	2.3	.5	3.5	274
Squash						
Acorn, cooked	½ cup	57	1.1	.1	14.9	4
Butternut, cooked	½ cup	41	.9	.1	10.8	4
Spaghetti, cooked	½ cup	22	.5	.2	5.0	14
Yellow, sliced, cooked	½ cup	14	.9	.2	2.8	1
Winter, cooked, mashed	½ cup	65	1.9	.4	15.8	1
Zucchini, sliced, cooked	½ cup	11	.9	.1	2.3	1
Strawberries, fresh, whole	1 cup	55	1.0	.7	12.5	1
Sugar						
Brown, packed	1 tablespoon	51	0	0	13	4
Granulated	1 tablespoon	48	0	0	11.9	Tr
Powdered	1 tablespoon	28	0	0	8.0	Tr
Sunflower kernels, unsalted	¼ cup	203	8.7	17.2	7.2	11

Tr = Trace amount of nutrient   Dash (-) indicates insufficient data available

FOOD	APPROXIMATE MEASURE	FOOD ENERGY (CALORIES)	PROTEIN (GRAMS)	FAT (GRAMS)	CARBOHYDRATES (GRAMS)	SODIUM (MILLIGRAMS)
Sweet potato						
Whole (about 2½ per pound), baked	1 potato	148	2.2	.5	34.1	13
Boiled, mashed	½ cup	146	2.2	.5	33.6	13
Syrup, maple	1 tablespoon	50	0	0	12.8	2
Tangerine, fresh	1 medium	39	.7	.2	10.0	2
Tapioca, dry	1 tablespoon	30	.1	Tr	7.3	Tr
Tofu	4 ounces	80	8.7	4.7	2.7	8
Tomato						
Juice	1 cup	46	2.2	.2	10.4	486
Fresh, raw	1 medium	27	1.4	.2	5.8	4
Fresh, cooked	½ cup	32	1.6	.3	6.7	5
Canned, regular pack	½ cup	26	1.2	.3	5.2	157
Paste, regular pack	1 (6-ounce) can	139	5.8	.7	31.6	65
Puree, regular pack	1 (29-ounce) can	321	14.0	1.6	73.2	3,280
Turkey, roasted						
Dark meat, without skin	3 ounces	173	25.5	7.1	0	84
Light meat, without skin	3 ounces	150	28.0	3.3	0	70
Turnip, cubed, cooked	½ cup	18	.6	.2	3.8	27
Turnip greens						
Fresh, cooked	½ cup	15	1.6	.2	2.6	-
Canned, regular pack	½ cup	21	1.8	.4	3.7	274
Veal, trimmed of excess fat						
Loin cut, broiled	3 ounces	199	22.4	11.4	0	55
Round, broiled	3 ounces	184	23.0	9.4	0	56
Vegetable juice cocktail	1 cup	41	2.2	.2	8.7	484
Vinegar	1 tablespoon	2	Tr	0	.9	Tr
Water chestnuts, Chinese	4	20	.4	.1	4.8	-
Watercress, leaves with stems, raw, chopped	1 cup	4	.8	0	.4	14
Watermelon, fresh, diced	1 cup	42	.8	.3	10.2	2
Yeast, dry	1 package	20	2.6	0.1	2.7	4
Yogurt, plain						
Fruit varieties, low-fat	1 cup	225	9.0	2.6	42.3	120
Low-fat	1 cup	123	8.3	4.2	12.7	125
Made from whole milk	1 cup	152	7.4	8.3	12.0	115

Sources of Data:

Adams, Catherine F. *NUTRITIVE VALUE OF AMERICAN FOODS.* Washington: U. S. Government Printing Office, 1975.

Church, Helen Nichols, and Jean A. T. Pennington. *BOWES AND CHURCH'S FOOD VALUES OF PORTIONS COMMONLY USED.* Philadelphia: J. B. Lippincott Company, 1980.

Index

Subject Index

Acknowledgments

Project Consultants

Editorial Coordinator: Elizabeth Pearce
Exercise Physiologist: Kathy A. Alexander, M.S.
Medical Consultant: Julius Linn, M.D.
Recipe Consultant: Susan M. McIntosh, R.D.
Menus & Recipe Developer: Georgia Downard
Recipe Developers: Miriam Gordon, Ann Hodges, Bonnie Keeler,
   Karen Pickus, Miriam Rubin
Recipe Testers: Lana Benson, Colleen Carr, Ellyn Kendrick
Copy Editor: Virginia G. Perrin

Photographers & Stylists

Arie deZanger, Food Art Director & Photographer;
   Wilma G. deZanger, Food Stylist.
      9, 24, 26, 30, 33, 34, 39, 40, 45, 53, 54, 56, 58, 60, 62, 64, 70,
      72, 74, 76, 78, 90, 92, 102, 109, 119, 125, 133, 135, 157, 159, 169,
      175, 191, 224.
Charles E. Walton, *Southern Living* Senior Foods Photographer;
   Beverly Morrow, Photo Stylist.
      Cover, backcover, ii, vi, 6, 20, 29, 49, 69, 82, 94, 99, 122, 137, 151,
      193, 196, 202, 212, 215, 218, 223.
Jim Bathie, *Southern Living* Foods Photographer;
   Kay Clarke, Food Stylist.
      15-17, 37, 46, 67, 128, 143, 149, 205, 207.
Courtland W. Richards, *Southern Living* Photographer;
   Sara Jane Ball, Food Stylist.
      28, 42, 89, 91, 97, 179, 200.